INTERNATIONAL TERRORISM

Characteristics, Causes, Controls

Edited by

CHARLES W. KEGLEY, JR.

University of South Carolina

Senior Editor: *Don Reisman*
Production management: *Publication Services, Inc.*
Cover design: *Tom McKeveny*

Library of Congress Catalog Card Number: 89-10440

For information, write:
    St. Martin's Press, Inc.
    175 Fifth Avenue
    New York, NY 10010

ISBN 0-312-03667-1 (cloth)
ISBN 0-312-00734-5 (paper)

Library of Congress Cataloging-in-Publication Data

International terrorism: characteristics, causes, controls / edited
    by Charles W. Kegley, Jr.
        p. cm.
    ISBN 0-312-03667-1
    1. Terrorism.   2. Terrorism–Prevention.   I. Kegley, Charles W.
HV8431.I5568   1990
    363.3'2–dc20   89-10440
                                                                        CIF

Published and distributed outside North America by:

MACMILLAN EDUCATION LTD.

Houndsmills, Basingstoke, Hampshire RG21 2XS and London

Companies and representatives throughout the world.

ISBN: 0-333-53015-2

Acknowledgments
   Acknowledgments and copyrights are continued at the back of the book on page 281,
which constitutes an extension of the copyright page.

   Brian M. Jenkins. Excerpt from *International Terrorism: The Other World War*. A project
AIR FORCE Report prepared for the USAF (Santa Monica: Rand, Nov. 1985).
   Richard A. Falk. Excerpt from *Revolutionaries and Functionaries: The Dual Face of Terrorism*,
by Richard A. Falk. New York: Dutton, 1988. Copyright © by Richard A. Falk. Reprinted
by permission of the author and publisher, E. P. Dutton, a division of Penguin Books USA,
Inc.

PREFACE

The growth of international terrorism has stimulated revision of the way collegiate instruction about international affairs and national security is organized. Increasingly, the syllabi of many courses give expanded coverage to international terrorism as a topic, and numerous new courses dealing exclusively with the subject have been added to the undergraduate and graduate curriculum. However, the available scholarship in terrorism has not been assembled in a way that accomodates the need for instructional materials for use in the classroom.

It is the purpose of *International Terrorism: Characteristics, Causes, Controls* to respond to this need. This anthology brings together under one cover authoritative but contending interpretations that clearly communicate the major ideas presently being advanced about international terrorism. The readings represent diverse analytic orientations and ideological positions, informed by theory and not bound by time or setting for their relevance.

The subject of international terrorism is covered in three parts, with the readings organized according to three general questions: What is terrorism and how might its characteristics best be defined? What are its immediate and underlying causes? What approaches have been proposed to bring it under control? The organization employed does not restrict the way the instructor might utilize the book; though it conveniently divides major issues and questions into three categories, the volume does not necessarily require that a particular sequence of presentation be followed for presenting the articles. Depending on the needs and preferences of the individual instructor, the parts (and the selections within them) may be reorganized without violating the meaning of the essays. Yet the whole of *International Terrorism* remains greater than the sum of its parts, for the ideas presented in each reading contribute synergistically to the understanding of the others.

Although there already exists abundant technical (and often esoteric) literature on terrorism, *International Terrorism: Characteristics, Causes, Controls* seeks to make a distinctive contribution. Assembling the major arguments, most authoritative statements, and most compelling empirical descriptions, it introduces students to key concepts to which they can refer for analyzing future incidents of international terrorism. By design, therefore, the book is intended to do more than cover previous incidents of terrorism; it provides a framework for analyzing present and future acts of terrorism.

International Terrorism's contribution resides in its effort to expose the multifarious parts of a puzzle, thereby allowing the broad picture to be visualized, and illuminating the extensive range of opinion that can be brought to bear to describe, account for, and control terrorist activities. Specifically prepared for pedagogical purposes, *International Terrorism* has been constructed to provoke interest, arouse controversy, and educate by demonstrating the inadequacy of simplistic theories and stereotypic images and by illustrating the tensions between contending interpretations and schools of thought. Given that existing literature on terrorism is rife with ambiguity, impassioned rhetoric, and unsubstantiated claims, it is hoped that *International Terrorism* will demonstrate to students that how terrorism is defined will shape the conclusions that are reached about its causes and remedies, and that, as with the study of any complex subject, rational discourse and rigorous methodology are the most likely ways to yield understanding and insight.

No book can succeed without the help of many people. Intellectually, this book has been guided by the advice provided by Steven W. Hook, the University of South Carolina; Lloyd Jensen, Temple University; Gregory A. Raymond, Boise State University; and Eugene R. Wittkopf, Louisiana State University; as well as helpful comments provided in reviews for St. Martin's by Richard Immerman, University of Hawaii, Manoa; Felix Moos, the University of Kansas; John Stack, Florida International University; and Robert Wood, North Dakota State University. In addition, those experts who authored original contributions to the book—Louis René Beres, Martha Crenshaw, David C. Rapoport, Peter C. Sederberg, and Michael Stohl—made valuable suggestions. The administrative assistance provided by Steven W. Hook and Cindy Powell is also gratefully acknowledged, as is the support offered by Don Reisman, Emily Berleth, and Abigail Scherer of St. Martin's Press, and Melissa G. Madsen of Publication Services, Champaign, Illinois. The admirable tolerance for my preoccupations while preparing this manuscript displayed by those closest to me, my daughter Suzanne and Ms. Lisa Jarrett, likewise is deeply appreciated.

CONTENTS

The Characteristics, Causes, and Controls of International Terrorism: An Introduction

Charles W. Kegley, Jr.

Terrorism is dangerous ground for *simplificateurs* and *generalisateurs*. To approach it, a cool head is probably more essential than any other intellectual quality.
— Walter Laqueur

Picture yourself a passenger on an international flight from New York to London. Without warning, the pilot announces that gunmen claiming to represent the Third World Liberation Army have seized control of the aircraft and intend to hold you and the other passengers hostage until their demands are met by the governments of the North Atlantic Treaty Organization. Moreover, the pilot announces that the commandos have declared that the failure to receive compliance with their demands will result in the death of the entire crew and passengers.

Your immediate response to this announcement is likely to be one of alarm, fear, and outrage, followed by hopelessness and despair. That is precisely the intended reaction—to inspire fear and submissiveness on the part of the hostages and compliance through intimidation on the part of governmental authorities, so that the terrorists' demands will be met. To punctuate their intense commitment to their cause and the sincerity of their threat—but more importantly to exercise their leverage with the news media, which have been informed by telecommunications of the crisis—the next step is taken: An unsuspecting executive sitting in first class is assassinated.

Now contemplate how you, an innocent bystander yourself and a potential victim of the same brutal atrocity, are to make sense of this seemingly senseless situation. A flood of emotions is certain to rush through your mind. But your actions are limited because you are merely a helpless pawn in a deadly international showdown.

But, assuming the crisis is ultimately "managed" and your release is eventually negotiated, a number of deeper, intellectual questions are bound to surface as you attempt to bring meaning to the trauma you have experienced. Who were these people? What beliefs could they hold so

1

strongly that they would be willing to take extreme risks and violate every ethical precept for their cause? What psychological drives, ideological convictions, institutional loyalties, cultural or ethnic affiliations, financial rewards, or sense of desperation led them to such acts? And why did they act the way they did—killing innocents, advertising their crime to the entire world, and defining themselves as freedom fighters seeking justice? Why, indeed, was their message directed to particular governments and not just to those they claimed deprived them of their legitimate rights? Why had their claims fallen on deaf ears? Did the terrorists receive external assistance for the acts they committed? And finally, why was this act not prevented? What could have been done to deter its occurrence? Is there a solution available to control this menace, so that others will be spared in the future?

This chilling scenario of air piracy is imaginary. Unfortunately, however, it is based on fact. On a regular basis, headlines report that this kind of event—hijackings, kidnappings, hostage takings, assassinations— is a prominent and horrifying feature of our times. Consider a real-world event, as described by the *Wall Street Journal*:

> The attractive couple and their young child appeared to be on vacation, flying on a Pan American World Airways jet from Hong Kong to Tokyo, on Aug. 11, 1982. But the man quietly and unobtrusively slipped a tiny, powerful bomb beneath his seat cushion before he and his family got off in Tokyo.
> On the plane's next flight, as the Pan Am jet neared Honolulu, the bomb went off. The blast tore the legs off a Japanese teen-ager who happened to be in that seat, and he bled to death. Fifteen other passengers were injured.
> The event brought new actors and increasingly sophisticated bombs onto the stage of international terrorism. The man who put the bomb beneath the seat allegedly is . . . a member of . . . terrorist groups that have since placed bombs in planes around the world.[1]

The unspeakable horror that surrounds this and other equally unsettling incidents of terrorism are not the products of imagination. Acts of ruthless terrorism are real. They have been committed on a regular basis, and their primary purpose is the production of fear and alarm. To instill paralyzing fear—to terrorize—has unfortunately become a common way of expressing grievances and attempting to realize political objectives. The bombing of Pan Am flight 103 over Scotland on December 21, 1988, which claimed 270 lives, provides another conspicuous real-world example of this kind of recurrent human tragedy, and exemplifies the potency of terrorism and the frustration and failure of efforts to contain it.

DEFINING INTERNATIONAL TERRORISM

Since the 1960s, when they first became frequent, these kinds of nightmares have been termed, for lack of a better label, "terrorist." Terrorism, perversely like theater, has become "popular," attended by press and public. Its popularization has accelerated its growth as a political issue.

As acts of international terrorism began to increase, growing attention was paid to terrorists' existence and motives—just as its perpetrators intended. Since the 1960s, acts of international terrorism have recurred with sufficient frequency for terrorism to rise steadily on the global agenda. Regarded as a chronic condition potentially of epidemic proportions, it has commanded increasing resources to combat. As the affliction has contagiously spread, it has changed from a problem once overwhelmingly identified with obscure insurrectionists in remote areas to one that today might strike anyone, anyplace. In response, vigorous counterattacks against this pernicious new threat have been mounted, but these vigilant and expensive programs have met with only limited success.

International terrorism represents one of the defining elements of politics on the world's stage today. The ubiquitous threat of terrorism intrudes into the lives and thinking of people throughout the world. Its story is a human story, deeply personal and often tragic, that provokes great fear and intense outrage. It is high drama, the subject of widespread commentary.

Given its psychological impact, the extensive attention increasingly paid to the nature and roots of international terrorism is understandable, as is the frantic search in recent years for methods to control it.

Despite the growth of this attention, however, international terrorism remains a phenomenon that has not been clearly understood, adequately explained, or effectively controlled. Throughout the world, people are perplexed and frightened by terrorism, not able to understand the seemingly incomprehensible problems associated with it. Governments, likewise, remain unable to forge an effective policy to combat this new menace, and have yet to achieve agreement about its nature. The scholarly literature that has emerged to deal with terrorism, while voluminous, has not produced a definitive conceptualization.

Indeed, international terrorism is a topic surrounded by myth and cant. It is a phenomenon that few people can ignore (and about which, it seems, everyone has an opinion, either ill- or well-informed). Polemics abound, and divergent interpretations compete for acceptance and dominance. But debate has failed to result in consensus about international terrorism's essential attributes, determinants, or cure.

The purpose of *International Terrorism* is not to resolve the many semantic, epistemological, and evaluative issues confronting its analysis, or to propose solutions to them. Instead, its educational mission is to illuminate these disagreements and the implications that result from alternate conceptualizations. International terrorism is a multidimensional concept; it refers to a diverse set of observable phenomena. Observers often bring very different assumptions to discussions of international terrorism, and their conclusions customarily spring from radically different perceptions, beliefs, and preferences. As a result, the considerable disagreement that exists is unlikely to be resolved because terrorism seems destined to remain a highly subjective, sensational, and emotional phenomenon. It is a strategy consciously perpetrated to outrage the sensibilities of others, and terrorists are likely to continue to succeed in that goal.

To manage the task of comprehending terrorism in its diverse manifestations by reducing it to a single definition would mask complexities and thereby conceal its diverse and changing nature. It is the goal of this book to highlight, not minimize, this diversity by exposing the many perceptions of and disagreements about international terrorism. Hence, this book aspires to evaluate a representative sample of the broad spectrum of opinion about the nature, sources, and solutions to the problem of international terrorism. Readers of this book are invited and challenged to evaluate for themselves the relative worth of incompatible ideas, and to refine their thinking by seeking to identify the criteria by which they made these assessments. *International Terrorism* will provide discussion of the organizing concepts and interpretations necessary for engaging in these tasks.

Underlying the entire approach of this book is the premise that contemporary terrorism is primarily and intrinsically an *international* phenomenon. As Paul Wilkinson has argued, "Terrorism is inherently international in character, so that, paradoxically, the more individual states improve their national measures [to combat international terrorism], the more it becomes attractive for the terrorist to cross national frontiers."[2] In an age of growing interdependence, terrorism may be seen as a phenomenon that increasingly colors every aspect of international relations, while simultaneously facilitated by global trends in world politics. It is difficult to conceive of terrorism as a prominent problem in the absence of the pressures exerted by certain global developments. These have created a hospitable environment for the practice of terrorist tactics and contributed to the transformation of terrorism from a sub-national instrument of political change to one whose methods today almost invariably transcend national boundaries. For these reasons, we shall inspect terrorism in this book as it typically unfolds through actions directed toward and addressed by actors beyond the home territory of those practicing terrorist acts. This follows the conceptualization of Brian Jenkins, who suggests that "what is called international terrorism may refer broadly to any terrorist violence that has international repercussions, or to acts of violence which are outside the accepted norms of international diplomacy and rules of war."[3]

This is not to deny the existence of occasional acts of terrorism that are primarily domestic in origin or orientation. Many terrorist movements undoubtedly are provincial in outlook and conceive of their activities exclusively as a response to internal circumstances.

For this reason it has been conventional analytic practice to distinguish domestic and nationalist terrorism from international terrorism, with the former identified by activities confined within the borders of a single nation and carried out by people seeking their own homelands, and the latter associated with attacks on third-party targets in foreign territory or supported by state sponsors. For example, one expert writing in the 1970s felt it useful to differentiate four types of terrorism: *international* (terrorism conducted by people controlled by a sovereign state), *transnational* (terrorism practiced by autonomous non-state actors, but not necessarily' with the support of sympathetic states), *domestic* (terrorism involving the nationals of only one state), and *state terrorism* (terrorist tactics practiced by a state within its own borders, such as the genocide performed by Nazi Germany).[4] This classification allowed the *types* of terrorism to be isolated, as depicted in Table 1.

TABLE 1   Four Forms of Terrorism*

		Are Nationals of More than One State Directly Involved?	
		yes	*no*
Are Activities Controlled	*yes*	International	State
or Directed by Governments?	*no*	Transnational	Domestic

*Adapted from Edward Mickolus, "Trends in International Terrorism," in Marius H. Livingston, et al., eds., *International Terrorism in the Contemporary World* (Westport, Conn.: Greenwood Press, 1978), 45.

However interesting and informative, this kind of distinction has become increasingly difficult to draw. Since the 1970s, acts of terrorism have almost invariably transcended national borders in one way (violence on foreign soil) or another (through publicity communicated across international borders by the news media or by state sponsorship of terrorist activities abroad). Almost all acts of terrorism have international consequences. The increasingly international face of modern terrorism has blurred (if not totally erased) the distinction between national and international terrorism. Whereas it was once analytically useful to distinguish intranational from international aspects of terrorism, these categories increasingly refer to a distinction without a difference. It is exceedingly difficult to locate cases of terrorist activity—however defined and identified—that are not internationally supported, targeted abroad, fomented by prevailing global circumstances, international in their repercussions, or addressed to the international community in some manner.

Accordingly, despite the acknowledgment that terrorism may sometimes originate exclusively from internal conditions and be directed only at national governments, this type of purely indigenous terrorism today is statistically rare. Therefore, this book operates on the assumption that contemporary terrorism possesses a decidedly international character, and that terrorism's assessment requires exploration of the foreign implications of terrorist acts. Our object of analysis will be the generic phenomenon of international terrorism—those acts of terror that cross "national boundaries, through the choice of a foreign victim or target, the commission of the terrorist act in a foreign country, or an effort to influence the policies of a foreign government."[5] The inquiry undertaken will be guided by (but not restricted to) those forms of terrorism international in scope, origin, and effects, wherein terrorism is seen as a particular "form of political violence, directed at governments but often involving ordinary citizens, whose aim is to create a climate of fear in which the [demands] of the terrorists will be granted by the government in question [but] extended to apply to acts perpetrated by governments themselves in order to instill a sense of fear."[6]

ORGANIZING PERCEPTIONS OF TERRORISM: BREAKING THE TOPIC INTO COMPONENTS

To organize thinking about international terrorism, the book divides the subject into three parts, centered on three central questions: What is international terrorism, what are its predominant causes, and what are the methods proposed for its control?

Part I is definitional and descriptive. It presents essays that provide alternative definitions of international terrorism and illuminate the different attributes of the phenomenon. The essays in this section place terrorism in historical perspective and survey the properties commonly ascribed to it. Thus, the various ways in which contemporary international terrorism has been conceived are introduced so that the characteristics connecting it to other aspects of national and international politics can be appreciated. This coverage encourages the reader to contemplate the incompatible ways in which international terrorism has been defined and the implications of those differences.

Part II presents inquiries that address the sources or causes of international terrorism. Here the focus shifts to the multiple causes commonly believed to have contributed to the growth of international terrorism. At issue is the question: What conditions and factors have made international terrorism so prevalent?

The competing interpretations offered here advance theories and evidence about terrorism's probable causes and evaluate popular and allegedly "mythical" beliefs about the panoply of sources claimed to precipitate its occurrence. The readings were selected to stimulate debate about terrorism's determinants.

To many, international terrorism is appropriately likened to a disease, and to them the contagious disease requires a remedy. For those of this persuasion, essays are presented here whose insights enable the reader to play the role of a physician in an attempt to diagnose the causes of the disease and to separate the immediate or precipitating symptoms from the underlying sources. On the other hand, to those who see terrorism as a legitimate response to unjustified repression, and accordingly see it not as a curse, but as a cure, essays are presented from the perspective of terrorism's perpetrators and defenders to illuminate the diverse mentalities, ideologies, and circumstances which motivate terrorists' actions. The coverage is designed to treat not only the background factors, beliefs, and circumstances which lead individuals to become involved in terrorist movements, but especially the internal (national) and external (global) conditions which stimulate terrorist activity. The former include indigenous sources of terrorism, such as discontent emerging from perceived political, social, and economic inequities within states, and the latter include the transnational links between terrorist groups such as the networks between these movements and their state sponsors (for example, the alleged support of bomb-throwing dissidents in Lebanon by Iran, Libyan revolutionaries by the USSR, and Nicaraguan *contras* by the United States).

A key assumption of this and other sections is that the observer's definition of international terrorism is inevitably tied to underlying inferences made about terrorism's cause(s); and, vice versa, one's presumptions about terrorism's causes will shape images of its characteristics and how it should be defined. For example, those who perceive terrorism as undertaken primarily by the impoverished or persecuted will tend to see terrorism as rooted in conditions of oppression and inequality, whereas those who characterize it as merely another mode of violent conflict will tend to attribute terrorist activities to ideologies which justify aggression for political purposes.

Finally, **Part III** deals with the various solutions which have been proposed to bring international terrorism under control and to arrest its spread. Here the discussion focuses on how international terrorism might be most effectively combated and considers the limitations and dangers inherent in the various proposals for the control of terrorism that have been contemplated or practiced. These range from counterterrorist tactics using force to nonviolent remedies, with a host of institutional, legal, and political responses in between. Again, the selections highlight contending arguments in order to enable readers to understand the motives underlying efforts to combat violence with violence or to counter threats to freedom by restricting citizens' freedom. Accordingly, an inventory of specific policy programs and counterterrorist measures is provided, along with materials required to consider the problems and controversies those responses to terrorism entail.

By breaking them into separate categories, this tripartite organizational design allows the most important issues to be introduced and ordered in a way that makes the consideration of rival ideas manageable. In many respects, however, this separation is misleading. Whereas the organization divides these three dimensions into distinct categories, their occasionally overlapping nature should be recognized. The reader is encouraged to contemplate the ways in which characteristics, causes, and controls are intimately linked. The readings provide a rich set of materials which demonstrate that how terrorism is defined will necessarily shape the conclusions reached about its causes and remedies. Similarly, the readings will suggest how inferences about terrorism's causes will structure images of both its character and the best policy response to it. And, to round out the circle, the ways in which counterterrorist policy options are viewed will shape, and be shaped by, views of its character and the factors that produce it. The "tyranny of assumptions"—the way in which prior beliefs and expectations may lead to misperceptions of reality and inaccurate conclusions—is thus revealed by the discordant messages presented by the book's essays.

This overriding theme follows J. Bowyer Bell's warning that "the posture of the investigator quite often determines the result of his or her analysis."[7] As he notes, there "has at times been more interest in accumulating sympathetic 'evidence' or defining the nature of terrorism so as to buttress long-held positions, than in value-free investigation."

To illustrate this (inevitable?) deficiency in the analysis of terrorism, Bell notes the inescapably tight relationship between analysts' definitions of terrorism and their recommendations for its control. He observes that "a number [of analysts] have begun at the end, with prescription, rather than at the beginning," with description and definition, and that their positions can be collapsed into

> . . . two general postures. At one extreme are those who feel that most terrorists are warped, their politics pathological and consequently unamenable to accommodation. Since [terrorists'] demands are essentially nonnegotiable . . . the appropriate response is placed on coercion, protection, and punishment. . . . At the other pole are those who concentrate on the reasoned demands of the revolutionaries, who believe that in many cases accommodations or at least a dialogue is possible. They stress the reasons behind the massacres, the roots of violence, and the remedies to ease real frustration. They put less stress on maintaining order by coercive law and more on the necessity for justice.[8]

Another way of illustrating this connection among controls, characteristics, and causes is to note that those who think that international terrorism demands a military response are prone to define terrorism as a substitute form of warfare, caused primarily by the foreign sponsorship of governments. There exist many other examples where conclusions about one facet of international terrorism are colored and contaminated by the premises embraced about the others. If we recognize and take into account the inherent overlap of analysts' beliefs about terrorism's characteristics, causes, and controls, we can gain better understanding of the intellectual barriers to unlocking the mystery of terrorism and better avoid reaching erroneous conclusions about what international terrorism is, what produces it, and what can be done about it. In reading the essays in *International Terrorism,* it is essential to inquire how each analysis has been influenced by the assumptions of the interpreter. The introduction to each part will facilitate this requirement by outlining the major assumptions made in approaches to the subject by different interpreters.

This tripartite organizational scheme, it might be noted, parallels the scholarly convention to separate the analysis of international behavior into three tasks: description, explanation, and prescription. But again, this division, while common in the study of interpersonal and international behavior,[9] is artificial; for how a subject is observed and described is closely related to explanations of the factors that cause it. Likewise, the success of prescriptions about how people *ought* to deal with a perceived phenomenon is contingent on the accuracy with which those phenomena are observed and the validity of the causes identified to explain them. Hence the descriptive, explanatory or causal, and prescriptive policy analyses of international terrorism are heavily intertwined; none of these analytic tasks can be conducted wholly in isolation from the others, and the adequacy of each influences the adequacy of the others.

To introduce the contents, let us turn to the descriptions, explanations, and prescriptions presented in the readings. We shall expose the themes and contending interpretations by following the organizational scheme described above, so as to treat sequentially, in three discrete parts, leading ideas about the characteristics, causes, and control of contemporary international terrorism.

NOTES

1. William M. Carley, "Terrorist Blueprint," *The Wall Street Journal* (27 February 1989), A1.

2. "Trends in International Terrorism and the American Response," in Lawrence Freeman, et al., eds., *Terrorism and International Order* (London: Routledge and Kegan Paul, 1986), 49.

3. *International Terrorism: A New Mode of Conflict* (Los Angeles: Crescent Publications, 1975), 11.

4. Edward Mickolus, "Trends in International Terrorism," in Marius H. Livingston, with Lee Bruce Kress, and Marie G. Wanek, eds., *International Terrorism in the Contemporary World* (Westport, Conn.: Greenwood Press, 1978), 45.

5. Robert A. Fearey, "Introduction to International Terrorism," in Livingston, et al., 25.

6. David Miller, ed., *The Blackwell Encyclopedia of Political Thought* (New York: Basil Blackwell, 1987), 514.

7. "Terror: An Overview," in Livingston, et al., 43.

8. Ibid., 42.

9. For a critical discussion and application, see William D. Coplin and Charles W. Kegley, Jr., eds., *Analyzing International Relations: A Multimethod Introduction* (New York: Praeger, 1975).

I

The Characteristics
of Contemporary
International Terrorism

Throughout human history, our species has experienced many forms of
"terror." From the threats posed by predators to the devastation left by
natural disasters, people's survival has always depended on their response
to constant, life-threatening dangers. This timeless form of "terror" is an
emotion that is difficult to define but, like love, is easily recognized by
those who experience it.

This book is about another, more modern kind of terror: the deliberate
threat or use of violence by groups demanding changes.

This newer form creates similar psychological responses—uncertainty,
fear, outrage—which cast a dark shadow over the world. These responses
may be either highly visible or subtle, but they, too, are easily recognized
by those confronted with demands and threats.

THE DEFINITIONAL PROBLEM

To understand this kind of terror, it is necessary first to define it and
identify its distinguishing characteristics. But agreement has not been
reached about the phenomenon to which the term *terrorism* is meant
to refer. Unfortunately, with no consensus on its meaning, the term
is used in quite different and often contradictory ways. Furthermore,
criteria have not been consensually established for differentiating terrorist
activities from related phenomena, such as guerrilla warfare and protest
movements, in order to determine when a terrorist act has occurred.

At the heart of the definitional problem is the difficulty of distinguishing illegal acts of violence against governments from so-called "legitimate resistance" by groups fighting for their right of self-determination.
Christopher C. Joyner observes that

> Politically, academically, and legally, the phenomenon of terrorism eludes
> clear and precise definition. In a real sense, terrorism is like pornography:
> You know it when you see it, but it is impossible to come up with a universally

agreed-upon definition. The hackneyed bromide "One man's terrorist is another man's freedom fighter" still remains a truism in international political perceptions. "Terrorism" still lies in the eye of the beholder. A criminal act of terrorism to some will embody a legitimate act of self-determination to others. Thus, careless application of the term "terrorism" can lead to confusion and blurring between the crime and the method, as well as between the criminal and the motive. For the sake of legal clarity, utility resides in describing these acts by their familiar domestic legal labels—extortion, assault and battery, kidnapping, blackmail, murder, arson, and assassination. Recognizing this does not obviate the difficulty of distinguishing between the application of these acts as municipal crimes in contrast to their espoused legitimacy as acts of self-determination by a national liberation group. In addition, attribution by government officials of other related politico-legal terms such as "insurgents," "guerrillas," "freedom fighters," "democratic resistance," and "commandos" serves to complicate the conceptual, legal, and moral debate over terrorism even further.[1]

It is not certain that the analytic issues facing the accurate characterization and definition of international terrorism can be satisfactorily overcome. It may be that, as a committee of the French Senate concluded in 1984, "any definition is practically guaranteed to fail."

Why do disagreements over the characteristics of terrorism prevail and why have the controversies over its definition remained unresolved? One reason is that *terrorism* is so convenient to stigmatize a staggeringly diverse array of behaviors. The meaning of the term remains vague because it has been stretched to refer to widely disparate actions and actors; it is "used as a synonym for rebellion, street battles, civil strife, insurrection, rural guerrilla war, coups d'etat, and a dozen other things."[2] Consequently, "no definition of terrorism can possibly cover all the varieties of terrorism that have appeared throughout history."[3] This may explain why one scholar was able to identify 109 different definitions advanced between 1936 and 1981.[4]

Another reason why "no commonly agreed definition can in principle be reached [is] because the very process of definition is in itself part of a wider contestation over ideologies or political objectives."[5] *Terrorism* is often used not to analyze, but to attack and to advocate, that is, to voice disapproval or approval. The term is a handy noun in polemics because, as Barry Gewen notes,

> ... "terrorism" is a pejorative. As one recent writer has put it, "To call an act of political violence terrorist is not merely to describe it but to judge it." This makes things easy for those wishing to score propaganda points. Only one's enemies are terrorists. Others, striving for objectivity, have a harder time.[6]

Conor Cruise O'Brien astutely elaborates on the political and ideological connotation and denotation intrinsic to the definition of terrorism by noting

> Those who are described as terrorists, and who reject that title for themselves, make the uncomfortable point that national armed forces, fully supported by democratic opinion, have in fact employed violence and terror on a far vaster scale than what liberation movements have as yet been able to attain. The

"freedom fighters" see themselves as fighting a just war. Why should they not be entitled to kill, burn and destroy as national armies, navies and air forces do, and why should the label "terrorist" be applied to them and not the national militaries?[7]

We shall return to this issue shortly. Here let it simply be observed that in addressing terrorism, we are dealing with a value-laden subject that resists precise definition and whose description is often motivated by the desire to condemn, not to offer detached analysis. We must proceed with awareness of this terminological aspect of the terrorism debate and be attentive to the fact that with respect to terrorism there may be no "pair of researchers in the field using the same definition [or] even a single tradition that has crystallized as the dominant one, with others competing for recognition."[8]

The task of objective analysis is complicated because it requires comparing different ways in which international actors threaten violence and extracting valid generalizations about the characteristics terrorists share with other actors and those which set them apart. A definition must balance the need to identify commonalities against the need to recognize unique features of individual cases. Should Palestinian skyjackers, Basque separatists, Irish revolutionaries, and South American kidnappers be seen as similar? Are they properly classified with the insurgents who produced the American, French, and Russian revolutions? Do their actions resemble the tactics of the Red Brigade, the Ku Klux Klan, or big-time drug-trafficking street gangs? Are the methods of the African National Congress, Afghan rebels, or the French resistance during World War II a part of the same "terrorist" syndrome? What about the "state terrorism" of Pol Pot, Adolf Hitler, Joseph Stalin, Mao Tse-Tung? Should the Ayatollah Khomeini's order in 1989 to kill novelist Salman Rushdie (author of *The Satanic Verses*) and "execute quickly wherever they are found" everyone who helped publish or distribute the book be seen as an act of terrorism or as a call to expiate blasphemy by a religious fundamentalist? Is an attack on a principle, freedom of the press, different from a terrorist attack on human life? And what about the nuclear deterrence strategies of the United States and the Soviet Union, which rely on terror to prevent attack?[9] Where does one draw the line?

How one addresses these questions will structure one's image of terrorism. It will shape views about terrorism's purpose, challenge, and ultimate significance. Whether some forms of terrorism are found acceptable will similarly be shaped by our subjective images of it. What we see depends on what we look at, what we look for, what we expect to see, what we wish to see, and how we react to what we discern.

In this context, consider for example the seemingly simple question of whether international terrorism has increased in frequency since the 1960s. On the surface, this would appear to be an easy question to answer, yet estimates vary considerably. Each estimate depends on the indicator system developed to define what terrorism is, to identify individual acts of terrorism, and to measure changes in their occurrence. And secondarily, each depends on the assumptions built into the operational definitions and indices that select, screen, and filter what is perceived about international terrorism. For instance, the U.S. Department of State's Office of Counter-Terrorism, which employs the broad definition for international terrorism as any premeditated activity using force against noncombatants for political means involving the citizens or territory of more than one country,[10] arrives at the conclusion that international terrorist activity has increased dramatically between 1968, when it identified 125 individual international terrorist incidents, and 1988, when 855 incidents were identified (see Figure 1). Another account, by Brian M. Jenkins, similarly perceives "the total volume of international terrorism [to have] increased . . . [and] become bloodier." According to his estimating procedure, "since 1977 the number of international terrorist incidents resulting in fatalities has increased each year."[11]

However, other estimates, using different criteria, paint a much less alarming picture of the level of international terrorist incidents.[12] Still other observers don't even see international terrorism as a major threat, but envision it as a relatively rare, sporadic, and ineffectual activity whose incidence pales in comparison with other modes of violence.[13] And from another angle, there are those who believe that what matters is not the frequency of the acts but the amount of destruction caused. These observers insist that what is significant is the small number of deaths resulting from international terrorism; they note, for example, that "the 23 American lives lost overseas [in 1985] in terrorist incidents are greatly overshadowed by the 18,000 murders in the U.S. each year,"[14] and that "the number killed worldwide in an entire year by all international terrorist episodes has never reached 700, or less than the average weekly toll from either the Iran-Iraq War [in the 1980s] or America's highways."[15] Descriptions rest on what is inspected; for the paradox is that the victims of terrorism are few in number, but acts of terrorism are substantial and their symbolic impact dramatic. Terrorism takes few lives but generates a powerful shock effect.

These differences of opinion indicate that reasonable people can arrive at reasonable but divergent conclusions about something as basic as whether international terrorism is a growing, stable, or declining activity and that the picture of its occurrence and significance depends greatly on the way it is described and defined. As one study advised, differences "in defining terrorism will affect the coding and recording of data on terrorist [incidents]. . . . In examining any set of terrorist statistics, hence, the reader is cautioned to examine closely the counting rules employed."[16] What we see *is* what we will get; reality is what we perceive it to be.

Perhaps this accounts for the fact that experts hold diametrically opposed opinions about so many of international terrorism's attributes. Some of the issues about which expert opinions are polarized, J. Bowyer Bell summarizes, include whether the present epidemic of terrorism is

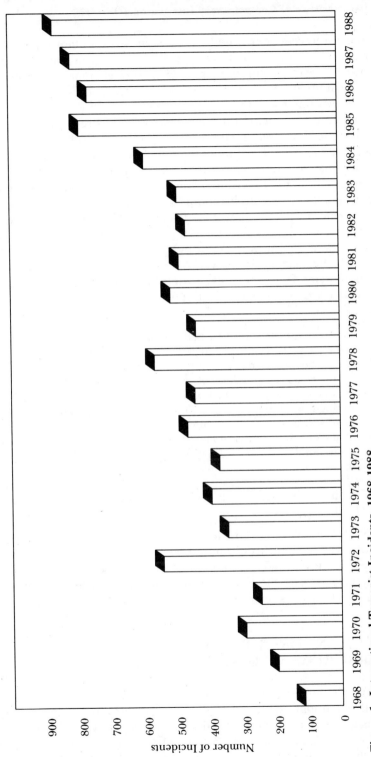

Figure 1. International Terrorist Incidents, 1968-1988

Source: Office of Counter-Terrorism of the U.S. Department of State

novel and unprecedented, whether terrorism is important or unimportant, whether the emergent wave of modern terrorism since the 1960s is a transient development or a growing threat, whether terrorism is an effective or ineffective strategy, and whether terrorism is controllable or is a danger with no solution.[17]

The opinions of experts on a host of other, more challenging and descriptive questions also remain contested, as demonstrated by the readings that follow and the voluminous literature on terrorism (see Table 1). Definitional questions, the source of great confusion, are largely responsible for the existing disagreement over such philosophical issues as whether terrorism is merely a poor man's war, a form of low-intensity conflict practiced by states, or an instrument of liberation. They are also the source for continuing debate over the validity of the claim that one man's terrorist is another's freedom fighter.

As noted, the inability to arrive at consensus about terrorism's characterization stems from the great variety of aims, actors' motives, and practices that are associated with it. This variety is described by Walter Laqueur:

> Terrorism . . . has been waged by national and religious groups, by the left and by the right, by nationalist as well as internationalist movements, and it has been state-sponsored. . . . Terrorist movements have frequently consisted of members of the educated middle classes, but there has also been agrarian terrorism, terror by the uprooted and the rejected, and trade union and working-class terror. . . . Terror has been directed against . . . autocratic regimes as well as democracies; sometimes there has been an obvious link with social dislocation and economic crisis, at other times there has been no such connection. Movements of national liberation and social revolution (or reaction) have turned to terrorism after political action has failed. But elsewhere, and at other times, terrorism has not been the consequence of political failure, but has been chosen by militant groups even before other options were tried.[18]

This variability alerts us to the need to be sensitive to the different modes of terrorism and to the misunderstandings that can result when too narrow or too broad a definition is adopted. Let us examine some efforts to grapple with these issues by introducing the selections that have been chosen to discuss terrorism's characterization and definition.

REFLECTIONS ON THE CHARACTER OF TERRORISM: SELECTIONS

In "International Terrorism: The Other World War," Brian M. Jenkins frames the boundaries for discussion by describing the multiple forms terrorism assumes, the variety of tactics terrorists employ, and the purposes that inspire terrorist acts. In describing what terrorists do, how they do it, and why they do it, his essay confronts many of the definitional issues

TABLE 1   What is International Terrorism? Opposed Positions on Four Issues

Are Revolutionary Terror and Regime Terror Different?

Yes: "The words 'terror' and 'terrorism' have become semantic tools of the powerful in the Western world. In their dictionary meaning these words refer to 'intimidation' by the 'systematic use of violence' as a means of both governing and opposing existing governments. But current Western usage has restructured the sense, on purely ideological grounds, to the retail violence of those who oppose the established order."

—Noam Chomsky and Edward Herman, 1979

No: "... the world, and especially the public at large, is not excessively interested in government terrorism, which tends to be accepted as unavoidable and is often viewed as inevitable if a government is to retain its authority against threats emanating from woolly-headed or vicious revolutionaries. [Such] acts of terrorism ... are only likely to be condemned by revolutionaries ..., idealists, libertarians, starry-eyed academics, and similar radicals."

—L. C. Green, 1979

Is State Support a Component of International Terrorism?

Yes: "... the term 'state-terrorism' is fundamentally a tautology, with the occasional exception of ... random, that is to say purposeless, violence. All terrorism is in fact state terrorism."

—U. S. Ambassador to the United Nations Charles Lichtenstein, 1986

No: "... there are basic differences in motive, function and effect between oppression by the state (or society, or religion) and political terrorism. To equate them, to obliterate these differences, is to spread confusion and to impede understanding of both."

—Walter Laqueur, 1987

Is Violence a Necessary Element of Terrorism?

Yes: "What characterizes modern terrorism, and makes for its basic strength, is the slaughter of generally defenseless persons."

–Roger Trinquier, 1964

No: "... terror ... does not necessarily include violence; just as some violence involves no terror, some terror (e.g. intimidation) requires no violence."

–Alexander Dallin and G. W. Breslauer, 1970

Can War and Terrorism Be Distinguished?

Yes: "As soon as the leaders of [a terrorist] movement cease their attacks against noncombatants and focus their military strength against the army of the entrenched government, they have ceased technically (if not in the minds of their enemies) to be terrorists."

–J. Schreiber, 1978

No: "Terrorism as well as war constitutes a form of use of violence for political purposes ... the aim being to force the opposing party in the conflict to a certain behavior."

–H. W. Tromp, 1978

surrounding terrorism, as well as the objectives and principles of action that distinguish international terrorism from other modes of conflict.

Although he does not dismiss the historical origins of modern terrorism, Jenkins views its current practice as a very "new" form of conflict—a surrogate, unique method of pursuing political objectives by threat of force, that in earlier eras was pursued by conventional warfare. His introduction stresses the attributes of the contemporary international environment which, especially since the 1960s, have inhibited recourse to war between the most heavily armed states[19] while providing an atmosphere conducive to the internationalization of terrorist practices heretofore largely confined to within-state tactics. As he might describe it, terrorism is "a form of political violence that falls between war and peace."[20] In depicting terrorism as a "new substitute" to conventional war and as part of a long-range trend toward the privatization of violence, Jenkins assumes a position that departs from those who see terrorism springing from many historical precedents and counterparts and who maintain that modern terrorism shares with warfare many characteristics such as the failure to discriminate between civilians and combatants. But to Jenkins, contemporary terrorism is different from warfare, and these differences require a definition which accommodates the transfer of terrorism from a domestic to an international concern and which illuminates why states find sponsorship of terrorists such a tempting method for the pursuit of foreign policy goals.

If the question of whether terrorism is a distinct new form of violence is debatable, the issue of whether terrorism is justifiable might appear to be beyond debate. No one publicly praises terrorism; it is universally reproached. Thus on December 9, 1985, the United Nations General Assembly passed a resolution that condemned terrorism. But symptomatically, that resolution failed to face the difficult problem of defining precisely what was being condemned. The resolution therefore avoided the *political* question of attempting to differentiate permissible violence from unjustified violence. That issue lies at the center of debate about what terrorism encompasses, and whether there are "acceptable" acts of terrorism. Many contested positions exist on this controversy. That issue *is* debatable; despite its public censure, "the long history of terrorism is littered with attempts at justification,"[21] and "terrorists have found admirers and publicity agents in all ages."[22]

To broaden understanding, Richard A. Falk's "Revolutionaries and Functionaries: The Dual Face of Terrorism" exposes a major semantic problem in efforts to specify the meaning of terrorism. Falk contends that terrorism is best defined by the kinds of actions undertaken and the purposes terrorists seek to achieve, not by the identity of the actor. In contrast to "the dangerously misleading mainstream image," Falk submits that terrorism should refer to "any type of political violence that lacks an adequate moral and legal justification, regardless of whether the actor is a revolutionary group or a government." He asks us to distinguish revolutionary terror from regime terror, while recognizing the similarities between terrorism practiced by insurgents and terrorism practiced by states. Terrorism, he observes, displays a "dual face"; it is used at times by those seeking to resist tyranny, as well as by governments against their own citizens and foreign governments and populations. The former use of terror tactics may sometimes be justified, as Aristotle, Cicero, Plutarch and other ancient philosophers maintained, and as the revolutionaries who authored the Declaration of Independence in America proclaimed. The use of terror by the latter is perhaps much more widespread and institutionally entrenched, but difficult to condone; how can we possibly justify the use of force and terrorism to subjugate and repress the population ruled by a government, or, for that matter, violence toward foreign adversaries authorized by government officials? Should terrorism by functionaries be accepted merely because international law gives states wide license to violate, in the name of preservation of order, the human rights of those it rules and permits some forms of external aggression in the name of self-defense? Is "functionary" or establishment terror to be justified because it seeks to preserve the status quo, whereas revolutionary terror is to be condemned because it seeks political change? Like some others,[23] Professor Falk answers in the negative and strongly castigates terror by government functionaries while defending certain types of insurgent terror for the purpose of resisting tyranny (but not the depravity of some dispossessed political extremists). There is, he would claim, a fundamental difference between aggression and self-defense. Moreover, he asserts, it is mistaken to overlook the "often calculating character of recourse to wanton and indiscriminate political violence from a variety of sources, including the deepest recesses of governmental bureaucracy operating in an entirely cool, calculating, rational style."

Falk offers an enlightened critique of the propagandistic tendency to define terrorism as the acts practiced by one's enemies when those same acts practiced by governments or by allies are defended. *Terrorism* is a dirty word, but merely using it to describe certain actors does not clarify the meaning of the behaviors to which it is meant to refer. As a former Italian intelligence officer, Franco Ferracuti, points out, "The Boston Tea Party was a historical event or a terrorist act, depending on which side you sat."[24]

By revealing the danger of assuming that terrorists can be defined simply as those who seek to overthrow governments (by showing that governments also engage in terrorism), Professor Falk enlarges our vision of the problem "How to Tell a Terrorist."[25]

Beyond the quality of their tactics and motives, which other attributes of terrorism should we study to construct an appropriate definition? In "Conceptualizing Political Terrorism," Richard Shultz provides a comprehensive inventory of the multiple dimensions of terrorism and the diverse questions they provoke. Although he approves of Brian Jenkins' view of terrorism as "acts of violence . . . designed primarily to instill fear," that is, as "violence for effect," Shultz differs from Jenkins' psychological approach and even more from some other students who see terrorism as the irrational or pathologically mindless behavior of maniacs. Instead, terrorist activity is assumed to be the product of rational choice—that is, it is "calculated violence directed at affecting the views and behavior of specific groups." Thus, it is best defined as "the threat and/or use of extranormal forms of political violence . . . with the objective of achieving certain political objectives."

This definition does not dismiss "the immense complexity of terrorism." To capture it, Shultz prescribes that terrorism be subdivided into three types: Revolutionary, Sub-Revolutionary, and Establishment, and that seven key variables relevant to these categories be considered: causes, environment, goals, strategy, means, organization, and participation. This typology of terrorism's basic components not only suggests the properties of international terrorism worthy of examination; it also delineates those aspects (such as patterns of organization and participation in terrorist movements) that fall outside the the coverage provided in *International Terrorism: Characteristics, Causes, Controls.* Accordingly, his essay serves as an aid to understanding the other essays in this book and their relationship to other literature on the subject. Shultz's survey highlights concepts around which analysis can be organized.

A primary facet of terrorism is its political inspiration, for unless one conceives of terrorism as purposeless behavior, the desire to practice politics (that is, exercise influence) clearly is characteristic of terrorist activity. In contrast to those who define international terrorism in terms of actors and their needs, Gary G. Sick in "The Political Underpinnings of Terrorism" emphasizes terrorism's political essence; it is "the continuation of politics by other means. Terrorists become terrorists," he observes, not "for motives of simple profit or passion . . . [but] for reasons associated with politics." Indeed, despite the observable differences among terrorist activities, terrorism nonetheless is essentially a particular approach to the general political goal of getting others to do what they would not otherwise do. In a balanced evaluation, Sick exposes the dangers of reducing the complexities of terrorism to convenient stereotypes, such as the image of the terrorist as a deranged, fanatically driven subversive whose willingness to die for his beliefs and efforts to shock and terrorize are not calculated. What most terrorists are up to is politics, not passion. (Yet to be asked is whether, by equating terrorism with politics, Sick broadens its conceptualization so widely that it encompasses *every* activity; politics is ubiquitous and cannot easily be separated from any form of behavior—a property that risks making the definition tautological and the phrase "political terrorism" a redundancy.)

If terrorism is a distinguishable phenomenon, how is it different from other types of political activity? How might the concept be refined further? Is it distinguishable from politically motivated violence? In "The Strategy of Terrorism" David Fromkin avers that terrorism receives its character primarily from the approaches terrorists take to pursue their political goals, but more specifically from the kind of *strategies* they devise to realize their objectives. Fromkin provides a summary of the strategy of terrorism that separates it from other types of political activities and, in so doing, provides a description of the various principles of action that highly diverse groups labeled by their opponents as terrorists practice to achieve their goals. In this context, Fromkin would undoubtedly agree with the view that it is "important to take terrorism seriously as a strategy and not just regard it as an outrage."[26] Terrorism is regarded by governments as a respected military weapon of national policy;[27] it is not just the strategy of lunatics and desperados. Nor, for that matter, is it synonymous with politics.

The controversies surrounding the characterization of terrorism may be highlighted through inspection of still other interpretations. One such insightful characterization is provided in Paul Johnson's "The Seven Deadly Sins of Terrorism." Taking exception to those such as Walter Laqueur who do not view terrorism as a new or major ascendant threat, Johnson attacks the proposition that terrorism is merely a response to political problems that on occasion may be justified. On the contrary, argues Johnson, international terrorism is a rising menace that threatens to undermine the very foundation of civilization. This is true because terrorism relies on insidious and lethal methods that are inherently sinful and virulent methods best recognized as such. Seven sins ascribed to terrorism prevent it from being venial, pardonable, or acceptable: It exalts violence, suppresses moral instincts, repudiates politics, spreads totalitarianism, destroys democracy, exploits freedom, and saps the will of civilized society to defend itself. As Johnson would have it, terrorism is unjustifiable because it employs methods that directly violate basic ethical precepts. (One might ask whether Johnson's moral position would lead him to chastize terrorist activities engaged in by *all* actors, and not just by those targeted against Western governments in the First World.)

To most, international terrorism is a highly effective (if repugnant) instrument for achieving the aims of terrorist movements. That efficacy, maintains Walter Laqueur in "The Futility of Terrorism," is greatly exaggerated. Asking us to measure objectively terrorism's *actual* record, he concludes that the extraordinary power often ascribed to terrorism is not warranted. Contrary to popular impressions, and despite the visibility and drama of terrorists' endeavors, that record attests instead to terrorists' essential failure. In reviewing that record, Laqueur advances a number of perceptive observations about why terrorism is, ultimately, *bound* to fail. These characteristics define further the nature of contemporary international terrorism, and provide an antidote to those who, reacting with revulsion to terrorism's intimidating methods, often distort the modest impact terrorist movements actually exert. Their methods are surely to be feared, but he concludes that their influence should not be overestimated. That hyperbole, he suggests, is just one component of a larger set of misperceptions about international terrorism. Also discussed in Laqueur's demythologization endeavor are additional alleged "myths" about terrorism's character. (Of course, one man's myth is another man's reality.)

The need to draw distinctions about the alternative forms of terrorism is convincingly argued by William D. Quandt in "The Multi-Dimensional Challenge of Terrorism: Common Misconceptions and Policy Dilemmas." Written primarily from the perspective of Americans, who since the 1960s consistently have been the major targets of international terrorism,[28] this essay highlights the ambiguous properties that divide opinions about describing terrorism accurately and forging an effective response to it. Berating the tendency to view terrorism in ahistorical and apolitical terms, Quandt does not share the belief that terrorism is new, on the rise, or a preeminent threat to democratic societies. The major threat, he argues, is over-reaction (indiscriminate retaliation against terrorism's perpetrators) resulting from exaggerated fears of terrorism's challenge.

To cope with terrorism's challenge, Quandt stresses the need to differentiate the multifaceted forms of terrorism and formulate a response that recognizes its diverse types. (He thereby introduces a theme to which we shall return in **Part III.**) Two basic categories are distinguished: "hardcore terrorism" and "terrorism by popular movements." This distinction has implications for the way responses to terrorism should be evaluated. The first "can be dealt with primarily as a police problem, whereas the second affords no easy solutions" because punitive retribution against leaders who have gained popular support can easily strengthen their position and resolve and incite their further use of terrorism. Likewise, the diverse nature of "state-sponsored terrorism" poses dilemmas because no policy to counter state-supported terrorism can effectively manage the different cases that are destined to arise. Because international terrorism is perceived to be "a multi-dimensional phenomenon which allows no easy answers," he concludes that "to deal effectively with the threat we must think clearly about the kind of terrorism we confront."

Terrorism, which is "theater," resembles legitimate theater in many ways, argues Michael Stohl, in that its drama involves many characters performing many roles. But, he observes, "only certain plays are given prominent reviews and fewer still become hits. Likewise, only a few actors and directors achieve stardom." The result is that popular images of international terrorism are often built around sensationalism and stereotypes that fail to reflect the subtle differences encompassed in the myriad ways in which international terrorism is practiced. To reduce the distance between fact and fiction, closer inspection of this obscure variation is required. That is Stohl's purpose in "Demystifying the Mystery of International Terrorism."

An accurate definition of terrorism should incorporate, argues Stohl, the key words *purposeful, violence, fear, victim,* and *audience,* and it must distinguish the victims from the actual target (the "audience" of the violence committed). Examination reveals that "the process of terrorism arises for a number of quite different purposes, purposes that are dependent upon the position of both the agents and the targets of terror."

To illustrate the misunderstandings that can result from failure to observe terrorism by reference to these organizing concepts, Stohl classifies ten characteristics often attributed to terrorism as "myths" or erroneous images.

1. Political terrorism is exclusively the activity of nongovernmental actors.
2. All terrorists are madmen.
3. All terrorists are criminals.
4. One man's terrorist is another man's freedom fighter.
5. All insurgent violence is political terrorism.
6. Terrorism's purpose is to produce chaos.
7. Governments always oppose nongovernmental terrorism.
8. Political terrorism is exclusively a problem relating to internal conditions.
9. Contemporary terrorism is caused by the evil actions of one or two major actors.
10. Terrorism is a futile strategy.

Each of these widely embraced beliefs about terrorism (some of which are articulated in the preceding readings, such as Walter Laqueur's contention that terrorism is futile or Paul Johnson's belief that terrorism is carried out by sinful and irrational actors), Stohl concludes, is founded on false premises, fallacious logic, or unrepresentative evidence. If terrorism is to be unmasked so that its real nature can be revealed, these myths must be exposed.

Professor Stohl's provocative essay serves as an appropriate conclusion to **Part I**, for it forces us to question the validity of many popular assumptions about the character and definition of terrorism. Rather than definitively resolving debate about the subject (which is perhaps an unachievable goal, given terrorism's manifest complexity and relentlessly changing nature), Stohl sets the stage for subsequent discussion and analysis. He puts forward questions that are destined to remain pertinent well into the twenty-first century. Efforts to tie the loose threads together by listing the images of terrorism regarded as "mythical" also organize perceptions about the nature of international terrorism (see Table 2). These should be compared to develop an inventory of the issues being debated.

But these efforts to separate myths from reality are unlikely to resolve controversies about the nature of international terrorism and the most meaningful way of characterizing and defining it. On the contrary, they are likely to stimulate further debate. The basic questions are likely to remain relevant. Is international terrorism new, or is it rooted in practices dating back to antiquity? Is it increasing in frequency and impact as a force in world politics, or is its incidence and influence receding? Is it a

TABLE 2   Will the Real "International Terrorism" Please Present Itself? Some Popular Images of Terrorism Hypothesized by Two Authorities to Be "Myths"

Peter C. Sederburg:

1. Violence signifies the breakdown of politics.
2. One man's terrorist is another man's freedom fighter.
3. Terrorism is the weapon of radical revolutionaries.
4. Terrorism is the weapon of the weak.
5. Terrorism is senseless violence.
6. An international terrorist conspiracy directs a war against the West.
7. Terrorism can be cured by swift, severe retribution.
8. Terrorism can only be cured by addressing the root causes of extreme discontent.

Walter Laqueur:

1. Terrorism is a new and unprecedented phenomenon.
2. Terrorism is one of the most important and dangerous problems facing mankind today, and it should figure uppermost on our own agenda.
3. Terrorism will grow in importance as the destructiveness of its methods increases.
4. Terrorism is highly effective.
5. One man's terrorist is another man's freedom fighter.
6. Terrorists are poor and their inspiration is deeply ideological.
7. Terrorists are more intelligent and less cruel than "ordinary" criminals.
8. Terrorists are fanatical believers driven to hopelessness by intolerable conditions.
9. Terrorism is the natural response to injustice, oppression and persecution.
10. The only means to reduce the likelihood of terrorism is through reduction of the grievances underlying it.
11. Terrorism is left-wing and revolutionary in character.
12. Terrorism can happen anywhere.
13. Terrorism is essentially a Middle Eastern problem, and most of the targets of terrorism are American.
14. State-sponsored terrorism presents a new dimension and is a far more dangerous threat than any past terrorist movements.

Sources: Sederburg, *Terrorist Myths* (Englewood Cliffs, N.J.: Prentice-Hall, 1989); Laqueur, *The Age of Terrorism* (Boston: Little, Brown, 1987), pp. 5–8, merged with material extracted from his article reprinted in this Part of *International Terrorism*.

true threat and menace to national and international security or merely a psychologically frightening nuisance whose threat to liberal democracy and global stability is greatly exaggerated? Is it best distinguished by the fear it instills, the violence it employs, the strategies on which it relies, the methods it uses, the political goals it seeks to promote, or the actors who practice it? Is it extranormal and unlawful, or a mode of conflict bearing many similarities to other forceful means of conflict resolution? Is international terrorism a term applicable only to those seeking to overthrow governments and thus best identified by the kinds of actors who practice it? Or should one consider the nature of the liberation or national causes at stake? And, depending on the posture taken on these issues, is international terrorism a justifiable practice, or one inherently sinister and inexcusable, whether engaged in by sub-national or national actors? What are the criteria by which we might evaluate the adequate response to these questions, in order that the mythology surrounding the mystery of international terrorism might be managed and more adequate understandings developed? These analytical tasks will continue to challenge the student and policymaker.

Among the paths to greater understanding, perhaps none is more important to the discovery of the character of international terrorism and the appropriate response to it than is greater appreciation of the *causes* that produce it. These essays, especially Stohl's, lay a foundation for examining the causes of contemporary international terrorism. As will become evident in the essays in **Part II**, definitions of terrorism strongly affect perceptions of terrorism's sources (and conversely, views about terrorism's determinants shape images of its character). To prepare the way for analyses of the causes of terrorism, let us now turn to rival ideas about its character as presented in the essays in **Part I**.

NOTES

1. "In Search of an Anti-Terrorism Policy: Lessons of the Reagan Era," *Terrorism: An International Journal* 11 (No. 1, 1988), 30.

2. Walter Laqueur, ed., *The Terrorism Reader* (New York: New American Library, 1978), 262.

3. Walter Laqueur, *The Age of Terrorism* (Boston: Little, Brown, 1987), 11.

4. Alex P. Schmid, *Political Terrorism* (Amsterdam: North Holland Publishing Co., 1983), 119–158 passim.

5. Cited in Schmid, ibid., 7.

6. "Taking on Terrorism," *The New Leader* 70 (7 September 1987), 17.

7. "Liberty and Terrorism," *International Security* 2 (Fall 1977), 56–57.

8. Johan Galtung, as cited in Schmid, *Political Terrorism*, 9.

9. See Charles W. Kegley, Jr., and Eugene P. Wittkopf, eds., *The Nuclear Reader: Strategy, Weapons, War* (New York: St. Martins Press, 1989), which presents evidence supporting the view, in the words of Lawrence Freeman, that "much of nuclear strategy is concerned with the manipulations of threats" and that "legitimate forms of military strategy" are predicated on terrorism; see "Terrorism and Strategy," in Freeman, et al., eds., *Terrorism and International Order* (London: Routledge and Kegan Paul, 1986), 59–60. This thesis is forcefully advanced by Thomas C. Schelling in *Arms and Influence* (New Haven: Yale University Press, 1966).

10. U.S. Department of State, *Patterns of Global Terrorism: 1987* (August 1988), v.

11. "Defense Against Terrorism," *Political Science Quarterly* 101 (No. 5, 1986), 777.

12. For example, see John L. Scherer, *Terrorism: An Annual Survey* (Minneapolis: Sherer, 1982), as well as Edward F. Mickolus and Todd Sandler, and Jean M. Murdock, *International Terrorism in the 1980s* (Ames: Iowa State University Press, 1989).

13. Most representative of this thesis is Walter Laqueur, *The Age of Terrorism.*

14. Rushworth M. Kidder, "The Fear of Fear Itself," *The Christian Science Monitor* (13 May 1986), 17.

15. Patrick Clawson, "Terrorism in Decline?" *Orbis* 32 (Spring 1988), 264.

16. José Luis Nunes and Lawrence J. Smith, Rapporteurs, *Terrorism* (Brussels: North Atlantic Assembly, 1989), 2–3.

17. *A Time of Terror: How Democratic Societies Respond to Revolutionary Violence* (New York: Basic Books, 1978), 95–104 passim.

18. *The Age of Terrorism,* 72–73.

19. For discussions of the reasons why war between the great powers since World War II has been virtually nonexistent and the general frequency of warfare among all states has in many respects declined, see Charles W. Kegley, Jr., ed., *The Long Postwar Peace: The Sources of Great Power Stability* (Chicago: Scott, Foresman/Little, Brown, 1991).

20. Bell, *A Time of Terror, op. cit.,* 3.

21. Adam Roberts, "Terrorism and International Order," in Freeman, et al., 17.

22. Laqueur, *The Age of Terrorism,* 3.

23. For example, Noam Chomsky, *Pirates and Emperors: International Terrorism in the Real World* (New York: Claremont Research and Publications, 1986).

24. Cited in Rushworth M. Kidder, "Acts of Terror?" *The Christian Science Monitor* (13 May 1986), 19.

25. *The Economist* 30 (26 July 1986), 9–10. This interpretation by *The Economist*'s editors suggests that terrorists are best identified by the illegal kinds of actions undertaken (skyjacking, arson, bombing, kidnapping, sabotage), but that other considerations (Are the means just? Is the cause just?) ought to be factored into the definition.

26. Freeman, "Terrorism and Strategy," 51.

27. See Jay Mallin, "Terrorism as a Military Weapon," in Marius H. Livingston, ed., *International Terrorism in the Contemporary World* (Westport, Conn.: Greenwood Press, 1978), 389–401, as well as Thomas C. Schelling, "Thinking About Nuclear Terrorism," *International Security* 6 (Spring 1982), 61–77.

28. U.S. State Department, 1–2.

1

International Terrorism: The Other World War

Brian M. Jenkins

"The Third World War has started," the notorious terrorist Carlos told his hostages in Vienna in 1975. A French soldier in Beirut, a survivor of the suicide terrorist bombing that killed 58 of his comrades, made a similar observation: "Our 58 comrades are perhaps the first deaths of the Third World War." Unlike the wars of the past, this war did not begin with one identifiable event. Indeed, no one can say for certain when or where it began.

It is not the war the . . . military [of national governments] has trained for. There are no massed armor formations pouring across a central front, no divisions on the march, no scramble of fighter aircraft. It is, rather, a hundred wars waged by elusive and ruthless foes. They operate under diverse banners: the Red Army Faction, the Red Brigades, the Armed Forces of National Liberation, the Revolutionary Armed Forces, the Revolutionary Army of the People, the Popular Front, the Holy War.

It is a conflict for which we are inadequately prepared . . . [Embassies] have been destroyed, . . . citizens have been kidnapped and killed . . . jet fighters have been blown up on the ground. . . .

If [the] losses are numerically small compared to those suffered in more conventional combat, they are nevertheless symbolically and politically significant. Terrorists have . . . demonstrated the difficulties . . . in striking back. They have compelled us to divert increasing resources to protect ourselves and our facilities against their attacks. [In the United States, the] Joint Chiefs of Staff, the Secretary of Defense, the Secretary of State, and even the President live behind concrete barriers, visible reminders of [their] vulnerability.

THE DEFINITION OF TERRORISM

When we talk about terrorism, what exactly are we talking about? How does terrorism differ from ordinary crime? Is all politically motivated violence terrorism? Is terrorism synonymous with guerrilla war, or is

Note: footnotes have been deleted.

the term properly reserved for those trying to overthrow governments? Can governments also be terrorists? What is the distinction between driving a truck loaded with explosives into an embassy and dropping high explosives on a city? How do we make useful distinctions? Virtually all discussions about terrorism sooner or later wander into the swamp of definition.

The term "terrorism" has no precise or widely accepted definition. If it were a mere matter of description, establishing a definition would be simple: Terrorism is violence or the threat of violence calculated to create an atmosphere of fear and alarm—in a word, to terrorize—and thereby bring about some social or political change. This is pretty close to the definition offered by a South American jurist more than [25] years ago, i.e., terrorism consists of acts that in themselves may be classic forms of crime—murder, arson, the use of explosives—but that differ from classic crimes in that they are executed "with the deliberate intention of causing panic, disorder, and terror within an organized society."

But while this definition puts terrorism in the realm of crime, we live in a world that recognizes the legitimacy of war and the right of revolution. At the turn of the century, socialist revolutionaries in Russia were proud to call themselves terrorists. They had a terrorist arm called appropriately the Terrorist Brigade, and they hoped through selective assassination to inspire terror among Russia's ruling elite. They were careful not to injure bystanders, and if their intended victim was accompanied by members of his family, they would abort their attack. Ironically, today's terrorists are less fastidious about their actions and more concerned about their public image. In the age of mass media, *terrorism* has become a pejorative term. Terrorists now call themselves anything but terrorists.

Nobody is a terrorist who "stands for a just cause," Yasir Arafat told the United Nations. If we accept Arafat's statement, the problem of definition is further complicated, since the validity of causes must be inserted into the criteria. As a result, only to the extent that everyone in the world can agree on the justice of a particular cause is there likely to be agreement that an action is or is not a terrorist action.

Some governments are prone to label as terrorism all violent acts committed by their political opponents, while antigovernment extremists frequently claim to be the victims of government terror. Use of the term thus implies a moral judgment. If one group can successfully attach the label *terrorist* to its opponent, then it has indirectly persuaded others to adopt its moral and political point of view, or at least to reject the terrorists' view. Terrorism is what the bad guys do. This drawing of boundaries between what is legitimate and what is illegitimate, between the *right* way to fight and the *wrong* way to fight, brings high political stakes to the task of definition.

Terrorism in recent years has become a fad word that is promiscuously applied to a variety of violent acts which are not necessarily intended to produce terror. It is important to distinguish between actions that are intended to terrorize and actions that just happen to terrify. Muggers may terrify the population of a large urban area, but they produce terror as a by-product of their crimes; their objectives are wallets and watches, not alarm.

The difficulty in defining terrorism has led to the cliché that one man's terrorist is another man's freedom fighter. The phrase implies that there can be no objective definition of terrorism, that there are no universal standards of conduct in conflict. However, civilized nations have through law identified modes of conduct that are criminal. Homicide, kidnapping, threats to life, and the willful destruction of property appear in the criminal codes of every country. True, some of the prohibitions may legally be violated in times of war—the law against killing, for example, may be violated by those we call "lawful combatants." Terrorists claim to be not criminals, but soldiers at war who are therefore privileged to break ordinary laws. But even in war, there are rules that outlaw the use of certain weapons and tactics.

The rules of war grant civilian noncombatants who are not associated with "valid" targets at least theoretical immunity from deliberate attack. They prohibit taking hostages. They prohibit violence against those held captive. They define belligerents. They define neutral territory. These rules are sometimes violated—and in these cases, those responsible for the violations become war criminals. But violations in no way diminish the validity of the rules.

Some international lawyers see the laws of war as a possible solution to the dilemma of definition. They suggest that rather than trying to negotiate new treaties on terrorism which are not likely to be ratified or enforced, nations should apply the laws of war, to which almost all have agreed. Terrorists, they say, should be dealt with as soldiers who commit atrocities. Nearly all countries have agreed to try or extradite soldiers who commit atrocities in international armed conflicts. Why should persons not explicitly granted soldiers' status be given greater leeway to commit violence than soldiers have? Under the laws-of-war approach, terrorism would comprise all acts committed in peacetime that, if committed during war, would constitute war crimes.

Terrorism can be objectively defined by the quality of the act, but not by the identity of the perpetrators or the nature of their cause. All terrorist acts are crimes, and many would also be war crimes or "grave breaches" of the rules of war if we accepted the terrorists' assertion that they wage war. All involve violence or the threat of violence, sometimes coupled with explicit demands. The violence is frequently directed against civilian targets. The purposes are political. The actions are often carried out in a way that will achieve maximum publicity. The perpetrators are usually members of an organized group. Their organizations are by necessity clandestine, but unlike other criminals, terrorists often claim credit for their acts. And finally—the hallmark of terrorism—the acts are intended to produce psychological effects beyond the immediate physical damage.

While these criteria do not eliminate all ambiguity, they enable us to draw some limits and answer some of the questions. Terrorism differs from ordinary crime in its political purpose and in its primary objective. Neither the ordinary bank robber nor the man who shot President Reagan is a terrorist. Likewise, not all politically motivated violence is terrorism. The Minuteman of the American Revolution and the rebel in Central America both have political motives, but they are not automatically terrorists. Terrorism is not synonymous with guerrilla war or any other kind of war, and it is not reserved exclusively for those trying to overthrow governments. The leftist assassin and the right-wing death squad secretly working under the direction of a Ministry of Interior both use the same tactics for the same purpose—to instill fear and alter a political situation.

DIFFERING CONCEPTS OF CONFLICT

International terrorism comprises those terrorist incidents that have clear international consequences: incidents in which terrorists go abroad to strike their targets, stay at home but select victims because of their connections to a foreign state (e.g., diplomats or the executives of foreign corporations), or attack international lines of commerce (e.g., airliners). It excludes the considerable amount of terrorist violence carried out by terrorists operating within their own country against their own nationals and in many countries by governments against their own citizens. For example, Irish terrorists blowing up other Irishmen in Belfast would not be counted as international terrorists, nor would Italian terrorists kidnapping Italian officials in Italy.

This definition of international terrorism reflects the particular concern of the United States and the handful of other governments frequently targeted by terrorists abroad. The issue here is not the general problem of political violence or terrorism, or the causes of the conflicts that give rise to terrorist violence. These are domestic matters. The unit of measure is the spillover of this violence into the international domain. But why, terrorists might ask, should they play by the established rules of diplomacy and war when these rules were contrived by a small group of primarily Western nations for their own advantage, and when they deprive groups without recognized governments, territory, or armies from exercising their "right" to resort to violence?

The terrorists of today see no essential difference between the local authority they fight against and the diplomatic and commercial representatives of foreign powers. All terrorists, from the urban guerrillas in South America to the Palestinian fighters in the Middle East, have incorporated the Marxist concept of imperialism. It has become an article of faith in Third World thinking. The banker in Manhattan, the embassy in Montevideo, the local subsidiary of the multinational corporation, the President in his office are all links in a chain of economic exploitation and political repression. It is a concept shared also by the "irregulars" in North America, Western Europe, and Japan who consider themselves to be the auxiliary forces of a Third World revolution.

Many Third World governments, particularly those in Africa and Asia, do not always cooperate with American and European efforts to identify and combat international terrorism, not because these governments approve of terrorist tactics, but because they see the antiterrorist efforts as part of a broader campaign aimed at outlawing the irregular methods of warfare that were developed in the Third World during the civil war in China and the anticolonial struggles in Asia and Africa. Not a few of the Third World's insurgent chiefs—and today's leaders—were once called terrorists themselves. Their governments, particularly the ones that lack the tools of modern conventional war, therefore deliberately exclude from their definition of terrorism other means of struggle—"wars of liberation," or guerrilla warfare—which they once employed or which are now being employed on behalf of causes they support.

The position on international terrorism taken by the Third World governments is consistent with the position they took at the Geneva negotiations to revise the laws of war. There, they sought to extend the rights and protections of the original Geneva Conventions to irregular forces as well as regular soldiers in international wars. They noted that the Geneva Conventions and other treaties regulating war had been drafted by Europeans to regulate warfare among Europeans, but that they omitted from "international warfare" military force used by the Europeans in gaining and maintaining colonies. In other words, when Europeans shot at Europeans, it was a closely regulated affair, but when Europeans shot at Africans or Asians, they could do what they wanted. The Third World governments feared that the Americans and Europeans now wanted to brand the irregular methods used by the natives to fight back as "terrorism" and thereby outlaw them.

Their rejection of this unequal state of affairs was reflected in the long-winded definition of international terrorism proposed by a group of nonaligned nations in 1973, which included "acts of violence and other repressive acts by colonial, racist and alien regimes against peoples struggling for their liberation . . .; tolerating or assisting by a State the organizations of the remnants of fascists or mercenary groups whose terrorist activity is directed against other sovereign countries; acts of violence committed by individuals or groups of individuals which endanger or take innocent human lives or jeopardize fundamental freedoms, [provided this definition does] not affect the inalienable rights to self-determination and independence of all peoples under colonial and racist regimes and other forms of alien domination."

It must be remembered that this debate about what constitutes international terrorism originally began in the early 1970s, when guerrilla armies still fought for independence in Portugese Angola and Mozambique, against white supremacist governments in Rhodesia and South

Africa, for "national liberation" in Indochina, and for the recovery of a Palestinian homeland in the Middle East—causes which evoked considerable support in the Third World.

Even though governments have not been able to agree on a common definition of terrorism, they have achieved a modest degree of cooperation in dealing with certain aspects of the problem. This has been attained by avoiding definition altogether and identifying specific terrorist tactics that concern all nations. For example, most nations have signed and generally have abided by the various international conventions against hijacking and sabotage of aircraft. Not surprisingly, the world's diplomats have been able to agree that diplomats should not be targets of terrorist violence and have signed the Convention on the Prevention and Punishment of Crimes Against Internationally Protected Persons. A broader degree of cooperation has been achieved in smaller international forums, such as the Summit Seven or the European Economic Community, where political consensus is more easily reached.

THE THEORY OF TERRORISM: AIMED AT THE PEOPLE WATCHING

Present-day terrorism derives largely from twentieth century theories of guerrilla warfare, for which Mao Zedong deserves the most credit, although his paramount concern for winning the support of the masses would probably have made him reject the tactics of contemporary terrorism. During the civil war in China, Mao formulated a series of relationships that differed both from conventional military strategies and from earlier Marxist theories of revolution. He placed greater emphasis on military power than the earlier Marxists did. They relied primarily on political organization, seeing the military portion of the revolution as a final assault on government buildings. This had not worked in China. Mao had to wage a long war, but because his forces were numerically and technologically inferior to those of his opponents, he had to substitute political power for conventional military power. With superior political motivation, Mao reasoned, guerrillas strengthened by the support of the Chinese peasants could survive military reverses and wage a protracted military campaign that would wear down their opponents.

Mao's concept of a "people's war," elaborated in the insurgent movements of the 1950s and 1960s, freed strategists from thinking about warfare exclusively in terms of more soldiers and better armaments. It allowed determined revolutionaries who lacked conventional military power to take on militarily superior forces, with some hope of ultimately defeating them. Perhaps it accorded too much weight to political motivation and determination—both very subjective factors—because it has convinced later revolutionaries that a few pistols and their own political convictions (which they always judge superior to everyone else's) could guarantee them eventual victory.

Mao suggested that guerrillas must aim for and depend upon the political mobilization of people who are mere bystanders in a conventional military conflict. Mao thus introduced a relationship between military action and the attitude and response of the audience. This added a new dimension to armed conflict: Instead of gauging success primarily in terms of the physical effect that military action had on the enemy, strategists could now say that the effect a violent action has on the people watching may be independent of, and may equal or even exceed in importance the actual physical damage inflicted on the foe. Terrorism is that proposition pursued to its most violent extreme, though terrorists have not been very good at explaining it.

"Political power grows from the barrel of a gun," wrote Mao, a phrase contemporary terrorists are fond of repeating. Their own thinking apparently stops at the muzzle. In recent years, terrorists have turned out thousands of pages of manifestos, manuals, assessments, directives, claims, communiqués, commentaries, critiques, and self-criticisms, but they have yet to articulate a clear and convincing theory to explain just how laying a bomb here or pulling a trigger there relates to the achievement of their objectives. What emerges from this vast body of angry literature are declarations, slogans, exhortations, unjustified assumptions, unproved assertions, and generally poor analysis. Carlos Marighella's *Mini Manual of the Urban Guerrilla*, which is supposed to have inspired and instructed the first generation of terrorists in Latin America and Western Europe, offers at best a discussion of terrorist tactics. (Marighella, a renegade from the Brazilian Communist Party, died in a gun battle with Brazilian police—hardly a model of success to be emulated.) Today's terrorists offer no theory, no doctrine, no strategy, not even an inspiring vision of the future.

Most outsiders find it difficult to understand how the killing of Olympic athletes in Munich or the hijacking of an airliner in Rome is supposed to ease the plight of Palestinians in the Middle East, or how blowing up an office in Manhattan will help topple a dictator in Latin America. And terrorists themselves may argue with each other over whether a particular action helps or hurts their cause. Some terrorist attacks may appear to be random or directed against targets that are not directly related to the terrorists' cause. For this reason, terrorist acts are often dismissed as *mindless* violence, *senseless* violence, or *irrational* violence; but terrorism is seldom mindless or irrational.

If it is not mindless, terrorism must have purpose—but what? To answer that question, we must try to think like terrorists and see beyond the apparent meaninglessness—sometimes even the tragic absurdity—of a single terrorist act, to discern its objectives.

The objectives of terrorism are not those of conventional combat. Terrorists do not try to take and hold ground or physically destroy their opponent's forces. They usually lack the kind of power needed to pursue such goals. Instead, terrorists attempt by their acts to inspire and manipulate fear, for a variety of purposes.

Terrorism may be aimed at gaining publicity. Terrorists hope that dramatic and shocking incidents of violence will attract attention to their cause and make them appear to be a force to be reckoned with. The atmosphere of fear and alarm they create frequently causes people to exaggerate the importance of the terrorists' cause and the strength of their forces and their movement. Because most terrorist groups are small and weak, the violence they carry out must be all the more dramatic and deliberately shocking.

Terrorist attacks are often carefully choreographed to attract the attention of the electronic media and the international press. The victims themselves often mean nothing to the terrorists. Terrorism is aimed at the people watching, not at the actual victims. Terrorism is theater.

Individual acts of terrorism also may be aimed at extracting specific concessions, such as the payment of ransom, the release of prisoners, or the publication of a terrorist message. Terrorists often seek to improve their bargaining power by creating a dramatic hostage situation that might coerce a government into meeting their demands.

The seizure of Israeli athletes at the 1972 Munich Olympiad had two objectives: publicity and concessions. The terrorists demanded that the government of Israel release a number of their imprisoned comrades. Israel rejected the demands, but the millions of people watching the Olympics on worldwide television guaranteed the terrorists the publicity they sought. Abu Iyad, the reputed architect of the attack, summarized the results: "The sacrifices made by the Munich heroes were not entirely in vain. They didn't bring about the liberation of any of their comrades imprisoned in Israel . . . but they did obtain the operation's other two objectives: World opinion was forced to take note of the Palestinian drama, and the Palestinian people imposed their presence on an international gathering that had sought to exclude them."

Terrorism also may be aimed at causing widespread disorder, demoralizing society, and breaking down the existing social and political order. These objectives are typical of revolutionary, nihilistic, or anarchistic terrorists. Terrorists condemn society's normal rules and relationships as intolerable complacency. Dramatic acts of terrorism, they think, will awaken an army of potential supporters who slumber in apathy. If the benefits of political obedience are destroyed, if the complacency of uninvolvement is not allowed, if the government's inability to protect its citizens (which is the origin of and basic reason for the existence of government) is revealed, if there is no place to hide in the ensuing battle, if people are forced to choose sides, then, terrorists presume, the "people" will join the opponents of the government and a revolution will be carried out.

Impatient at the reluctance of the "people" to join them, terrorists may deliberately aim at provoking repression. In the terrorists' mind, the government, alarmed by continued terrorist attacks, will be compelled to strike back brutally, and perhaps blindly. The heavy hand of repression will fall upon the masses, whose discontent can then be mobilized by the terrorists.

This idea was colorfully expressed by the Basque terrorists who wrote, "The enemy, as a massive animal, stung by many bees, is infuriated to the point of uncontrollable rage, and strikes out blindly to the left and right—on every side. At this point we have achieved one of our major objectives, forcing him to commit a thousand atrocities and brutal acts. The majority of his victims are innocent. Then the people—to this point more or less passive and waiting—become indignant and in reaction turn to us. We could not hope for a better outcome."

Another powerful motivation for terrorist actions is revenge. Small groups who have lost close comrades are particularly likely to strike back ferociously. A Puerto Rican separatist group detonated a bomb in a Wall Street restaurant in an obvious effort to cause casualties. The attack was in revenge for a bomb that was allegedly detonated by government authorities in a cafe frequented by separatists in Puerto Rico. Revenge becomes less important in larger organizations, where the deaths of comrades are accepted as losses in combat.

Finally, terrorism may be used to enforce obedience. This is the usual purpose of state or official terrorism, but terrorists themselves may also employ violence against their own members to discourage betrayal. The outcome desired is a prescribed pattern of behavior: obedience to the state or to the cause, and full cooperation in identifying and rooting out infiltrators or enemies. In recent years, governments have extended their reach to émigrés and exiles, hiring terrorists or employing their own agents to attack foes of the regime in other countries. Libya openly avowed its campaign to murder "traitors living abroad" as a warning to all dissidents. Syria, Iran, Yugoslavia, Bulgaria, and Romania have all been accused of killing defectors and troublesome exiles in Western Europe.

The success of such terrorism again depends on the creation of an atmosphere of fear, reinforced by the seeming omnipresence of the internal security or terrorist apparatus. Like other forms of terrorism, that aimed at enforcing obedience contains elements of deliberate drama: defectors are abducted or mysteriously assassinated, stories (often real) are spread of dungeons and torture. The objective is to frighten and alarm the target audience. In contrast to other forms of terrorism, however, terrorism for the purpose of enforcement seldom involves victims chosen at random, and the terrorists do not usually seek widespread publicity. It aims at the influence and control of its "own" population or organization. . . .

TERRORIST TACTICS:
A LIMITED REPERTOIRE

Terrorists operate with a limited tactical repertoire. Six basic terrorist tactics comprise 95 percent of all terrorist incidents: bombings, assassinations, armed assaults, kidnappings, barricade and hostage situations, and hijackings. No terrorist group uses all of them. Bombings, generally the least demanding of the tactics, predominate. Explosives are easy to obtain or manufacture, and a bombing requires little organization—one person can do the job, with little risk. Bombings alone account for roughly half of all international terrorist incidents.

This tactical repertoire has changed little over time. Terrorists appear to be more imitative than innovative, although their tactics have changed in response to new defenses. For example, seizing embassies, a popular terrorist tactic in the 1970s, declined in the 1980s for several reasons. Nations began turning their embassies into virtual fortresses, making takeovers more difficult. Governments also changed their policies. Whereas they were initially inclined to yield to the demands of terrorists holding hostages, governments began to adopt hardline policies as terrorist kidnappings and hostage seizures continued. Officials refused to release prisoners (the most frequent terrorist demand) or make other serious concessions.

The Israeli government refused to offer concessions to the terrorists holding Israeli athletes hostage at the Munich Olympics in 1972. In 1973, the United States refused to yield to the demands of terrorists holding American diplomats in Khartoum. In 1975, the German government refused to yield to the demands of terrorists holding the German embassy in Stockholm, the Irish government refused to yield to the demands of the surrounded kidnappers of a Dutch businessman, the Dutch government refused to yield to terrorists who had seized the Indonesian consulate, and the British government refused to yield to the terrorists holding hostages in London. There were exceptions, of course; terrorists occasionally won concessions. But overall, the likelihood that their demands would be met declined almost 50 percent in the latter half of the 1970s.

Unwilling to make concessions or stand by and do nothing while terrorists shot hostages, governments increasingly resorted to force to end barricade and hostage episodes at home and abroad, using forces they had created for the task. In the wake of the 1972 Munich incident, which ended in a disastrous shootout and the deaths of all of the hostages, governments began to develop specialized hostage-rescue units.

The tide turned in the second half of the 1970s. In 1976, Israeli commandos successfully rescued hostages held at Entebbe Airport in Uganda. In 1977, German commandos successfully rescued passengers aboard a hijacked airliner in Mogadishu. That same year, Dutch commandos successfully stormed a hijacked train and a school both held by South Moluccan terrorists. In 1980, British commandos rescued hostages held in the

Iranian embassy in London. Some of the rescue attempts failed, notably the American attempt to rescue U.S. hostages held in Iran. But the message was clear: Terrorists who barricaded themselves with hostages risked capture or death.

As security measures improved, the terrorists' chances of obtaining concessions declined, and the probability of their being captured or killed went up. Not surprisingly, seizing embassies declined as a terrorist tactic. At the same time, however, terrorist attacks in general, and attacks on diplomats in particular, increased. Terrorists merely changed their tactics, turning to assassinations and bombings.

This ability to switch tactics is a major reason why defending against terrorism is so difficult. Security measures can protect one set of targets against one type of attack, but terrorists can alter their tactics or shift their sights to other targets, obviating rather than overcoming the security measures, thus requiring new security measures to be devised. Unfortunately, the situation is asymmetrical. Unlike regular soldiers, terrorists do not have to attack at a certain time and place. Since many possible targets will satisfy their political needs, terrorists can strike practically anything or anyone they decide is a suitable target; they can attack almost anywhere, at any time. Because of limitations on resources, however, and because they prefer not to become garrison states, governments cannot protect everything, everywhere, all the time. This asymmetry also means an inequality of effort between terrorist attackers and antiterrorist defenders. The amount of resources required for defense against terrorism is determined not by the very small number of the terrorists, but rather by the virtually unlimited number of targets to be defended. This makes terrorism a cheap way to fight and a costly kind of threat to defend against. . . .

STATE-SPONSORED TERRORISM:
A NEW MODE OF CONFLICT

[State] sponsorship of terrorism [represents another disturbing trend]. A growing number of governments are using terrorist tactics themselves or employing terrorist groups as a mode of surrogate warfare. These governments see in terrorism a useful capability, a "weapons system," a cheap means of waging war against domestic foes or another nation rather than against a political or social structure. Terrorists offer a possible alternative to open, interstate armed conflict. Modern conventional war is increasingly impractical—it is destructive, it is expensive, and it is dangerous. World, and sometimes domestic, opinion imposes constraints. Some nations that are unable to mount a conventional military challenge see terrorism as the only alternative: an "equalizer."

Growing state sponsorship of terrorism has serious consequences. It puts more resources in the hands of the terrorists: money, sanctuary, sophisticated munitions, intelligence, and technical expertise. It also reduces the constraints on them, permitting them to contemplate large-scale operations without worrying so much about alienating their perceived constituents or provoking public backlash, since they need not depend on the local population for support.

Without the need to finance themselves through bank robberies or ransom kidnappings, and without the need to carry out operations just to maintain group cohesion, state-sponsored terrorist groups operate less frequently than groups that receive little or no state support, but they are many times more lethal and have far greater operational reach.

Middle Eastern groups like Black June (*Al-Assifa*), which has carried out assassinations in Western Europe, the Middle East, and Asia, and Islamic Jihad, the Shi'ite Moslem extremist group that claimed credit for the suicide bombings of the American and French embassies in Beirut and Kuwait and the U.S. Marine barracks, fall under the heading of state-sponsored groups. The 1983 bombing that killed 17 South Korean officials in Rangoon was an example of a country, in this case North Korea, sending its own agents to assassinate another country's leaders.

We may be on the threshold of an era of armed conflict in which limited conventional warfare, guerrilla warfare, and international terrorism will coexist, with governments and sub-national entities employing them individually, interchangeably, sequentially, or simultaneously—and having to defend against them.

Warfare in the future may be less destructive than that in the first half of the twentieth century, but it may also be less coherent. Warfare will cease to be finite. The distinction between war and peace will become more ambiguous and complex. Armed conflict will not be confined by national frontiers. Local belligerents will mobilize foreign patrons. Terrorists will attack foreign targets both at home and abroad. It will be necessary to develop capabilities to deal with—if not wage—all three modes of armed conflict, *perhaps simultaneously. . . .*

2

Revolutionaries and Functionaries: The Dual Face of Terrorism

Richard A. Falk

. . . To act effectively against terrorism, we must first learn to think clearly about what it is. . . . There exists great confusion, some genuine, some insidious, about the true character of terrorism in our world. As well, there are several strange, even startling, inconsistencies between what our government in Washington tells us as citizens about terrorism and the actual policies it pursues.

So far, the subject matter of terrorism has been dominated, with a few notable exceptions, by polemical treatments of the topic that encourage the illusion that terrorism is something alien to American patterns of conduct in the world, that it is done unto us, and that what we do violently unto others is legitimate counterterrorism, or, in the language of the polemics, "fighting back."

The general view is that the deepest roots of terrorism involve some mixture of desperation and depravity within dispossessed political extremists, especially those on the Left. My claim is that this mainstream image of terrorism is dangerously misleading. It overlooks the often calculating character of recourse to wanton and indiscriminate political violence from a variety of sources, including the deepest recesses of governmental bureaucracy operating in an entirely cool, calculating, rational style.

My argument is that it is futile and hypocritical self-deception to suppose that we can use the word *terrorism* to establish a double standard pertaining to the use of political violence. Unless we are consistent and self-critical in our use of language we invite the very violence we deplore.

Terrorism, then, is used here to designate any type of political violence that lacks an adequate moral and legal justification, regardless of whether the actor is a revolutionary group or a government. Of course, such a definition is open to interpretation. The word *adequate* suggests that legal and moral judgments are unavoidably somewhat subjective and that the process of justification is necessarily grounded in the realms of private morality and partisan ideology. To justify political violence adequately means seeking a generally persuasive and objective interpretation of prevailing

Note: footnotes have been deleted.

community norms as embodied in international law and in a shared ethos that restricts political violence to a defensive role and unconditionally protects those who are innocent. Seeking such an objective interpretation is not easy in a world of rival belief systems and cultural backgrounds, but neither is it impossible.

A pitfall of repudiating terrorism is the question of its effectiveness, especially in war. So long as terrorist methods are relied upon by states to avoid defeat or hasten victory in war, bolstered by the claim of saving lives, terrorists of all persuasions gain validation, provided only that they express some plausible justification that an indiscriminate attack or a sacrifice of innocent lives is reasonably consonant with their political goals. Programs of counterterrorism must renounce certain forms of political violence even if they seem effective and even if they are selected by leaders of governments or battlefield commanders in the heat of war.

It is foolish moralism to suppose that revolutionary groups would be prepared to follow a higher morality than that accepted by states. And it is hypocritical to insist that they do so; besides, it has no effect, except possibly as an example of self-deluding propaganda. On occasion, revolutionary groups adopt a higher morality, either renouncing violence altogether or being much more careful than their governmental adversaries about the protection of innocents. A comparison between the tactics of the African National Congress and the South African government over the course of several decades discloses such a persistent normative gap favorable to the revolutionary group in relation to the role of political violence in the South African struggle. Similar claims have been advanced on behalf of the conduct of the Sendero Luminoso ("shining path") in Peru, both as to its care in confining violence to appropriate targets given the reality of revolutionary struggle and its relatively greater care as to the protection of innocents as compared to the governement of Peru, especially during the period of Fernando Belaúnde Terry's presidency (1980–1985).

Similarly, we cannot argue conclusively that terrorism never works, and that therefore its renunciation on all sides could be undertaken as a practical political step. It is true that terroristic methods often harden opposition and alienate the perpetrators from the citizenry. But it is also true that acts of terrorism under certain circumstances focus attention on grievances and may induce an adversary to back down. Arguably, the British decisions to quit Ireland after World War I and Palestine and Cyprus after World War II were influenced by the terrorist tactics of their opponents, and surely the French defeat in Algeria was a consequence, in part, of terrorist challenges by revolutionary nationalists. Similarly the Allied powers in World War II may have weakened the will of Germany and Japan to resist by large-scale indiscriminate air attacks against heavy concentrations of the civilian population on cities.

The embodiment of terrorism in the modern war-fighting mentality is, at present, a fact of international life. Without using the word *terror-*

ism, Thomas Schelling accurately and typically associates the essence of military strategy with calculated recourse to terrorism:

> Military strategy can no longer be thought of, as it could for some countries in some eras, as the science of military victory. It is now equally, if not more, the art of coercion, of intimidation and deterrence. The instruments of war are more punitive than acquisitive. Military strategy, whether we like it or not, has become the diplomacy of violence.

The essence of our problem is that terrorism has been routinized on every side of the main political equations of our day.

In various forms, terrorism is as old as government and armed struggle, and as pervasive. The modern torment over terrorism arises because our lives and societies are more interconnected than ever before through mass media and because we live in an era of pervasive turmoil and high-technology weaponry that threaten the very idea of a human future.

It is too easy to blame the terrorist menace on the evil other. To end terrorism, in my view, requires a cultural resolve to avoid indiscriminate and unjustified political violence and to respect the integrity of civilian life at all costs. As soon as the choice of violent means is entrusted to human evaluations of effectiveness in supporting a political cause in a given setting, a terrorist ethos is bound to hold sway in circumstances of crisis and pressure.

Another strong temptation is to turn from terrorism to pacifism. After all, our world is saturated with violence, and we seem locked into a series of cultural patterns that sustain spirals of violence within and between nations. To move from violence to nonviolence is also to solve the problem of ambiguity. We do away with the dilemmas of assessment if we agree that violence is *never* justified. And further, nonviolence enjoys a strong mandate in several leading world religions, including Christianity and Buddhism, providing a basis for challenging the war system at a time of great jeopardy to the entire human species.

Yet pure nonviolence is not the course proposed here. For one thing, the opposite of terrorism is not nonviolence, but permissible violence. In other words, we don't want to claim that a war fought in self-defense is an instance of terrorism. That would be abuse of language as damaging as that of now associating terrorism only with the political violence of enemies while reserving to ourselves the right to engage in comparable practice.

Furthermore, given the way the world is organized—repressive governments, aggressive foreign policies—it is unrealistic and arrogant to insist that victims acquiesce in injustice. We may be exceedingly skeptical about violent strategies, and yet there does not seem to be either an ethical basis or a political structure that could sustain an invariable practice of nonviolence.

What we can do, and need to try, although it is difficult, is to oppose at the very least those forms of political violence that seek to gain their ends by striking fear into hearts and minds and that refuse to respect the innocence of civilian life. Such a position demands a lot, including the practice of warfare in a principled way. But unless we demand this much we are fooling ourselves if we think we are opposing terrorism. How can we claim to be antiterrorists unless we have ourselves renounced terrorism? . . .

In the end there are two principal ways to frame the debate on terrorism: the mainstream focus on the political violence of revolutionary groups and their supporters and the emphasis [placed here] on impermissible forms of political violence, regardless of the identity of the actor. The attempt here is to persuade readers of the importance of moving from the narrow to the broader conception of terrorism. . . .

. . . One notices that the torch of dignity is kept lit among suppressed and mutilated nationalist causes by terrorist practices. Whether among the Irish, Croatians, Basques, Moluccans, Ukrainians, Sikhs, Palestinians, Puerto Ricans, or others, the common impulse seems to be an incredibly deep urge to keep faith with the past and with one's specific identity. The mode of doing this is to make the victors or their representatives share some of the pain. Such recourse to terrorism is not mainly instrumental (a means to a political end), but rather symbolic or expressive (seeking to register a statement of grievance as powerfully as possible, by inducing shock, even trauma). In some settings, the main terrorist purpose is to mobilize the victims, challenging their indifference and ignorance. Recovering a sense of cultural identity need not require such violence: witness efforts to revive cultural identity by encouraging language study, music and art, and observance of folk rituals. Powerful experiences of national recovery have taken place among various indigenous peoples throughout the world. Among these peoples there is no project to dispossess the settler civilization, nor does such a capability exist, but there is a sense that cultural vitality can overcome the humiliations of the historical past. Some indigenous peoples, such as the Maoris in New Zealand, have made impressive progress despite the great difficulty of reestablishing cultural identity in opposition to the whole weight of modern industrial civilization.

But there is another distinctive source of terrorism in the modern world. It is the general suspension of limits with respect to political undertakings by, for, or against the state. The state claims for itself an unconditional security rationale, a rationale that culminates in making preparations to wage nuclear war and in envisioning a nuclear winter or other forms of catastrophic collapse. Many leading states have established intelligence agencies that engage in covert operations against foreign enemies without respect to the limits of law or morality. Analogously, those who aspire to statehood regard their nationalist aspirations as unconditional, therefore not subject to limits on their tactics.

But it is not only extremists who reject limits on their tactics, including recourse to violence. The pervasiveness of the terrorist phenomenon reflects a generalized breakdown of moral and legal inhibition to violence throughout society. To the extent that terrorism is perceived by the players to be "useful" it will be authorized even by liberal democracies that proclaim their *raison d'être* to be human dignity and the worth of the individual. In a quasi-official publication of the Rand Corporation, Brian Michael Jenkins (a prominent specialist on terrorism) summarizes his belief that the United States government must use terrorism to fight terrorism, as part of its need to engage in what he calls "indirect forms of warfare:"

> Indirect forms of warfare include clandestine and covert military operations carried out by other than the regular armed forces of a nation, providing asylum and support for guerrillas in an adjacent country, *providing support — and sometimes operational direction — to terrorist groups opposing a rival or enemy regime, and governmental use of terrorist tactics, such as assassinating foreign foes or troublesome exiles.* [emphasis added]

Only ignorance could excuse the view that the United States or other major governments renounce terrorist practices even when they serve accepted foreign policy goals. All that is unusual about the Jenkins formulation is its candor. Any examination of official practices would disclose the adoption of a wide series of terrorist undertakings, veiled in secrecy and disguised by the antiseptic semantics of covert operations, low-intensity warfare, and indirect modes of conflict.

So it is misleading in the extreme to characterize a few Arab states as international pariahs because they alone sponsor terrorist activities. It is equally misleading to construct an elaborate conspiracy theory that links instances of terrorism with a network masterminded and financed in Moscow. Opportunistic support of terrorist activity is an ingredient of geopolitical rivalry. No one would deny that the Soviet government has lent support to groups using political violence in a manner that qualifies it as terrorism under most accepted definitions, and that these groups have transnational links. But it is equally undeniable that the United States is similarly engaged. Indeed, given the relative openness of the American political system, it is impossible to mount a denial. The attempt is rather to provide a justification, in the form of either promoting democracy or resisting the expansion of Soviet interests. The debate over the Nicaraguan Contras [did not seriously draw] into question the reality of U.S. official support for political violence against civilians that could generally be identified as terrorism. The attempt [was] rather to provide an abstract justification for support by reference to democracy and strategic interests.

This second source of terrorism is the absolutism of secular politics, whether statist or antistatist. Terrorism is deployed (more or less intelligently and successfully) as a rational instrument by policymakers on *all sides* of the political equation.

This kind of idolatry finds its theoretical validation in a tradition of Western realist thought, especially that of Machiavelli, Hobbes, and Clausewitz. The terrorist sensibility is only one manifestation of the Machiavellian mind-set that proclaims the absolute primacy of state interests. We condemn the political adversary who engages in indiscriminate violence as a barbarian and outlaw and reward our own officials with accolades for their "statecraft," even conferring a Nobel Peace Prize from time to time on those who oversee this second type of terrorism.

I believe that it has become as essential to eliminate terrorism from our world as it is to eliminate nuclear weapons, and that it is possibly more difficult. To overcome terrorism we must respond to both of its sources: the unrelieved pain of groups who are victims of severe abuse and the unconditional pretension that political goals associated with state power can be pursued without respect for the limits of law or morality. In the foreground of this undertaking is a new consideration of the place of political violence in human affairs.

Admittedly, there are additional types of terrorism that do not flow from the two sources discussed, as well as depraved behavior that exerts a terrorist impact on the community even if it is derived from purely personal motives. There is the kind of nihilistic violence that is directed at modern societies by alienated intellectuals who feel betrayed on all sides, not least of all by the collapse of a viable Left project for the seizure of state power. The Baader-Meinhof Red Army Faction, Red Brigades, [and] the Symbionese Liberation Army are illustrative, expressing as much rage against the accommodationist politics of nationalist Communist parties as against the established order.

There is also the kind of pseudo-political private pathology that is associated with drug-induced, antisocial random violence that was frighteningly displayed by "the Manson family" in the Sharon Tate murders. This is not terrorism, but it spreads fear and acute anxiety throughout the society and may also be self-aggrandizing in the sense of seeking personal notoriety, even leadership among those sharing the same antisocial ethos.

Although pain and abuse seem to lie in the background of the terrorist personality in both these instances, the problems these individuals pose can usually be dealt with locally by standard law enforcement techniques. True, this kind of normative breakout is not nearly so likely to occur in societies that aspire actively to social justice and that sustain the social fabric of child development and community, but neither can complex societies tolerate expressive and symbolic violence, nor are such activities likely to put down deep roots. Unlike the two sources of terrorism, these variants cannot acquire potency from the notion of a sacred struggle, mutilated or thwarted by oppressive political arrangements that may currently have ascendancy, but not in the hearts and minds of those vanquished.

In any event, . . . those forms of political violence that are tied to the existence of states *and* to the vitality of nationalist strivings [must be emphasized]. Hence the two critical terrorist types for my purpose are revolutionaries (who act to oppose the state or to gain control over the state) and functionaries (who act on behalf of the state). There is a period of overlapping identity that occurs in the time after revolutionaries acquire control of the state and functionaries lose control. Some of the worst orgies of political violence occur in the aftermath of revolution when the fear of counterrevolution is both a pretext and explanation for bloody terror.

3

Conceptualizing Political Terrorism

Richard Shultz

Throughout history, the strategies and tactics of political terrorism have maintained a trenchant position in the political calculus within and between nations. However, since World War II, the practice of political terrorism has undergone a frightful proliferation at the national and transnational levels. Given this proliferation, and given the immense complexity of political terrorism, it would seem fruitless to attempt to analyze this process without first developing a systematic typology. . . .

As a first step, it is necessary to define, in a generalized sense, what constitutes political terrorism. . . . Brian Jenkins presents one of the more perceptive delineations of the characteristic attributes of political terrorism. According to Jenkins:

> the threat of violence, individual acts of violence, or a campaign of violence designed primarily to instill fear—to terrorize—may be called terrorism. Terrorism is violence for effect: not only, and sometimes not at all, for the effect on the actual victims of the terrorists. In fact, the victim may be totally unrelated to the terrorists' cause. Terrorism is violence aimed at the people watching. Fear is the intended effect, not the by-product, of terrorism.[1]

In essence, political terrorism is goal directed, employed in pursuit of political objectives. It is calculated violence directed at affecting the views and behavior of specific groups. While we generally agree with this definition, there are certain points with which we would take issue. First of all, while the instilling of fear characterizes the use of terrorism by many groups, it is not the principal aim of all terrorist acts. Furthermore, such acts may have certain tactical and strategic aims quite remote from instilling fear. Based on the above observations, the following working definition of political terrorism is proposed:

> Political terrorism may be defined as the threat and/or use of extranormal forms of political violence,[2] in varying degrees, with the objective of achieving certain political objectives/goals. Such goals constitute the long range and short-term objectives that the group or movement seeks to obtain. These will

Note: some footnotes have been deleted and others have been renumbered to appear in consecutive order.

differ from group to group. Such action generally is intended to influence the behavior and attitudes of certain targeted groups much wider than its immediate victims. However, influencing behavior is not necessarily the only aim of terrorist acts. The ramifications of political terrorism may or may not extend beyond national boundaries.

. . . Three categories of political terrorism—Revolutionary, Sub-Revolutionary, Establishment—may be defined as follows:

Revolutionary Terrorism may be defined as the threat and/or employment of extranormal forms of political violence, in varying degrees, with the objective of successfully effecting a complete revolutionary change (change of fundamental political-social processes) within the political system. Such means may be employed by revolutionary elements indigenous to the particular political system or by similar groups acting outside of the geographical boundaries of the system.

Sub-Revolutionary Terrorism may be defined as the threat and/or employment of extranormal forms of political violence, in varying degrees, with the objective of effecting various changes in the structural-functional aspects of the particular political system. The goal is to bring about certain changes within the body politic, not to abolish it in favor of a complete system change. Perhaps the broadest of the three categories, groups included here span the political spectrum from left to right (i.e., ethnic, religious, linguistic, regional, anticolonial, secessionist, reactionary, restorationist, etc.). Such means are employed primarily by groups or movements indigenous to the particular political system, though similar elements beyond the system's geographical boundaries may also rely on such means.

Establishment Terrorism may be defined as the threat and/or employment of extranormal forms of political violence, in varying degrees, by an established political system, against both external and internal opposition. Specifically, such means may be employed by an established political system against other nation-states and groups external to the particular political system, as well as internally to repress various forms of domestic opposition/unrest and/or to move the populace to comply with programs/goals of the state.

Although a long list of possible variables could be selected, for the sake of parsimony, we have chosen seven: causes, environment, goals, strategy, means, organization, and participation. Together, they yield the typology of political terrorism presented in Table 1.

As was noted above, the axiom that political terrorism is goal directed underlies the whole approach of this typology. Although various writers have attributed the use of political terrorism to various notions/forms of irrational behavior, it is our position that most extranormal political violence is employed to achieve certain political goals. Although certain forms of violence may result from irrational behavior, organized goal-directed political terrorism does not fall into this category. We define goals and the other variables that make up this typology [as follows].

TABLE 1 A Typology of Political Terrorism

General Categories	Selected Variables						
	Causes	Environment	Goals	Strategy	Means	Organization	Participation
Revolutionary Terrorism	Economic, Political, Social, Psychological factors	Internal (urban or rural revolutionary groups)	Long Range/Strategic Objectives	Primary or Secondary role in the overall strategy	Various capabilities and techniques employed	Nature—degrees of organizational structures	Participant profiles
		External (autonomous non-state revolutionary actors)	Short Term/Tactical Objectives				Leadership style/attitude
Sub-revolutionary Terrorism	Economic, Political, Social, Psychological factors	Internal (urban-rural non-revolutionary groups)	Long Range/Strategic Objectives	Primary or Secondary role in the overall strategy	Various capabilities and techniques employed	Nature—degrees of organizational structures	Participant profiles
		External (non-revolutionary, autonomous, non-state actors)	Short Term/Tactical Objectives				Leadership style/attitude
Establishment Terrorism	Economic, Political, Social, Psychological factors	Internal (repression of urban or rural opposition)	Long Range/Strategic Objectives	Primary or Secondary role in the overall strategy	Various capabilities and techniques employed	Nature—degrees of organizational structures	Participant profiles
		External (aimed at other nation-states or non-state actors)	Short Term/Tactical Objectives				Leadership style/attitude

Causes
Causes may be broadly conceptualized as any one or array of observable economic, political, social, and/or psychological factors. Conditions underlying the decision to resort to the use of extranormal political violence are quite varied and complex. These generalized causal factors may be sub-divided into two categories: long-term factors (preconditions extending over a lengthy period of time), and short-term factors (igniting events). In the case of non-revolutionary terrorism, long-term causal factors might include prolonged societal inequities, political disfranchisement, or economic depression; while short-term causes could be the result of a rapid upsurge of ethnicity, relative deprivation, or government repression.

Environment
This concerns the various forms political terrorism can take within the typology's three general categories. Conceptualized on the basis of geographical spheres, these environmental variations may be broadly classified into internal environmental (within the nation-state) and external environmental (global, or systemic levels) categories. For example, in the case of revolutionary terrorism, internal variations include the use of varying degrees of extranormal violence by urban and/or rural movements, while the external variation would include such actions when carried out by basically autonomous, non-state, actors.

Goals
Goals are the objectives at which terrorism is directed, categorized in terms of long range (broader strategic objectives) and short term (specific tactical objectives) political ends. Political terrorism may be directed towards both types of objectives simultaneously. For example, in the case of revolutionary terrorism, the long range/strategic objective would be to assist in the overthrow of the established order, while short term/tactical objectives might include disruption of the government's controls, demonstrations of the movement's strength, and building solidarity within the movement. In this case, the goals are a reflection of the ideology underlying the movement.

Strategy
For our purposes, this may be conceptualized as the overall plan—all necessary actions, policies, instruments, and apparatus—for the achievement of one's goals. It entails the deployment of men, materials, ideas, symbols, and forces in pursuit of these goals. With regard to political terrorism, the issue to be determined concerns whether it constitutes the primary or secondary tactics in the overall strategy. For example, in rural insurgency strategy, political terrorism has tended to be relegated to a secondary tactical position, while in the urban guerrilla and transnational variation, political terrorism has been elevated to a primary tactical consideration, and, in certain situations, to the level of a strategy.

Means
Means are categorized as any and all capabilities and techniques utilized within the broader strategic framework to achieve the goals projected. Capabilities available may include the most primitive or the most sophisticated forms of weaponry, mobility, electronic media manipulation, tactical commu-

nications, etc. The techniques utilized can range from kidnapping, barricade and hostage, bombing, armed assault or ambush, hijacking, incendiary attack or arson, assassination, chemical, bacteriological or radiological pollution.

Organization

As a fundamental adjunct to political terrorism, organization provides the formalized structure utilized for the planning, coordination, and application of extranormal forms of political violence. The success or limitations in the use of such forms of violence will be determined, in part, by the nature of the organization. For example, in the case of rural insurgent movements, an essential feature in the use of political terrorism is its detailed preparation. The effective use of terrorism is predicated on a thorough knowledge of localities, people, customs and habits. In essence, a great deal of time is spent in preparation, and organization is inextricably linked to this preparation.

Participation

This variable is broadly conceptualized to refer to the type of individual who takes part in political terrorism, as well as the various types of political leaders who employ political terrorism to achieve their particular goals. Thus, with regard to the profile of the terrorist, pertinent factors to be examined include age, social background, occupation, education, ideology, personality, and belief system. While many of these factors would also be pertinent to the examination of leadership involved, we would suggest focusing on the issues of "willingness to employ" and "attitude towards employing" terror and violence.

. . . The typology draws attention to the complex nature of political terrorism, and the various pertinent factors involved in such activity. Given the emotionalism, controversy, and outrage surrounding political terrorism, monistic explanations such as the notion that all those who resort to such tactics are "abnormal . . . in the sense of being psychologically disturbed,"[3] are pervasive in the literature. In fact, the literature in general has tended to be descriptive, prescriptive and obliquely emotive in form. Hopefully, this typology will move the study of political terrorism away from such subjective analysis.

. . . This typology is . . . more than simply a device for pigeonholing data. Classifying data is only the first step in explaining and predicting social phenomena. In addition, from a well-developed typology, assayable propositions can be derived. This will then result in the clarification of specific differences and similarities within and between the three terrorist categories. In effect, this suggests that once this skeletal typology is fleshed out, we will find that while the general categories tend to differ when compared as integrated systems of factors, similarities among categories will emerge in terms of specific variables. For example, with respect to manipulation of the media, little difference may exist between a conservative ethnic or regional sub-revolutionary group employing terrorism and a radical left terrorist group. However, in terms of long range goals and strategic objectives, significant differences will probably exist between two such divergent groups. . . .

NOTES

1. Brian Jenkins, *International Terrorism: A New Mode of Conflict* (Los Angeles: Crescent Publications, 1975), p. 1.

2. Extranormal forms of political violence would consist of very extreme and brutal tactics that would be considered even beyond the conventions of war if they were used in a declared war between two nations. Such acts are too numerous to list. Examples would include blowing up a school with children present, torture of political prisoners, kidnapping, execution, etc.

3. Albert Parry, *Terrorism from Robespierre to Arafat* (New York: The Vanguard Press, Inc., 1976).

4

The Political Underpinnings of Terrorism

Gary G. Sick

Terrorism, to paraphrase Clausewitz, is the continuation of politics by other means. The political content of the terrorist act distinguishes it from such ordinary criminal activities as murder, robbery, hijacking and extortion—all of which are committed with far greater frequency by vastly larger numbers of non-terrorists for motives of simple profit or passion.

Terrorists become terrorists, at least initially, for reasons associated with politics. After a certain amount of time, of course, terrorists may *continue* to be terrorists for no reason except that they *are* terrorists. More than most vocations, terrorism does not easily lend itself to career changes. But the initial impulse that led a group to adopt terrorism as a method of operation or that persuaded an individual to participate in such activities almost certainly had its origins in political circumstances.

Indeed, the political nature of their origin and proclaimed purpose is the most important common characteristic shared by such disparate groups as the Sendero Luminoso of Peru, the Provisional Irish Republican Army, the dissident Sikhs of India, the Moro National Liberation Front of the Philippines, the Armenian Secret Army for the Liberation of Armenia, the Italian Red Brigades, the Popular Front for the Liberation of Palestine, and in the United States, organizations as diverse as the Puerto Rican Front for National Liberation, the Weather Underground, the Jewish Defense League, and a scattering of neo-fascist groups.

There are, of course, other similarities among such groups, including many of the methods they employ, the organizational structures they adopt, and, some would argue, personality attributes. However, those similarities (to the extent they exist at all) do not adequately explain terrorism. Instead, they appear to be a by-product of the conditions and choices common to the terrorist experience. Individuals with a taste for violence and extremist beliefs may be attracted to terrorist activity, but such individuals exist in every population, including those that are relatively free of terrorism. Their choice of terrorism, as opposed to other possible forms of behavior, is a function of the political environment.

The political nature of terrorism endows it with a special quality of generalized menace. Acts of violence against person or property for whatever

Note: footnotes have been deleted.

reason may be terrifying, but when such acts are performed in conscious defiance of an existing political order and, as is often the case, in the pursuit of radical political alternatives, they acquire an added sinister weight. Terrorist acts may be directed at almost anyone, anywhere. The fact that such attacks are statistically rare is counterbalanced by the realization that, at least in principle, no one is entirely safe.

Furthermore, the political underpinnings of the terrorist philosophy provide a convenient rationalization—perhaps even a perpetual incentive—to escalate both the frequency and the shock value of operations. Neither the calculus of the common criminal nor the constraints of conventional morality apply. Since terrorism occurs in an ethical netherworld where ordinary notions of good and bad, right and wrong, can be—and frequently are—reversed, the normal defense mechanisms of society seem less relevant and hence less comforting. Terrorists typically demand fundamental structural changes in the status quo (or the concessions that are politically humiliating) and seem to be willing to employ any means—however repugnant—to dramatize and advance their cause. They not only operate outside the law (which is common enough) but reject the ultimate legitimacy of the law itself.

Terrorists attempt to rewrite the rules of the game and to transcend the barriers that societies erect for deterrence and self-protection. It is small consolation that they seldom succeed. The mere combination of outrageous demands and outrageous behavior commands our attention, in spite of ourselves. Terrorism is capable of inspiring a kind of horrified paralysis—like a cobra hypnotizing its prey. It is precisely that reaction that terrorists strive to achieve, and our susceptibility to such tactics ensures that terrorism will always remain a tempting strategy of coercion for those marginal groups and individuals devoted to a cause that has lost its power to persuade.

The political dimension of terrorism bedevils our attempts to study it in a scholarly or systematic fashion. The word *terrorism* itself is hopelessly loaded and is normally applied only to activities of which we disapprove, implicitly or explicitly. Even those who practice terror and who openly seek credit for bombings, hijackings, and other such activities prefer to be known by other, less pejorative, titles. The cliché that "one man's terrorist is another man's freedom fighter" is no less true for being trite.

Thus, whether we like it or not, the study of "terrorism" lends itself most often and most easily to the excoriation of political enemies and the production of political tracts. The heavy overload of political baggage attached to the term also helps explain why it has proven so difficult to devise a definition that is acceptable to a wide range of opinion.

If a study is primarily intended to launch an assault on certain political movements or tendencies, then the central methodological problem is how to define "terrorism" in a way that will include the enemy while excluding other activities that the author finds congenial. . . .

Similarly, the recent preoccupation with *state-sponsored terrorism* has had the effect of focusing attention on a few key countries that are hostile to the United States and its allies while brushing over the activities of many domestic terrorist groups, even though their combined frequency and destructiveness dwarf the "state-sponsored" variety. It now seems quaint to recall that only a few years ago students of the subject were at pains to draw distinctions between the actions of small groups dedicated to the overthrow of the state and the actions of the state itself. State behavior was granted a degree of legitimacy denied to those committed to its downfall, perhaps in uncomfortable acknowledgment of the fact that states have historically employed tactics that could reasonably be described as terrorism in the pursuit of their political objectives.

For those who would go beyond the denunciation of political enemies to a more objective and systematic examination of the terrorist phenomenon, the definitional problem is not so easily resolved. One possibility is to replace the loaded term *terrorism* with more neutral phrases, such as *political violence* or *low-intensity conflict*. However, such terms are often unsatisfactory, since they may include activities not normally regarded as terrorism and because they fail to convey one of the essential elements of the phenomenon, to wit, that it evokes "terror."

The serious scholar may find it necessary to strike a balance, continuing to use the word *terrorism* but adhering to a rigorous definition that attempts to remove the most obvious ideological and emotional connotations. A particularly lucid example is the formulation proposed by Martha Crenshaw.

> Terrorism is the deliberate and systematic use or threat of violence to coerce changes in political behavior. It involves symbolic acts of violence, intended to communicate a political message to watching audiences.

By focusing on the objectives and methods of political terror, rather than the identity or political affiliation of those who practice it, this definition provides a useful basis for thinking about terrorism in its many guises while avoiding the more obvious value judgments.

Nevertheless, it is probably illusory to imagine that even the most elegant definition will succeed in dissolving—except perhaps for a highly specialized audience—the encrusted impressions and misperceptions that have accumulated around this highly emotional word. Certainly in the political sphere, *terrorism* is a "fighting word." It is much too valuable as a rhetorical weapon and as a proven instrument for mobilizing public opinion to permit its sharp edge to be blunted—even if it sometimes cuts both ways.

The high political content of terrorism, the absence of an agreed definition, the emotional response that terrorist acts typically provoke, and the intensity of public interest during periods of conspicuous terrorist activity all suggest that the subject will continue to receive a great deal of public and media attention but that this coverage will, for the most part, generate more heat than light. . . .

Terrorism is a calculated and deliberate assault on our most cherished values. To the extent that it seems to threaten us personally, it assumes the attributes of pure evil. Our instinctive response to terrorism is therefore more emotional than logical. We are appalled by the impersonal, implacable nature of an alien ideology that refuses to respect the most fundamental rules of civilized behavior, that takes aim at us personally by disregarding everything we believe and stand for. We are angry. We are frustrated. We are frightened.

At the same time, we need to be aware of the explosive potential terrorism represents for public policy. As we struggle to devise policies to deal with terrorism, several general observations are worth bearing in mind:

- Terrorism is a form of political defiance that has been used for many centuries. Like vice or corruption, it can be (and often is) confronted, contained, and defeated in specific instances. But the phenomenon itself cannot be eliminated.
- Definitions of terrorism are suspect, since they are frequently used to condemn and denigrate political enemies. We also reveal our political preferences by distinguishing between those terrorist actions we deplore and those we are prepared to tolerate.
- For those reasons a consistent national policy to deal with terrorism in all its manifestations may be impossible, or politically undesirable.
- In a free society the media will play a key role in shaping public attitudes toward terrorism and generating pressures for actions that may have to be resisted. However, "shooting the messenger" will not make the problem go away, and attempts to impose restrictions on free expression are probably as futile as they are ill-advised.
- Because of its salience and fascination, terrorism is an effective instrument for mobilizing public opinion and can be used to generate support for a wide range of policies—wise or unwise. It is more likely than many other issues to provoke consideration of the use of military force.
- Foreign-policy actions relating to terrorism are intimately connected with domestic political considerations and perceptions. The risk is therefore always present that initiatives will be undertaken primarily for domestic reasons, without adequate regard for the long-term international consequences.

Awareness of these general principles offers no guarantee of an effective and rational policy. They may be useful, however, because they remind us that policymaking in this complex and contentious area is subject to a special set of risks that we ignore at our peril.

5

The Strategy of Terrorism

David Fromkin

I

. . . The generations that have come to maturity in Europe and America since the end of the Second World War have asked only to bask in the sunshine of a summertime world; but increasingly they have been forced instead to live in the fearful shadow of other people's deadly quarrels. Gangs of politically motivated gunmen have disrupted everyday life, intruding and forcing their parochial feuds upon the unwilling attention of everybody else.

True, other ages have suffered from crime and outrage, but what we are experiencing today goes beyond such things. Too small to impose their will by military force, terrorist bands nonetheless are capable nowadays of causing enough damage to intimidate and blackmail the governments of the world. Only modern technology makes this possible—the bazooka, the plastic bomb, the submachine gun, and perhaps, over the horizon, the nuclear mini-bomb. The transformation has enabled terrorism to enter the political arena on a new scale, and to express ideological goals of an organized sort rather than mere crime, madness, or emotional derangement as in the past.

Political terrorism is a distinctive disorder of the modern world. It originated as a term and, arguably, as a practice, less than two centuries ago and has come into the spotlight of global conflict in our lifetime. Whereas both organized and irregular (or guerrilla) warfare began with the human race, political terrorism emerged as a concept only in 1793 [during Robespierre's Reign of Terror in revolutionary France]. As a political strategy, it is both new and original; and if I am correct, its nature has not yet fully been appreciated.

Of course nobody can remain unaware of the upsurge of global terrorism that has occurred in recent years. But the novelty of it has not been perceived. Force usually generates fear, and fear is usually an additional weapon. But terrorism employs the weapon of fear in a special and complicated sort of way.

II

. . . [Political] terrorism has become especially notorious in a different cause from that in which Robespierre used it. It has been used to destroy governments rather than to sustain them. This changed the way in which many people thought of it as a political strategy and how they viewed its adherents. As revolutionaries, terrorists have come to seem romantic figures to many. Their life of dangers and disguises, risks and betrayals, conspiracies and secret societies, exerted a powerful fascination. As torn and tormented characters, they provided authors with the stuff of which complex and interesting novels can be made.

Though the terrorists seemed romantic, until recently they also seemed ineffective. Until the Irish Treaty of 1921, they scored no significant political successes. The most famous of the terrorist groups up to that time was the Terrorist Brigade of the Russian Socialists-Revolutionists; and not merely did they fail to change the Tsarist government in the ways in which they desired, they also failed to pick up the pieces when it was overthrown by others. Plekhanov, Lenin, Trotsky and the other Russian disciples of Marx had seen more clearly in placing their emphasis on mass organization rather than on individual terrorism. The Bolsheviks came to power by winning the metropolitan workmen, the sailors of the Baltic fleet, and the soldiers to their side. Organization proved to be the key to victory. It was not individual gunmen but armed masses who seized power in Russia. Revolution, like war, is the strategy of the strong; terrorism is the strategy of the weak.

It is an uncertain and indirect strategy that employs the weapon of fear in a special sort of way in which to make governments react. Is fear an effective method? Is fright any kind of weapon at all? What can terrorists hope to accomplish by sowing fear? How can it help their side to vanquish its opponents? Clearly it can do so in many ways. Fright can paralyze the will, befuddle the mind, and exhaust the strength of an adversary. Moreover, it can persuade an opponent that a particular political point of view is taken with such deadly seriousness by its few adherents that it should be accommodated, rather than suffering casualties year after year in a campaign to suppress it. . . .

Terrorism can also make heroes out of gunmen, and thereby rally popular support to their cause. The problem this creates for them is that when the time comes to make the compromises necessary in order to negotiate the terms of their victory, the glamour wanes, and with it, the political support. . . .

Just as it can make gangsters into heroes, terrorist provocations can also make policemen into villains. . . .Brutality is an induced governmental response that can boomerang. It is this ability to use the strength of repression against itself, in many different ways, that has enabled terrorist strategies to succeed in many situations that have, rightly or wrongly, been described as colonialist in the modern world.

III

Sophisticated approaches have been developed along these lines. One of these was explained to me and to others at a meeting in New York City sometime in 1945 by one of the founders of the Irgun Zvai Leumi, a tiny group of Jewish militants in what was then the British-mandated territory of Palestine. His organization had no more than 1,000 or 1,500 members, and it was at odds with the Palestinian Jewish community almost as much as it was with the mandatory regime. Yet he proposed to combat Great Britain, then a global power whose armed forces in the Second World War numbered in the millions, and to expel Great Britain from Palestine.

How could such a thousand-to-one struggle be won? To do so, as he explained it, his organization would attack property interests. After giving advance warning to evacuate them, his small band of followers would blow up buildings. This, he said, would lead the British to overreact by garrisoning the country with an immense army drawn from stations in other parts of the world. But postwar Britain could not afford financially to maintain so great an army either there or anywhere else for any extended period of time. Britain urgently needed to demobilize its armed forces. The strain would tell; and eventually economic pressure would drive the Attlee-Bevin government either to withdraw from Palestine or else to try some reckless and possibly losing gamble in an effort to retrieve the situation.

It can be argued that such is in fact what happened. Of course Britain might have withdrawn anyway, at some other time or for some other reason. But that is really beside the point, for the Irgun wanted independence then and there, in order to open up the country to refugees from Hitler's Europe. They got what they wanted when they wanted it by doing it in their own way. . . .

[Despite] its flaws, the strategy was sufficiently ingenious so that the Irgun played a big part in getting the British to withdraw. Its ingenuity lay in using an opponent's own strength against him. It was a sort of jujitsu. First the adversary was made to be afraid, and then, predictably, he would react to his fear by increasing the bulk of his strength, and then the sheer weight of that bulk would drag him down. Another way of saying this is that the Irgun, seeing that it was too small to defeat Great Britain, decided, as an alternative approach, that Britain was big enough to defeat itself.

IV

In the 1950s, the nationalist rebel group in Algeria developed yet another method of using the strength of an occupying power against itself. Their method was to induce that strength to be used as a form of persuasion.

For, in Algeria, the whole question was one of persuasion. The problem initially faced by the miniscule band of Algerian nationalists that called itself the National Liberation Front (or, in its French initials, FLN) was that Algeria at that time had little sense of national identity. Its population was not homogeneous; and the Berbers, the Arabs, and the settlers of

European descent were peoples quite different from one another. The name and separate existence of Algeria were only of recent origin. For most of recorded history, Algeria had been no more than the middle part of North Africa, with no distinct history of its own. Legally it was merely the southern part of France. The French had treated Morocco and Tunisia as protectorates, with separate identities, but not Algeria, which was absorbed into France herself. With sarcasm, Frenchmen used to reply to Americans who urged independence for Algeria by saying that, on the same basis, the United States should set Wisconsin free or give back independence to South Carolina.

It was a jibe that went to the heart of the matter. Colonial empires were coming to an end in the 1950s and 1960s. If Algeria was a nation, then inevitably it would be set free to govern itself. Only if it were genuinely a part of France could it continue to be ruled from Paris. All depended, therefore, on whether the indigenous population could be convinced by the French government that Algeria was not a separate country, or upon whether they could be persuaded by the FLN to change their minds so as to think of themselves as a nation.

The FLN strategy of terrorism addressed itself to this central and decisive issue. By itself, as has been said, terror can accomplish nothing in terms of political goals; it can only aim at obtaining a response that will achieve those goals for it. What the FLN did was to goad the French into reacting in such a way as to demonstrate the unreality of the claim that there was no distinct Algerian nation. Unlike the Irgun, the FLN did not set out to campaign merely against property; it attacked people. It used random violence, planting bombs in market places and in other crowded locations. The instinctive French reaction was to treat all persons of non-European origin as suspects; but, as Raymond Aron was to write, "As suspects, all the Muslims felt excluded from the existing community." Their feeling was confirmed when, in the middle 1950s, the authorities further reacted by transferring the French army units composed of Muslim Algerian troops out of Algeria and into mainland France, and replacing them in Algeria by European troops. By such actions they showed in the most unmistakable way that they regarded no Algerians as Frenchmen except for the European settlers. They spoke of we and us, and of they and them, and did not realize that their doing so meant the end of Algérie Française.

Thus the French conceded the issue of the war at its very outset. They threw away the potential support of Muslim Algeria because they were skeptical of the possibility that it could be obtained. From that moment the conclusion of the conflict was foregone. Once the sympathies of the population had shifted to its side, the FLN was able to outgrow mere terrorism and to organize a campaign of guerrilla warfare. It also was enabled to appeal to world sympathies on behalf of a people fighting for its freedom. From the French point of view all had become hopeless; for no amount of force can keep an unwilling population indefinitely in subjection. Even though the FLN had written the script, the French, with suicidal logic, went ahead to play the role for which they had been cast.

The FLN success was therefore a special case. It required a particular kind of opponent. It could not be duplicated in other circumstances and conditions.

V

[Since the 1950s] revolutionist-terrorists . . . have failed to perceive the special characteristics of the colonialist situation that facilitated success for . . . Irgun and Algerian terrorists. They have tried to apply the strategy of terrorism in situations that are essentially different. This has been true, for example, of extremist groups seeking to overthrow liberal-pluralistic regimes . . . . Their theory has been that their terrorist attacks would force hitherto liberal regimes to become repressive, a change which in turn would alienate the masses, thus setting the stage for revolution. But it has not worked out that way in practice. In the United States, for example, terrorist bomb attacks have not led to any change at all in the form of government, much less to a transformation of America into a police state. On the other hand, in Uruguay, once the model democracy of Latin America, the terror of the Tupamaro bands has led to a military dictatorship that brutally destroyed the Tupamaros, but that does not seem, at least as yet, to have led to the predicted reaction by the masses in favor of revolutionary action.

Other revolutionary groups have taken a somewhat different approach. They have argued that liberal democracies are already police states. Thus, the object of revolutionary terrorist action should be to reveal this hidden reality to the population at large. Unthinking reaction by the authorities to terrorist provocation would accomplish the desired result. Thus the aim of terrorism would be to trick the government into taking off its mask.

In open societies such as Great Britain and the United States, the liberal democratic features have proved to be a face and not a mask: there is nothing to take off, and the strategy failed because its factual premise proved to be untrue.

In closed societies, the strategy has been to show that authoritarian regimes are actually impotent despite their outward show of virility. In such circumstances, supposedly, by demonstrating that the public author- ities are powerless to enforce law and order, a campaign of terror can cause a government to collapse; but the flaw in the theory is that the ter- rorists usually are not strong enough to take its place. Either some more broadly based group will seize power, or else . . . private groups will take the law into their own hands and retaliate in kind against murder and extortion, so that society relapses into a semi-anarchic state of reprisals and blood feuds, where terrorists are buried with their victims. . . .

VI

If this is an age of terror, then it has become all the more important for us to understand exactly what it is that terrorism means. Terrorism, as has been seen, is the weapon of those who are prepared to use violence but who believe that they would lose any contest of sheer strength. All too little understood, the uniqueness of the strategy lies in this: that it achieves its goal not through its acts but through the response to its acts. In any other such strategy, the violence is the beginning and its consequences are the end of it. For terrorism, however, the consequences of the violence are themselves merely a first step and form a stepping stone toward objectives that are more remote. Whereas military and revolutionary actions aim at a physical result, terrorist actions aim at a psychological result.

But even that psychological result is not the final goal. Terrorism is violence used in order to create fear; but it is aimed at creating fear in order that the fear, in turn, will lead somebody else—not the terrorist—to embark on some quite different program of action that will accomplish whatever it is that the terrorist really desires. Unlike the soldier, the guerrilla fighter, or the revolutionist, the terrorist therefore is always in the paradoxical position of undertaking actions the immediate physical consequences of which are not particularly desired by him. An ordinary murderer will kill somebody because he wants the person to be dead, but a terrorist will shoot somebody even though it is a matter of complete indifference to him whether that person lives or dies. He would do so, for example, in order to provoke a brutal police repression that he believes will lead to political conditions propitious to revolutionary agitation and organization aimed at overthrowing the government. The act of murder is the same in both cases, but its purpose is different, and each act plays a different role in the strategies of violence.

Only an understanding of the purpose for which such an act is undertaken can enable us to know the nature of the act. When Julius Caesar was murdered in the Roman Senate, it was an assassination of the traditional sort, intended to eliminate a specific figure from the political scene; but had he been killed there by the representative of a subversive sect, intent on plunging his dagger into the first Roman leader he encountered in order to provoke a certain political response from the Senate, it would instead have been an act of political terrorism.

It is because an action of the same sort may be undertaken by two different groups with two quite different ends in view that terrorism is so often confused with guerrilla warfare, for terrorists and guerrillas often seem to be doing the same sorts of things. . . .

The distinction is of more than academic importance. The French lost their empire over Algeria when they mistook terrorism for guerrilla warfare. They thought that when the FLN planted a bomb in a public bus, it was in order to blow up the bus; whereas the real FLN purpose in planting the bomb was not to blow up the bus, but to lure authorities into reacting by arresting all the non-Europeans in the area as suspects.

The terrorist is like a magician who tricks you into watching his right hand while his left hand, unnoticed, makes the switch. It is understandable that the French authorities in Algeria became totally obsessed by the need to stamp out criminal attacks, but it was fatal to their policy to do so, for the violent attacks were merely a subsidiary issue. The tiny FLN band of outlaws could have blown up every bus in all of Algeria and never won a convert to their cause of independence. Failing to understand the strategy of terrorism, the French did not see that it was not the FLN's move, but rather the French countermove, that would determine whether the FLN succeeded or failed. . . .

The tragedies that befall great public figures can sometimes seem to have been deserved; but when a man on the street is killed at random on behalf of a cause with which he had nothing to do, it is a different matter and provokes a different reaction. In a homogeneous society, at any rate, it leads to a reaction against the terrorism, and it renders it vulnerable to a campaign that politically isolates it in order to physically destroy it, for the nature of the attacks tends to demonstrate that terrorists are enemies of the people rather than merely of the government. . . .

[In] view of its inherent weakness, it is remarkable how many political successes have been scored by the strategy of terrorism in the last few decades. Its success seems to be due in large part to a miscomprehension of the strategy by its opponents. They have neglected the more important of the two levels on which terrorism operates. They have failed to focus on the crucial issue of how the manner in which they, as opponents, respond affects the political goals of the terrorists. Discussion instead has centered on the criminal justice aspects of the question: prevention and punishment. . . .

The overriding questions are not legal or technological; they are philosophical and political. Terrorism is the indirect strategy that wins or loses only in terms of how you respond to it. The decision as to how accommodating or how uncompromising you should be in your response to it involves questions that fall primarily within the domain of political philosophy.

VII

Those who are targets of terrorism—and who are prepared to defend themselves by doing whatever is necessary in order to beat it—start with a major advantage. The advantage is that success or failure depends upon them alone. Terrorism wins only if you respond to it in the way that the terrorists want you to; which means that its fate is in your hands and not in theirs. If you choose not to respond at all, or else to respond in a way different from that which they desire, they will fail to achieve their objectives.

The important point is that the choice is yours. That is the ultimate weakness of terrorism as a strategy. It means that, though terrorism cannot always be prevented, it can always be defeated. You can always refuse to do what they want you to do.

Whether to pay the price of defeating terrorism is increasingly going to be a major question in our time. The answer is relatively easy in most kidnapping and ransom situations: experience has shown that blackmailers and extortionists usually are encouraged to try it again if you give in to their demands the first time. So, if you can do so, you should accept the consequences, however terrible, of standing firm in order to avoid an infinite sequence of painful events.

But the price of doing so is constantly rising, as technology increases the range and magnitude of horrible possibilities. Terrorist outrages, when they occur, are bound to become more deadly. Increasingly, we will be under pressure to abridge our laws and liberties in order to suppress the terrorists. It is a pressure that should be resisted.

In our personal lives we sometimes have to choose between these alternatives: whether to live a good life or whether to live a long life. Political society in the years to come is likely to face a similar choice. An open society . . . is especially vulnerable to terrorist violence, which seems to threaten us with ever more dreadful and drastic fates. Have we the stoicism to endure nonetheless? Will we be tempted to abandon our political and moral values? Will we be willing to go on paying an ever higher price in order to defeat the terrorists by refusing to respond in the way they want us to?

Of course it would make things easier if terrorism simply would go away. It seems unlikely to do so. The weapons are at hand, and they probably will be used, for terrorism will never cease until the day when the Old Man of the Mountain loses his last disciple. The old man was grand master of the sect called the Assassins (hashish-ins) because of the hashish which he gave them. The old man, according to Marco Polo, used to drug his young disciples and transport them while they were asleep to his secret pleasure garden, persuading them when they awoke in it that it was paradise itself. Drugging them again, he would transport them back to the everyday world while they slept. Never afterward did they doubt that their Master could and would reward them with eternal paradise after death if they did his killing for him while they were alive. And so they did do his killing for him.

If anything, the modern world seems to breed more and more votaries of this peculiar sect. They seem to thrive and multiply everywhere in the world, bomb or machine gun in hand, motivated by political fantasies and hallucinations, fully convinced that their slaughter of the innocent will somehow usher in a political millennium for mankind. "*Voici le temps des* ASSASSINS," as Rimbaud wrote in the dawn of the industrial age; and we do indeed live in the time of the Assassins.

6

The Seven Deadly Sins of Terrorism

Paul Johnson

Before indentifying the correct approach to the terrorist problem, let us look at the wrong one. The wrong approach is to see terrorism as one of many symptoms of a deep-seated malaise in our society, part of a pattern of violence which includes juvenile delinquency, rising crime rates, student riots, vandalism and football hooliganism, and which is to be attributed to the shadow of the H-bomb, rising divorce rates, inadequate welfare services and poverty. This analysis usually ends in the meaningless and defeatist conclusion that society itself is to blame: "We are all guilty."

The truth is, international terrorism is not part of a generalized human problem. It is a specific and identifiable problem on its own; and because it is specific and identifiable, because it can be isolated from the context which breeds it, it is a remediable problem. That is the first point to get clear.

But to say it is remediable is not to underestimate the size and danger of the problem. On the contrary: it is almost impossible to exaggerate the threat which terrorism holds for our civilization because, unlike many other current threats, it is not being contained. Quite the reverse, it is increasing steadily, and one reason is that very few people in the civilized world—governments, parliaments, journalists and the public generally—take terrorism seriously enough.

Most people, lacking an adequate knowledge of history, tend to underestimate the fragility of a civilization. They do not appreciate that civilizations fall as well as rise, that they can be, and have been, destroyed by malign forces. In our recoverable history, there have been at least three Dark Ages. One occurred in the third millenium B.C., and smashed the civilization of the Egyptian Old Kingdom—the culture which built the pyramids. Another occurred towards the end of the second millenium B.C., and destroyed Mycenaean Greece, Minoan Crete, the Hittite Empire, and much else. We are more familiar with the third, which destroyed the Roman Empire in the West in the fifth century A.D.; it took Europe 800 years to recover, in terms of organization, technical skills and living standards. The great catastrophes had varying causes, but there was a common factor in all of them. They occurred when the spread of metals technology and the availability of raw materials enabled the forces of barbarism to equal or surpass the civilized powers in the quality and quantity of their weapons, for in the last resort, civilizations stand or fall, not by covenants, but by the sword.

ENEMIES OF SOCIETY

Edward Gibbon, at the end of his great book, *The Decline and Fall of the Roman Empire*, wrote: "The savage nations of the globe are the common enemies of civilized society, and we may well inquire with anxious curiosity whether Europe is still threatened with a repetition of those calamities which formerly oppressed the arms and institutions of Rome." Writing in the 1780s, on the threshold of the Industrial Revolution, Gibbon thought he could answer his own question with a reasonably confident negative. He rightly estimated the strength of the civilized world to be increasing, and he believed the scientific and rational principles on which that strength was based were becoming more firmly established with every year that passed.

Now, . . . 200 years later, we cannot be so sure. The principles of objective science and human reason, the notion of the rule of law, the paramountcy of politics over force, are everywhere under growing and purposeful challenge; and the forces of savagery and violence, which constitute this challenge, are becoming bolder, more numerous and, above all, better armed. The arms available to terrorists, the skills with which they use them and, not least, the organizational techniques with which these weapons and skills are deployed, are all improving at a fast and accelerating rate—a rate much faster than the countermeasures available to civilized society. . . .

These menacing improvements in weaponry and organization have been brought about by the international availability of terrorist support, supply and training services. Terrorism is no longer a purely national phenomenon, which can be destroyed at a national level. It is an international offensive—an open and declared war against civilization itself—which can only be defeated by an international alliance of the civilized powers.

To the argument that terrorists are not enemies of civilization in that they are often idealists pursuing worthy ultimate aims, I would answer that the terrorist can never be an idealist, and that the objects sought can never justify terrorism. For what is terrorism? It is the deliberate, systematic murder, maiming and menacing of the innocent to inspire fear in order to gain political ends. By this definition, the impact of terrorism, not merely on individuals, not merely on single nations, but on humanity as a whole is intrinsically evil, necessarily evil and wholly evil. It is so for a number of demonstrable reasons—what I call the Seven Deadly Sins of Terrorism.

EXALTATION OF VIOLENCE

First, terrorism is the deliberate and cold-blooded exaltation of violence over all forms of political activity. The modern terrorist does not employ violence as a necessary evil but as a desirable form of action. There is a definite intellectual background to the present wave of terrorism. It springs not only from the Leninist and Trotskyist justification of violence, but from the postwar philosophy of violence derived from Nietzsche through Heidegger, and widely popularized by Sartre, his colleague and disciple. . . .

Some of those influenced by Sartre went much further—notably Franz Fanon. His most influential work, *Les Damnés de la Terre*, which has a preface by Sartre, has probably played a bigger part in spreading terrorism in the Third World than any other tract. Violence is presented as liberation, a fundamental Sartrean theme. For a black man, writes Sartre in his preface, "to shoot down a European is to kill two birds with one stone, to destroy an oppressor and the man he oppresses at the same time." By killing, the terrorist is born again—free. Fanon preached that violence is a necessary form of social and moral regeneration for the oppressed. "Violence alone," he writes, "violence committed by the people, violence organized and educated by its leaders, makes it possible for the masses to understand social truths and gives the key to them." The notion of "organized and educated violence" conducted by elites is, of course, the formula for terrorism. Fanon goes further: "At the level of individuals, violence is a cleansing force. It frees [the oppressed] from his inferiority complex and from his despair and inaction."

It is precisely this line of thought, that violence is positive and creative, which enables the terrorists to perform the horrifying acts for which they are responsible. Of course the same argument—almost word for word—was used by Hitler, who repeated endlessly, "Virtue lies in shedding blood." Hence the first deadly sin of terrorism is the moral justification of murder not merely as a means to an end but for its own sake.

MORAL INSTINCTS SUPPRESSED

The second is the deliberate suppression of the moral instincts in man. Terrorist organizers have found that it is not enough to give their recruits intellectual justifications for murder: the instinctive humanity in us all has to be systematically blunted, or else it rejects such sophistry. In the Russia of the 1870s and 1880s, the Neznavhalie terror group favored what it called "motiveless terror" and regarded any murder as a "progressive action." Once indiscriminate terror is adopted, the group rapidly suffers moral disintegration—indeed the abandonment of any system of moral criteria becomes an essential element in its training. The point is brilliantly made in Dostoevsky's great anti-terrorist novel, *The Possessed*, by one of the gangsters, who argues that the terror-group can be united only by fear and moral depravity: "Persuade four members of the circle to murder a fifth," he says, "on the excuse that he is an informer, and you will at once tie them all up in one knot by the blood you have shed. They will be your slaves." This technique is undoubtedly used by some terror groups today, on the assumption that neither man nor woman can be an effective terrorist so long as he or she retains the moral elements of a human personality. One might say, then, that the second deadly sin of terrorism is a threat not merely to civilization but to humanity as such.

REJECTION OF POLITICS

The third, following directly from the first two, is the rejection of politics as the normal means by which communities resolve conflicts. To terrorists, violence is not a political weapon, to be used *in extremis*: it is a substitute for the entire political process. Middle East terrorist groups, the IRA, the Bader-Meinhoff gang, Red Armies or Brigades in Japan, Italy, and elsewhere, have never shown any desire to engage in the democratic political process. The notion that violence is a technique of last resort, to be adopted only if all other attempts to obtain justice have failed, is rejected by them. In doing so, they reject the mainstream of civilized thought, based, like so much of our political grammar, on the social-contract theorists of the 17th century. Hobbes and Locke rightly treated violence as the antithesis of politics, a form of action characteristic of the archaic realm of the state of nature. They saw politics as an attempt to create a tool to avoid barbarism and make civilization possible: politics makes violence not only unnecessary but unnatural to civilized man. Politics is an essential part of the basic machinery of civilization, and in rejecting politics, terrorism seeks to make civilization unworkable.

SPREADS TOTALITARIANISM

Terrorism, however, is not neutral in the political battle. It does not, in the long run, tend towards anarchy: it tends towards despotism. The fourth deadly sin of terrorism is that it actively, systematically, and necessarily assists the spread of the totalitarian state. The countries which finance and maintain the international infrastructure of terrorism—which give terrorists refuge and havens, training-camps and bases, money, arms, and diplomatic support as a matter of deliberate state policy—are, without exception, totalitarian states. The governments of all these states rule by military and police force. The notion that terrorism is opposed to the "repressive forces" in society is false—indeed, it is the reverse of the truth. International terrorism, and the various terrorist movements it serves, are entirely dependent on the continuing good will and active support of police states. The terrorist is sustained by the totalitarian paraphernalia of tanks, torture and the secret police. The terrorist is the direct beneficiary of the Gulag Archipelago and everything it stands for.

ENEMY OF DEMOCRACY

Which brings us to the fifth deadly sin. International terrorism poses no threat to the totalitarian state. That kind of state can always defend itself by judicial murder, preventative arrest, torture of prisoners and suspects, and complete censorship of terrorist activities. It does not have to abide by the rule of law or any other consideration of humanity or morals. Hence, the fifth deadly sin is that terrorism can destroy a democracy, as it destroyed Lebanon, but it cannot destroy a totalitarian state. All it can do is to transform a nation struggling towards progress and legality into a nightmare of oppression and violence.

EXPLOITS FREEDOM

This leads us to another significant generalization about terrorism. Its ultimate base is in the totalitarian worlds—that is where its money, training, arms, and protection come from. But at the same time, it can only operate effectively in the freedom of a liberal civilization. Terrorists are the advance scouts of the totalitarian armies. The sixth deadly sin of terrorism is that it exploits the apparatus of freedom in liberal societies, and thereby endangers it.

In meeting the threat of terrorism, a free society must arm itself. But that very process of arming itself against the danger within threatens the freedoms, decencies and standards which make it civilized. Terrorism then—and it is this we must get across to intelligent young people who may be tempted to sympathize with it—is a direct and continuous threat to all the protective devices of a free society. It is a threat to the freedom of the press and television to report without restraints. It is a threat to the rule of law, necessarily damaged by emergency legislation and special powers. It is a threat to *habeas corpus*, to the continuous process of humanizing the legal code and civilizing our prisons. It is a threat to any system designed to curb excesses by the police or prison authorities or any other restraining force in society.

INDUCEMENT TO SUICIDE

Yet the seventh deadly sin of terrorism operates, paradoxically, in the reverse direction—and is yet more destructive. A free society which reacts to terrorism by invoking authoritarian methods of repression necessarily damages itself. But an even graver danger—and a much more common one today—is of free societies, in their anxiety to avoid authoritarian excesses, *failing* to arm themselves against the terrorist threat, and so abdicating their responsibility to uphold the law. The terrorists succeed when they provoke oppression: but they triumph when they are met with appeasement.

The seventh and deadliest sin of terrorism therefore is that it saps the will of a civilized society to defend itself. We have seen it happen. We find governments negotiating with terrorists—negotiations aimed not at destroying or disarming them, for such negotiations may sometimes be necessary—but negotiations whose natural and inevitable result is to concede part of the terrorists' demands. We find governments providing ransom money to terrorists—or permitting private individuals to do so, even assisting the process whereby such funds reach terrorist hands. We find governments releasing convicted criminals in response to terrorist demands, according terrorists the status, rights and advantages, and above all, the legitimacy, of negotiating partners. We find governments conceding to terrorist convicts the official and privileged status of political prisoners. We find governments yielding to demands—an invariable and well-organised part of terrorist strategy—for official enquiries, or international investigations, into alleged ill-treatment of terrorist suspects or convicts. We find newspapers and television networks—often, indeed, state networks—placing democratic governments and the terrorists on a level of moral equality. We find governments failing, time and again, in their duty to persuade the public that terrorists are not misguided politicians: they are criminals, extraordinary criminals indeed, in that they are exceptionally dangerous to us all and pose a unique threat not merely to the individuals they murder without compunction but to the whole fabric of society—but criminals just the same.

In short, the seventh and deadliest sin of terrorism is its attempt to induce civilization to commit suicide.

These seven mortal dangers must be seen in the light of the fact that terrorism is not a static threat but a dynamic one. Not only is the international infrastructure of terrorism becoming better organized and more efficient, but the terrorists' own sights are being raised by their successes. We must expect and prepare for yet further improvements in the types of weapons which they deploy. We cannot rule out the possibility that terrorists will obtain access to nuclear devices or even to their production process.

Terrorism, in short, is no longer a marginal problem, something to be contained and lived with, a nuisance. It is a real, important and growing threat to the peace and stability of all legitimate states—that is, all those states which live under the rule of law. It is an international threat—therein lies its power. That power can only be destroyed or emasculated when there is international recognition of its gravity and international action by the united forces of civilization to bring it under control.

7

The Futility of Terrorism

Walter Laqueur

... The current terrorist epidemic has mystified a great many people, and various explanations have been offered—most of them quite wrong. Only a few [myths] will be mentioned here:

Political terror is a new and unprecedented phenomenon. It is as old as the hills, only the manifestations of terror have changed. The present epidemic is mild compared with previous outbreaks. There were more assassinations of leading statesmen in the 1890s in both America and Europe, when terrorism had more supporters, than at the present time. Nor is terrorist doctrine a novelty... The basic ideas of Mao and Castro all appeared at least a hundred years ago.

Terrorism is left-wing and revolutionary in character. Terrorists do not believe in liberty or egality or fraternity. Historically, they are elitists, contemptuous of the masses, believing in the historical mission of a tiny minority. It was said about the Tupamaros [of Uruguay] that one had to be a Ph.D. to be a member. This was an exaggeration but not by very much. Their manifestos may be phrased in left-wing language, but previous generations of terrorists proclaimed fascist ideas. Nineteenth-century European partisans and guerrillas fighting Napoleon were certainly right-wing. The Spanish guerrilleros wanted to reintroduce the Inquisition; the Italian burned the houses of all citizens suspected of left-wing ideas. Closer to our own period, the IRA and the Macedonian IMRO at various times in their history had connections with fascism and communism. The ideology of terrorist movements such as the Stern gang and the Popular Front for the Liberation of Palestine encompasses elements of the extreme left and right. Slogans change with intellectual fashions and should not be taken too seriously. The real inspiration underlying terrorism is a free-floating activism that can with equal ease turn right or left. It is the action that counts.

Terrorism appears whenever people have genuine, legitimate grievances. Remove the grievance and terror will cease. The prescription seems plausible enough, but experience does not bear it out. On the level of abstract reasoning it is, of course, true that there would be no violence if no one had a grievance or felt frustration. But in practice there will always be disaffected, alienated, and highly aggressive people claiming that the present state of affairs is intolerable and that only violence will bring a change. Some of their causes may even be real and legitimate—

69

but unfulfillable. This applies to the separatist demands of minorities, which, if acceded to, would result in the emergence of nonviable states and the crippling of society. It is always the fashion to blame the state or the "system" for every existing injustice. But some of the problems may simply be insoluble, at least in the short run. No state or social system can be better than the individuals constituting it.

It is ultimately the perception of grievance that matters, not the grievance itself. At one time a major grievance may be fatalistically accepted, whereas at another time (or elsewhere) a minor grievance may produce the most violent reaction. A comparison of terrorist activities over the last century shows, beyond any shadow of doubt, that violent protest movements do not appear where despotism is worst but, on the contrary, in permissive democratic societies or ineffective authoritarian regimes. There were no terrorist movements in Nazi Germany, nor in fascist Italy, nor in any of the communist countries. The Kurdish insurgents were defeated by the Iraqi government in early 1975 with the greatest of ease, whereas terrorism in Ulster continues for many years now and the end is not in sight. The Iraqis succeeded not because they satisfied the grievances of the Kurds but simply because they could not care less about public opinion abroad.

Terror is highly effective. Terror is noisy; it catches the headlines. Its melodrama inspires horror and fascination. But seen in historical perspective, it has hardly ever had a lasting effect. Guerrilla wars have been successful only against colonial rule, and the age of colonialism is over. Terrorism did have a limited effect at a time of general war, but only in one instance (Cuba) has a guerrilla movement prevailed in peacetime. But the constellation in Cuba was unique and, contrary to Castro's expectations, there were no repeat performances elsewhere in Latin America. The Vietnam war in its decisive phase was no longer guerrilla in character. There is no known case in modern history of a terrorist movement seizing political power, although terror has been used on the tactical level by radical political parties. Society will tolerate terrorism as long as it is no more than a nuisance. Once insecurity spreads and terror becomes a real danger, the authorities are no longer blamed for disregarding human rights in their struggle against it. On the contrary, the cry goes up for more repressive measures, irrespective of the price that has to be paid in human rights. The state is always so much stronger than the terrorists, whose only hope for success is to prevent the authorities from using their full powers. If the terrorist is the fish—following Mao Tse-tung's parable—the permissiveness and the inefficiency of liberal society is the water. As Regis Debray, apostle of the Latin-American guerrillas, wrote about the Tupamaros: "By digging the grave of liberal Uruguay, they dug their own grave."

The importance of terrorism will grow enormously in the years to come as the destructive power of its weapons increases. This danger does indeed exist, with the increasing availability of missiles, nuclear material, and highly effective poisons. But it is part of a wider problem, that of individuals blackmailing society. To engage in nuclear ransom, a "terrorist movement" is not needed; a small group of madmen or criminals, or just one person, could be equally effective—perhaps even more so. The smaller the group, the more difficult it would be to identify and combat.

Political terrorists are more intelligent and less cruel than "ordinary" criminals. Most political terrorists in modern times have been of middle- or upper-class origin, and many of them have had a higher education. Nevertheless, they have rarely shown intelligence, let alone political sophistication. Larger issues and future perspectives are of little interest to them, and they are quite easily manipulated by foreign intelligence services. As for cruelty, the "ordinary" criminal, unlike the terrorist, does not believe in indiscriminate killing. He may torture a victim, but this will be the exception, not the rule, for he is motivated by material gain and not by fanaticism. The motivation of the political terrorist is altogether different. Since, in his eyes, everyone but himself is guilty, restraints do not exist.

Political terror therefore tends to be less humane than the variety practiced by "ordinary" criminals. The Palestinian terrorists have specialized in killing children, while the Provisional IRA has concentrated its attacks against Protestant workers, and this despite their professions of "proletarian internationalism." It is the terrorists' aim not just to kill their opponents but to spread confusion and fear. It is part of the terrorist indoctrination to kill the humanity of the terrorist—all this, of course, for a more humane and just world order.

Terrorists are poor, hungry, and desperate human beings. Terrorist groups without powerful protectors are indeed poor. But modern transnational terrorism is, more often than not, big business.... [Governments] give millions to terrorist movements from Ulster to the Philippines. This abundance of funds makes it possible to engage in all kinds of costly operations, to bribe officials, and to purchase sophisticated weapons. At the same time, the surfeit of money breeds corruption. The terrorists are no longer lean and hungry after prolonged exposure to life in Hilton hotels. They are still capable of carrying out gangster-style operations of short duration, but they become useless for long campaigns involving hardship and privation.

All this is not to say that political terror is always reprehensible or could never be effective. The assassination of Hitler or Stalin in the 1920s or 1930s would not only have changed the course of history, it would have saved the lives of millions of people. Terrorism is morally justified whenever there is no other remedy for an intolerable situation. Yet it seldom occurs, and virtually never succeeds, where tyranny is harshest.

THE TERRORIST'S FRIENDS

Events in recent years offer certain obvious lessons to terrorists. These lessons run against the terrorist grain, and have not yet been generally accepted. For example, terror is always far more popular against foreigners than against one's own countrymen. The only terrorists in our time who have had any success at all are those identifying themselves with a religious or national minority. It is sectarian-chauvinist support that counts, not drab, quasirevolutionary phraseology; Irish, Basques, Arabs, and the rest have found this out by trial and error. The media are a terrorist's best friend. The terrorist's act by itself is nothing. Publicity is all. Castro was the great master of the public-relations technique, from whom all terrorists should learn; with less than 300 men he created the impression of having a force of overwhelming strength at his disposal. But the media are a fickle friend, constantly in need of diversity and new angles. Terrorists will always have to be innovative; they are the super-entertainers of our time. . . .

The timing of the operation is also of paramount importance, for if it clashes with other important events, such as a major sports event or a natural disaster, the impact will be greatly reduced. Whenever terrorists blackmail governments, it is of great importance to press realistic demands. Democratic authorities will instinctively give in to blackmail—but only up to a point. The demand for money or the release of a few terrorist prisoners is a realistic demand, but there are limits beyond which no government can go, as various terrorist groups have found out to their detriment.

Psychiatrists, social workers, and clergymen are the terrorist's next-best friends. They are eager to advise, to assuage, and to mediate, and their offer to help should always be accepted by the terrorist. These men and women of goodwill think they know more than others about the mysteries of the human soul and that they have the compassion required for understanding the feelings of "desperate men." But a detailed study of the human psyche is hardly needed to understand the terrorist phenomenon; its basic techniques have been known to every self-respecting gangster throughout history. It is the former terrorist, the renegade, who has traditionally been the terrorist's most dangerous opponent. Once again, the terrorist should never forget that he exists only because the authorities are prevented by public opinion at home and abroad from exercising their full power against him. If a terrorist wishes to survive, he should not create the impression that he could be a real menace, unless, of course, he has sanctuaries in a foreign country and strong support from a neighboring power. In this case political terrorism turns into surrogate warfare and changes its character, and then there is always the danger that it may lead to real, full-scale war.

Recent terrorist experience offers some lessons to governments too. If governments did not give in to terrorist demands, there would be no terror, or it would be very much reduced in scale. . . . However, it would be unrealistic to expect determined action from democratic governments in present conditions. In wartime these governments will sacrifice whole armies without a moment's hesitation. In peace they will argue that one should not be generous with other people's lives. Western politicians and editorialists still proclaim that terrorism is condemned "by the whole civilized world," forgetting that the "civilized world" covers no more than about one-fifth of the population of the globe. Many countries train, equip, and finance terrorists, and a few sympathetic governments will always provide sanctuary. Western security services may occasionally arrest and sentence foreign terrorists, but only with the greatest reluctance, for they know that sooner or later one of their aircraft will be hijacked or one of their politicians abducted. . . .

Terrorism is, of course, a danger, but magnifying its importance is even more dangerous. Modern society may be vulnerable to attack, but it is also exceedingly resilient. A plane is hijacked, but all others continue to fly. A bank is robbed, but the rest continue to function. All oil ministers are abducted, and yet not a single barrel of oil is lost.

Describing the military exploits of his Bedouin warriors, Lawrence of Arabia once noted that they were on the whole good soldiers, but for their unfortunate belief that a weapon was dangerous in proportion to the noise it created. Present-day attitudes towards terrorism in the Western world are strikingly similar. Terrorism creates tremendous noise. It will continue to cause destruction and the loss of human life. It will always attract much publicity but, politically, it tends to be ineffective. Compared with other dangers threatening mankind, it is almost irrelevant.

8

The Multi-Dimensional Challenge of Terrorism: Common Misperceptions and Policy Dilemmas

William B. Quandt

The topic of terrorism understandably arouses such strong emotions that it is often hard to discuss it in analytical terms or to think clearly about the policy choices and dilemmas that confront us in reacting to terrorism. When Americans are held hostage . . . there is intense public preoccupation with the issue and strong pressures develop to strike out at the perpetrators of these actions. But public and press attention can also quickly fade, and in such periods we tend not to think about the long-term problems posed by terrorism and political violence. But it is precisely at such times that balanced consideration of policy should take place, not in the midst of crises. . . .

COMMON MISPERCEPTIONS

There is a tendency . . . to look at terrorism in somewhat ahistorical and apolitical terms. This leads, on occasions, to rather apocalyptic warnings about the rising threat of terrorism or the unraveling of the fabric of free societies, and the need to react decisively to every threat in order to prevent even greater dangers in the future. Some of our public officials have even spoken of terrorism as if it were the greatest threat to our nation. There is a danger in all this of becoming obsessed with terrorism, of becoming paralyzed by our preoccupation with it, and of diverting more resources to combatting it than are warranted.

There is little evidence that terrorism is the wave of the future or that democratic societies are unable to defend against it. There is little reason to believe that terrorism is on the rise. Indeed, there is not much that is new about terrorism, except for the technology now available and its lethality. This is not to belittle the problem, but rather to warn against exaggerating its importance.

74

Like crime in the United States, terrorism cannot be completely eliminated. Our goal in fighting it is to reduce the danger it poses and to insure that our society can continue to function even with the occasional threats from terrorists that will doubtless occur in the future.

To prepare ourselves for a future in which some degree of political violence is likely to be directed against Americans, we need a sense of history and a comparative perspective. Not all acts of violence directed at the United States, its citizens, and its interests are identical, nor are the preferred courses of action by our government the same. By distinguishing among types of political violence, we may begin to understand which policies are appropriate in each set of circumstances. This is not an argument for adopting an understanding posture toward terrorism, but rather to understand it so as to combat it most effectively.

HARD-CORE TERRORISM

I propose the category of "hard-core terrorism" to describe the actions of small groups of extremists like the Red Army faction, the Baader-Meinhof groups, and the Weather Underground, to name just a few. What distinguishes them is not their methods—they bomb, kidnap, and seek to disrupt society, as do other terrorists—but rather the extremism of their goals and their relative isolation within the society surrounding them. Because of their isolation and small numbers, they do not pose a threat of taking over the central institutions of their societies. They are not much of a political problem, since their extremist goals have little backing in the society at large.

Because hard-core terrorists are relatively isolated, they can be dealt with primarily as a police problem. Most citizens will be more than happy to cooperate in passing along information and intelligence on their activities. To use the classic formulation, these are fish operating in an unfriendly sea, perhaps even out of water. Good police work, good intelligence, and heightened public awareness are the keys to reducing the threat from these groups. They may not be easy to eliminate completely, but they can be kept isolated, kept underground, and generally contained. Since society at large supports the authorities against the terrorists, tough methods can be used without the danger of creating new waves of recruits for the terrorists.

To date, the United States has not had much experience with this kind of terrorism, with the exception of the Weather Underground. In fact, the United States has been remarkably free of this form of terrorism. It is considerably more common in Europe. It is more the product of advanced industrial societies than developing countries, more a problem of democracies than authoritarian states.

TERRORISM BY POPULAR MOVEMENTS

For democratic societies, the most difficult form of terrorism to combat is that carried out by political movements with actual or potential broad-based support. The tactics of these movements are familiar—the bombs, the attacks on military and civilian targets, assassinations, kidnappings, and hijackings. The use of violence in these cases is part of a deliberate strategy to build support within one's own community and to weaken the legitimacy of the existing regime. To this end, terrorist acts are designed to gain publicity, to provoke indiscriminate retaliation in the hope of undercutting competing moderate leaders, and to demoralize the target community.

Terrorism is only one of several tactics used by political leaders in these circumstances. It can be turned on and off, depending on results. The reactions of one's own political constituents are therefore crucial. If the goals of the movement are widely supported, and if the target of the terrorist attacks is seen as illegitimate, the conditions are ripe for continued use of these forms of political violence as a deliberate tactic. This has been the case in numerous third-world contexts where the goal of independence enjoyed broad support and the colonial authorities had little legitimacy. Terrorism then became the weapon of the weak, especially in the early phases of their nationalist struggles.

In cases like Algeria, the French fought back by imitating many of the methods of the terrorists. In the famous Battle of Algiers, the urban terrorist network of the FLN was essentially uprooted, but at the cost of driving most of the Muslim population of Algeria to support the FLN, and at the cost, as well, of creating deep divisions within French society over the use of torture as an instrument of counter-terrorism. Once independence was achieved by the FLN, terrorist attacks against France came to an end. The use of violence was tied to the achievement of specific goals that had broad support within the Algerian population.

In the end, French President Charles de Gaulle realized that the cost to French society of fighting to save French Algeria was too high. By negotiating with the "terrorists," as they were commonly called in France at the time, de Gaulle reached a solution that brought the violence to an end and set the stage for a new and surprisingly cordial era in French-Algerian relations.

Today, all of the leaders of Algeria come from the ranks of those who supported the FLN in its struggle against France. But Algeria today cannot be considered a country which practices terrorism. The [U.S.] State Department long ago dropped it from the list of countries supporting terrorism. In fact, [in 1985 the U.S. began to offer] to sell military equipment to the Algerian government, and earlier [the same year it hosted] a visit from the Algerian head of state. Looking back, few would question that de Gaulle made the right decision in agreeing to negotiate with the FLN. Only a few die-hard supporters of French Algeria accused de Gaulle of appeasing terrorists by acceding to their basic demands.

The Algerian model has no exact parallels, but there are similarities in the IRA, the Shia in Lebanon, the ANC in South Africa, the Sikhs in India, the PLO, and countless other examples around the world. In each case, regimes confront demands from political movements that have broad support but are not prepared to play by the rules of the game established by the authorities. In fact, they do not accept the legitimacy of the regime, and their resort to violence, including terrorism, is meant to demoralize adversaries and to rally support among a defined political community.

The dilemmas posed to governments in such situations are well-known. Indiscriminate retaliation or repression can play into the hands of the extremists. Concessions in the face of terrorist attacks may be seen as signs of weakness. Negotiating with proponents of terrorism is unpalatable to established regimes, and yet often that seems to be the only way to reduce the violence. Experience suggests that there are no easy choices confronting authorities when terrorism has gained widespread support. The time to have acted was much earlier, but of course that can often only be seen with hindsight.

Let us take the example of Lebanon to see if any useful lessons can be learned. Before 1982, no Americans were threatened by Shiite extremists. Nor had Israel confronted Shia terrorism. By 1984, however, both the U.S. and Israel had suffered anguishing losses at the hands of militant Shiites, and these extremists seemed to have substantial support within their communities. What happened between 1982 and 1984?

Quite simply, [the Americans] and the Israelis became involved in an internal Lebanese struggle for primacy between Christian factions and Shia factions. Any careful observer of the Lebanese scene could have predicted that these two communities were headed for conflict, but the presence of the PLO in Lebanon until 1982 kept the direct clash from coming to a head. Once the Israelis had succeeded in driving the PLO out of Beirut, the question arose of how Israel and the United States would use their influence within the Lebanese political arena. [They] both opted for a solution that put [them] at odds with the Shia community. The fact that [U.S. officials] did not see [their] policies in Lebanon in those terms is irrelevant. That is how they were seen by the bulk of the Shiites, especially after summer 1983.

Had [the U.S.] understood Lebanese politics better, [it] would have been wary of being dragged into the internal struggle. [It] would have also recognized that moderate leaders among the Shiites were fighting for control against extremists, and [it] would have thought of how [its] actions might contribute to the outcome of that contest. In [contrast, during] the ... TWA hostage crisis [in 1985, U.S. officials] seemed to recognize that leaders such as Nabih Berri were deserving of support against the radicals, and therefore they wisely refrained from adopting policies of indiscriminate retaliation that would have weakened Berri and strengthened the extremists.

It is appropriate here to say a word about the rising tide of violence in South Africa. The United States, as a matter of principle and policy, has been opposed to apartheid. And yet [its] policy of "constructive engagement" with the regime in South Africa [has come] under severe criticism. If [the U.S. government is] seen to be supporting apartheid [it] should not be surprised if American interests come under attack in South Africa, and perhaps elsewhere in Africa. If the efforts of moderate leaders such as Bishop Tutu fail, more extreme leaders will come to the fore. They will be called terrorists, and they will doubtless resort to terror.

By [its] policies in South Africa, [the U.S.] can determine to a significant degree whether Americans will or will not be targets of that violence if and when it occurs. Fortunately, by taking a stand in favor of principles in which [Americans] as a nation believe, [it] will also be reducing the risk to American lives and interests.

There are no easy lessons here. But the beginning of sound policy is to recognize the political dimension of the problem of this form of terrorism. Pure retaliation will not work against a political movement that has broad support. Instead, the goal should be to isolate extremists within their own community, while seeking to build up moderate voices by demonstrating a willingness to meet legitimate political demands. A mixture of forcefulness in dealing with genuine extremists and nuance in encouraging moderate forces is what is called for. Inevitably, this means a policy which will combine elements of accommodation and toughness. It will be condemned by some as appeasement of terrorism and by others as mindlessly repressive.

No democracy has an easy time conducting such policies, but we should not conclude from this that the situation is hopeless. After all, the United States faces relatively few situations around the world where it is the target of attack by terrorists. . . .

STATE-SPONSORED TERRORISM

How should the United States react when it has evidence that a state is engaged in promoting terrorism? We often hear that Libya, Iran, Syria, the Soviet Union and some of its East European allies, and a few other countries are engaged in recruiting and training terrorists. We all know that there are numerous examples of intelligence agencies of various powers conducting operations against one another, often in the form of terrorism. Even some of [America's allies] resort to political assassination in the higher interest of the state. Where do we draw the line on behavior of this sort?

Once again, I have no easy answers. But it does seem to me that certain points should be made. First, rhetoric is no substitute for action. . . .

A second point is that we must be very sure of the facts when we seek to counter state-sponsored terrorism. It is a weighty matter to hold another government responsible for acts of terrorism, and, if we make such charges based on faulty information or deliberate disinformation, we are playing a dangerous game. If we expect to win in the important court of both domestic and international opinion [in] our efforts to build pressures against state-sponsored terrorism, we had better be sure of our facts. When Egypt managed to unmask a Libyan plot by faking the assassination of a Libyan political dissident, it did more than all our rhetoric to convince many in Africa and the Middle East that Qaddafi was committed to policies of terror against his enemies.

A third point to make in dealing with state-sponsored terrorism is that sometimes . . . broader national interest will dictate that we not act on what we know to be true. There will be cases when we see the hand of the KGB or Iran in some act of international terrorism, but for reasons of state we will choose not to react. This may have to do with other important common interests, such as arms negotiations, or with a judgment about the struggle for power in Tehran and the likely consequences of any direct action we might take. [The U.S.] will have to ask . . . if it serves [American] interests to cancel a U.S.-Soviet summit meeting, for example, because [it suspects] the KGB or its Bulgarian accomplices of involvement in the assassination attempt against the pope.

There will be difficult judgments to make and to explain. It does little good, then, to raise the rhetorical level about state-sponsored terrorism in ways that may commit us to certain unwise courses of action. Far better to be restrained in rhetoric and effective in our actions, when those actions will advance our national interests. In some instances, forceful private communications to the state in question are the most effective step.

CONCLUSIONS

[Terrorism] is a multi-dimensional challenge which allows no easy answers. To deal effectively with the threat, we must think clearly about what kind of terrorism we confront. Are we dealing with hard-core terrorists, isolated from the society at large? Are we dealing with terror as a tactic employed by a popularly-based movement? Is state-sponsored terrorism the issue? The distinctions will not always be easy to make, and there may be some mixed cases, but we must try to approach the question of terrorism with such analytical categories in mind if we are to get the policies right.

We must be wary of dealing with the terrorist threat by striking poses that are attractive to domestic opinion but do nothing, or may even be counterproductive, in terms of the real problem. Much of our public rhetoric falls into this category.

To act effectively against terrorism, we must obviously be well informed. This means good intelligence and good analysis. It sometimes means cooperating with people we are not very comfortable with in order to get information on even less desirable ones. All of this is standard practice in the intelligence community and they need to be given support to learn what they can about threats from political extremists. They should not, however, have carte blanche to act on the basis of the information they gather. Responsibility for counter-terrorist action must always remain in the hands of the highest responsible authorities of . . . government.

We must be wary of the advice given by so many of the so-called experts on terrorism. There are very few genuine experts in this field. When you hear about the necessity of retaliating against someone, somewhere, even if we do not know who was responsible for a terrorist attack, be careful. To follow such advice is often to play into the hands of the terrorists. They know, even if we do not, that such blind lashing out will ensure more recruits for their cause. They are cynical about the loss of innocent lives in a way that we cannot, or at least should not, be.

Remember that [the U.S.] did retaliate for the bombing of the Marine headquarters [in Lebanon] in October 1983, but [it] almost certainly did so against the wrong targets. Those who planned and organized the attack almost certainly were not hurt by [the] retaliation. The communities which were hit, however, were probably among those who provided the political support for the next wave of terrorist attacks against Americans in Lebanon. At a minimum, we can say with certainty that retaliation did not remove the threat to American interests in Lebanon. It may have even made it worse.

We have short memories. During the TWA hostage crisis, one American woman from New Jersey could not understand why the hijackers kept yelling the name of her state. Perhaps she had never known that the battleship New Jersey had lobbed its shells into Shia-controlled areas in the latter part of 1983. Certainly the hijackers had not forgotten.

In the end, we must realize that terrorism, like crime, cannot be eliminated. We can, however, reduce our vulnerability. . . . Finally, we must be aware that our policies entail consequences. When we take positions that align us against groups that are committed to violent political struggle, we must be prepared for all forms of violence, conventional and unconventional. If we are not ready for that, then we should stay out of such quarrels. If we do choose sides, we owe it to ourselves, to our military personnel, and to our citizens, to prepare for the consequences. War is a serious business, and when we engage in it, directly or indirectly, covertly or openly, we must be prepared for the violence that comes with it. Today that violence assumes many forms, and civilians are often the targets—all the more reason to be extremely careful about the commitments [made] abroad that entail the use of force.

9

Demystifying the Mystery of International Terrorism

Michael Stohl

Political terrorism is theatre. It is profound and often tragic drama for which the world is the stage. Violence, death, intimidation, and fear are the theatrical ingredients. The plot often involves hostages, deadlines, and high-level bargaining. Tension and anxiety levels are immediately raised. National and international news media frequently monitor and broadcast terrorist events as they unfold. Law enforcement officials and sometimes insurgent terrorists are interviewed via on the scene minicams, and speculations abound as to the nature of the forthcoming responses that we might expect from both the authorities and the terrorists.

But while the central ingredients are present in all forms of terrorism, as in the legitimate theatre, only certain plays are given prominent reviews and fewer still become hits. Likewise, only a few actors and directors achieve stardom.

In the past decade, the American public's attention has been drawn to the problem intermittently as particular terrorist acts have caught the President's and media's attention. While the fear, frustration, and often anger have remained just below the surface of public consciousness throughout the decade, an active continuous attention has been lacking.

From November 4, 1979–January 20, 1981, 53 American hostages in Iran occupied the media center stage. At the time, it was believed that none of them suffered major physical abuse and none were killed. The hostages were certainly under severe psychological stress and it is likely that many if not most were traumatized, perhaps permanently, by the experience. Their situation remained fairly constant and the public learned very little, if anything, of substance that was new each evening when the daily record of captivity was broadcast. The Ayatollah Khomeini, however, achieved stardom as the villain Americans loved to hate.

In 1985 American hostages of a TWA airline hijacking and passengers on the cruise ship Achille Lauro were placed on the media center stage. After hundreds of column inches, banner headlines, and days of video tape, the two terrorist crises came to an end. In each case, one hostage was a tragic victim. In the first crisis, Nabih Berri of the Shi'ite Amal and Shaykh Fadallah of the Hezballah achieved instant stardom. In the second crisis, Abul Abbas was accorded his notoriety. In both crises the stardom proved fleeting.

While these cases attracted the media's attention, it is time to recognize that terrorism is a political strategy that is not practiced merely by the insurgent hijackers and other extremist groups that attract the Western media. The embassy takeover and the hijacking of TWA flight 847 and the hijacking of the cruise ship Achille Lauro were traumatic events (as have been the taking of the almost all but forgotten hostages in Lebanon for those hijacked and for their families), and by virtue of media coverage and government responses to the action became significant events. But they are not as significant nor as devastating in terms of human life as the numbers of everyday, "quiet" murders, torture, and other state terrorist acts perpetrated by more than one half of the world's governments on a daily basis.

Insurgent terrorism may make the headlines, but the fact is that most of the terrorism in the world goes unnoticed and unreported by the Western media. United States Department of State reports on the incidence of international terrorism worldwide cite approximately 5,000 events and threats of events in the ten years between 1975 and 1985. These events resulted in fewer than 5,000 deaths. In the worst year, 1983, 720 deaths were reported from events, most of which occurred in Europe and the Middle East.

During the period that the Department of State has kept statistics on international terrorism, tens of thousands of people have perished at the hands of government terrorism and death squads, and even more have been the direct victims of torture and intimidation in places such as Guatemala, Uganda, South Africa, East Timor, Chile, and Kampuchea. The actions of Latin American governments in the 1970s turned a verb, to "disappear," into a tragic and intimidating noun, the "disappeared," the desaparecidos. This terror far outstrips the insurgent terror that gains most Western press notice.

THE PROCESS AND PURPOSES OF POLITICAL TERRORISM: VICTIMS AND TARGETS

Terrorism is not simply violence. It includes violent acts intended to influence a wider audience, to send a message. When practiced by insurgents, it may be used to publicize a cause or to demonstrate the weakness of a government so as to put pressure on governments and their supporters. How the audience reacts is as important as the act itself. In the Teheran Embassy takeover, the students who seized the embassy originally intended only to hold the staff hostage for three to five days. They sought to demonstrate their displeasure with the Shah's admittance to the United States and their ability to strike a blow against the much more powerful United States. As time progressed, they realized they could achieve much greater results and manipulate the United States government, media, and public as well as gain influence within their own society. In the TWA hijacking, the U.S. government was not the only intended audience. The Shi'ite hijackers were also attempting to influence the United States public and the publics of the other Western nations and their own supporters and opponents in Lebanon and the Middle East. Thus, in both these cases, the U.S. government reaction and more importantly the public and media overreaction served to accomplish the major purposes of the terrorist act.

What, then, is terrorism? It may be defined as *"The purposeful act or the threat of the act of violence to create fear and/or compliant behavior in a victim and/or audience of the act or threat."*

The key words are purposeful, violence, fear, victim, and audience. It is crucial to understand that we must distinguish the victims of the violent act from the targets (the audience of that violence). The terrorists are primarily interested in the audience and not the victims. The process of political terrorism consists of three component parts: The act or threat of violence, the emotional reaction to such an act or threat, and the social effects resultant from the acts and reaction. The initiation of the process of terrorism arises for a number of quite different specific purposes, purposes which are dependent upon both the position of the agents and targets of terror.

An important key to the understanding of terrorism is to recognize that while each of the component parts of the process is important, the emotional impact of the terrorist act and the social effects are more important than the particular action itself. In other words, the targets of the terror are far more important for the process than are the victims of the immediate act. The act or threat of violence is but the first step.

Let us examine the case of the Algerian FLN terrorist campaign in the 1950s. One particular tactic employed was the bombing of public transportation. The victims of the terrorist act were the relatively limited number of passengers and bystanders in the area of the bombing. The targets of the bombing were many and varied. The French Colons in Algeria perceived the attack as aimed at them, became fearful and demanded greater protection and an increase in security measures. Many began to question the ability of the French government to provide that most basic of governmental services—security. Some formed vigilante groups to engage in activity that they perceived the government as unwilling or incapable of performing. A campaign of terror aimed at the native Algerian populations was initiated. The campaign, of course, only further undermined the legitimacy and authority of the French regime. The Algerian population, having been singled out by the regime as a group distinct from "normal" Frenchmen and having become the object of terror by the Colons, began to question the legitimacy of the regime and became more receptive to the message of the FLN. In addition to these two primary targets, the population and government of Metropolitan France began to see the Algerian colony as an economic, military, and political liability, and sought a way out of the dilemma. The initial reaction of increased force, while providing a temporary halt to the Algerian revolution, in the end created severe strains within Metropolitan France. In Algeria as a result of the campaign of terror and the reaction of the French government and the Colons, victory came to the FLN, [as one observer summarized it,] "less through its own brave and desperate struggle during seven and one-half years of war than through the strain which the war had produced in the foundations of the French polity."

While the ultimate strategic purposes of terrorism are either to maintain a regime or create the conditions for a new one, there are a number of more immediate tactical considerations for which regimes and insurgents employ terror. The first (and according to many, the principal) purpose of terrorism is the advertising of the cause. The violence of the terrorist act is not intended simply to destroy but also to be heard. For regimes, the terror is a message of strength, a warning designed to intimidate, to insure compliance without the need to physically touch each citizen. For insurgents, the terror is a message; i.e., we exist, we must be heard, and you may choose not to listen only at great risk. The impact of the violent act thus extends far beyond the immediate victims and the moment. It is a message wide in time and space. The more extensive the message, the more successful the act. Terrorists of the left and the right, governments and insurgents, are thus likely to choose their victims and targets with care to achieve maximum impact. This doesn't mean that they will not target "innocents" or avoid mass casualties, but rather that they will make their choice on the basis of what will create maximum impact with maximum chance of success.

A second purpose of terrorism is the winning of specific concessions through coercive bargaining. It is a purpose and tactic that governments are quite familiar with in international relations. The idea of the tactic is to make the possibility of noncapitulation "terrible beyond endurance." The United States employed such a strategy with the dropping of the atomic bombs on Hiroshima and Nagasaki and the Christmas bombings of Hanoi in 1972. We are all quite familiar with the war movie version of relations between the occupying force and the occupied nations wherein the occupying commander threatens the lives of 50 or 100 villagers unless information about the "resistance" is forthcoming from the village. Insurgents employ kidnapping, bomb threats, and other weapons to seek a tactical advantage in regard to recognition of their group and cause, information, money, release of prisoners, and ultimately the capitulation of a regime.

A third purpose of terrorism is to create or enforce obedience, either of the population at large or within the ruling party. In the image of the war movie introduced above, we remember also the occupying commander taking the lives of 30 villagers in retaliation for an assassination by the resistance and the assassination of the informer by the resistance for sharing information with the occupying forces. These actions are intended to ensure greater future reluctance to assist the opposing side and greater obedience to the wishes of the insurgent cause or the security forces. We are also quite aware of the employment of terror within revolutionary movements and in revolutionary regimes to create obedience within the ruling elites (employed with perhaps the greatest scope and vigor by Stalin in the Great Terror of the 1930s and defended with vigor by Robespierre, the first of revolutionary regime leaders). In the contemporary world, the tactic of terror to ensure obedience has been widely used by right wing movements in Latin America who seek to provide assistance to governments in ensuring the loyalty of the population to the regime.

A fourth purpose, illustrated by the case of the Algerian FLN discussed above, is the provoking of indiscriminate reactions or repression to expose the true nature of the "regime" or "insurgent." Many analysts are of the opinion that overreactions and repressive countermeasures often work in the terrorists' own interests. It is important here to note that it is for both insurgent terrorists and regime terrorists that this is the case. Regimes and their "agent provocateurs" (both official and self-identified) have both encouraged insurgent groups to plan and execute terrorist actions, not only to provide grounds for arrest, but also to alienate potential supporters within the population.

A further derivative of this purpose has been a particular favorite of right wing Latin American governments and vigilante groups operating on their behalf. This is the creation and then the "elimination" of a threat from an opposing political movement or possible political movement so as to demonstrate the need for greater resources and powers for "law and order" campaigns. States have also employed such a strategy in the international arena.

There are a myriad of other purposes and uses of terrorism that are variations of these four major purposes. Both domestically and internationally, regimes and insurgents seek to destabilize opposition forces, provide an excuse for intervention, military buildups, or less costly meddling. The techniques for the implementation of these purposes are as unlimited as the terrorist imagination, but there are a number that have been consistently employed: public executions, kidnapping, bombing, hijacking, arson, assassination, armed attack, hostage-barricade situations, reprisal, publishing of "death lists," and other serious threats to persons and property such as kneecapping.

Reading the professional and general literature on political terrorism, it is my conclusion that it has not been only the French colonial regime in Algeria that has misunderstood the purposes and politics of terrorism. The misunderstandings persist and they are widespread. These misunderstandings have important implications for our reactions to and our consideration of terrorism as a political problem. In the remainder of this chapter, I review ten persistent myths found in the current literature on terrorism.

MYTHS OF CONTEMPORARY POLITICAL TERRORISM

The ten myths discussed below are

1. Political terrorism is exclusively the activity of non-governmental actors.
2. All terrorists are madmen.
3. All terrorists are criminals.
4. One man's terrorist is another man's freedom fighter.
5. All insurgent violence is political terrorism.
6. The purpose of terrorism is the production of chaos.
7. Governments always oppose non-governmental terrorism.
8. Political terrorism is exclusively a problem relating to internal political conditions.
9. Devil theories of cause: The source of contemporary political terrorism may be found in the evil of one or two major actors.
10. Political terrorism is a strategy of futility.

A note of caution and explanation prior to the discussion of these myths is appropriate here. While each of the myths presented is widely accepted, it is doubtful that the set of myths as a whole is accepted by any individual. The discussion of the myths is meant to introduce the reader to the complexities of terrorism and to elucidate many of the contentious issues surrounding the employment of terrorist strategies and possible responses to the problem.

Myth 1: Political Terrorism Is Exclusively the Activity of Non-Governmental Forces

The most important place to begin our survey of the myths of contemporary terrorism is with the myth that terrorism is the exclusive province of insurgents, dissidents, or anti-governmental forces.

The particular irony of this myth is that the first usage of the term "terror" developed in response to the systematic employment of violence and the guillotine by the Jacobin and Thermidorian regimes in France. Etymologists claim that the English terms "terrorism," "terrorists," and "terrorize" did not come into use until the equivalent French words "terrorisme," "terroriste," and "terrorister" had developed in the revolutionary period between 1793 and 1798.

The singular exception to this myth that is proposed by most liberal Western authors is the recognition that non-democratic, totalitarian, fascist, or communist states practice terrorism or are only able to remain in power because of their utilization of terrorist practices. The implicit conclusion of these writers is that terrorism is not something that is practiced by the governments of liberal Western democracies. The recent action by the French against the Greenpeace ship *Rainbow Warrior* in Auckland Harbor and the revelations of the last fifteen years of state behavior in the Southern Cone of Latin America, in El Salvador and Guatemala, in Indonesia, Southern Africa, the Philippines, and a further score of nations make clear the widespread use of state terror.

Yet the myth persists. The important point to be considered before leaving this myth is that the Reign of Terror, which characterized the Jacobin period in France, was not an isolated phenomenon. There have been, are, and most likely will continue to be regimes that are dependent upon or employ terror as a basic component of their rule.

Myth 2: All Terrorists Are Madmen

A second myth, one that finds a particularly warm reception in the American media and in governmental statements concerning terrorism, is that terrorists are mentally unbalanced. The position taken in such statements and commentaries takes the form that only madmen would resort to many of the actions that terrorists have undertaken. This comfortably accepted notion would be the reasonable conclusion of many casual observers as they peruse their evening newspapers or sit watching the evening news and learn of the latest "exploits" of individual terrorist groups or actors, each treated as an isolated event, devoid of any political meaning except that which the audience can decipher from the presentation of the immediate terrorist demands or messages. Rarely are the actions of insurgent terrorists presented as part of an ongoing political struggle, related to any particular goals, and rarely are these goals presented as reasonable or even meaningful.

A corollary to this myth is found in the penchant of American and English observers to psychologize, to reduce structural and political problems to ones of individual pathologies and personal problems. If the perpetrators of terrorism have such severe psychological hangups, why look for any particular political source for their acts?

In addition to the theoretical difficulties that this approach to terrorism entails, there is a very immediate and practical shortcoming in accepting this myth. There are direct and unfortunately too obvious policy implications in accepting the myth of terrorists as madmen. When confronted by an insurgent terrorist action in progress, whether it be hijacking, kidnapping, or other "hostage-barricade" situations where innocent civilians are directly involved, a policy-maker accepting this myth might very well assume that negotiations and bargaining with the terrorists could not proceed on a rational basis. Thus, the only avenue left open to the policy-maker is the use of force in an attempt to overpower the perpetrators with all the added risk that such behavior entails for the saving of hostages (witness the unfortunate results in Munich, 1972). However, more hostages have died as the result of assaults than from direct killing by terrorists. Further, the evidence is overwhelming, at least in the case of criminal hostage-barricade situations, that negotiations conducted by trained police personnel will most likely produce a non-violent conclusion to the situation. The single clearly political hostage-barricade situation that occurred in the United States took place in March 1977 in Washington, D.C. The District of Columbia police employed a negotiating strategy in their confrontation with the Hanafi Muslims, which from the standpoint of saving of lives had quite successful results.

There is much criticism of such a strategy. Many suggest that if governments did not give in to terrorist demands there would be no further terror or it would be much reduced in scale. Many also assert that the media who broadcast the terrorists' exploits and the psychologists who advocate negotiation are amongst the best friends that the terrorists have.

The official policy of the United States Department of State (in contradistinction to the policy of most domestic American law enforcement agencies) during the Nixon-Kissinger-Ford tutelage was no negotiation, no ransom or yielding of any kind to terrorist demands. The Carter administration officially kept to this policy, but obviously did talk. The Reagan administration stressed a tough American image and a declaratory policy which stressed the reaffirmation of the no negotiation, no ransom position, coupled with threats of force and retaliation, with one such threat of retaliation carried out in its April 1986 raid on Libya. The official Israeli government position also disavows any possibility of negotiation. This is not to say that governments which hold such a policy never "talk" to terrorists (as opposed to holding serious "negotiations").

The Israeli case provides both counterfactual evidence to the simple hard-line thesis and an excellent example of the problem of discussing terrorism without reference to the actual political situation. After more than a decade of a clearly stated and consistent policy of no negotiations with and no concessions to terrorists that confront them, and furthermore delivering swift and brutal reprisals for any such confrontations, the problem of political terrorism in Israel has not by any means been alleviated. It has in fact been argued that the non-negotiation policy may have been viewed as a challenge to Palestinian terrorists to escalate the level and horror of their attacks. The Israelis did not alter their position. The Israelis felt then and continue to so argue that any such negotiation would provide the Palestinians the forum they were seeking and in an important political sense "legitimate" their existence as far as "official" Israeli actions were concerned. Thus, the Israelis refused to sacrifice the long-term policy of non-recognition (as much as it obviously pained them to do so) to the short term possibility of saving lives.

The path out of the maze constructed by terrorists is not simple or inexpensive to travel. The important point is that if policy-makers and the public refuse to recognize that terrorists are not universally psychopathic but are quite often serious political actors, the options for dealing with terrorists will be foreclosed. It is obvious that it is the policy-makers' responsibility to balance costs of the terrorists achieving their aim with the investment in lives that may or may not be saved now and in the future. It is also clear that a simple strategy of no negotiation, while obviously evidence of firm resolution, does not have any evidence on its side that it will prevent future terrorism. It is equally clear that a policy of negotiation with terrorists does not prevent future terrorism, but it does have a remarkable record of success in saving lives in the present.

Myth 3: All Terrorists Are Criminal

A myth directly related to the psychopath explanations of terrorism is one that is subscribed to, and promoted by, virtually all governments, that is, terrorism is the activity of criminals. The purpose of this myth is to deny the insurgent any possible "legitimacy" with the population they are trying to influence by their terrorist actions.

Most contemporary systems of jurisprudence do not recognize "political" crimes as distinct from "purely" criminal acts and thus governments consistently portray acts which terrorists conceive of as acts against the state for political ends as criminal activities with purely individual motives. The waters of this myth become particularly murky, however, when governments that are engaging in terrorist activities themselves are caught not only consorting with organized crime operatives but also perpetrating "political" acts that surely appear "criminal" to their populations (from CIA involvement with the Mafia, to Central American security forces' relationship to death squads, to Bulgarian security agencies' involvement with Turkish smugglers). Governments, of course, justify their behavior by referencing national security needs, but a population should certainly pause to consider what makes governmental behavior in these instances political and acceptable when the same act, if perpetrated by insurgent "terrorists," would surely be condemned as a wanton criminal act.

We must distinguish the propaganda and law enforcement requirements where we discuss terrorists as criminals. Naturally, most terrorist acts are violations of the criminal code. Therefore, in the narrow sense their activities are "criminal," and they should be tried under such codes. However, if we are attempting to respond to the threat of such actions, it is important to recognize the source and motive of such "criminal" acts so that our enforcement techniques do not alienate the populations that we seek to both protect and draw support from.

Myth 4: One Man's Terrorist Is Another's Freedom Fighter

This cliché confuses what terrorism is with the terrorist actor. An actor is a terrorist when the actor employs terrorist methods. While one may wish to argue that the particular ends justify particular means, that does not alter what those means are. Likewise, all actions by groups which have performed terrorist action in the past are not ipso facto terrorism. Until we are willing to treat one man's terrorist as everyone's terrorist we will make very little progress in either our understanding of the problem of terrorism or begin to take steps to effectively reduce its occurrence.

Myth 5: All Insurgent Violence Is Political Terrorism

A fifth myth is that all insurgent violence and attacks are terrorist in nature. It is a commonplace for commentators as well as governments to portray regime opponents as terrorists because, as analysts have argued, terrorism is seen as more evil than other strategies of violence if public opinion sometimes can be rallied against it. Commentators on guerrilla war often speak of the tactic of terrorism within the strategy of guerrilla warfare so as to effectively treat them as one phenomenon. They then assert that in only one non-colonial, peacetime case has guerrilla war (read terrorism) been successful in bringing the guerrillas to power. That victory by guerrillas was Castro's. The irony however, is that Castro's leading theorist of guerrilla war, Che Guevara, disavowed the use of terrorism because terrorism made victims of innocent people and therefore had the potential of alienating the support of the masses necessary for a revolutionary victory.

Thus, the important point to be kept in mind is that while some guerrillas may resort to terrorist tactics (for example, the Vietcong and FLN of Algeria), for tactical and strategic reasons most do not terrorize the populations within which they operate so they may, following Mao's dictum, "swim like fish in water." It may be useful to argue that they do for propaganda purposes but we should not assume that popular support arises merely out of fear of retribution.

Myth 6: The Purpose of Political Terrorism Is the Production of Chaos

A sixth myth, intimately related to the first five, is that terrorism both in purpose and in practice produces chaos. In fact, a primary purpose of terrorism, as practiced by challengers to governmental authority, is the production of chaos to accelerate social disintegration, to demonstrate the inability of the regime to govern, and to challenge the legitimacy of attempts by such regimes to impose order. That insurgent terrorists have been successful, at least in the short term, of producing chaos is not often disputed. However, the most persistent and successful use of terror both in the past and in the modern era has been demonstrated by governments and authorities for the purpose of creating, maintaining, and imposing order.

The justification and necessity of state terror in postrevolutionary societies for the purpose of establishing and protecting the revolutionary society has now here been more vigorously presented than in Leon Trotsky's *Terrorism and Communism*, which was a reply to the criticism of the methods of the new Soviet regime by Karl Kautsky. Trotsky discussed the origin of the terror in the revolutionary struggle and takeover and argued that the stronger the enemies of the revolution, the more the revolutionary government must, if it is to survive, resort to state terror.

Terrorism thus becomes the weapon of the new regime in the takeover stage as it attempts to consolidate and protect its position. It is important to remember that the use of terror at this stage is characteristic of revolutionary regimes in general, not simply a characteristic of communist takeovers.

This is not to say, however, that the official communist position is one of support for terrorism at all stages of revolutionary action. Quite the contrary is the case. The official Soviet formulation has not changed since Lenin characterized terrorism as a form of "infantilism."

The reasons are quite simple. Soviet theorists do not believe that insurgent terror has positive long term effects for the building of revolutionary mass movements. As did Che Guevara (noted above), they have made their assessment on the basis of utility. This is not to say that the Soviet Union has no interactions with groups and organizations which use terrorism. There is no doubt that, for example, various Palestinians have received weapons and military training in the Soviet Union and elsewhere under the auspices of the Soviet Union and have subsequently become involved in terrorist operations. Soviet agents have also interacted with other terrorist organizations. However, there is little doubt that the Soviets would prefer Leninist party building and the development of a mass revolutionary strategy, if they had the choice (for further analysis of the Soviet role, see myth 9).

Myth 7: Governments Always Oppose Non-Governmental Terrorism

Contemporary research on violence and politics has traditionally considered government as society's neutral conflict manager, interested primarily in creating the conditions, and enforcing the maintenance of political order, within which a healthy society may function. However, for most of the world's states, the state may more usefully be considered as a party to conflict and as such not necessarily a neutral one.

The myth that governments view all non-governmental terrorism as disruptive and therefore are against non-governmental terrorism occurring within their own borders arises from this misunderstanding of the role of government. It is quite clear that vigilantes, whether from the right or the left, often employ terrorist tactics. When vigilantes seek to assist the established government in the performance of the maintenance of order they are not only tolerated, but also too frequently encouraged by governments. Two of the most notorious contemporary illustrations of this phenomenon which have now been exposed to full public view were found in Brazil and Argentina. In the late sixties and early seventies, the Esquadrao de Morte (Death Squad) in Brazil, thought to be mainly off-duty policemen, executed an estimated five hundred to twelve hundred persons. According to spokesmen claiming to be Esquadrao members, the death squads took these actions because of the inefficiency of Brazil's established judicial institutions. In Argentina, the Anti-Communist Alliance (the Triple A) was established by Jose Rega, then the chief advisor to and Minister of Social Welfare in the Isabel Peron regime. Within a ten-month period in 1974 and 1975, the Triple A is believed to have assassinated over two hundred persons. Any doubts as to the nature of the Triple A were dispelled after the 1976 military coup when the vigilante apparatus was incorporated in its entirety into the government security services.

The death squads operating in Guatemala and El Salvador throughout the decade of the 1980s are sufficient proof that governments have not abandoned their support for and complicity with "private" vigilante organizations. It is a thinly-veiled illusion that these organizations, working within a repressive, military milieu, could continue to operate in an open and deadly manner without either the full connivance or the direct support of the government in power.

Government tolerance of vigilante organizations is not, by any means, confined to the South American continent nor the present. The activities of the Ku Klux Klan in the American South during and following Reconstruction and in the South and Midwest following World War I were intended to terrorize blacks and others. It was always vaguely apparent that police and other law enforcement agencies were either employing Klan members, or that the local sheriff, for example, was working in a kind of tacit agreement with the Klan. In Northern Ireland, the Protestant establishment tolerated and encouraged vigilante organizations to maintain the status quo. The silence of the United Kingdom government in Westminster was viewed as tacit approval of the policy by Northern Irish politicians. Countless other examples are available. The important point for our consideration is the recognition that just as governments employ their own terrorism to impose or maintain internal order, they will sometimes tolerate and even encourage terrorism by non-governmental groups if they perceive these actions as useful for their own purposes of maintaining control.

Myth 8: Political Terrorism Is Exclusively a Problem Relating to Internal Political Conditions

There is yet another myth about the role of government and the practice of terrorism that needs exploration. This is the myth that terrorism is primarily a problem for governments threatened with insurgency. That is, we tend to think of terrorism as something having to do with the revolutionary overthrow of regimes or, as in our previous examples, with the prevention of that overthrow by governments and their supporters. However, to complicate the picture, in addition to revolutionary terrorism and repressive terrorism, there is government terror that is exported. All types of governments export terror. Colonel Qaddafi of Libya has been reported to have supported the I.R.A. (Provisional Branch), the Baader Meinhof "Red Army Faction," factions of the Palestine Liberation Organization and death squads to eliminate expatriate Libyans. The Israelis, in addition to their widely publicized commando raids into Lebanon in retaliation for Palestinian terrorist actions, have also conducted in the 1970s a clandestine campaign of assassination against Palestinian and Arab agents and overt bombing raids against "suspected" PLO organizational outposts and locations.

The covert operations of the American C.I.A. through "dirty tricks" and the harassment and assassination of Soviet defectors also are illustrative of the covert export of governmental terror. But, in addition to the secret use of terror by governments outside their own borders, there is the overt employment of terror to coerce other governments to capitulate or submit to the wishes of the dominant. In *Arms and Influence*, Thomas Schelling refers to this use of terror as the "diplomacy of violence." Two well known uses were demonstrated by Nixon and Kissinger in the Christmas bombings of 1972 against the North Vietnamese and by the Israeli mock bombings of Beirut prior to their invasion in 1982. The idea of this tactic is to make the possibility of non-capitulation "terrible beyond endurance." It is not because governments are weak that they employ this tactic but rather because another tactic might be costlier in time, lives or material. Consider the following passage by Schelling and its implications:

> These (the two atomic bombs on Hiroshima and Nagasaki) were weapons of terror and shock. They hurt, and promised more hurt, and that was their purpose. The few small weapons we had were undoubtedly of some direct military value, but their enormous advantage was in pure violence. In a military sense the United States could gain a little by destruction of two Japanese industrial cities; in a civilian sense, the Japanese could lose much. The political target of the bomb was not the dead of Hiroshima or the factories they worked in, but the survivors in Tokyo. The two bombs were in the tradition of Sheridan against the Comanches and Sherman in Georgia and South Carolina. Whether in the end those two bombs saved lives or wasted them, Japanese lives or American lives; whether punitive coercive violence is uglier than straight-forward military force or more civilized; whether terror is more or less humane than military destruction; we can at least perceive that the bombs on Hiroshima and Nagasaki represented violence against the country itself and not mainly an attack on Japan's material strength. The effect of the bombs, and their purpose, were

not mainly the military destruction they accomplished but the pain and the shock and the promise of more.

Within this single paragraph Schelling has amply demonstrated how and why as a policy terror may be effective.

Myth 9: Devil Theories of Terrorism: The Source of Contemporary Political Terrorism May Be Found in the Evil of One or Two Satanic Actors

In his first news conference as President Reagan's newly-appointed Secretary of State, Alexander Haig charged that the Soviet Union was deeply involved in international terrorism. Haig indicated that the Soviet role included training, funding, and equipping international terrorists. Haig's charges focused public attention on an issue which has continued to find increasing attention in the last half decade—the role of states in the apparently increasing activities of terrorists who operate both within and across state boundaries.

There have been two major thrusts in the interconnected argument concerning the role of the Soviet Union in international terrorism. The first concerns the question of cooperation and possible organizational coordination among terrorists and the second Soviet involvement and possible organizational control. Despite the assurance with which many have spoken, there has been little evidence publicly available of Soviet control and of an actual organizational infrastructure.

Few dispute the existence of working relations among some terrorist groups resulting in relatively low level cooperation regarding safe houses, travel documents, weapons information and the like. However, much of the cooperative network doesn't appear any more sophisticated than the "ordinary" criminal network that exists for the purchase of visas, weapons, and silence throughout the world. That groups cooperate at this level should come as no surprise to anyone familiar with organized criminal or insurgent terrorist behavior. It is a long leap to assert that this cooperation implies any coordinated effort or long term policy agreement.

When all the charges and evidence are carefully reviewed, rather modest conclusions appear warranted. The Soviets have trained, funded, and equipped some Palestinians for what they would describe as guerrilla warfare. Some Palestinians are Marxists and have developed links with other Marxist and non-Marxist political organizations, governments, and also terrorist organizations, including most member states of the United Nations and all of the states in the Arab League. Radical Arab states who have purchased arms from the Soviet Union have made some of these arms available to Palestinians. (Conservative Arab states who have purchased arms from the United States and other Western states have also made arms available to the Palestinians.) We can and should thus make the argument that the Soviet Union, by training Palestinian guerrillas and others in military techniques, weapons use, and tactics at bases within the Soviet Union and the Middle East must bear a share of the responsibility for the practices for which that training is employed. But in the Palestinian case the same argument about responsibility may be directed at others with very different and often anti-Soviet aims. In addition, we only would fool ourselves were we to believe that without the Soviet Union and/or the Palestinians terrorism would no longer be a major problem.

In the mid-1980s a second popular "devil," the subject of Western media and particularly United States government attention as the source of much of the world's international terrorism, was Colonel Qaddafi. The case against Qaddafi, despite its popularity with the Reagan administration and the American public, was appallingly weak to have been sustained for so long.

The obsession with Qaddafi in the Reagan administration began with the so-called Libyan Hit Squads of November 1981. The *New Statesman* reported in August 1985 that the so-called hit team members were actually senior functionaries of the Lebanese Amal, including Nabih Berri. This did not stop Mr. Reagan's continuing charges leading right up to the charges of Libyan complicity in the Rome and Vienna airport attacks of December 1985 and the West Berlin disco bombings which were given as the *causus belli* for the April 1986 raid on Tripoli and Benghazi. It is now clear that the evidence for state support and sponsorship leads more clearly and heavily towards the Syrians for each of these actions, and that Qaddafi, for all his bluster, had very little direct connection to terrorist operations outside his own quite limited campaign against Libyan dissidents, which had claimed the lives of 14 Libyan expatriates by 1985.

Myth 10: Political Terrorism Is a Strategy of Futility

This brings us to the last myth that we will discuss, the myth of the futility of terrorism. Many analysts, such as Walter Laqueur [see Chapter 7 above], have argued that terrorism creates noise but has no political success.

We may easily refute Laqueur's argument by reference to the above Schelling passage, the Stalinist terror of the 1930s, Robespierre and the Thermidorians, and numerous other examples of the successful employment of terror by governments. It is important to stress, of course, that most of the world's terror is in fact of this variety and continues to be quite effective.

However, most commentators refer only to insurgent terror, and thus the argument should be confronted on its own ground. It is true that terrorism and terrorists by themselves have probably not been militarily responsible for a revolutionary victory or the end of colonial rule, but is this the single proper measure to judge the success or failure of terrorist actions?

Let us briefly consider the case of the Palestinians. It is clear that the various terrorist groups have not accomplished their major purpose of dislodging the Israelis from any portion of the territory that they consider their homeland, nor have they achieved any significant military victories.

However, when more than 800 million persons were the live audience for the hostage-barricade drama at the Olympic Village in Munich in 1972 and witnesses of the eventual shoot-out involving the Palestinian group Black September, the Israeli Olympic athletes and the West German authorities, the question of Palestinian demands was forced onto the public agenda regardless of the success or failure of the operation in tactical or strategic terms. More such failures followed. Despite the human cost, it cannot be denied that the terrible price in lives and fear was in large part responsible for the elevation of the "Palestinian situation" into the "Palestinian Question" or the "Palestinian Problem." It cannot be denied that Western leaders, the Israelis, and the Arab states developed a much greater interest in providing a solution to the Palestinian question in the Middle East because the Palestinians made it ever more costly for all parties to continue to ignore the Palestinians in considerations of the Middle East future. The continuing tragedy of the Palestinians has been the inability of the Palestinian community to transform the attention that the original wave of terrorism brought to their cause into actual political gains. While noting that the terrorism of the Palestinians has not brought about the political ends that they originally sought, it must be stressed that the terrorism which has engulfed the Middle East during the past decade and one half has certainly been in large part responsible for the political transformation of Lebanon and has had important political ramifications within the other Arab states, including the transformation of the status of Palestinians within these societies.

On the other hand, the thesis gets much greater support from the fact that thus far it has indeed proved a futile and counterproductive strategy in liberal democratic societies. However, when we judge terrorism as a strategy for revolutionary change, a different conclusion surfaces: a strategy of terror is unlikely to produce changes in liberal societies even while it may produce tactical successes. Nevertheless, we should recognize that there are precious few societies in the world today that meet democratic standards, and thus terrorist strategies have a wide world in which to operate with some chance of success no matter how abhorrent we may find the strategy and its consequences.

II

The Causes
of Terrorism

International Terrorism shifts attention in this Part, from debate about terrorism's defining characteristics to debate about its causes. For the student of international terrorism, this analytic task is also challenging. Like disagreement about the definition of international terrorism, there also exists great disagreement about the variables that influence terrorism's occurrence.

The essays in **Part II** illustrate these unresolved controversies very well. They capture the diverse causes observers from differing analytic traditions have identified as the most potent factors responsible for international terrorism. And they demonstrate the principle that how terrorism is characterized shapes the inferences drawn about its causes (and the paths to its control).

TRACING CAUSAL INFLUENCES:
TWO ORIENTING DISTINCTIONS

In order to organize inquiry about rival theories of terrorism's causes, let us introduce two basic issues. The first centers on the question, Does international terrorism emanate primarily from influences internal or external to the state? Most efforts to discover causes can be classified by this dichotomy or distinction between two "levels of analysis."[1] Those persuaded that *internal* factors are powerful emphasize the domestic sources of terrorist activity—the personal, societal, cultural, and governmental variables nested within nations that may prompt terrorist activities. Those emphasizing *external* sources stress the attributes of the international system that influence terrorists' decisions, such as the foreign policies of other states and the global circumstances in general that create a conducive environment for terrorist activity. This "systemic" category consists of *all* the developments sweeping the global arena, including trends in the global diffusion of military capabilities, the worldwide expansion of telecommunications, the unequal distribution of international wealth, and the political and economic deprivation experienced by the powerless and poor in a highly stratified system of unequals.[2]

This division between internal and external levels of analysis helps to organize perceptions about the potential sources of terrorism. But if we are able to peel away the interacting layers that conduce to acts of international terrorism, quite clearly some terrorist incidents would be shown to be concomitantly caused *both* by developments occurring within states and by forces transcending national borders. Nonetheless, even though drawing distinctions between internal and external influences on behavior often is difficult in an age of interdependence, it is useful to analyze terrorism's causes by estimating the relative causal weight attributable to influences originating in these two spheres. The exercise of classifying causal levels facilitates identification of the multiple causes that collectively shape terrorist activities as well as estimation of the relative power exerted by each. That undertaking forces the mind to evaluate the broad array of equally plausible contributing factors; it reduces the risk of riveting attention on only one explanatory factor while dismissing from consideration the influence of other potentially powerful determinants; and it prompts us to contemplate how different causes, acting in conjunction, may converge in different ways under different conditions to produce terrorist acts. Merely asking the question, "Is a particular act of terrorism accounted for by domestic or external influences?" requires us to consider the possibility that it was not determined exclusively by only one set of factors, but by a number in combination. This allows complexity to be captured and serves as an antidote to inaccurate stereotypes and invalid inferences.

For example, some analysts are drawn hastily to the reassuringly simple theory that international terrorism is the product of a conspiracy orchestrated by state sponsors, who are alleged to direct and manage terrorism worldwide through an elaborate network of terrorist organizations. This theory depicts international terrorism as a phenomenon determined exclusively by a single "external" influence. But if there exists some evidence that fits this theory, are there also possible exceptions? Are some cases of terrorism caused primarily by indigenous factors? Could some incidents, for instance, be better explained as a product of terrorists' psychological impulses and their movements' ideological beliefs, of nationalistic passions and ethnic hostilities within a country, or of ruthless governmental repression? Perhaps these, not external sponsorship, were actually more critical. Indeed, possibly it was the confluence of internal civil strife and external support which produced the incendiary conditions from which the acts ignited. And a panoply of intermediate or intervening causal influences possibly were at work which, if unrecognized, might lead us to mistake spurious connections for the actual causal relationships. Attention to the force of influences at different causal levels can help prevent those kinds of unwarranted conclusions.

Analytic leverage also can be obtained by consideration of a second basic distinction found in discussion of terrorism's causes. In the study of terrorism two traditions stand in opposition about the question of whether terrorism stems from "root" causes. The first tradition subscribes to the view that terrorism is rooted primarily in *conditions* which deprive politically oppressed and economically deprived groups of their ability to meet their basic needs, motivating them to turn to terror as a means of overturning circumstances they find intolerable. Hopelessness, despair, deprivation, and persecution are among the experiences shared by many members of terrorist movements. According to the "root causes" theory of terrorism, these experiences are the cause of their recourse to terrorism. For example, Moorhead Kennedy contends that the existence of one or more of a small number of common circumstances, such as colonialism, ethnic separation, or political oppression, are catalysts to terrorism.[3] Proponents of this theory maintain that terrorism is caused primarily by poverty and misery, that it is bred by exploitation and repression, and that it is best controlled by alleviating the frustration and despair experienced by the disadvantaged. Richard E. Rubenstein's declaration exemplifies this posture: "Our policy must be to uproot the causes of terrorism by putting an end to . . . oppression of classes, nations, and ethnic communities."[4] At the heart of this orientation is the presumption that terrorism is a reaction to particular kinds of circumstances and that the threat of political violence to instill fear and promote radical change is made by desperate people experiencing desperate conditions.

Against this school of thought are those who adamantly reject the "root causes" theory that "terrorism is a pathological contagion that can be best understood when placed in a broader political/historical context."[5] Instead, these see terrorism as disconnected from unfortunate conditions; it is caused by the decision to wage a campaign of violence outside the accepted rules of warfare, produced by actors without principles choosing to rationalize the destruction of innocents and noncombatants. To them, what makes terrorism distinctive is that it

> . . . abides by no rules. It avoids military targets. Its victims are virtually invariably unarmed, undefended, unwary civilians. The terrorist murders, maims, kidnaps, hijacks, tortures, bombs and menaces the innocent without the justification of military necessity.[6]

From this perspective, to think of terrorism as resulting from "root causes" is misguided because terrorism is not an experience but a heinous practice. It is mistaken to focus on the conditions which motivate some people to engage in terrorism to express grievances because many people throughout the world suffer intolerable conditions, but only a particular type of person will turn to terrorism to vent frustrations. The terrorist is different. Terrorism is practiced by a small number of extremists who choose to step outside the boundaries of accepted norms for behavior. The circumstances in which they live do not determine or dictate that choice. Terrorists are moved by politics, not ideals; and therefore it is dangerous to even approach the origins of terrorism by searching for its root causes, because, as Moshe Decter warns, "explanations of terrorists' motivations and aspirations effectively function to justify terrorist acts."[7]

Hence, some observers seek to explain the outbreak of terrorism in terms of the national and international *conditions* in which individuals' terrorist actions are alleged to be rooted, while an opposed tradition treats terrorism as a political activity defined by the intentions and tactics of its perpetrators. The former is represented by the view stated in "The Origins and Fundamental Causes of International Terrorism" prepared in 1972 by the United Nations' Secretariat, which concluded:

> ... It thus appears that the "misery, frustration, grievance and despair" which lead to terrorism have many roots in international and national political, economic and social situations affecting the terrorists, as well as in his personal circumstances. The precise chain of causation cannot be traced with scientific exactitude.[8]

The latter interpretation sees terrorism as a political strategy encompassing a repertoire of techniques practiced by a diverse range of individuals, groups, and states, operating in very diverse conditions, whose choice of terrorist tactics is not influenced heavily by past experiences. And, to the extent they are, the people facing these grievous conditions are very dissimilar; therefore terrorism should not be correlated with a particular type of circumstance such as oppression. Correlation is not causation. This school is represented by the causal perspective of L. C. Hamilton, who emphasizes that "the root causes of terrorism are obscure" because:

> It has arisen among rich and poor, oppressive and relatively unoppressive societies. It has been used to promote causes with no popular support as well as causes endorsed by a large majority. And it has emerged to fight against the overwhelming forces of foreign invaders and has been used, by other invaders, as an extension of interstate war.[9]

To trace the potential causes of international terrorism, inquiry can be informed and guided by reference to the preceding two sets of distinctions or rival theoretical orientations.

To explain acts of terrorism requires uncovering the cause(s) that produced them.[10] The causes hypothesized by analysts to influence and therefore explain terrorist acts may be categorized in terms of the debaters' positions nested within these two dichotomies. To illustrate, a non-exhaustive list of causes frequently posited to promote international terrorism are classified in Table 1.

Note that some of these illustrative causes are difficult to classify because they are highly related to others and influenced by them—a feature that alerts us to the difficulty of drawing distinctions, disentangling causal influences, and identifying temporal sequences in the chain

TABLE 1   The Etiology of International Terrorism: Classifying Some Hypothesized Causes

Are the Causes Primarily "Internal" or "External"?	Are There Root Causes?	
	Yes	*No*

Internal	· Government repression
	· Economic deprivation
	· Political oppression
	· Ethnic persecution
	· Class cleavage
		· Uncompromising
		  nationalism
		· Cultural pluralism
		· Religious fanatacism
		· Media attention
		· Random, irrational
		  or pathological
		  violence

External	· Global disparities
	  between the rich
	  and poor
	· Territorial disputes
	· Ineffective and
	  permissive international
	  legal system
	· Absence of supernational
	  institutions (anarchy)
	· Colonialism
		· State-sponsorship
		· Terrorist networks
		· Foreign financing
		· Publicity made
		  possible by global
		  communications
		· Arms sales and
		  weapons dispersion
		· Superpower policies

of causation. For example, does a terrorist become a terrorist because of his or her fanatical religious beliefs, or because severe religious persecution intensified loyalty to those convictions, made dedication to them fanatical and all-consuming, and rationalized reliance on terror to combat that persecution? Which cause comes first—the actor and the act, or the prior grievance that molds the actor and prompts the act? It is exceedingly difficult to resolve these "chicken-or-egg" issues. Yet despite the inherent challenge of unraveling the chronological sequence of causal influences, reference to these categories nevertheless is recommended to organize thinking about the determinants of international terrorism, to understand better the tradition from which others' interpretations of terrorism's origins are based, and to heighten awareness of the causal inferences made. When reading the essays about terrorism's causes that follow, ask yourself where the variables identified by the author are best placed. Then, consider the assumptions about the determinants of terrorism that are embedded in the author's selection of causal factors and how these are associated with other catalytic or causal influences. And finally, contemplate the ways in which the author's interpretation of causes is related to his or her characterization of terrorism's definition as well as to the policy response that is prescribed, if one is advanced, to combat the problem of terrorism.

REFLECTIONS ON THE DETERMINANTS
OF TERRORISM: SELECTIONS

The preceding categories identify the major questions which frame much of the debate about terrorism's sources. Within them are contained an epistemological issue: assuming we can define and identify terrorist behavior, *how do we know* what produces it?

The epistemological obstacles to the discovery of terrorism's causes and to valid generalization about them are treated lucidly in Martha Crenshaw's "The Causes of Terrorism," which was prepared especially for publication in this book. Her broad-ranging review displays sensitivity to the need to disentangle the *preconditions* "that set the stage for terrorism in the long run" from the *precipitant* causes or "specific events that immediately precede the occurrence of terror." In addition, it artfully outlines an approach to the study of the sources of terrorism by inviting us to separate treatment of terrorism's causes, processes, and effects. In exploring the major schools of thought regarding these three dimensions of contemporary terrorism, she asks us to distinguish different levels of causation and to recognize the importance of contextual factors and both internal and external variables explaining terrorism.

Like Richard Shultz, David Fromkin, and Gary Sick (recall **Part I**), Professor Crenshaw characterizes terrorism as a product of deliberate choice—the selection of terrorist methods for pursuing political goals is seen as a result of rational decisions. Inspection of the intra-organizational dynamics of terrorist organizations and the behavior of participants in them will clearly disclose, she maintains, that terrorists make efforts to construct coherent strategies to achieve defined ends. There is little reason to accept the "mental disorder" image of terrorists as deranged individuals driven by pathological impulses beyond their conscious control.[11] She concurs with Brian M. Jenkins, who asserts:

> Terrorism is often described as *mindless* violence, *senseless* violence, or *irrational* violence. If we put aside the actions of a few authentic lunatics, terrorism is seldom mindless or irrational. There is a theory of terrorism, and it often works. To understand the theory, it must be understood first that terrorism is a means to an end, not an end in itself.[12]

Terrorism, Crenshaw insists, is thus best seen as a "logical" (albeit repugnant) choice; it "is an attractive strategy for groups of varied ideological persuasions who challenge the state's authority." This property, she avers, makes the effort to trace the causes possible; because terrorism is not a random practice it therefore is possible to generalize about the patterns of causation that produce it. To illustrate, Professor Crenshaw examines the perspectives of the individuals joining terrorist movements and explores prominent propositions about the psychological influences on that decision.

The differences of opinion which have emerged about the causes of terrorism are illuminated further in Richard E. Rubenstein's "The Non-causes of Modern Terrorism." Given its diversity, is it possible to generalize about terrorism's causes? Like Professor Crenshaw, Rubenstein also answers in the affirmative, but warns about the barriers to valid conclusions that will result when a narrow definition of terrorism's causes is adopted. This error is evident, he asserts, in the current "fashion . . . to explain terrorism exclusively in terms of external causes—for example, outside sources of training, supplies, planning, or ideological inspirations." If one only looks at terrorism from the orthodox Western perspective, Rubenstein argues, then one will see it as either a development entirely dependent on external support or as a development produced by inefficient or permissive government policies.

Neither the "outside-agitator" theory stressing the impact of terrorist networks and external sponsors, or the "permissive-society" theory stressing terrorism as a practice made possible by lenient governments, are seen as valid. These are not true causes. Although there are elements of truth in these theories, Rubenstein argues that the real causes of terrorism are *situational*: "the constellation of economic, political, and psychological factors that have the effect, in a particular society, of inciting young people to engage in conspiratorial violence." Rubenstein stresses the indigenous origins of terrorism, the soil in which he perceives terrorism to be rooted. He thus recommends the "root causes" theory as a convincing way of accounting for many of the diverse strains of terrorism and rejects its rival theory as a "non-cause." His position takes him close to adopting a definition of terrorism as a fight for freedom, a position that interprets political violence as an almost natural form of revolutionary justice in the historical process.

The forms international terrorism have assumed in the twentieth century's last quarter are, to many, unprecedented in frequency and impact. What is responsible? Another interpretation is offered by Rushworth M. Kidder, who argues in "Why Modern Terrorism?" that contemporary international terrorism springs from three seeds planted in the 1960s. As a counterpoint to Rubenstein and others, Kidder explains "the peculiar epicycle that sprouted up suddenly" as a product of three causes: broad historical changes, ideological shifts, and technological advances. The first are symbolized by the end of colonialism, the independence of new nations, the military stalemate of the great powers, and the prohibitive costs of conventional war that pushed guerrilla uprisings, low-intensity conflict, and terrorist activities to center stage as the predominate mode of violence. Second, the 1960s witnessed the rise of Islamic fundamentalism, the intense ideological repudiation of Western culture and modernity in the developing countries, and the radicalization of young people and growth of urban terrorism in the developed nations. And third, the expansion of mass communications and air travel, and technological improvements in weaponry, made terrorist tactics potent weapons. In contrast to others, this interpretation focuses on both the "external" and "internal" causes while departing in emphasis from the "root causes" school of thought.

Another way of interpreting Kidder's explanation of contemporary international terrorism is to note that it supports the proposition that "ideas have consequences," the indisputable principle that how we think shapes how we behave. This theory assumes that the best way of tracing the origins of terrorism is through examination of terrorists' attitudes and convictions. Terrorists' beliefs, however, may not be products of ideas emerging only from the 1960s. They derive as well from a much older intellectual legacy. Hence another way of viewing the origins of the wave of terrorism since the 1960s is by recognizing that

> In the case of terrorism that now afflicts the nations of the West, there is a long intellectual history behind it—one which is rather unflattering to those who see themselves as the main victims of terrorism. The intellectual roots of terrorism lie in three philosophical ideas which, ironically, are peculiarly Western: popular sovereignty, self-determination and ethical consequentialism. The diffusion of political responsibility that results from popular sovereignty, the belief that every group has a right to its own state, and the decline in the belief in absolute human rights have together fostered a hospitable intellectual climate for terrorism.[13]

This interpretation stressing the intellectual sources of terrorism is associated with the posture toward causation assumed by Paul Wilkinson, who contends in "The Sources of Terrorism: Terrorists' Ideologies and Beliefs" that one of the most useful ways of understanding the determinants of terrorism is through inspection of terrorists' convictions. For Wilkinson, it is not wise "to link the onset of political terrorism to particular socio-economic conditions or to psychopathology." "If it is argued that political terrorism is a function . . . of marginality and deprivation in an affluent society," he rhetorically asks, "why is the incidence of terrorism so much lower in the United States . . .?" A "much more powerful tool for understanding the roots" of terrorism, he avers, is "to identify . . . the political motivations of terrorists and to relate them to particular ideologies, régimes, conflicts, and strategic and political conditions." In examining these causes, Wilkinson distances himself from the "root cause" school of thought while accepting the thesis that international terrorism is conditioned by internal variables.

Religion is a conspicuous component of the ideas commonly associated with terrorist movements and the individuals drawn to them, for, as Andrew J. Pierre notes, although the "motivations for international terrorism vary from case to case . . . the terrorist [often] is dedicated to a political goal which he sees as one of transcendent merit."[14] David C. Rapoport explores this aspect of the intellectual origins of terrorism by focusing on the religious convictions of terrorist groups in "Religion and Terror: Thugs, Assassins, and Zealots."

Observing that modern terrorism is highly influenced and justified by religious beliefs and that the "holy terrorist believes that only a transcendent purpose which fulfills the meaning of the universe can justify terror," Rapoport explores causes largely internal in nature that offer a counterpoint to those who conceive of terrorism as a product of deliberate, calculated choice. In a period where professional terrorists are able to draw from a deepening pool of religious zealots and militant fundamentalists to terrorize on behalf of their faith, his perspective on the origins of terrorism is both timely and timeless.

To investigate the religious sources of modern terrorism, he compares in an essay prepared especially for this book the doctrines of three of the best-known terrorist movements inspired by religious precepts in antiquity, the "Thugs," "Assassins," and "Zealots." This comparison shows that each group "displayed strikingly different characteristics," differences that raise questions about "the appropriateness of contemporary definitions" of terrorism which fail to appreciate the ancient lineage of modern terrorism and the relationship of holy or sacred terror and secular terror. Rapoport's evidence casts doubts upon the wisdom of contemporary efforts to make *any* activity, including terrorism, rational, because he shows that terrorism characteristically stems from irrational and messianistic impulses. Terrorism's primary characteristic is its perpetrators' fanaticism; terrorists today as in the past are true believers whose most telling attribute is their willingness to die for their cause. Terrorism, he shows, "entails extranormal violence, and as such, is almost guaranteed to evoke wild and uncontrollable emotions. Indeed, the people attracted to it may be so intrigued by the experience of perpetrating terror that everything else is incidental."

An approach different from those accentuating mental states and ideological causes is to treat terrorism's origins not as an intellectually or psychologically-animated phenomenon, but rather as one that arises from particular kinds of environmental circumstances. Here the view is advanced that terrorism is best explained by ecological factors, not by motives, needs, experiences or beliefs. Terrorism arises in particular *situations*, and to understand its origins, the "ecology of terrorism"—the atmosphere which makes terrorism so convenient and tempting—needs to be considered.[15]

This perspective thus shifts away from the identity and motives of actors and accounts for terrorism by reference to the climate or environment which shape actors' thinking and actions. It sees modern terrorism occurring because modern circumstances make terrorist methods exceptionally easy.

Let us shift focus and explore this alternative interpretation by examining some of its variants that stress different ecological causes and conditioning factors. Many aspects of the contemporary environment might be identified as influential in explaining the ascendance of international terrorism in the twilight of the twentieth century. Limitations of space enable only the most salient ecological influences to be addressed. We shall concentrate on several.

For example, modern technology is often interpreted as a powerful causal influence. Technology is alleged to have increased the magnitude of terrorists' means, making it possible for very small groups to achieve the minimal critical mass necessary for the perpetration of terrorism. The standardization of air communications, for example, can be cited as a feature of the contemporary environment created by technology that has made air transportation systems such an easy target for air pirates: "The circumstances of air travel present the terrorist hijacker with a perfectly insulated hostage group more completely at the mercy of the terrorist than almost any other imaginable."[16] But the impact of technology extends beyond air transport and is more pervasive and generic; it has contributed to the growth of terrorism and its internationalization in a number of ways. As Brian M. Jenkins summarizes:

> Contemporary international terrorism is well suited to the technology of our era. Modern jet travel provides terrorists with worldwide mobility. Conflicts need no longer be local—terrorists can strike on any continent. Radio, television, and communications satellites provide almost instantaneous access to a global audience. Weapons and explosives are increasingly available, and modern industrial society presents many vulnerable targets.[17]

In addition to technological determinants, also conspicious among the diverse ecological factors cited as a cause of terrorism is the powerful impact widely assumed to be exerted by the mass media. Journalists, it is often assumed, play into the hands of terrorists by dramatizing their activities; the media don't just mirror reality, they create it and thereby aid terrorists:

> . . . Journalism, which shines lights at people, not electrons, does more than alter. It creates. First, out of the infinite flotsam of "events" out there, it makes "stories." Then, by exposing them (and their attached people, ideas, crimes), it puts them on the map. "As seen on TV" gives substance to murder as surely as it does to Ginzu knives. The parade of artifacts is varied, but the effect is the same: coverage makes them real. . . . No one knows this better than terrorists.[18]

If it were not for media coverage, so this reasoning claims, terrorists could not create the hysteria they seek and require to succeed. It is the media therefore that are believed largely responsible for modern terrorism's rise.

Of course, this view is debatable. The thesis that the media assist terrorists and that media coverage is a cause of terrorism's growth can and has been questioned.[19] The effects of media coverage of terrorist activities are disputable. So it may be asked, when terrorist acts are reported, "Do they contribute to the free marketplace of ideas, helping the citizens to understand the central issues of the day? Or do they give terrorists a megaphone through which to spread their message of fear to their ultimate target, the public at large?"[20]

L. John Martin's "The Media's Role in Terrorism" reviews the theories addressing the proposition that, in explaining terrorism's causes, we may have a case of newsmen, in search of a story, creating one. Martin sees a symbiotic relationship existing between terrorism and the mass media: "Each exploits the other and terrorism has no meaning without media coverage in this age of mass communication. Terrorists use the mass media for both tactical and strategic purposes." But the content of the coverage is important, and not just the publicity of terrorist actions which, he estimates, receive attention at a rate of nine incidents per day worldwide. He finds it noteworthy that the press uses the term "terrorist" sparingly and that journalists often omit "the propaganda message the terrorists would like to see accompanying reports of their exploits, thus reducing terrorism to mere crime or sabotage." His analysis provides an interpretation which enables the thesis of the media's influence to be evaluated, and raises important questions about the media's contribution to terrorism's rise on the global agenda.

Still other background factors and environmental influences may be especially important in conjunction with other causes in explaining the growth of international terrorism. The vast number of sophisticated weapons at the disposal of terrorists, for example, must be cited as well. But the foregoing examples suggest the line of reasoning that is followed by those who see emergent trends having coalesced to create an environment that has made the practice of terrorism attractive to extremists. As a result, these observers postulate, contemporary terrorism has changed

> into an independent, self-sufficient, self-fulfilling business organization . . . which is no longer an ephemeral and marginal phenomenon of contemporary society. Unless conditions are drastically changed, one can only predict that the strategy and tactics of terrorism will become further entrenched.[21]

Having examined several major perspectives on the origins of terrorism, let us contemplate still another major causal theory, which starts with the point that most terrorist activities are conducted by people without power. To exercise power and make an impact, resources are required. "Modern terrorists unlike their predecessors do not live by enthusiasm alone; they need a great deal of money."[22] Accordingly, substantial financing may be a precondition for international terrorism as well as a contributing cause of it.[23] Where, therefore, do terrorist movements turn to acquire the resources they lack? To another school of thought, contemporary international terrorism is seen as driven primarily by the matériel and financial support and propaganda assistance provided by *states* – that is, by government *sponsors*. According to this thesis, international terrorism is made possible by the simultaneous existence of two factors: motivated and mobilized actors willing to turn to terrorism to pursue their political objectives, and governments willing, for their own foreign policy objectives, to support them.

This thesis underlies one of the most popular theories of the causes of international terrorism, which contends that terrorism results from and is maintained primarily through the assistance provided by governments.[24] This argument rests in part on the logical fact that many terrorist organizations could not survive in the absence of encouragement, financial and matériel backing, and political support supplied by states from abroad. It also derives its credibility from the substantiated fact that many governments have indeed provided terrorist movements assistance, both overtly and covertly. Hence a school of thought has emerged which assigns great weight to the influence of "state-sponsored terrorism" as an explanation for the growth of international terrorist activity since the 1960s. It rejects the "root cause" thesis but unreservedly aligns itself with the "external causes" school of thought.

This theory has been embraced most enthusiastically and has been expressed most vociferously in the United States. It gained currency in the Reagan administration and attracted many adherents in part as a result of Claire Sterling's influential book, *The Terror Network: The Secret War of International Terrorism*,[25] which seeks to trace international terrorism to the sponsorship of the Soviet Union. In particular, that book alleges that an international terrorist "network" orchestrated from Moscow exists whose active and generous support of various revolutionary movements relying on terrorism makes terrorism so ubiquitous worldwide. (It should be noted that Sterling and other subscribers to this theory[26] reject the view that Western democracies and especially the United States might be included in the category of state sponsors of international terrorism, but that other scholars[27] subsequently have produced evidence showing that the United States and other non-communist regimes within the First World also have been active sponsors of terrorist movements outside their borders.)

The state-sponsorship theory and its corollary, that international terrorism is a form of "undeclared war," is critically examined in Martha Crenshaw's second contribution to *International Terrorism*. In "Is International Terrorism Primarily State-Sponsored?" she focuses on the core hypotheses of the state-sponsorship view of Sterling and others.

It is tempting to ignore the available evidence and accept the theory of a Soviet conspiracy because "ascribing terrorist motivation to world Communist aggression provides an easy answer to a hard question." However, warns Crenshaw, "simplicity of explanation is a virtue, but terrorist organizations are in reality extremely complicated. . . .[To interpret] terrorism as a reflection of state rivalries, particularly the Cold War struggle, is an attempt to draw universal principles from a particular picture of reality. State sponsorship of terrorism," she concludes, "is a part of the problem of terrorism but it is not all of the problem." The record, she demonstrates, refutes the basis for "the belief that terrorism is part of the international power struggle between East and West." A more comprehensive, integrated theory of terrorism is required if international terrorism is to be adequately explained.

Addressing her rejection of this single-factor explanation of international terrorism to an America audience, Professor Crenshaw persuasively shows why other variables must be factored into the equation to account for the advent of international terrorism. In particular, she stresses the potency of indigenous or internal sources of terrorism, and illustrates how many terrorist activities are better explained by reference to local conditions, nationalism, and political grievance than they are by reference to the alleged influence of an international terrorist network led by the Soviet Union and its allies. She also presents insightful comments about the sponsorship of terrorism by dictatorships and totalitarian governments in the Western orbit, and criticism of the views that the mass media contribute powerfully to terrorism or that terrorism springs from ideological or religious sources.

In the search for an adequate account of terrorism, one must focus on the most powerful actors whose actions more than those of any others shape the international atmosphere in which terrorism emerges. Since World War II, the international system has been profoundly altered by the global impact of the United States and the Soviet Union. Accordingly, the role they have played and the response they have made to international terrorism must be given consideration as a potentially powerful "external" influence on terrorism's development.

In "The Superpowers, Foreign Policy, and Terrorism," Donna M. Schlagheck explores controversies about the role of the United States and the Soviet Union in the advent and control of international terrorism. Her reflective comparative examination of the superpowers' foreign policies reveals many similarities and differences, and documents the extensive involvement of both superpowers in the processes giving rise to contemporary international terrorism. Terrorism has been exported. But her examination reduces confidence in theories which assign the superpowers great responsibility for the emergence of international terrorism and the diffusion of terrorism worldwide: while there has been *involvement* and both overt and covert encouragement of terrorist tactics, there has not necessarily been direct *influence*. The power to dominate world politics has not translated to the power to control.

As the preceding essays in **Part II** disclose, because international terrorism is complex and constantly changing, the search for a compelling general theory of its cause(s) has not proven successful. Many rival explanations have been advanced but none has managed to command widespread respect. "All want answers," notes J. Bowyer Bell, but after decades of inquiry "there is still no consensus about the people, the terrorists, about their goals, avowed and perceived, and about what might be done. There are, however, all sorts of explanations concerning the phenomenon, some self-serving, often discipline-based, many speculative, and most arising from long-held political and ideological positions."

"Explaining International Terrorism: The Elusive Quest," by Dr. Bell, concludes discussion of the obscure nature of terrorism's cause(s). He advises us to recognize that "terror arises from all sorts of conditions." Accordingly, it is mistaken to grasp for certainty by reducing the complexities to a simple, singular, and certain answer about terrorism's causes. A sophisticated observer should discern the radical differences and subtle similarities of international terrorist movements and the diverse motives and conditions that animate terrorist activity.

To illuminate the inadequacies of such simple explanations, Bell, like Professor Crenshaw, criticizes the theoretical fad to stress "the nets, the links, the contacts and conspiracies" believed by some to account for contemporary terrorism: "Thus to explain the present apparent wave of world terrorism the simplest answer is that a communist conspiracy most easily fits the evidence." Reviewing the selectively cited evidence by this theory's proponents, Bell, like Professor Crenshaw, uncovers some indicators to which advocates of such a network theory legitimately may point. But closer inspection reveals a different reality, one in which communist agitation and support have had little to do with many terrorist movements which "often operate far beyond the control of a Moscow center."

Given its multidimensional characteristics and multiple determinants, there probably does not exist a single factor which, if manipulated, could eradicate terrorism. Instead, "the contemporary revolutionary ocean is murky, cut with layered temperatures and often ateem with fish elegant or awful." As Bell pessimistically concludes, "The problem is there is no solution." In the absence of a panacea, the search for programs to arrest the spread of international terrorism is also complicated and has proven ineffectual. It is to the policies proposed to control international terrorism that consideration will be given in the concluding Part of *International Terrorism: Characteristics, Causes, and Controls.* But first, various interpretations of the causes of terrorism must be examined. The essays which follow in this Part are presented for that purpose.

NOTES

1. For a discussion of alternate "levels of analysis" and the implications of their application to the study of international phenomena, see J. David Singer, "The Level-of-Analysis Problem in International Relations," in Klaus Knorr and Sidney Verba, eds., *The International System* (Princeton: Princeton University Press, 1961), 77-92.

2. For a "systemic" or "structural" interpretation of the sources of terrorism, see Charles W. Kegley, Jr., T. Vance Sturgeon, and Eugene R. Wittkopf, "Structural Terrorism," in Michael Stohl and George Lopez, eds., *Terrible Beyond Endurance? The Foreign Policy of State Terrorism* (Westport, Conn.: Greenwood Press, 1988), 13-31.

3. "The Root Causes of Terrorism," *The Humanist* 46 (September-October 1986), 5-9, 30.

4. *Alchemists of Revolution: Terrorism in the Modern World* (New York: Basic Books, 1987), 236.

5. Moshe Decter, "Terrorism: The Fallacy of 'Root Causes,'" *Midstream* 33 (March 1987), 8.

6. Ibid.

7. Ibid.

8. Cited in Alex P. Schmid, *Political Terrorism* (Amsterdam: North-Holland Publishing Co., 1983), 161.

9. Cited in Schmid, ibid., 165.

10. What does it mean to "explain" an event? There are several approaches among philosophers. For our purposes, it is useful to employ a "nomological" or "law-like" model of explanation, which assumes that events are explained by reference to generalizations or covering laws attaching cause to effect, that is, linking independent variables (causes) to dependent variables (effects) stated in terms of the probability that the linkage will apply to many cases and will not be highly bound by time or place for their validity. Thus to "explain" an act of international terrorism is to cite it as an instance of a general law that identifies the "causes" or "determinants" that tend to produce or lead to terrorist acts. These laws are defined in terms of a general tendency or probability describing the discerned causal relationship. For a discussion of this and other types of explanations, see Gregory A. Raymond, "Comparative Analysis and Nomological Explanation," in Charles W. Kegley, Jr., et al., eds., *International Events and the Comparative Analysis of Foreign Policy* (Columbia: University of South Carolina Press, 1975), 41-51.

11. See Raymond Corrado, "A Critique of the Mental Disorder Perspective of Political Terrorism," *International Journal of Law and Psychiatry* 4 (Nos. 3-4, 1981), 293-309.

12. *International Terrorism: A New Mode of Conflict* (Los Angeles: Crescent Publications, 1975), 3.

13. Robert L. Phillips, "The Roots of Terrorism," *The Christian Century* 103 (April 1986), 355.

14. "The Politics Of International Terrorism," *Orbis* 19 (Winter 1976), 1254.

15. Representative of this thesis and causal logic is D. V. Segre and J. H. H. Adler, "The Ecology of Terror," *Encounter* 40 (February 1973), 17-24.

16. Graham Norton, "Tourism and International Terrorism," *The World Today* 43 (February 1987), 31.

17. "Defense Against Terrorism," *Political Science Quarterly* 101 (No. 5, 1986), 776.

18. Charles Krauthammer, "Looking Evil Dead in the Eye," *Time* 126 (15 July 1985), 80.

19. For example, see Jonathan Harris, *The New Terrorism* (New York: Simon and Schuster, 1983).

20. Rushworth M. Kidder, "Manipulation of the Media," *The Christian Science Monitor* (16 May 1986), 18.

21. Serge and Adler, "The Ecology of Terror," 22.

22. Walter Laqueur, *The Age of Terrorism* (Boston: Little, Brown, 1987), 96.

23. For a comprehensive treatment of this causal factor, see James Adams, *The Financing of Terror* (New York: Simon and Schuster, 1986), as well as his summary update, "The Financing of Terror," *TVI Report* 7 (No. 3, 1987), 30-35.

24. Non-state actors of considerable wealth also play a substantial role in the financing of international terrorism. Increasingly, international terrorism is financed through monies acquired through illicit trade in narcotics. Hence "narco-terrorism" has become a relatively recent ingredient in the causal chain. For a case study, see Alan Riding, "Cocaine Billionaires: The Men Who Hold Colombia Hostage," *The New York Times Magazine* (8 March 1987), 28; see also Charles C. Frost, "Drug Trafficking, Organized Crime, and Terrorism: The International Cash Connection," in Uri Ra'anan, *et al.*, eds., *Hydra of Carnage* (Lexington, Mass.: Lexington Books, 1986), 189-198.

25. New York: Holt, Rinehart & Winston, 1981.

26. For example, see Ray S. Cline and Yonah Alexander, *Terrorism: The Soviet Connection* (New York: Crane, Russak, 1984), and Desmond McForan, *The World Held Hostage: The War Waged by International Terrorism* (New York: St. Martin's Press, 1987).

27. Noam Chomsky and Edward S. Herman, *The Washington Connection and Third World Fascism* (Montreal: Black Rose Books, 1979). For another example of an argument that if the practices engaged in by states and accepted as custom were undertaken by insurgent groups these would be regarded as terrorist, see Michael Stohl and George Lopez, eds., *The State as Terrorist* (Westport, Conn.: Greenwood Press, 1984).

10

The Causes of Terrorism

Martha Crenshaw

In focusing on terrorism directed against governments, we are considering the premeditated use or threat of symbolic, low-level violence by conspiratorial organizations for purposes of political change. Terrorist violence communicates a political message; its ends go beyond damaging an enemy's material resources. The victims or objects of terrorist attack represent an audience from whom terrorists seek a reaction.

The study of terrorism can be organized around three issues: causes, processes, and effects. Here the objective is to outline an approach to the analysis of the causes of terrorism.

We can begin explaining terrorism by establishing a theoretical order for different types and levels of causes. We initially approach terrorism as a deliberate choice. A comprehensive explanation, however, must also account for the environment in which terrorism occurs and address the question of whether political, social, and economic conditions make terrorism more likely in some contexts than in others. What sort of circumstances lead to the formation of a terrorist group? On the other hand, only a few people with similar experiences practice terrorism. Not even all individuals who share the same ends agree that terrorism is the best means. Psychological variables may encourage or inhibit individual participation in terrorist actions. The analysis will consider first situational variables, then strategies of terrorism, and last individual participation.

This essay represents only a preliminary set of ideas about the problem of causation; historical cases of terrorism are used as illustrations, not as demonstrations of hypotheses. The historical examples referred to here are significant terrorist campaigns since the French Revolution of 1789; terrorism is considered as a facet of secular modern politics, principally associated with the rise of nationalism, anarchism, and revolutionary socialism. The term *terrorism* was coined to describe the systematic inducement of fear and anxiety to control and direct a civilian population, and the phenomenon of terrorism as a challenge to the authority of the state grew from the difficulties revolutionaries experienced in trying to recreate the mass uprisings of the French Revolution. Most references are drawn from the best-known examples: Narodnaya Volya and the Combat Organization of the Socialist-Revolutionary party in Russia from 1878 to 1913; anarchist terrorism of the 1890's in Europe, primarily France; the Irish Republican Army (IRA) and its predecessors and successors from

1919 to the present; the Irgun Zvai Leumi in Mandate Palestine from 1937 to 1947; the Front de Libération Nationale (FLN) in Algeria from 1954 to 1962; the Popular Front for the Liberation of Palestine from 1968 to the present; the Rote Armee Fraktion (RAF) and the 2nd June Movement in West Germany since 1968; and the Tupamaros of Uruguay, 1968–1974.

THE SETTING FOR TERRORISM

The absence of significant empirical studies of relevant cross-national factors is an obstacle to identification of propitious circumstances for terrorism. There are a number of quantitative analyses of collective violence, assassination, civil strife, and crime, but none of these phenomena is identical to a campaign of terrorism. Little internal agreement exists among such studies, and the consensus one finds is not particularly useful for the study of terrorism.[1]

To analyze the likely settings for terrorism, we must distinguish different types of factors. *Preconditions* are factors that set the stage for terrorism over the long run, while *precipitants* are specific events that immediately precede the occurrence of terrorism. Preconditions can be enabling or permissive, providing opportunities for terrorism to happen, or situations that directly inspire and motivate terrorist campaigns.[2]

Modernization produces an interrelated set of factors that is a significant permissive cause of terrorism, as increased complexity on all levels of society and economy creates opportunities and vulnerabilities. Sophisticated networks of transportation and communication offer mobility and publicity to terrorists. The terrorists of Narodnaya Volya would have been unable to operate without Russia's newly established rail system, and the Popular Front for the Liberation of Palestine could not indulge in hijacking without the jet aircraft. In Algeria, the FLN only adopted a strategy of urban bombings when they were able to acquire plastic explosives. In 1907, the Combat Organization of the Socialist-Revolutionary party paid 20,000 rubles to an inventor who was working on an aircraft in the futile hope of bombing the Russian imperial palaces from the air.[3] Today we fear that terrorists will exploit the potential of nuclear power, but it was in 1867 that Nobel's invention of dynamite made bombings feasible.

Urbanization is part of the modern trend toward aggregation and complexity which increases the number and accessibility of targets and methods. The popular concept of terrorism as "urban guerrilla warfare" grew out of the Latin American experience of the late 1960s. Yet, cities became the arena for terrorism after the urban renewal projects of the late nineteenth century such as the boulevards constructed by Baron Haussman in Paris made them unsuitable for a strategy based on riots and the defense of barricades.[4] Cities may be significant because they provide an opportunity (a multitude of targets, mobility, communications, anonymity, and audiences) and a recruiting ground among politicized and volatile inhabitants.[5]

Social habits and historical traditions may sanction the use of violence against the government by making it morally and politically justifiable, and may even dictate appropriate forms of resistance, such as demonstrations, coups, or terrorism. In Ireland, for example, the tradition of physical force dates from the eighteenth century, and the legend of the Irish Republican army in 1919-21 still inspires and partially excuses the much less discriminate and less effective terrorism of the contemporary Provisional IRA in Northern Ireland.

Moreover, the attitudes and beliefs that condone terrorism are communicated transnationally. Revolutionary ideologies have always crossed borders with ease. In the nineteenth and early twentieth centuries, such ideas originated in Europe, stemming from the French and Bolshevik Revolutions. Since the Second World War, Third World revolutions— China, Cuba, Algeria—and intellectuals such as Frantz Fanon and Carlos Marighela have significantly influenced terrorist movements in the West.

The most salient political factor in the category of permissive causes is probably the government's inability or unwillingness to prevent terrorism. The absence of adequate prevention permits the spread of conspiracy. However, since terrorist organizations are small and clandestine, prevention is extremely difficult. Inefficiency or leniency can be found in a broad range of all but the most brutally efficient dictatorships, including incompetent authoritarian states such as tsarist Russia as well as modern liberal democratic states whose desire to protect civil liberties constrains security measures.

Turning to the direct causes of terrorism, we focus on background conditions that encourage resistance to the state. These instigating circumstances go beyond creating an environment in which terrorism is possible; they provide motivation and direction for the terrorist movement. We are dealing here with reasons rather than opportunities.

The first possible direct cause of terrorism is the existence of grievances among a subgroup of a larger population, such as an ethnic minority discriminated against by the majority. A social movement develops in order to redress these grievances and to gain equal rights or autonomy; terrorism is then the resort of an extremist faction of this broader movement.

This is not to say, however, that dissatisfaction is a necessary or sufficient cause of terrorism. Not all those who are discriminated against turn to terrorism, nor does terrorism always reflect deprivation. In West Germany, Japan, and Italy, for example, terrorism has been the chosen method of the privileged, not the downtrodden. Some theoretical studies have suggested that the essential ingredient that must be added to real deprivation is the perception on the part of the deprived that this condition is not what they deserve or expect, in short, that discrimination is unjust. An attitude study, for example, found that "the idea of justice or fairness may be more centrally related to attitudes toward violence than are feelings of deprivation. It is the perceived injustice underlying the deprivation that gives rise to anger or frustration."[6]

A second condition that motivates terrorists is lack of opportunity for political participation. In this case, grievances are primarily political, without social or economic overtones. Discrimination is not directed against any subgroup of the population. The terrorist organization is not necessarily part of a broader social movement; indeed, the population may be largely apathetic. In situations where paths to the legal expression of opposition are blocked, but where the regime's repression is inefficient, revolutionary terrorism is doubly likely, as permissive and direct causes reinforce each other. An example is Russia in the 1870s.

Terrorism is the result of elite disaffection; it represents the strategy of a minority, who may act on behalf of a wider popular constituency who have not been consulted about, and do not necessarily approve of, the terrorists' aims or methods. There is considerable relevance in E.J. Hobsbawn's comments on the secret societies of post-Napoleonic Europe: "All revolutionaries regarded themselves, with some justification, as small elites of the emancipated and progressive operating among, and for the eventual benefit of, a vast and inert mass of the ignorant and misled common people, which would no doubt welcome liberation when it came, but could not be expected to take much part in preparing it."[7]

Perhaps terrorism occurs precisely where mass passivity and elite dissatisfaction coincide. Discontent is not generalized or severe enough to provoke the majority of the populace to action against the regime, yet a small minority, without access to the power resources that would permit overthrow of the government through coup d'état or subversion, seeks radical change. Terrorism may thus be a sign of a stable society rather than a symptom of fragility and impending collapse.

We must also ask whether a precipitating event immediately precedes outbreaks of terrorism. Although it is generally thought that precipitants are unpredictable, there does seem to be a common pattern of government actions that act as catalysts for terrorism. The resort to unexpected and unusual force in response to protest or reform often invites retaliation. The development of an action-reaction syndrome then establishes the structure of the conflict between the regime and its challengers. There are numerous historical examples of a campaign of terrorism precipitated by a government's reliance on excessive force to quell protest or squash dissent. The tsarist regime's severity in dealing with the populist movement was a factor in the development of Narodnaya Volya in 1879. The French government's persecution of anarchists was a factor in subsequent anarchist terrorism in the 1890's. The British government's execution of the heroes of the Easter Rising set the stage for Michael Collins and the IRA. The Protestant violence that met the Catholic civil rights movement in Northern Ireland in 1969 pushed the Provisional IRA to retaliate. In West Germany, the death of Beno Ohnesorg at the hands of the police in a demonstration against the Shah of Iran in 1968 contributed to the emergence of the RAF.

THE REASONS FOR TERRORISM

Campaigns of terrorism may be considered to depend on political choice. As purposeful activity, terrorism is the result of an organization's decision that it is politically useful. The argument that terrorist behavior should be analyzed as "rational" is based on the assumption that radical organizations possess internally consistent sets of values and regularized procedures for making decisions. Terrorism is seen collectively as a logical means to advance desired ends. The terrorist organization engages in decision-making calculations that an analyst can approximate.

Terrorism is not restricted to any particular ideology. Terrorists may be revolutionaries (such as the Combat Organization of the Socialist-Revolutionary Party in the nineteenth century or the Tupamaros in the twentieth); nationalists fighting against foreign occupiers (the Algerian FLN, the IRA of 1919-21, or the Irgun); minority separatists combating indigenous regimes (such as the Corsican, Breton, and Basque movements, and the Provisional IRA); anarchists or millenarians (such as the original anarchist movement of the nineteenth century and modern millenarian groups such as the Red Army faction in West Germany, the Italian Red Brigades, and the Japanese Red Army); or reactionaries acting to prevent change from the top (such as the Secret Army Organization during the Algerian war or the contemporary Ulster Defence Association in Northern Ireland).[8]

Saying that extremist groups resort to terrorism in order to acquire political influence does not mean that all groups have equally precise or realistic objectives. The leaders of Narodnaya Volya, for example, lacked a clear conception of how the assassination of the tsar would force his successor to permit liberalization. Other terrorist groups are more pragmatic: the IRA of 1919-21 and the Irgun, for instance, understood the utility of a war of attrition against the British. Degree of skill in relating means to ends seems to have little to do with ideological sophistication. The French anarchists of the 1890s, for example, acted in light of a well-developed philosophical doctrine but were ambiguous about how violence against the bourgeoisie would bring about freedom.

However diverse the long-run goals of terrorist groups, there is a common pattern of proximate or short-run objectives, defined in terms of the reactions that terrorists want to produce in different audiences.[9] A basic reason for terrorism is to gain recognition or attention—what Thomas P. Thornton called advertisement of the cause. Violence and bloodshed always excite human curiosity, and the theatricality, suspense, and threat of danger inherent in terrorism enhance its attention-getting qualities. Publicity may be the highest goal of some groups. Today, in an interdependent world, the need for international recognition encourages transnational terrorist activities, with escalation to ever more destructive and spectacular violence. As the audience grows larger, more diverse, and more accustomed to terrorism, terrorists must go to extreme lengths to shock.

Terrorism is also often designed to disrupt and discredit the processes of government. As a direct attack on the regime, it aims at producing insecurity and demoralization. An excellent example is Michael Collins's campaign against the British intelligence system in Ireland in 1919-21. This form of terrorism often accompanies guerrilla warfare, as insurgents try to weaken the government's control.

Terrorism aims at creating either sympathy in a potential constituency or fear and hostility in an audience identified as the "enemy." These two functions are interrelated, since intimidating the "enemy" impresses both sympathizers and the uncommitted. At the same time, terrorism may be used to enforce obedience in an audience from whom the terrorists demand allegiance.

Terrorism may also be intended to provoke a counterreaction from the government, to increase publicity for the terrorists' cause, and to demonstrate that criticism of the regime is well founded. The terrorists mean to force the state to show its true repressive face, thereby driving the people into the arms of the challengers. For example, in Brazil, Carlos Marighela argued that the way to win popular support was to provoke the regime to measures of greater repression and persecution.[10] The FLN against the French, the Palestinians against Israel, and the RAF against the Federal Republic all appear to have used terrorism as provocation.

In addition, terrorism serves internal organizational functions of control, discipline, and morale building within the terrorist group and even becomes an instrument of internecine rivalry. Factional terrorism has frequently characterized the Palestinian resistance movement. The victims are Israeli civilians or anonymous airline passengers, but the immediate goal is influence within the resistance movement.

Terrorism is a logical choice when oppositions are extreme and when the power ratio of government to challenger is high. The observation that terrorism is a weapon of the weak is hackneyed but apt. Terrorism is initially the strategy of a minority that by its own judgment lacks other means. When the group perceives its options as limited, terrorism is attractive because it is relatively inexpensive and simple; and its potential reward is high.

Weakness and consequent restriction of choice can stem from different sources. Weakness may result from the regime's suppression of opposition. Resistance organizations who lack the means of mounting more extensive violence may then turn to terrorism because legitimate expression of dissent is denied. Lack of popular support initially does not mean that the terrorists' aims lack general appeal. Over the course of the conflict they may acquire the allegiance of the population. For example, the Algerian FLN used terrorism to mobilize mass support.

Yet, it is wrong to assume that terrorism is always a sign of oppression. An extremist organization may reject nonviolence and adopt terrorism because they are impatient with time-consuming legal methods of eliciting support or advertising their cause, because they distrust the regime or are not capable of, or interested in, mobilizing majority support. Most terrorist groups operating in Western Europe and Japan in the 1970s are cases in point.

Thus, the weakness of some groups is imposed by the political system on others, by unpopularity. In some cases resistance groups are genuinely desperate; in others they have alternatives to violence. Nor do we want to forget that nonviolent resistance is a choice in some circumstances; Gandhi and Martin Luther King made this choice. Terrorists may argue that they have no alternative, but their perceptions may be flawed.[11]

In addition to weakness, an important reason for terrorism is impatience. For a variety of reasons, the challenge to the state cannot be left to the future. Given limited means, the group often sees the choice as between action as survival and inaction as the death of resistance.

One reason for haste lies in the situation; the historical moment seems to present a unique opportunity. For example, the resistance group facing a colonial power recently weakened by a foreign war exploits a temporary vulnerability: the IRA against Britain after World War I, the Irgun against Britain after World War II, and the FLN against France after the Indochina war. We might even suggest that the stalemate between the United States and North Vietnam stimulated the post-1968 wave of anti-imperialist terrorism, especially in Latin America.

A sense of urgency may also develop when similar resistance groups have apparently succeeded with terrorism. The contagion effect of terrorism is partially based on an image of success that recommends terrorism to groups who identify with the innovator. The Algerian FLN, for example, was pressured to keep up with nationalists in Tunisia and Morocco, who won independence in 1956. Terrorism spread rapidly through Latin America after 1968 as revolutionary groups worked for a continental solidarity.

Dramatic failure of alternatives may also fuel a drive toward terrorism. The Arab defeat in the 1967 war with Israel led Palestinians to realize that they could no longer depend on the Arab states to further their goals. Extreme weakness, traditions of violence, and the intolerability of the status quo made it likely that militant nationalists should turn to terrorism. Since international recognition of the Palestinian cause was a primary aim (given the influence of outside powers in the region) and attacks on Israeli territory were difficult, terrorism developed into a transnational phenomenon.

These external pressures to act are often intensified by internal politics. Leaders of resistance groups act under constraints imposed by their followers. They are forced to justify the organization's existence, quell restlessness among militants, satisfy demands for revenge, enforce unity, and maintain control.

In conclusion, terrorism is an attractive strategy for groups of varied ideological persuasions who challenge the state's authority. Groups who want to dramatize a cause, demoralize the government, gain popular support, provoke regime violence, inspire followers, or dominate a wider resistance movement, who are weak vis-à-vis the regime, and who are impatient to act, often find terrorism a reasonable choice. This is especially so when conditions are favorable, providing opportunities and making terrorism a convenient and economical option, with immediate and visible payoff.

INDIVIDUAL MOTIVATION AND PARTICIPATION

Terrorism is neither an automatic reaction to conditions nor a purely calculated strategy. Terrorists are only a small minority of people with similar personal backgrounds and experiences who might be expected to reach identical conclusions about the utility of terrorism. What psychological factors motivate the terrorist and influence his or her perceptions? What limited data we have on individual terrorists suggest that the outstanding common characteristic is normality. Terrorism often seems to be the connecting link among dissimilar personalities. Franco Venturi observed that "the policy of terrorism united many very different characters and mentalities" and that agreement on using terrorism was the cement that bound the members of Narodnaya Volya together.[12] The West German psychiatrist who conducted a pretrial examination of four members of the RAF concluded that they were "intelligent," even "humorous," and showed no symptoms of psychosis or neurosis and "no particular personality type."[13]

In his study of the pre-1933 Nazi movement, Peter Merkl abandoned any attempt to classify personality types and instead focused on factors such as level of political understanding.[14] An examination of conscious attitudes might be more revealing than a study of subconscious predispositions or personalities. If terrorists see the state as unjust, morally corrupt, and violent, then terrorism may seem legitimate and justified. The evidence also indicates that many terrorists are activists with prior political experience in nonviolent opposition to the state. How do these experiences in participation influence later attitudes?

Analyzing these issues involves serious methodological problems. As the Blumenthal study emphasizes, there are two ways of analyzing the relationship between attitudes and political behavior.[15] If our interest is in identifying potential terrorists by predicting behavior from the existence of certain attitudes, then it would be best to survey a young age group in a society determined to be susceptible. If terrorism subsequently occurred, we could then see who became terrorists. (A problem is that the preconditions would change over time and that precipitants are unpredictable.) The easier way of investigating the attitudes-behavior connection is to select people who have engaged in a particular behavior and ask them questions about their opinions. Yet attitudes may be adopted subsequent to behavior and serve as rationalizations, rather than as motivations. These problems would seem to be particularly acute when the behavior in question is illegal.

Another problem is that terrorists are recruited in different ways. Assuming that people who are in some way personally attracted to terrorism actually engage in such behavior supposes that potential terrorists are presented with an appropriate opportunity, which is a factor over which they have little control. Moreover, terrorist groups often discourage or reject potential recruits who openly seek excitement or danger. William Mackey Lomasney, a member of the Clan na Gael or American Fenians in the nineteenth century (who was killed in 1884 in an attempt to blow up London Bridge) condemned the "disgraceful" activities of Jeremiah O'Donovan Rossa:

> Were it not that O'Donovan Rossa has openly and unblushingly boasted that he is responsible for those ridiculous and futile efforts ...we might hesitate to even suspect that any sane man, least of all one professedly friendly to the cause, would for any consideration or desire for notoriety take upon himself such a fearful responsibility, and, that having done so, he could engage men so utterly incapable of carrying out his insane designs.[16]

Lomasney complained that the would-be terrorists were:

> such stupid blundering fools that they make our cause appear imbecile and farcical. When the fact becomes known that those half-idiotic attempts have been made by men professing to be patriotic Irishmen what will the world think but that Irish revolutionists are a lot of fools and ignoramuses, men who do not understand the first principles of the art of war, the elements of chemistry or even the amount of explosive material necessary to remove or destroy an ordinary brick or stone wall. Think of the utter madness of men who have no idea of accumulative and destructive forces undertaking with common blasting powder to scare and shatter the Empire.[17]

Similarly, Boris Savinkov, head of the Combat Organization of the Socialist-Revolutionary party in Russia, tried to discourage an aspirant whom he suspected of being drawn to adventure:

> I explained to him that terrorist activity did not consist only of throwing bombs; that it was much more minute, difficult and tedious than might be imagined; that a terrorist is called upon to live a rather dull existence for months at a time, eschewing meeting his own comrades and doing most difficult and unpleasant work—the work of systematic observation.[18]

Similar problems in linking attitudes to behavior arise from role differentiations within organizations. Degree of organization varies from the paramilitary hierarchies of the Irgun or the IRA to the semiautonomous coexistence of small groups in contemporary West Germany or Italy or even to the absence of central direction in the nineteenth century anarchist movement in France. There are thus likely to be psychological or background differences between leaders and cadres. If there is a predisposition to terrorism, the terrorism-prone individual who obtains psychic gratification from the experience is likely to be a follower, not a leader who commands but does not perform the act.

An alternative approach to analyzing the psychology of terrorism is to use a deductive method based on what we know about terrorism as an activity, rather than an inductive method yielding general propositions from statements of the particular. What sort of characteristics would make an individual suited for terrorism? What are the role requirements of the terrorist?

One of the most salient attributes of terrorist activity is that it involves significant personal danger. Furthermore, since terrorism involves premeditated, not impulsive, violence, the terrorist's awareness of the risks is maximized. Thus, although terrorists may simply be people who enjoy or disregard risk, it is more likely that they are people who tolerate high risk because of intense commitment to a cause. Their commitment is strong enough to make the risk of personal harm acceptable and perhaps to outweigh the cost of society's rejection, although defiance of the majority may be a reward in itself. In either case, the violent activity is not gratifying in itself.

Terrorism is group activity, involving intimate relationships among a small number of people. Interactions among members of the group may be more important in determining behavior than the psychological predispositions of individuals. Furthermore, the group operates under conditions of stress and isolation.

Terrorists can only trust each other. The nature of their commitment cuts them off from society; they inhabit a closed community that is forsaken only at great cost. Isolation and the perception of a hostile environment intensify shared beliefs and make faith in the cause imperative. A pattern of mutual reassurance, solidarity, and comradeship develops, in which the members of the group reinforce each other's self-righteousness, image of a hostile world, and sense of mission. Because of the real danger terrorists confront, the strain they live under, and the moral conflicts they undergo, they value solidarity. Terrorists are not necessarily people who seek "belonging" or personal integration through ideological commitment; but once embarked on the path of terrorism, they desperately need the group. Isolation and the need for internal consensus explain how the beliefs and values of a terrorist group can be so drastically at odds with those of society at large. An example of such divergent conceptions is the idea of the RAF that terrorism would lead to a resurgence of Nazism in West Germany that would in turn spark a workers' revolt.

In their intense commitment, separation from the outside world, and intolerance of internal dissent, terrorist groups resemble religious sects or cults. Michael Barkun has explained the continued commitment of members of millenarian movements, a conviction frequently expressed in proselytizing in order to validate beliefs, in terms of the reinforcement and reassurance of rightness that the individual receives from other members of the organization. He also notes the frequent practice of initiation rites that involve violations of taboos, or "bridge-burning acts," that create guilt and prevent the convert's return to society. Thus the millenarian, like the terrorist group, constitutes "a community of common guilt."[19] J. Bowyer Bell commented on the religious qualities of dedication and moral fervor characterizing the IRA: "In the Republican Movement, the two seemingly opposing traditions, one of the revolution and physical force, and the other of pious and puritanical service, combine into a secular vocation."[20]

If a single common emotion drives the individual or group to terrorism, it is vengeance. A government that creates martyrs encourages terrorism. Anger at what is perceived as unjust persecution inspires demands for revenge.

There are numerous historical demonstrations of the central role of vengeance. It is seen as one of the principal causes of anarchist terrorism in France in the 1890s. The infamous Ravachol acted to avenge the "martyrs of Clichy," two possibly innocent anarchists who were beaten by the police and sentenced to prison. Subsequent bombings and assassinations, for instance that of President Carnot, were intended to avenge Ravachol's execution. In Russia, the cruelty of the sentences imposed for minor offenses at the "Trial of the 193," the hanging of eleven southern revolutionaries after Soloviev's unsuccessful attack on the tsar in 1879, and the "Trial of the 16" in 1880 deeply affected the members of Narodnaya Volya. During the Algerian war, the French execution of FLN prisoners; in Northern Ireland, British troops firing on civil rights demonstrators; in West Germany, the death of a demonstrator at the hands of the police—all served to precipitate terrorism.

Willingness to accept high risks may also be related to the belief that one's death will be avenged. The prospect of retribution gives the act of terrorism and the death of the terrorist meaning and continuity, even fame and immortality. Vengeance may be not only a function of anger but of a desire for transcendence.

Shared guilt binds members of the terrorist group together. Almost all terrorists seem compelled to justify their behavior, and this anxiety cannot be explained solely as public relations. Justifications include past suffering, the glorious future to be created, and the regime's illegitimacy and violence. Shared guilt and anxiety increase the group's interdependence and mutual commitment and may also make followers more dependent on leaders and on the common ideology as sources of moral authority.

Guilt may also lead terrorists to court danger. The motive of self-sacrifice influenced many Russian terrorists of the nineteenth century. Kaliayev, for example, felt that only his death could atone for the murder he committed. A member of the Irgun High Command felt "high spirits" and "satisfaction" when arrested by the British because he now shared the suffering that all fighters had to experience. He almost welcomed the opportunity to prove that he was prepared to sacrifice himself for the cause. In fact, until his arrest he had felt "morally uncomfortable," whereas afterwards he felt "exalted."[21] Vera Figner of the Narodnaya Volya insisted on participating in terrorism, although her comrades accused her of seeking personal satisfaction instead of allowing the organization to make the best use of her talents. She found it intolerable to bear a moral responsibility for acts that endangered her comrades. She could not encourage others to commit acts she would not herself commit; anything less than full acceptance of the consequences of her decisions would be cowardice.[22]

Willingness to face risk may be related to what Robert J. Lifton has termed "survivor-guilt" as well as to feelings of group solidarity or of guilt at harming victims.[23] Sometimes individuals who survive disaster or escape punishment when others have suffered seek relief by courting a similar fate. This may explain why terrorists often take enormous risks to rescue imprisoned comrades, as well as why they accept danger or arrest with equanimity or even satisfaction.

Once a group embarks on a strategy of terrorism, whatever its purpose and whatever its results, psychological factors make it very difficult to halt. Terrorism gathers an independent momentum.

CONCLUSIONS

Terrorism need not reflect mass discontent or deep social cleavages. More likely it represents the disaffection of a fragment of the elite who take it upon themselves to act on the behalf of a majority unaware of its plight, unwilling to take action to remedy grievances, or unable to express dissent. Terrorism is an attractive strategy for small organizations that want to attract attention, provoke the government, intimidate opponents, appeal for sympathy, impress an audience, or maintain the adherence of the faithful. Whether unable or unwilling to perceive a choice, the group reasons that there is no alternative. The ease, simplicity, and rapidity of terrorism strengthens its appeal, especially since terrorist groups are impatient. Traditions that sanction terrorism against the state further enhance its attractiveness.

There are two fundamental questions about the psychological basis of terrorism. The first is why the individual takes the first step and chooses to engage in terrorism: why join? Does the terrorist possess specific psychological predispositions, identifiable in advance, that suit him or her for terrorism? That terrorists are people capable of intense commitment tells us little, and the motivations for terrorism vary immensely. To explain why terrorism happens, a second question is more useful: Why does involvement continue? What are the psychological mechanisms of group interaction? We are not dealing with a situation in which certain types of personalities suddenly turn to terrorism in answer to some inner call. Terrorism is the result of a gradual growth of commitment both to political objectives and to a group. The psychological relationships within the group—the interplay of commitment, risk, solidarity, loyalty, guilt, revenge, and isolation—discourage members from altering the course they have taken. This may explain why opposition persists even after grievances are met or nonviolent alternatives opened.

NOTES

An earlier version of this article was published in *Comparative Politics*, 13 (1981), 370-399.

1. A sampling would include Douglas Hibbs, Jr., *Mass Political Violence: A Cross-National Causal Analysis* (New York, 1983); William J. Crotty, ed. *Assassinations and the Political Order* (New York, 1971); Ted Robert Gurr, *Why Men Rebel* (Princeton, 1971), and Ted Robert Gurr, Peter N. Grabosky, and Richard C. Hula, *The Politics of Crime and Conflict* (Beverly Hills, 1977). For a summary of these findings, see Gurr, "The Calculus of Civil Conflict," *Journal of Social Issues*, 28 (1972), 27-47.

2. A distinction between preconditions and precipitants is found in Harry Eckstein, "On the Etiology of Internal Wars," *History and Theory*, 4 (1965), 133-62. Kenneth Waltz also differentiates between the framework for action as a permissive or underlying cause and special reasons as immediate or efficient causes. In some cases we can say of terrorism, as he says of war, that it occurs because there is nothing to prevent it. See *Man, the State and War* (New York, 1959), 232.

3. Boris Savinkov, *Memoirs of a Terrorist*, trans. Joseph Shaplen (New York: A. & C. Boni, 1931), 286-87.

4. E.J. Hobsbawm, *Revolutionaries: Contemporary Essays* (New York, 1973), 226-27.

5. P.N. Grabosky, "The Urban Context of Political Terrorism," in Michael Stohl, ed., *The Politics of Terrorism* (New York, 1979), 51-76.

6. Monica D. Blumenthal, et al., *More About Justifying Violence: Methodological Studies of Attitudes and Behavior* (Ann Arbor: Survey Research Center, Institute for Social Research, University of Michigan, 1975), 108. Similarly, Peter Lupsha, "Explanation of Political Violence: Some Psychological Theories Versus Indignation," *Politics and Society*, 2 (1971), 89-104, contrasts the concept of "indignation" with Gurr's theory of relative deprivation, which holds that expectations exceed rewards (see *Why Men Rebel*, especially 24-30).

7. E.J. Hobsbawm, *Revolutionaries*, 143.

8. For a typology of terrorist organizations, see Paul Wilkinson, *Political Terrorism* (New York, 1975).

9. Thomas P. Thornton, "Terror as a Weapon of Political Agitations," in Harry Eckstein, ed. *Internal War* (New York, 1964), 82-88.

10. Carlos Marighela, *For the Liberation of Brazil* (Harmondsworth: Penguin, 1971), 94-95. The West German RAF apparently adopted the idea of provocation as part of a general national liberation strategy borrowed from the Third World.

11. See Michael Walzer's analysis of the morality of terrorism in *Just and Unjust Wars* (New York, 1977), 197-206. See also Bernard Avishai, "In Cold Blood," *The New York Review of Books* (8 March 1979), 41-44, for a critical appraisal of the failure of recent works on terrorism to discuss moral issues.

12. Franco Venturi, *Roots of Revolution: A History of the Populist and Socialist Movements in Nineteenth Century Russia* (London, 1960), 647.

13. Quoted in *Science* 203 (5 January 1979), 34, as part of an account of the proceedings of the International Scientific Conference on Terrorism held in Berlin, December 1978. Advocates of the "terrorist personality" theory, however, argued that terrorists suffer from faulty vestibular functions in the middle ear or from inconsistent mothering resulting in dysphoria. For another description see John Wykert, "Psychiatry and Terrorism," *Psychiatric News*, 14 (2 February 1979), 1 and 12-14.

14. Peter Merkl, *Political Violence Under the Swastika: 581 Early Nazis* (Princeton, 1974), 33-34.

15. Blumenthal, et al., 12.

16. Quoted in William O'Brien and Desmond Ryan, eds. *Devoy's Post Bag*, vol. II (Dublin: D.J. Fallon, Ltd., 1953), 51.

17. Ibid., 52.

18. Savinkov, *Memoirs*, 147.

19. Michael Barkun, *Disaster and the Millennium* (New Haven, 1974), 14-16. See also Leon Festinger, et al., *When Prophecy Fails* (New York, 1964).

20. J. Bowyer Bell, *The Secret Army* (London, 1970), 379.

21. Ya'acov Meridor, *Long Road to Freedom* (Tujunga [Ca.]: Barak Publications, 1961), 6 and 9.

22. Vera Figner, *Mémoires d'une révolutionnaire*, trans. Victor Serge (Paris: Gallimard, 1930), 131 and 257-62.

23. Such an argument is applied to Japanese Red Army terrorist Kozo Okamoto by Patricia Steinhof in "Portrait of a Terrorist," *Asian Survey*, 16 (1976), 830-45.

11

The Noncauses
of Modern Terrorism

Richard E. Rubenstein

In March 1976, at the height of the urban guerrilla explosion in Latin America and western Europe, the U.S. State Department sponsored a conference on terrorism. One might expect the two hundred foreign and American specialists in attendance to have done some serious thinking about the causes of terrorism—in particular, the social and economic causes that so often set the stage for political action. Instead, what the conference revealed was the profound aversion to social theory of those concerned exclusively with suppression of the urban guerrillas. Political scientist A. Chalmers Johnson summarized the results:

> Most conference participants believed that the direct causes of terrorism [that is, the socio-economic causes] had remained relatively constant in recent times and that the rise in transnational terrorist incidents was due almost entirely to changes in the permissive causes [foreign sponsorship, availability of publicity, etc.] ...Many members of the conference doubted that the direct causes of terrorism could be discovered in political or socio-economic conditions. They were skeptical of the argument that the way to stop terrorism was to "remove its causes," particularly when in concrete cases the causes seemed more psychological or pathological than socio-political.

What this really means is that most of these experts did not *care* to inquire more closely into the socioeconomic causes of terrorism, either because they believed that the inquiry was fruitless or because they felt that to identify causes might be to identify grievances, and thus provide terrorists with excuses. The academic formulations cited by Johnson barely conceal the commonest sort of conservative prejudices. That terrorism's "direct causes" have "remained relatively constant" means, I suppose, that the poor are always with us (or perhaps, that students will be students), while to assert that the "permissive causes" of the rise in terrorist acts have changed only restates in academic jargon the hoary outside-agitator theory of civil violence. Similarly, the reference to "psychological or pathological," rather than "socio-political," causes suggests the assumption that terrorists are simply fanatics, unreasoning and unreasonable, reproducing in history the essential disorder of their own minds. If this were true, the

Note: some footnotes have been deleted, and others have been renumbered to appear in consecutive order.

only form of analysis that would illuminate the subject is psychoanalysis. Fortunately, no less an authority than the Columbia University historian Walter Laqueur has pointed out the uselessness of the search for a "terrorist personality":

> Given that men and women at certain times and at various places have engaged in political violence, throwing bombs and firing pistols, does not necessarily prove that they had more in common with one another than have rose growers or stamp collectors ...That their members have been young is the only feature common to all terrorist movements, and that hardly requires explanation.

What does require explanation is why young people have thrown bombs and fired pistols at certain times and in certain places rather than others and, further, what the consequences of such behavior have been. Why, in particular, has there been such a significant increase in urban guerrilla activity in the industrialized nations since 1968? . . . What interests us, then, are both the immediate causes of modern terrorism and the longer-term causes that help to explain its persistence. . . .

Among American scholars and journalists, two explanations have achieved a certain currency: the "Red network" theory favored by many conservative writers, and the "permissive society" theory advocated by a number of centrists and liberal commentators.[1] Each theory expresses a modest truth that becomes an untruth when stretched too far. Thus, conservatives are certainly justified in believing that there exists a terror network or "terrorist international"—a number of cooperating organizations supported directly or indirectly by the Soviet Union and/or its allies. In fact, there seem to be several such networks, both "Red" and "Black," although American analysts have been far more interested in the former than in the latter. However (for reasons we will explore shortly), they are not justified in considering the existence of such networks to be a primary cause of terrorism. Similarly, although it is correct to assert that terrorists generally have an easier time of it in democratic societies than under effective dictatorship, to make a great deal of this distinction is surely misleading. How can democracy be a cause of terrorism, when small-group violence afflicts only certain democracies at certain times? And what makes some dictatorships more effective than others in avoiding or suppressing terrorism?

Confronting these hard questions means paying attention to terrorism's internal causes: the constellation of economic, social, political, and psychological factors that have the effect, in a particular society, of inciting young people to engage in conspiratorial violence. Unfortunately, it is the fashion nowadays to explain terrorism exclusively in terms of external causes—for example, outside sources of training, supplies, planning, or ideological inspiration. In The Terror Network, Claire Sterling goes to great lengths to prove the existence of "an international terrorist circuit, or network, or fraternity" financed and assisted by Soviet bloc forces.[2] Sterling's terminology is deliberately vague. What is a "network"? Not an organization, evidently, since Sterling concedes that the evidence "does not prove a closely planned and centrally commanded worldwide conspiracy." But she insists nevertheless that Communist states acting as external sponsors are primarily responsible for the wave of terrorism that has swept the Western World since the late 1960s. Sterling's thesis is as contradictory as it seems, for if the Soviets and their allies are not in command of a planned conspiracy, then at most their role is to provide advice or material assistance either to terrorists or to groups that supply terrorists. And a source of supply (however else it may be judged) can hardly be considered a primary cause of terrorism. As we know, determined combatants usually find material support somewhere, managing at times to milk both the Communist and Capitalist cows.

The intellectual villain here is the network concept, which, although lacking evidence of central control, is used to imply that terrorists are mere puppets of their suppliers. . . . The problem . . . is that in many nations [terrorist groups] exist, and persist, despite efforts to destroy them by shutting off their sources of supply. Conversely, when terrorists are uprooted and defeated, this is generally not because some network has been disrupted or because their foreign sponsorship has been terminated, but because they have been deprived of their base of support at home. In fact, the most powerful terrorist groups of modern times, such as the Argentine ERP and Italian Red Brigade, have also been the least dependent upon external suppliers.

Similarly oversimplified is the one-sided emphasis on a single terrorist network. Conservative analysts, for the most part, choose not to analyze the right-wing network, supported directly or indirectly by the United States and its allies, which has spread havoc from Turkey and Lebanon to Central America.[3] Thus, Claire Sterling has nothing to say about the joint CIA-Mafia attempts to assassinate Castro during the 1960s, the assassination of Chilean diplomat-in-exile Orlando Letelier in Washington, D.C., in 1976 by anti-Castro Cubans financed by the Chilean Agency for Intelligence and National Defense (DINA), or the Central American death squads, Nicaraguan Contras, South Korean Central Intelligence Agency (KCIA), Israeli Central Institute for Intelligence and Security (MOSSAD), and the South African-backed guerrillas now operating throughout Southern Africa, all of which are linked with the CIA and, to some extent, with each other. "Linkage," an intentionally blurry word, can mean anything from active sponsorship of a specific terrorist act to unintentional complicity in extremist violence. . . .

By the same token, although one can discover connections aplenty between "Carlos," the RAF and June 2d groups, the PFLP, the Libyans, and the KGB, it is impossible to state with conviction that any "Carlos" operation was performed under the orders or with the advice of the KGB. This is not to say that the Soviet Union and the United States are free of moral responsibility for the acts of their protégés' protégés; it is simply to affirm that the farther one moves down the chain of linkages from super-powers like the United States or the Soviet Union to relatively unpowerful extremist groups, the more questionable becomes the hypothesis of a tightly controlled network. *That* its why network theorists like Sterling have been unable to find concrete evidence of a "closely planned and centrally commanded" conspiracy. Moral responsibility may exist when the creature one has assisted to live runs amok, however indirect the assistance. And certain terrorist operations are surely undertaken with the connivance of outside sponsors. But network theory is not really a theory of terrorism at all. It is an avoidance mechanism: an invitation to consider internal causes as being of little consequence and external sponsorship as all-determining. Modern terrorologists are fascinated by *technique*—sophisticated weapons in the hands of underground grouplets, types of bombs, elaborate schemes for obtaining false papers, and the like. That is, they are fixated on supply, when what most requires explaining is demand—not the sources of terrorist matériel, but the sources of terrorism itself. . . .

People who want to make war on the state generally find the means to do so—a fact that would be too trite to mention had it not, apparently, been forgotten. At the turn of the century, anarchists armed with little more than knives, pistols, and homemade bombs terrorized Europe and North America quite effectively. In our own time, not just sporadic terrorist acts but extended violent campaigns have been fought with the weaker side relying largely on weapons taken from the enemy or obtained from curious sources. When one considers the whole range of civil violence, from individual acts of rage or martyrdom to civil war, supply appears to have increasingly more weight in determining the outcome as violence becomes more massive. Small groups have little need for exotic weapons; the European terrorists who obtained antiaircraft missiles during the 1970s never used one successfully, while the most devastating attacks of recent years have been made with car or truck bombs, submachine guns, and grenades.

Furthermore, the basic components of the terrorist infrastructure—terrorists' sources of forged papers, safehouses, transportation and communications links, personnel, and money, as well as weapons—are in plentiful supply locally. It is thus a myth that terrorist groups can be "crushed in the egg" by cutting off their external sources of supply. It is the local political base that makes the terrorist organization or breaks it. Politically isolated groups turn to banditry or disappear because of political weakness, not from a shortage of matériel. Others survive and expand, not because they have learned to master high technology, but because they generate their own sources of supply. . . .

Years ago, Karl Marx pilloried the terrorists, calling them "alchemists of the revolution" who "throw themselves on discoveries which should work revolutionary wonders: incendiary bombs, hell-machines of magical impact," instead of mastering the more complex and subtle science of political organization. Our terrorism experts, for the most part, are alchemists of the *counter*revolution. They hope to suppress terrorism, guerrilla wars, even social revolutions without recognizing the political and social conditions that produce them.

The liberal theory that attempts to correlate modern terrorism with "permissive" institutions has, at least, the virtue of looking for internal causes, although it hardly can be said to have found them. There are several variations on this theme. Some writers believe that democratic leniency encourages terrorism or makes it difficult to suppress, while others emphasize the prevalence of terrorism in inefficiently administered societies, be they democratic or totalitarian. A number of commentators have focused on racial or ethnic conflict in such societies as a generator of small-group violence.[4] Still others connect the increase in terrorism with the uninhibited media coverage of terrorist acts and demands, or with the psychological appeals of extremism to affluent, permissively reared youths.[5] Like the Red network theory of the conservatives, all of these notions combine a small bit of truth with large doses of question-begging. To say that terrorism flourishes in permissive societies, or that it is encouraged by media publicity, really tells us nothing about the origins of the phenomenon. Rather, it implies that terrorist impulses are somehow loose in society, just waiting to be realized, and that they *will* be realized unless effectively deterred. Some analysts assign a cause to this assumed tendency: the prevalence of social injustice, or a high level of frustration among certain groups, or the decline of traditional inhibitors of personal violence. But none of these general explanations is satisfactory. Oppression, frustration, and aggression have been with us always, but terrorism—the violence of the intelligentsia—has erupted only under certain conditions.

Which conditions? Liberal commentators, by and large, have been no more inclined than have conservatives to develop a theory that would specify them. "It may be misleading to search for the root causes of terrorism," says [Jan] Schreiber.[6] And along the same lines, [Walter] Laqueur explains that:

> Given the specific difficulties involved in the study of terrorism rather than political violence in general, it is not surprising that there has been no stampede to search for a general theory explaining the phenomenon.[7]

It seems to me that the reason for this uncharacteristic reticence is not just the inherent difficulty of the subject, but the fact that liberals are no less obsessed than law-and-order conservatives with the issues of short-term deterrence and control. The principal question, says Schreiber, is, "Who will bell the cat?"[8] One would like to know how the cat got loose in the first place—what relationship between social development, political institutions, and ideas generates modern terrorism—but governments and foundations that sponsor research in the field are looking for practical answers to immediate questions: how do you infiltrate a terrorist group? Do you or do you not negotiate in a hostage situation, and if so, under what guidelines? Should the mass media report the details of ongoing violent incidents? Should the government's antiterrorist activities be centralized? Officials are entitled to ask these questions and to pay for attempts to answer them, but the answers they get are necessarily limited by the narrow scope of the inquiry. Research that does not explain terrorism's origins cannot predict its likely course of development. Even worse, abandoning the search for social causes has the practical effect of substituting a theory of supply for a theory of causation. Foreign sponsorship (another evasive term, like "network") becomes the villain.

This does not mean that scholarship in the field of terrorism has been inaccurate or useless. Lacking a general theory, analysts have focused their attention on specific violent movements, thus providing us with a considerable amount of data. . . . Indeed, since 1976 a well-edited scholarly publication called *Terrorism: An International Journal* has been devoted primarily to this sort of empirical research, with results that are frequently enlightening. The major drawback of an approach that lacks a general theory, however, is a tendency to answer questions about the causes of terrorism by referring to the motivation of this or that group. The primary cause of Irish terrorism, for example, is sometimes said to be British policy in Ireland, sometimes Protestant or Catholic intransigence, sometimes the Irish personality, and even, on occasion, the alleged conversion of the IRA Provisionals to Marxism. While it is certainly true that one cannot understand behavior without appreciating its motivation, the underlying issue for social scientists is what *produces* the motivation both in particular cases and in general. The unfortunate result of the present theoretical impasse has been not only to "psychologize" the subject of terrorism but to fragment it. Each terrorist movement is considered in isolation from every other movement, except insofar as some foreign sponsorship or networking is judged to be taking place.

In his thoughtful article on terrorism in Northern Ireland, Alan O'Day remarks that

> Terrorism in Northern Ireland . . . has much to do with Irish history and is little inspired by movements elsewhere. It is a largely self-contained effort that reproduces its own heroic past and seeks ends that are entirely insular. The aims of the Irish are not at all like those of other groups engaging in terrorism; should the aims be achieved, other movements are unlikely to benefit from the success, except in the sense that their morale might receive a boost.[9]

All of this seems true enough; but whether the aims of the Irish are like those of other groups, and whether the IRA is supported politically or financially by other groups, are irrelevant to discovering the social causes and consequences of terrorism. The Irish cause is no more or less insular than that of the Basques in northern Spain, the Argentine Montoneros, the Palestinians, or for that matter, more doctrinaire formations like the

Red Brigade. No sizable terrorist movement can be comprehended in isolation from its own antecedents and its own society. Nevertheless, it is a fact that *all* of the groups just mentioned, as well as several hundred others, have engaged in significant campaigns of small-group violence during the past fifteen years. How do we account for this explosion of urban guerrilla activity in many nations, each with its own "insular" problems and history? When liberal scholars fail to explain this simultaneity — when they fail to demonstrate how similar social causes in diverse cultures can produce like effects — they leave the field to the conservatives, whose theories at least have the virtue of attempting to comprehend terrorism as a transnational phenomenon.

Similarly, rather than explore the consequences of terrorist violence with a view toward constructing a coherent social theory, most modern analysts focus on the effectiveness or ineffectiveness of official responses to the terrorist challenge. In general, liberal scholars have opted for more highly modulated responses to terrorism than conservatives. They caution against repressive overreactions that would weaken democratic institutions and emphasize the need [in Schreiber's words] "to reckon first with the subtler violence of legitimate power." Interestingly, the analysts who make such statements are often those who live in nations with little experience of serious terrorism. Let the frequency and seriousness of attacks in their own country rise . . . and they are unlikely to object to "special measures" directed against terrorists, suspected terrorists, suspected supporters . . . and anyone else who might be connected with the violence.

The tendency of liberals to harden their line as terrorism escalates is attributable in part to specific acts directed against them . . . and in part to their deep identification (when push comes to shove) with the sociopolitical establishment. But it also suggests that the differences between soft and hard responses over the proper methods of combating and controlling terrorism were not profound to begin with. Many scholars start out searching for terrorism's social causes, but when the search produces unacceptably complex results (for example, results suggesting the need for significant social change), their focus shifts to what they think is doable: making the target less accessible, strengthening police and intelligence capabilities, cutting off sources of supply — in short, counterterrorism. If, in the end, liberal and conservative analysts appear to speak with one voice, this may be because they accept the same implicit dogma: terrorism, like sin, is mysteriously rooted in human nature. It cannot be ended, it can only be deterred or combated. . . .

NOTES

1. Network theory is represented in Claire Sterling, *The Terror Network: The Secret War of International Terrorism* (New York: Holt, Rinehart, & Winston, 1981); Christopher Dobson, *The Terrorists* (New York: Facts on File, 1982); and Ray S.

Cline and Yonah Alexander, *Terrorism: The Soviet Connection* (New York: Crane Russak, 1984); among others. Permissive society theories are offered in Laqueur, *Terrorism* (Boston: Little, Brown, 1977); Paul Wilkinson, *Terrorism and the Liberal State* (New York: John Wiley, 1977); J. Bowyer Bell, *A Time of Terror: How Democratic Societies Respond to Revolutionary Violence* (New York: Basic Books, 1978); and Jan Schreiber, *The Ultimate Weapon: Terrorists and World Order* (New York: William Morrow, 1978).

2. New York: Holt, Rinehart & Winston, 1981, 10.

3. There is unfortunately no definitive work as yet on the "Black network(s)." But see Edward S. Herman, *The Real Terror Network* (Boston: South End Press, 1982). See also Hans Josef Horchem, "European Terrorism: A German Perspective," *Terrorism: An International Journal* 6 (1): 27ff.; Bruce Hoffman, "Right-Wing Terrorism in Europe," *Conflict* 5 (3): 185ff.; "The Contra/Nazi Connection," *Workers Vanguard*, 1985, no. 377: 1, 14-15.

4. See, for example, Paul Wilkinson, *Political Terrorism* (London and New York: Macmillan, 1974); Richard Clutterbuck, *Living With Terrorism* (London: Faber, 1975).

5. See theories summarized in Paul Wilkinson, "Social Scientific Theory and Civil Violence," in *Terrorism: Theory and Practice,* ed. Yonah Alexander et al. (Boulder, Colo.: Westview Press, 1979), 45-72. The most useful causal theory, which has influenced my analysis of terrorism's origins, is the "relative deprivation" theory originally outlined by Ted Gurr in *Why Men Rebel* (Princeton, N.J.: Princeton University Press, 1970).

6. *The Ultimate Weapon*, 27.

7. *Terrorism*, 144.

8. *The Ultimate Weapon*, 148 ff.

9. "Northern Ireland, Terrorism, and the British State," in *Terrorism: Theory and Practice*, ed. Yonah Alexander et al., 127.

12

Why Modern Terrorism? Three Causes Springing from the Seeds of the 1960s

Rushworth M. Kidder

"Nineteen sixty-eight really was the big upsurge."

In his book-lined office at the University of Aberdeen, Paul Wilkinson pinpoints the year that launched the latest epicycle of political violence.

"A number of different events came together [that year] to create a situation where terrorist violence was a more attractive mode of struggle," says Professor Wilkinson, an internationally recognized authority on terrorism.

Among the events of 1968:

- Three armed members of the Popular Front for the Liberation of Palestine seized an El Al airliner and forced it to fly to Algeria — launching a campaign of air piracy that has been a hallmark of terrorism ever since.
- In West Germany, the Baader-Meinhof gang gained prominence by torching a Frankfurt department store.
- In Egypt, the Palestine Liberation Organization, sobered by Israel's victory in the "six-day war" in 1967, made Yasser Arafat its leader.
- In the United States, Martin Luther King, Jr. was assassinated, unleashing a spate of domestic violence by groups such as the Black Panthers and Weathermen.
- In Mexico City, street marches culminated in protests at the Olympic Games, aiding growth of a terrorist movement with Cuban and Soviet connections.

Like any trend, the upsurge was not restricted to a single year. Ché Guevara had been killed in Bolivia in 1967. The Provisional Irish Republican Army took up terrorism in 1969, the year British soldiers were introduced into Northern Ireland. In 1970, terrorism took a new turn with the kidnapping and murder of Daniel A. Mitrione, a U.S. advisor to Uruguay's police, by Marxist urban guerrillas, the Tupamaros. That year, too, Italy's Red Brigades began their campaign of terror, and the Japanese Red Army sprang into view with robberies, kidnappings, and the hijacking of an airliner.

Since the late 1960s, the trend has risen steadily. . . . But terrorism itself is nothing new. "There is a long history of [terrorism]," notes Wilkinson, "going right back to the period of struggle of the Jews [known as the Zealots] against the Romans [66–73 AD]." History also records the eleventh-century rise of the Assassins, a sect based in Persia (modern-day Iran).

Yet the modern epicycle is peculiar, sprouting up fairly suddenly in a number of countries. What produced it? What happened in the late 1960s that provided such fertile ground for this ugly weed?

Terrorist experts point to a number of causes. Generally, however, they fall into three categories: broad historical changes, ideological shifts, and technological advances.

HISTORICAL PATTERNS

By the late 1960s, three things had become clear.

First, the world was living under the umbrella of a nuclear standoff between the superpowers. "Those states and factions which are interested in achieving their ends by force," says Wilkinson, "will be aware of the danger that, if they use even conventional war, it may easily escalate into a nuclear intervention."

"It is therefore all the more attractive in an age of nuclear stalemate for groups to use low-risk, potentially high-yield, and potentially very effective methods of struggle [such as terrorism]."

Second, European colonialism had pretty much ended, leaving a host of newly independent nations to grapple with unfamiliar problems. In some of these nations, restless minorities were no longer held in check by European-model police and military forces. In others, disputes arose with neighboring states over boundaries that had often been established arbitrarily by colonial administrations. The result: guerrilla uprisings and low-intensity warfare, often including terrorist activity.

Third, a growing emphasis on human rights had led Western democracies to place high value on the life of a single citizen. Unlike totalitarian regimes, democracies proved to be particularly susceptible to hostage-taking threats. Terrorists soon found that a kidnapping, mobilizing public opinion, could bring concessions unattainable in other ways.

IDEOLOGICAL SHIFTS

Several key religious and political changes also occurred around the late '60s.

- Islamic fundamentalism, growing out of a violent reaction against Westernization and modernity, provided a climate favorable to Shiite terrorism.

- The Vietnam war radicalized large numbers of young people in developed nations throughout the world. By the late '60s, some of them, impatient at the inefficacy of street protests, turned to violence. Citing inequalities between first- and third-world nations, they espoused Marxist-Leninist ideologies, went underground, and took up terrorism.
- Guerrilla warfare, long thought to be a rural phenomenon, became increasingly urbanized. "[Fidel] Castro and Guevara were firmly convinced that the city was the 'graveyard' of the revolutionary freedom fighter," writes historian Walter Laqueur in his pioneering book, *Terrorism*. "It was only in the middle 1960s that urban terrorism came into its own, mainly as a result of the defeat of the rural guerrillas in Latin America."
- The rise in world terrorism also coincides with the arrival of Yuri Andropov as head of the KGB, the Soviets' secret service, in 1967. Terrorism experts generally dismiss the notion that somewhere deep in the Kremlin is a "control room" coordinating international terrorism. But under Andropov's influence the Soviets, in the words of Rand Corporation scholar Paul B. Henze, seemed "ready for a rougher game."

TECHNOLOGICAL ADVANCES

Foremost among the new technological factors has been the growth of mass communications, especially television. The first live satellite broadcast of an Olympic Game came from Tokyo in 1964. Eight years later, some 500 million viewers around the world saw terrorists take the spotlight at the Munich Olympics, where 11 Israeli athletes were murdered by the Black September Organization. Since then, television has become the terrorists' medium of choice, allowing tiny, essentially powerless gangs to megaphone their demands.

By the early 1970s, air travel had also come of age. The number of passenger-miles flown throughout the world tripled between 1960 and 1970. That growth has provided quick and easy movement for terrorists between target nations and countries that provide safe havens. It has also increased the availability of hijacking targets. Terrorists have been quick to seize the latter opportunity. Between 1930 and 1968, there were 16 successful hijackings of scheduled US aircraft. In 1969 alone there were 33.

Weapons, too, have improved. Modern, rapid-fire submachine guns fit easily into a briefcase. The Austrian-made Glock 17, a 9-mm automatic pistol made almost entirely of plastic, is easy to disassemble—and therefore easy to hide in luggage passed through airport scanners. Weapons have also grown more widely available. It is common knowledge among terrorist groups and security experts that in Lebanon, for example, cold cash can buy some of the hottest weapons available: rifles, pistols, hand grenades, telescopic sights, flak jackets, antitank missile launchers, even (if the price is right) a tank.

Technology in the intelligence community, in a backhanded way, has also benefited the terrorist. As technical means of intelligence-gathering were coming to the fore (in satellite photography and sophisticated listening devices, for example), the aftermath of Vietnam and Watergate led to disillusionment with the U.S. Central Intelligence Agency. The result: cutbacks in staff, and increased reliance on technology. Interviews with present and former intelligence officers suggest, however, that the best intelligence tool for antiterrorism is not the high-tech "eye in the sky" but the agent on the ground. Such resources are being rebuilt, but the process takes time.

13

The Sources of Terrorism: Terrorists' Ideologies and Beliefs

Paul Wilkinson

[Because] terrorism constitutes a potentially grave problem for liberal democracy, one is driven to try to gain an understanding of its underlying causes. Attempts have been made to link the onset of political terrorism to particular socio-economic conditions or to psychopathology, but they have been singularly unsuccessful. It is true that political terrorism is a minority activity, but only a tiny proportion of those captured and convicted for terrorist offences have been found to be either psychotic or acutely deprived either in absolute or relative terms. Indeed much of the politically motivated terrorism in liberal democracies for the past decade has been committed by the spoilt children of affluence. The Baader-Meinhof gang, the Weathermen, the Japanese United Red Army and the Angry Brigade in Britain have all mainly comprised young people from comfortably-off middle class homes and with the 'advantages' of higher education. What chance would a mere poverty-stricken revolutionary have of retaining the massive retinue of legal advisers placed at the disposal of Ulrike Meinhof and her colleagues?

Northern Ireland is one of the few cases that lend support to this theory. The I.R.A.'s political front, Provisional Sinn Fein, is one of the small number of groups supporting terrorism with a genuine and growing base of mass support. . . .

If it is argued that political terrorism is a function, or at least a symptom, of marginality and deprivation in an affluent society, why is the incidence of terrorism so much lower in the United States, Canada and Australasia than in Europe and Latin America?

On the other hand, if it is seriously argued that political terrorism is a response to high levels of absolute poverty or deprivation, why is it that the annual rate of terrorist incidents in Western Europe far outstrips that of the least developed Afro-Asian countries? There *is* a much more powerful tool for understanding the roots of political terrorism, though it has been sorely neglected until recently. We can attempt to identify and explore the political motivations of terrorists and to relate them

Note: footnotes have been deleted.

to particular ideologies, régimes, conflicts, and strategic and tactical conditions. This approach affords us by far the richest insights into the dynamics of terrorism. . . .

Whatever their ideological coloring, terrorists in democratic societies are desperate people bitterly opposed to the prevailing régime, alienated from all liberal democratic values. Yet by definition, liberal societies contain overwhelming majorities in favor of liberal institutions and values. Knowing as he does that the liberal democratic government enjoys such universal support and legitimacy the fanatical dissident may give up all hope of gaining influence or political power by peaceful and legitimate means such as electoral struggle—if ever, indeed, he had such hopes— and may consider instead various violent alternative roads to power, including political terrorism. Hence the paradox that a growing popular consensus on the legitimacy of liberal democratic government renders a desperate internal challenge by minorities most fanatically opposed to it more probable.

The rational and well-informed terrorist knows full well that in taking on the liberal state he is likely to be at the dangerous end of an asymmetrical conflict. But if he has given up all hope of any other vehicle of fundamental change—such as the liberal state's defeat or assimilation at the hands of a rival state, or a total economic collapse or a mass insurrection—he may well conclude that terrorism is the weapon of last resort. . . . [The] advantages are by no means all on the side of the liberal democratic state in this asymmetrical conflict. However, the point to be made here is that the odds are stacked heavily against the terrorists in any well-ordered relatively stable liberal state. And the very vulnerability and isolation of the terrorist will tend to be intensified as the vast majority of citizens rally and close ranks to protect themselves, their community, and the constitutional order which they regard as legitimate. Hence, unless the liberal state's authorities grossly mishandle the situation, public hostility to the terrorists will tend to increase in proportion to the visibility of the terrorist campaign. As the public is roused to outrage and fury by terrorist attacks on life and property, the situation may well rebound upon the terrorist. They become still more marginal, hunted and desperate creatures more often than not flung into heavy dependence upon the criminal underworld or on foreign states for aid, succor and sanctuary.

One of the consequences of the terrorists' relative marginality in the liberal state is that it becomes far easier for the terrorist movement to terrorize the terrorist, to keep tabs on his or her movements and to control and discipline members. Because the bulk of the population support the authorities in their fight to defeat terrorists, the terrorists cannot melt away into the 'background' easily. And once he or she has been 'blooded' in a terrorist attack or venture, it becomes easy for the terrorist movement to hold them by threatening to betray them to the authorities: thus the mechanism for terrorist control of the group by means of blackmail and intimidation is all too effective.

Inevitably many who get caught up in the network of terrorist organizations become involved accidentally by virtue of criminal expertise or coercive exploitation by the terrorists. Some are bought. More than a few may be attracted by promises of power or the vicarious sense of power and excitement entailed in any underground organization. Many more are trapped into collaboration by weakness and fear. Many of the pathetic creatures employed as bomb planters by terrorist 'retailers' fall into this category. However, none of these sources of motivation can explain the genuine fanatics, the leaders and the militant activists who sustain both the terrorist movement and its propaganda and political warfare. We must take into account their ideological obsession and fanaticism which is the sustaining passion that drives them to strive to reap tactical gains, especially publicity, for their causes.

It is these aspects of terrorist ideology, and the use of terrorism to control and sustain terrorist movements that are now discussed . . . .

TERRORIST IDEOLOGIES AND BELIEFS

The lack of any generally agreed and adequate scientific theory of the causes of revolutionary terrorism is too well known to require emphasis. Few have bettered Feliks Gross' checklist of antecedent conditions for terrorism: a sense of oppression or a state of anomie and the availability of a terroristic organization, leadership, and ideology. I would argue that we can usefully add the diffusion of knowledge concerning terrorist "successes", methods, and technologies which facilitates emulation; the existence of a tradition of terrorism; and the intensification of hatred and the desire for vengeance which characterizes communal violence.

General theories of violence are remarkably unhelpful for the study of terrorism. If we examine, for example, the psychological theories of the frustration-aggression and relative deprivation schools we will discover that they build very sophisticated models of relative deprivation, from which many different socio-political implications can be derived. The difficulty is that whatever relationships between expectations and capabilities are posited, the theory only provides a basis for correlating them to manifestations of "frustration-aggression" in general. The theory cannot explain why, in similar socio-economic and political conditions, some groups resort to terrorism while others manifest other forms of violence or aggressive behavior. As [Emile] Durkheim shrewdly observed: "the psychological factor is too general to predetermine the course of social phenomena. Since it does not call for one social form rather than another, it cannot explain any of them."

Most social scientific attempts at a theory of terrorism suffer from a fatal flaw: they neglect the role and influence of terrorist ideologies and beliefs in inspiring and guiding revolutionary terrorist organizations and in nourishing hatred and violence.

Understanding terrorism is an historical and philosophical, as well as scientific, task. We should not lose sight of the individual values and goals which themselves determine and inform consciously willed social and political action. All too often social scientists regard ideology in vulgar Marxist fashion as a mere reflection or product of the prevailing socio-economic conditions. This neglect is in part a consequence of the influence of Marxism's mechanistic conceptions of ideology as false consciousness and as the legitimation of the ruling class. Marxist and mechanistic sociological theory has generally overlooked the crucial role of ideology in providing for the ageless human need for a meaning to existence. The insights of other social theorists such as de Tocqueville, Sorel and Mannheim, who saw that ideologies and social myths could constitute surrogate religions and guides to conduct, have tended to be overlooked.

It is an extremely difficult task to delineate the ideological development and background of contemporary revolutionary terrorism. A thorough study would necessitate what R.G. Collingwood terms the "mental re-enactment" of terrorist thought in each tiny terrorist group. All that is possible here is to identify some of their ideologies' dominant features and self-images. There are three major contemporary strands in revolutionary terrorist ideology; (i) "classical" anarchism and nihilism; (ii) Third World revolutionism; and (iii) New Left ideologies of violence. These elements are frequently combined and are often fused with Marxist, Marxist-Leninist and Nationalist doctrines.

However, the first point to clarify is that revolutionary terrorism is officially rejected by Marxist-Leninist and Maoist parties. They believe that the revolution cannot be made by the subjective act of will of revolutionaries: it must await the correct objective socio-economic conditions. Moreover, they regard individual revolutionary terrorism as being counter-productive. At best it is seen as misguided romanticism risking valuable lives of potential revolutionaries. At worst it is charged with hindering the real revolution by provoking police repression and hindering the work of the party among the workers. Despite this official stance, however, the Soviet leadership has clearly taken due note of the growth and potential influence of New Left and Third World revolutionary terrorist groups since the early 1960s. They have expanded their repertoire of opportunist tactics to include assistance and indirect financial and logistic support to groups as ideologically diverse as the Provisional I.R.A., Turkish extremists, and the P.L.O. Presumably they hope to benefit from the disruptive effects of terrorist operations within non-communist states. The pattern here is clearly opportunist "proxy" terrorism rather than real ideological affinity.

The anarchist and nihilist strands in terrorist ideology are still strong today as can be seen in the propaganda of groups such as Action Directe in France and Revolutionäre Zellen (Revolutionary Cells) in the Federal Republic of Germany. There was a strong tradition of physical violence in anarchism going back to Bakunin, Nechayev and Malatesta which declared war on the state and on all forms of government and legality. Some anarchist leaders such as Kropotkin and Ferrer developed elaborate projects for an anarchist form of society. Others, of course, favored purely peaceful methods of anarchist education and cultural influence to bring about liberation. The nihilists, of whom Nechayev is the most notorious example, emphasized the need to destroy above all else and did not articulate any vision of a post-revolutionary society. In his *Catechism of the Revolutionist*, Nechayev proclaimed:

> The revolutionary despises all doctrinairism and has rejected the mundane sciences, leaving them to future generations. He knows of only one science, the science of destruction. To this end, and this end alone, he will study mechanics, physics, chemistry, and perhaps medicine. To this end he will study day and night the living science; people, their characters and circumstances. . . . His sole and constant object is the immediate destruction of this vile order.

Several themes in "classical" anarchist terrorism have an extraordinarily modern ring: the notion that violence is ennobling and cathartic (for example, Bakunin's claim that the passion to destroy is a creative urge); the emphasis on "propaganda by the deed" as a technique of symbolic protest and publicity; and the hopelessly ambitious efforts to organize an anarchist revolution internationally. Mannheim was, we now know, premature in his claim, forty years ago, that radical anarchism had almost entirely disappeared from the political scene. It has come back to haunt us in new forms! Mannheim considered radical anarchism to be an outstanding example of what he termed the "Chiliastic utopian mentality." His ideology-utopia distinction has been generally discarded by contemporary sociologists but his brilliant analysis of what he terms the utopian mentality still has much to teach us about the character of present-day anarchism and revolutionary terrorism:

> Their thinking is incapable of correctly diagnosing an existing condition of society. They are not concerned at all with what really exists; rather in their thinking they already seek to change the situation that exists. . . . In the utopian mentality, the collective unconscious, guided by wishful representation and the will to action hides certain aspects of reality. It turns its back on everything which would shake its belief or paralyze its desire to change things.

Mannheim emphasizes the features of blindness to the existing order, a tendency to simplify everything and to blur all partial differences, and an obsessively Manichean view of history and society which divides everybody into friends and enemies. Above all he stresses constantly the Chiliastic utopians' need for illusions and for action to hide harsh realities. This characterization certainly holds for the mentality of revolutionary terrorism. Listen to the FLQ terrorist Vallières on Utopia:

... as soon as you begin to act, the old system hastens to turn you into a public menace and a criminal, so as to be able to bury you alive before your 'idealism' puts Molotov cocktails, dynamite, and rifles into the hands of the workers and the young people who are very receptive to the idea of Utopia, which is all they are waiting for to rise up *en masse* against those who organize, profit from, and defend oppression. For no matter what the ideologists of capitalism, neocapitalism, and imperialism may say about Utopia, it is not a philosopher's utopia: it sums up aspirations which cry out not only to be perceived and understood, but above all to be *realized*. Nor is Utopia the final point, the terminus of human evolution. On the contrary, it is only the point of departure, the beginning, the first stage of the new history which men will embark upon together once they are liberated from their present condition as niggers, as sub-men.

Here we have all the elements of Chiliastic utopianism laid bare. There is the nihilist total rejection of the present "vile order," the absurd illusion that the workers and youth are waiting to "rise up *en masse*" at the terrorists' first bomb blast, and the desperate impatience of the cry "Utopia must be realized now." As Dr. André Lassier, a Montreal psychiatrist, has observed: "The terrorist is a man who cannot wait. He is in a state of mental urgency."

Which elements in Third World revolutionist ideology have been most influential in molding revolutionary terrorist groups' beliefs? I believe the significance of Guevara, Debray, and Marighela in this respect has been exaggerated. It is true that all these guerilla war theorists departed radically from Marxist orthodoxies by stressing the subjective factors in revolutionary struggle. Revolution does not have to wait for the "ripening" of objective conditions. It can be brought about by violence, by military struggle based on the guerilla *foco*. In their emphasis on the fusion of political and military leadership in the guerilla they do have organizational affinities with certain terrorist groups. But it should be noted that none of the Cuban guerilla theorists advocate terrorism as a principal means of revolutionary struggle. Guevara argues that is is actually counter-productive and Debray allows it only a limited diversionary role. It is true that Marighela does advocate terrorist bombings and arson as valuable methods for the urban guerilla war, but it has an extremely minor role in his scenario for revolutionary struggle. He envisages a hypermobile urban guerilla war against the security forces to act as a catalyst and support for a general rural guerilla conflict. At no point does he advocate acts of indiscriminate terror against the population. Marighela sees a concerted urban and rural guerilla war as the road to revolutionary power.

Sartre and Fanon are of far greater significance in the development of terrorist thought. Their almost mystical view of violence as an ennobling and as a morally regenerative force has been widely diffused among revolutionary intellectuals. So too has their advocacy and championship of terrorism. Sartre claims that revolutionary violence is "man re-creating himself." Is Sartre so blinded by hate that he cannot see the roads to utopia strewn with the bodies of their victims? "O Liberté! O Liberté! que de crimes on commet en ton nom!"

Let us strip away the masks of terrorist illusions and expose the deathhead of murder beneath. Terrorists are fond of using romantic euphemisms for their murderous crimes. They claim to be revolutionary heroes yet they commit cowardly acts and lack the heroic qualities of humanity and magnanimity. They profess to be revolutionary soldiers yet they attack only by stealth, murder and maim the innocent, and disdain all rules and conventions of war. They claim to bring liberation when in reality they seek power for themselves. Some claim that their violence ennobles them: history shows that it is totally corrupting and ultimately is turned against the revolutionary society itself. They frequently profess that they administer "revolutionary justice": in truth they make war on all ethics and legality and substitute the whim of their own tyranny. . . .

14

Religion and Terror: Thugs, Assassins, and Zealots

David C. Rapoport

Modern revolutionary terror originated in the writings and deeds of 19th century Russian Anarchists, particularly Nechaev, Kropotkin, and Bakunin. At the same time we all know that the 19th century did not "invent" terror, and that while modern terror is associated with secular groups, the early form springs from religious sources. No one, to my knowledge, has either compared the terror of early religious groups or discussed the relations between secular and sacred experiences.[1]

The second point has had a more immediate import in recent years as sacred terror groups have begun to proliferate.

My principal object here is to compare the strategy and tactics of three early groups, the Thugs, the Assassins, and the Zealots and/or Sicariis. I have chosen them because they are the best known. (The words Thug, Assassin, and Zealot have even become part of our vocabulary, though, as we shall see, their original meanings have become lost.) Another reason for examining them is that they are so dramatically different. Those differences seem related to the specific religious traditions which nurtured them—the Hindu, Muslim and Jewish. A comparison of early and modern terror will be made *en passant*, and only in order to make the differences between the early forms more vivid.

After a few introductory remarks, I shall discuss first the Thugs, who were destroyed in the 19th century, then the Assassins, who gave up terror in the 13th, and finally the Zealots-Sicarii, who were destroyed in the first century. Ironically, there is an inverse relationship between proximity to us in time, and distance from us in spirit. The Assassins seem more comprehensible than the Thugs, and the Zealots at times seem positively contemporary.

The durability of all three groups is remarkable. The Thugs may have existed in the time of Herodotus and, hence, have survived for nearly two thousand five hundred years. At the very least, they persisted for seven hundred years. The Assassins endured for nearly two centuries. Zealot organizations lasted only around seventy years. But in the space of a century, two more Jewish terrorist uprisings, which seem to have been inspired by the Zealots, occurred. The convictions which rooted these three groups were too deeply implanted to be devastated by the occasional storm.

Inconceivable as it may seem, even the more conservative estimates reckon that the Thugs were responsible for at least thirty thousand murders a year for the last three centuries of their existence—somewhere around a million deaths.[2] In their longevity and in the actual number of murders committed, they outstripped every sacred or, for that matter, every modern secular "competitor." Yet, ironically, the Thugs were never a threat to the existing order; or at least it would be hard to imagine any significant terrorist group which represented a smaller challenge because they did their work in secret and struck at individuals rather than at institutions. For the largest portion of the life of this hereditary caste, its presence, strangely enough, was unknown to many outsiders.

The Assassins and the Zealots-Sicarii provide a striking contrast. They did not want simply to kill people; their purpose was to destroy existing arrangements and their atrocities were always performed publicly, often in venerated sites or on holy days. The aim was to spread the message and, therefore, the audiences, not the victims, were the targets.[3] The message was directed towards at least two kinds of people: those whose hostility could be exploited and those whose potential sympathies could be manipulated. Both the Islamic and Jewish terrorists, unlike the Thugs, depended upon gaining larger and larger numbers of recruits. Judaism and the religions it spawned (Christianity and Islam) have, as Max Weber pointed out, always been pre-eminently and uniquely message-oriented religions.[4] Judaism in this period, moreover, was in its greatest proselytizing phase; approximately one fifth of the eastern half of the Roman Empire was Jewish. Islam, unlike Judaism, has always been a proselytizing religion.

The anonymity of the Thugs makes it difficult to imagine a significant event or development which they could have influenced on the Indian sub-continent. The Zealot-Sicarii represent the other extreme. The revolt culminated in the destruction of the Second Temple, the mass suicide at Masada, and then the disaster of disasters—the Diaspora or Exile itself. The impact on Jewish consciousness was traumatic and persisted for two thousand years; and without stressing the centrality of this experience no discussion of Jewish character and life can ever be complete. The Assassins have less significance, but they were an important challenge to the Seljuk empire, and their gnosticism posed a serious intellectual problem which shaped the doctrines of orthodox Islam.[5]

I. THUGS

For the Thugs, religion prescribed both a purpose and a method. They considered themselves progeny of Kali—the Goddess of Destruction. According to Hindu legend, in early times a gigantic monster devoured humans as soon as they were created. Kali killed it with her sword, but from each drop of blood another demon sprang up. As she killed these demons, more would spring up from their blood. Orthodox Hindus maintained that Kali solved the problem of the multiplying demons by licking the blood from their wounds, blood necessary for her nourishment. But the Thug interpretation of this myth was that eventually Kali grew tired and sought assistance. She made two men, and giving them handkerchiefs cut from her garment, told them to strangle the demons and, hence, kill without shedding a drop of blood. When they completed their mission, they were commanded to keep the handkerchiefs for their descendants who would continue supplying her with the blood she needed.

The Thugs (often called Phansigars or Stranglers) attacked highway travellers only. While they confiscated property in the process, the primary object was murder. No property was taken without first killing and burying its owner; and when religious omens were favorable, many were murdered even when it was obvious that they had no property. Still the Thugs did need enormous quantities of loot to pay princes who provided international sanctuaries which allowed Thuggee to persist for such a long time.

There were two types of persons immune to attack—Europeans and all those considered descendants of Kali, i.e., women, vagabonds, lepers, the blind, and the mutilated. The second category provides a faint suggestion that the cult was inspired by political motives. And if this suggestion has merit, a parallel would exist with the Muslim and Jewish terrorists whose strongest appeal was to the less fortunate social elements. Still, in the absence of publicity, there can be no politics and Thuggee must be considered religious activity. Kali's cosmic role of keeping the world in balance required Thugs to supply blood constantly. The goal of the individual Thug was to survive for as long as possible so that he could keep killing. Each was supposed to have averaged three murders for every year of his life; one claimed to have strangled over nine hundred persons![6]

A Thug to us is a brute, ruffian, or cut-throat. But the word originally signified a "deceiver;" the name derives from the skill displayed in allaying apprehensions of travellers whose parties a Thug would join for the ostensible purpose of providing protection and company. In some cases, these intimate congenial associations would last months before the opportunity to strike was clear. (Strangling is a difficult art and requires exceptional conditions.) Usually, close contacts of this sort create bonds between the relevant parties which make cold-blooded murder difficult; indeed, the striking way in which intimacy can transform relationships between potential murderers and their victims has stimulated academics to invent a new concept—the "Stockholm syndrome." But the Thugs seemed indifferent to the emotions which make the transformations possible, for they testified that neither pity nor remorse prevented them from acting. They believed that the victim himself benefitted from his death because he would enter paradise. Moreover, if Thugs failed to comply with Kali's commands, they would become impotent, and their families would either become extinct or experience many misfortunes.

There were other valuable considerations for the good Thug. He was confident of being admitted to paradise—a view which, as we shall see, characterizes the Assassins and Zealots (as well as many modern terrorists). Finally, Thugs spoke of the personal pleasure their particular methods generated. "Do you ever feel remorse for murdering in cold blood, and after the pretense of friendship, those whom you have beguiled into a false sense of security?" a British interrogator asked. "Certainly not," his prisoner responded.

> Are you yourself not a hunter of big game, and do [you] not enjoy the thrill of the stalk, the pitting of your cunning against that of an animal, and are you not pleased at seeing it dead at your feet? So with the Thug, who indeed regards the stalking of men as a higher form of sport. For you *sahib* have but the instincts of wild beasts to overcome, whereas the Thug has to subdue the suspicions and fear of intelligent men . . . often heavily guarded, and familiar with the knowledge that the roads are dangerous. . . .Game for our hunting is defended from all points save those of flattering and cunning. Cannot you imagine the pleasure of overcoming such protection during days of travel in their company, the joy in seeing suspicion change to friendship until that wonderful moment arrives. . . .Remorse, *sahib*? Never! Joy and elation often.[7]

The children of the Thugs were initiated into the tradition early by a carefully calculated process—a gradual inculcation and a circumstance which contributed to their resoluteness. The only examples of revulsion cited occur among the young; invariably, these cases involved those who witnessed events "before they were supposed to." Drugs were used rarely, and then, only among the young.

For the greater portion of the year (sometimes 11 out of 12 months), Thugs were models of propriety, known for their industry, temperance, generosity, kindliness, and trustworthiness. British officers who unwittingly had employed them as guardians for their children, lavishly praised the reliability of particular Thugs who had strangled hundreds. The Thugs, however, never abused their victims. The British officer who exterminated the caste emphasizes that the records do not provide a single instance of "wanton cruelty."[8]

II. ASSASSINS

The Assassins (known also as the *Ismailis* or the *Nizaris*) seem to be a more understandable group or one closer to our own experiences. They formed a movement whose mission was to reconstruct the Muslim world and to prepare the way for the coming of the Mahdi (or Messiah) who would create the conditions for an earthly paradise where both law and oppression would disappear.

Initially, the movement depended entirely on missionaries (*dias*) to propagate its doctrine. But the capacities of the establishment to uproot and restrict the missions seemed too great, leading the Nizari to organize missionary training centers in virtually inaccessible mountain fortresses. The basic idea—a withdrawal to primitive places of refuge (*dar al-hijara*)— "was a deliberate imitation of that archetype from Mohammed's own career." When he failed to convert his own people in Mecca, he fled to remote Medina where the population was more receptive: "Medina was the first *dar al-hijara* of Islam, the first place of refuge—whence to return in triumph to the unbelieving lands from which one had to flee persecution."[9]

The Assassins restricted their armies to the *defense* of their places of refuge, and as long as those armies were able to perform that function the movement itself could not be seriously hurt by the orthodox.[10] Assassin terror, too, was largely defensive, designed to protect their missionaries. Hence, those who were assassinated were prominent political figures, princes or members of royal courts who were able to prevent the "New Preaching" from being heard, and religious personalities, who argued against it in schools and mosques. The terror, one professional soldier tells us, performed the role of the armed escort in a naval convoy which must avoid the enemy until the convoy itself is attacked.[11]

The Assassins were called *Fidayeen* (the devoted ones). The assault patterns seem so uniform that they must, like those of the Thugs, have been prescribed by religious ritual. The victims were assassinated in public places. The weapon was always "a dagger; never poison, never missiles— though there must have been occasions when those would have been easier and safer. [The assailant] is almost always caught, and usually indeed makes no attempt to escape; there is even a suggestion that to survive a mission was shameful." The words of a twelfth century Western author are revealing: "When, therefore, any of them have chosen to *die* in this way . . . he himself [i.e., the Chief] hands them knives which are, so to speak, consecrated . . ."[12] The successful Assassin who *lost* his life secured a place in paradise, a view which developed the conventional Muslim doctrine concerning the heavenly reward for those who fall in a Holy War.

The most remarkable and terrifying feature of the Fidayeen legend was the relationship between assailant and potential victim. A typical Fidayeen was placed in the service of a high official. By devotion and skill over a period of years, he gained his master's confidence; and then, in response to the movement's leader, the "faithful" servant would plunge a dagger into his master's back. Not a single instance is recorded of an Assassin whose personal feelings for the victim made him unable to act. So implausible did this immunity from personal feelings seem to ordinary Muslims that they described the group as hashish eaters (i.e., assassins), though there seems to be no evidence that drugs played a role in the movement. The imagination of the medieval Christian was so impressed by this picture that in European languages the term assassin was initially a synonym for devotion![13] The particular reasons for Fidayeen steadfastness may remain moot forever, but it is pertinent that they began their rigorous course of training as children, and that the doctrine of *taquiyya*, the obligation and art of concealing one's beliefs in dangerous situations, was especially developed among the Shi'a, the section of Islam from which the Assassins sprang.

The Assassins were detested as few heretics have ever been and assassinations regularly provoked furious awful indiscriminate massacres or atrocities on elements of the population deemed sympathetic to the New Preaching. When Assassin bases or armies were assaulted, Muslims felt no obligation to respect rules governing war between fellow Muslims. No prisoners were taken, and the few noncombatants spared were enslaved. Even Nizari peace or truce negotiators were occasionally lynched, embarrassing princes anxious to come to terms.

The intensity of the revulsion may seem surprising. Assassination was not an unusual feature of Muslim politics. Mohammed himself "encouraged" assassination several times and provided, therefore, a moral warrant for the practice.[14] Indeed, a tradition of millenarian Islamic sects dedicated to assassination tactics existed, and the Nizari were simply the latest, the most thorough, and the most successful.

In the eyes of the Nizari, assassination compared to war may have seemed just and even merciful, striking at a few, the great and "guilty," and leaving untouched the much larger mass who so often were quite indifferent to the cause at stake. Yet reactions to assassinations of this sort are potentially immense for they involve serious breaches of faith. This fact led the philosopher Immanuel Kant to condemn belligerents who employed assassins as detestable because they jeopardized the mutual faith necessary to restrain the scope of violence and simultaneously diminished the possibility of achieving a peace settlement before one party exterminated the other.[15] Similarly, to the orthodox community, the depth of Fidayeen perfidy suggested that the Nizaris sought no reconciliation or *modus vivendi*, only "total devotion or total enmity."[16]

Particular justifications could be (and were) adduced for specific assassinations, and the basis of Muslim power was so clearly personal that anyone could understand the immediate advantages of an assassination policy. When a Sultan died, his troops were automatically dispersed and the Nizaris saved. When an Amir died, his lands were in disorder and the Nizaris could raid. Although the implacable hatred this policy generated would soon have been obvious, the Nizari saw no reason to alter their tactics. Hence the massacres which the assassinations regularly provoked did not lead the Nizari to respond in kind. There was the occasional act of urban terrorism in retaliation (i.e., fire-bombing and the like), but these responses occurred so infrequently that one is led to think assassinations were the only legitimate response prescribed by religious doctrine.[17] In this respect, it is worth noting that the Thugs, too, were so circumscribed by their doctrine with regard to who might be attacked that they were unable to retaliate against the small, relatively unprotected group of British administrators who exterminated the caste.[18]

The Nizaris appealed to elements with serious grievances and their fortresses were notoriously hospitable to refugees. Peoples in Persia and Syria chafing under foreign (Turkish and Egyptian) rule and the urban lower classes were attracted. It is surprising, however, to see how often key persons in the "establishment" supported them. Of course, it is doubtful whether a policy of assassinating high officials could be sustained without access from within; and it was through infiltration, conversion, and intimidation that the Nizari achieved their objective. Since the likelihood of internal support was obvious to orthodox Moslems, the Assassins would manipulate the apprehension by implicating their enemies as accomplices—a tactic which will always multiply suspicion and confusion.

III. ZEALOTS/SICARII

There are similarities between the Muslim and Jewish terrorists. Both were inspired by the hope for messianic deliverance and believed that those who gave their lives in this struggle would gain immortality. The Sicarii also used daggers; indeed, their name means daggermen, and the method was, in their eyes, authorized by Scripture. Yet the experiences were not the same, for the ideas and precedents animating them had different meaning.

Jews believed that the Messiah would be preceded by an era of titanic natural and revolutionary cataclysms, when the forces of evil would be at their greatest height and apostasy would occur everywhere. All would witness the "desecration of God's name" and "the upsetting of all moral order to the point of dissolving the laws of nature."[19] For a generation preceding the genesis of Zealot and Sicarii activity, most Jews lived in a state of feverish expectancy: "almost every event was seized upon . . . to discover how and in what way it represented a Sign of the Times and threw light on the approach of the End of the Days. The whole condition of the Jewish people was psychologically abnormal. The strongest tales and imaginings could find ready credence,"[20] and new Messianic pretenders flourished everywhere.

In *all* apocalyptic visions, God is believed to determine the date of the Messianic delivery. Sometimes it is thought that repentance, prayer and martyrdom might induce God to speed the redemptive process. But when a period of unimagineable "woe" is perceived as the precondition of paradise, it would only be a matter of time before some would attempt to bring about that precondition. The Zealots and Sicarii were certain that God would intervene when the believers' actions were resolute and spectacular, when they "did not shrink from the blood-shed that might be necessary."[21] Perhaps the most striking action in this respect was the decision of Zealot leaders to burn their own food supplies during the Roman siege of Jerusalem. In the eyes of the faithful, this act seemed decisive proof that they had, indeed, placed all their trust in God, that there was no turning back; one might even say that it was a kind of moral blackmail. The Sicarii and Zealot strategy was to *provoke* a massive uprising against Rome and subsequently to frustrate reconciliation efforts. Their assumption was that although God might let His people experience vast defeats to test their resolution, He was, by the same token, bound to rescue them sooner.

In vivid contrast to the practices of the Thugs and Assassins, religious ritual did not prescribe detailed methods. It is true that the wave of assassinations which initially characterized Sicarii was inspired by an ancient religious example, namely that of Phineas, a High Priest during the Exodus, who killed two prominent persons observed in flagrant acts of apostasy and religious contempt. The victims of the Sicarii, like those of the Assassins, were influential persons, usually priests, who doubted that God's hand could be forced and feared a war with Rome. Still other forms of terror were used against the influential; and with regard to other aspects and other targets, the tactical flexibility seems enormous. To the extent that Phineas was emulated, the spirit of his action rather than the specific method was decisive. Phineas was known for his zeal or righteous rage, the quality which gives the Zealots their name; and, therefore, the assassinations he inspired originated in rage-provoking situations and made the premeditation and the close intimate relations between assailant and victim which characterized the Thugs and Fidayeen impossible. Phineas was also known for his initiative and audacity— qualities which influenced the range and timing of the assaults which often took place on the most holy days to indicate that not even the most sacred conventions could provide immunity. (Rage and audacity are the qualities most admired and cultivated by modern terrorists.)

Fidayeen terror was an auxiliary weapon designed to protect Nizari missions where the main work of the movement, converting a population to a doctrine, was done. Patient and deliberate, the Nizaris *expected* to absorb the Muslim world piecemeal. The Zealots and the Sicarii saw themselves less as propagators of a doctrine and more as persons capable of compelling a revolutionary uprising by the force of audacious zealous action. Terror, here, became what the anarchist later would call "propaganda by the deed," and, as in the anarchist instance, aggressive action in Judea often seems to have been undertaken more for the sake of its personal value to the actor than for its social effect.[22] The memorable climax at Masada was only the last of a similar series of events where Zealots and Sicarii chose suicide rather than surrender.

Fidayeen activity is terror in the classic and most conventional sense, for it is *always* violent and always meant to intimidate and disorganize. Terror of this sort can be sustained only against special social elements and then probably only for intermittent intervals. (The police customarily are the most convenient targets of terrorists.) In their effort to generate a mass uprising *quickly*, and in their need to sustain or even increase pressures constantly, Zealot and Sicarii activity took different and more comprehensive forms. Potential participants were pulled into the struggle by tactics aimed at producing outrage, sympathy, and guilt as well as fear. The consequences are produced both by deliberately perpetrated atrocities and by tactics which provoke the enemy into committing atrocities or exploit his anxiety about doing so. Terrorists of this sort need not use violence always. But when violence does occur, it takes the form of an atrocity or something which goes beyond the norms people expect to govern violence.

The uprising is developed in several distinct phases, and it might help to clarify those phases by reviewing them here. The first occurs when public opinion is shocked by a series of nonviolent acts of defiance. Always, the confrontations involve new claims for respect due to sacred symbols, and governments find that, willy-nilly, they have backed or been backed into situations where they must tolerate flagrant disobedience to the law or commit actions which many Jews feel threaten their religion.

This seems to be the first known instance of passive resistance tactics; it resulted in what could well be history's first terrorist campaign. We have become familiar with analogous patterns in our own world (i.e., Cyprus and Northern Ireland). In each case, many who would have shrunk from violence, let alone terror, found "legitimate methods" of rectifying grievances, not understanding how the ensuing drama would intensify and broaden commitments by simultaneously exciting hopes and fanning smoldering hostilities.

The Romans were determined *not* to offend Jewish religious sensitivities. Their officials found the courage, restraint, and intensity displayed in this novel form of resistance admirable, and they soon learned how morally difficult and politically dangerous it was to break up demonstrations that included women and children. Romans feared that a rebellion engulfing the entire eastern portion of the Empire would encourage intervention by neighboring foreign states with large Jewish populations. Roman restraint encouraged moderates to become more reckless, to go much further than they originally intended and to forget that however conciliatory Rome might be, she was still determined to retain her authority. On the other hand, the Roman tendency to retreat when a good opportunity was available made militants eager to deny Rome that possibility.

In the next phase, demonstrators are abusive, and bands of rock-throwing youths break off from the crowds. When Roman troops (trying to keep a "low profile" by discarding military dress and exchanging swords for wooden staves) are attacked, their discipline dissolves. The crowds panic and hundreds of innocent bystanders are trampled to death in the narrow streets and alleys. The pattern keeps repeating itself and the atrocities are made much more horrifying and enraging because they almost always occur on holy days when Jerusalem is crowded with pilgrims, many of whom are killed while attending religious services. The massive outrage generated by Roman atrocities and the assassination campaign against the moderates induce intimidated but very reluctant priests to refuse Roman sacrifices at the Temple, which is taken to be a rejection of Rome's sovereignty.

The third phase—a war—ensues; but many on both sides hope to conclude it quickly with a political settlement everyone can live with. These hopes are given a severe jolt immediately in the events following the first military engagement when a tiny Roman garrison in Jerusalem lays down its arms for a safe-passage promise, and the moderates prove unable to stop the terrorists from slaughtering them. Immediately the Greeks, the other residents of the area (and the local source of Roman military recruitment) massacre Jews in various cities, and the Jews respond in kind. The pattern of massacre and countermassacre then spread throughout the eastern portion of the Empire. Roman troops run amok. Yet when military discipline is finally restored, the campaign against Judea is characterized by restraint. Military advantages are not pressed, for hope remains that the olive branch offered will be seized. Rome knows that most Jews want peace; and she believes that the atrocity of Jew against Jew will eventually destroy the popular tolerance all terrorist movements need. A significant Jewish desertion rate, including many important personalities, keeps Roman hopes alive that they can win peace without strenuous military efforts. Various Jewish atrocities in the countryside, however, which finally culminate in the cold-blooded murder of Roman peace envoys, lead the Romans to conclude that total war is the only feasible policy.

To recapitulate: The distinctive quality of Zealot and Sicarii strategy was to exploit outrage in order to provoke a massive uprising. Consecutive atrocities kept narrowing the room for a political or mutually agreeable solution, and this served to destroy the credibility of moderates on both sides while expanding the conflict by steadily enlisting more and more participants. It should be emphasized that no single master hand could be detected in this process. Unlike the Fidayeen, who had no real millenarian competitor, Jewish terrorists reflected a bewildering assortment of forces. There are several Zealot, at least two Sicarii organizations, and many other groups as well whose names and activities have scarcely survived. Then, as now, the existence of competing groups compelled each element to perpetrate more heinous atrocities to prove the superiority of its commitment; and, in time, such groups tended to turn upon each other with the same ferocity with which they assailed the Romans. As these extraordinary actions increased, these groups, like so many modern counterparts, had to make even more unusual claims about their enemies and more radical promises about the social reconstruction victory would bring. Ferrero's comment on the dynamics of the French Reign of Terror is apt: "The Jacobins did not spill all that blood because they believed in popular sovereignty as a religious truth; rather they tried to believe in popular sovereignty as a religious truth because their fear made them spill all that blood."[23]

CONCLUSION

The study of ancient sacred terror yields some interesting conclusions and questions. The durability of the groups and their destructive capacities are astonishing by our standards, attributable in part to favorable international contexts. Yet these three features were developed in environments where technology (i.e., communications, transport, and weapons) was primitive. Despite the uniform character of their technology, the groups were strikingly different—differences which must be attributed to the unique doctrine of each and the vulnerability of society to those doctrines. What is the relevance of these matters for contemporary terrorist studies? Does an analysis of the distinctive doctrinal bases for the sacred terror give us insight into the distinctiveness of the secular form? What kinship does the sacred terror in recent years have with the ancient form?[24]

NOTES

1. A more detailed version of this essay was published as "Fear and Trembling: Terror in Three Religious Traditions," *American Political Science Review* 78 (September 1984), 658-77.

2. The estimate made by Col. James L. Sleeman is also the title of his book, *Thug or A Million Murders* (London, N.D.).

3. Discussions of terrorism invariably describe the modern phenomenon as *sui generis* because it is associated with the ability to reach huge audiences quickly and, in a very profound sense, is the creation of the mass media. I find this view unpersuasive for two reasons. All societies have communication mechanisms, and under certain circumstances the news of atrocities can spread to huge numbers quickly. Secondly, while the differences between communication processes are important, the more fundamental considerations are whether or not individuals perceive the possibility of using terror and whether their audiences are receptive. The last two considerations are absent often.

4. *The Sociology of Religion*, E. Fischoff, tran. (London, 1965), 2 ff.

5. Marshall G. S. Hodgson, *The Order of Assassins* (Gravenhage, 1955), esp. Ch. VI.

6. W. H. Sleeman, *History of the Thugs or Phansigars of India* (Philadelphia, 1839), 58, ff. Sleeman, the officer who "discovered" and destroyed them, is the most authoritative source. See also his *Ramaseeana* (London, 1836), 2 vols.

7. J. L. Sleeman, *Thug*, 3-4.

8. *Ramaseeana*, vol. 1, 8.

9. Hodgson, *The Order*, 78-79.

10. As Mohammed himself did while in hegira, Assassin raiding parties gathered booty regularly from caravans and surrounding lands.

11. Brigadier M.A.J. Tugwell, *Revolutionary Propaganda and Possible Counter-measures* (Kings College, London, Ph.D. dissertation, 1979), 62.

12. B. Lewis, *The Assassins: A Radical Sect in Islam* (London, 1967), 127.

13. *Ibid.*, 3.

14. The English king Henry II encouraged his knights similarly when he asked, "Who will rid me of this man [Becket]?" But how different were the results! It was the victim who became the martyr, the assassins were punished, and Henry himself did penance. For a discussion of Western attitudes towards assassination, see my *Assassination and Terrorism* (Toronto, 1971), Chapter 1.

15. *Perpetual Peace* trans. by M. Smith (New York, 1948) 6-7. "[From] the Ismaili point of view . . . assassination not only was heroic but was just and humane. One point lost sight of . . . was the relative perfidy of an assassination . . . [There] can be good faith even in war but not in an unannounced murder . . . [though] the Moslems at large . . . were commonly not backward in using assassination as an expedient. The adoption of such means as a regular and admitted policy horrified them and has horrified men ever since." Hodgson, *The Order*, 84.

16. *Ibid., loc. cit.*

17. The subject of many allegations, the sect was never charged with instigating counter-atrocities against groups or classes.

18. The Thugs numbered 10,000 while the number of British officers directly concerned varied from 30 to 40 persons.

19. Gershom Scholem, *The Messianic Idea in Judaism* (New York, 1971), 12.

20. Hugh J. Schonfield, *The Passover Plot* (New York, 1965), 19.

21. Josephus, *Antiquities of the Jews*, XVIII, 23, trans. by Louis Feldman, *Loeb Classical Library* (London, 1926).

22. See my "Terror and the Messiah," in Rapoport and Alexander, *The Morality of Terrorism*, second edition, revised (New York, 1989).

23. *The Principles of Power* (New York, 1972), 100.

24. For a discussion of this issue, see my "Sacred Terror: A Case from Contemporary Islam," in Walter Reich, ed., *The Psychology of Terrorism* (Washington, D.C.: Woodrow Wilson Center Press, 1989).

15

The Media's Role
in International Terrorism

L. John Martin

... Terrorism has much in common with propaganda. Both are forms or vehicles of communication. Both are persuasive in intent, rather than, say, informative. Both are expressed in verbal as well as nonverbal terms. And both are pejorative in connotation. One does not refer to friends as terrorists or propagandists. These are terms reserved for one's enemies. The mass media ... may quote someone verbatim using "terror" or "terrorism" in reference to an act performed by a group toward which the medium is either neutral or opposed, but the press will never use these terms in a headline unless it not only disapproves of the act but has no sympathy for its perpetrators.

TERRORISM AND THE MEDIA

By the 1870s, it was recognized that political violence could not be effective without communication. Various Italian anarchists provoked peasant uprisings and acts of terrorism in southern Italy to "educate" the masses and to draw them into the movement. But it was a French anti-parliamentarian, Paul Brousse, who is generally credited with coining the phrase "propaganda by the deed" in ... 1877. At about the same time, the Russian anarchist, Prince Peter Kropotkin, was advocating terrorism as a means of rousing the masses to revolution. ...

Terrorists know that the war that matters is the propaganda war, says [Richard] Clutterbuck. "The shooting war must support that propaganda war but must never supersede it," he continues. "The most powerful weapon in the terrorist war is the television camera." Without mass media, terrorism would have limited effect today.

The media, in turn, find that terrorism has high news value. ... The media cannot resist news of terrorism, which has visual possibilities for television and all the conflict and drama that are the ingredients of news for all media. Behind the media's attention to terrorism is, of course, public interest in it. ... Even if a newspaper or television station were willing to deny terrorism coverage, it could not hold out for long because

Note: footnotes have been deleted.

of the fierce competition among the media. The press—at least in the West—has to build up an audience and keep it to remain in business.

TERRORIST GOALS

Terrorist objectives are either tactical or strategic. Publicly, their long-range goal, of course, is the realization of their cause, although it is not improbable that some terrorists may be secretly apprehensive about reaching their goals. While tactical terrorist objectives, being short-range, appear most readily attainable, terrorists have, on the whole, had little success with tactical methods. These have included attempting to raise funds by holding hostages for ransom; freeing terrorist colleagues from prisons; strengthening the loyalty of group members by involving them in violence, which marks them for arrest and forces them to seek the protection of the group; creating diversions, e.g., drawing attention away from or to some incident, such as the martyrdom of a member as a means of recruiting new members.

Terrorism has generally been more successful in achieving strategic, or long-range goals. These are mainly publicity for the group and the cause as an intermediate step in realizing the cause itself. Many tactical terrorist incidents, while they fail in achieving their immediate objectives, such as release of prisoners, are highly successful in getting full publicity for the group, including extensive media explanation of their cause. *Tactical* terrorism includes kidnapings, hijacks, bomb and nuclear threats. *Strategic* terrorism includes assassinations and murder, arson, and bombings.

In general, one would suspect that terrorists prefer publicity to casualties. . . [A] member of the Palestine Liberation Organization. . . [has been reported to have said] "we would throw roses, if it would work" instead of bombs. "Publicity," say [John] Amos and [Russell] Stolfi, "can be seen generally to rank above the goal of forcing a target government to carry out some immediate action, for example, the release of prisoners, distribution of food, or payment of tribute." In fact, terrorist groups are often known to claim responsibility for bombings they did not commit.

Terrorism, in effect, is a form of nonverbal communication that the terrorist resorts to when verbal communication fails. The terrorist feels a strong need to discredit a government in power, to right or to avenge a wrong. Since trying to do this single-handedly would brand him or her as a criminal, the terrorist organizes a group of likeminded individuals and declares a "cause." Once the group has been formed, it needs to be maintained, and it turns to tactical terrorism to keep itself in arms, money, and fresh recruits. The visibility thus achieved also has long-range or strategic value. The PLO, for example, soon became a group to be reckoned with after a few terrorist incidents. Saudi Arabia and other Arab, as well as non-Arab, countries began to provide the group with lavish support so that it was able to use more traditional, less vio-lent methods of propaganda, such as advertising, participation in interna-tional discussion, and attendance at world forums, as well as broadcasting, newspapers, magazines, motion pictures, and a wire service.

Tactical terrorism does not have to succeed to have strategic value. And even negative publicity is better than no publicity at all. . . . All that terrorists want is a large audience, and they have learned to exploit the media's own modus operandi to maximize their reach. The Red Brigades, according to [Alex] Schmid and [Janny] de Graaf, pick Wednesdays and Saturdays as "their preferred communication days" to get into the thicker Thursday and Sunday newspapers . . .Terrorists prefer to operate in Wes-tern Europe because the publicity they can receive there is greater than anywhere else except in the United States. . . .

INTERNATIONAL TERRORISM

While terrorism in the early part of this century tended to be national rather than international, and was largely limited to the Ottoman Empire and to Czarist Russia, today it is often international in scope and occurs mostly in Western democracies. A CIA report in 1981 stated that 40 percent of all transnational terrorism occurred in Western Europe or North America and that 44 percent involved the United States. . . .

As mentioned earlier, international terrorism is treated as important news by all media in the Western world. In the Communist world and much of the third world, which place less emphasis on objective "hard news" reporting and more on advocacy journalism, terrorist incidents are mentioned only when they have some didactic value or when they serve the country's current policies or ideology. . . .

"Terrorism" as a pejorative flows trippingly on the tongue, as Shake-speare might have put it, in all cultures. . . .But, on the whole, the term is used sparingly by all countries. [Al] Hester, who monitored the English-language international broadcasts of ten countries in late 1981, found that the Communist world was most sparing in its coverage of crime and ter-rorism (5.4 percent of all broadcasts), while the third world was almost equally disinterested in the topic, using "considerably less news about crime and terrorism than did the developed countries" (7.1 percent vs. 17.8 percent). Although the Soviet Union is gradually expanding its hard news coverage, "bad" news on crime and terrorism is still rarely reported. . . .

DISCUSSION

While terrorist incidents are fairly frequent—the reported ones averaging at least nine a day—they are not always covered by the world's press, in spite of their "made for the news media" production. If, therefore, it is true, as [Philip] Devine and [Robert] Rafalko say, that "it would be utterly pointless to commit an act of terrorism in a society having rigid control over its press" because without publicity, terrorism is meaningless; if, as [Alex] Schmid and [Janny] de Graaf state, "the main sense, if not the only one . . . a massacre has is that sense it gains from being reported and explained by the media;" and if "the terror event enjoys an unparalleled power simply because of its media value," as [Robert H.] Kupperman puts it, then terrorism is not being too successful, unless it is a truly spectacular event. [But evidence exists that] few terrorist incidents [tend to be] reported cross-nationally—at least in the leading newspapers. . . .Kupperman is right, in that case, when he says that "to maintain the media spotlight, terrorist organizations must heighten the threshold for the spectacular assault."

Also under press control, terrorists may have to escalate their activities in order to get into the media, John Grice fears, since there must presumably be a critical mass of terrorism that would force itself through the barrier of media secrecy. However, Brian Jenkins does not believe terrorists want a lot of casualties. They want publicity and are not, therefore, likely to go nuclear, for example. This is a reasonable assumption, since there also is a critical mass of public tolerance of violence. "Acts of extraordinary violence would be counterproductive," says Kupperman. "Were they to occur, nations would unite to rout out the terrorists." A possible consequence of the muzzling of the press, as has been true in Latin America and also in several African countries, is that terrorists are forced to seize broadcasting stations to get their message across. "Radio stations in many African states," according to [L. John] Martin, "are as closely guarded as the presidential residence because they are among the first targets of insurgents."

How effective, then, can terrorism be? "There is no known case in modern history," says [Feliks] Gross, "of a terrorist movement seizing political power. . . ."

Of course, others have suggested that the last thing terrorists want is to achieve their goals. . . .[Terrorists] seldom demand the full realization of their cause, possibly because they don't expect it, but equally probably . . . because achieving their goals would force them to relinquish their accumulated power. If terrorists want political power above everything else, they will not trade it away by negotiating to achieve their ultimate goal. Frequently, therefore, when a cause is realized or becomes moot, terrorists continue to operate but change their causes. German student terrorists, for example, began as an anti-Vietnam War movement. After the war, they took up other causes.

What should be the role of the media? There is no doubt that people have the right to know not only about the "crazies" in their midst and the threats to life, limb, and property, but also about the causes people espouse and are willing to lay down their lives for. For all one knows, people may wish to support such causes, if not physically then with money and through moral suasion. "It is possible to imagine governmental officials doing more to destroy democracy in the name of counter-terrorism than is presently likely to be achieved by terrorists themselves," [Grant] Wardlaw warns.

On the other hand, one must distinguish between the need to know and the desire to be entertained. Entertainment should not be at the expense of law and order, life, limb, and property. Yet terrorism has become a form of mass entertainment, according to psychiatrist Frederick J. Hacker. Richard Salant, president of CBS News, argues that, "We present facts from which people draw their own conclusions . . . , whether it's politics or terrorists or anything else. . . .If we start playing God and say that fact or this viewpoint . . . might give people ideas, we would have to stop covering politics." But is he being completely objective? Isn't there a conflict of interest in his argument? Does CBS present all the news, or does it play God, selecting what it thinks will keep its ratings above those of other networks? And is such selection made on the basis of the need to know or in terms of the maximum entertainment value— the drawing power of the story?

16

Is International Terrorism Primarily State-Sponsored?

Martha Crenshaw

The belief that terrorism is primarily a state-sponsored activity, directed by governments hostile to the United States and its allies, has gained many adherents. . . . I would like to examine the assumptions that lie behind this viewpoint. Is the assessment of the threat to the American national interest plausible? Does the source of international terrorism lie in the foreign policies of states rather than in local conditions? Does the Soviet Union dominate an international network of terrorists and their state sponsors? Has the response of Western democracies been weak and ineffective? On the basis of these assumptions, the proponents of the state-sponsorship argument recommend U.S. military intervention in response to terrorism. Secretary of State [George] Shultz, while admitting that the sources of terrorism are diverse, . . . [in the 1980s repeatedly] called for the use of force to stop terrorists or retaliate against them. Is this policy advisable? Is it likely to win popular support?

In the view of the state-sponsorship school of thought, terrorism is [a] strategic peril . . . constituting a fundamental challenge to U.S. security and strategic interests. Democracies, the primary target of terrorists, risk destabilization as well as disruption. Terrorism, seen as an undeclared war, more dangerous than conventional warfare and even than Soviet intermediate range nuclear missiles targeted on Western Europe, could eventually alter the international balance of power. So far terrorism has shown remarkable success, threatening the decapitation of entire governments (in the cases of South Korea and Great Britain). Since the level of terrorism is rising rapidly, the prospects for the future are alarming unless drastic action is taken to halt the contagion.

Before accepting this dire prognosis we might question the method by which the threat is evaluated. Does experiencing a high frequency of terrorist attacks bring about significant changes in governments? Terrorism has been endemic in Northern Ireland since 1970 without producing major change in the British political system other than the assumption of direct rule from Westminster, which if anything strengthened democracy. What is meant by stability? What are the signs of impending destabilization? Is domestic violence more or less dangerous than attacks on a state's foreign interests? Terrorism differs in terms of frequency, destructiveness, targets, and locale. How do these variations affect its success rate? How is success defined?

Without doubt the West is an important target of terrorism. The United States has consistently furnished roughly one third of the victims and targets of international terrorism since 1968. But it may not be the case that terrorism is most severe for liberal democratic states. Domestic campaigns of terrorism have not significantly altered the distribution of political power or the constitutional structure of states such as West Germany, Italy, Great Britain, and Spain. Instead the major regime changes in the postwar period (excluding colonial wars) have involved coup d'etats in which the military seized power in order to combat terrorism weak civilian regimes had been unable to contain: Uruguay, Argentina, and Turkey. In no case did a terrorist organization come to power. Only in authoritarian regimes already prone to revolution have radical opponents who used terrorism come to power: Nicaragua and Iran. Terrorism frequently affects non-democratic states, such as the authoritarian regimes of Central and South America. Lebanon has suffered more civilian casualties and destruction from terrorism than any Western democracy. Even Syria has not been immune; the Muslim Brotherhood has been active against both Syrian and Soviet interests.

The contention that assassinations of the leaders of democracies . . . are evidence of destabilization is illogical. Surely the defining feature of a democratic system is that leaders are replaceable. It is in nondemocratic states that the succession problem has not been solved. Democracies can survive the loss of individual leaders, tragic though such loss may be.

If terrorism has not so far undermined the internal stability of democracies, what does it threaten? The belief that terrorism is a threat to international order is based primarily on the assumption that terrorism is an element of the foreign policy of totalitarian states, namely the Soviet Union, Iran, Libya, Syria, Nicaragua, and Cuba. This premise, however, is implied rather than demonstrated and the degree of influence of states over terrorists is only vaguely specified. Sometimes it is said that states only "influence" their clients; at other times terms such as "guide," "instigate," or "direct" are used. Terrorist organizations are generally regarded as pliant accomplices in the designs of hostile states whose influence ranges from encouragement to control. It is argued that the political and ideological identification between terrorist organizations and their sponsors makes it a simple matter for states to affect their actions. The large majority of existing terrorist groups are assumed to be Marxist-Leninist and claim the right to Soviet support.

Terrorist organizations and their government supporters are linked in a global network, according to the state-sponsorship view. The PLO is at the center of the subnational branch of this conspiracy, while the Soviet Union coordinates state assistance. Even the Ayatollah [Khomeini was] said to be unconsciously submissive to the Soviet Union although the Middle Eastern states sometimes act unpredictably. Terrorism is interpreted as a critical piece of the pattern of Cold War subversion, in which even peace demonstrations in Western Europe are orchestrated by the Soviet Union. In Central America, Cuba and Nicaragua serve Soviet interests and support terrorism organizations as third-class proxies. Even the Weather Underground is said to have been under Cuban influence.

The fact that governments often assist terrorist organizations is as undeniable as the existence of Soviet hostility and Iranian anti-Americanism. Supporting the opponents of one's enemies is a common practice in international conflict, as is labeling the other side terrorist and one's own side freedom fighter. Official and unofficial American assistance for the Contras in Nicaragua, whom many observers accuse of terrorist activity, is an example of state support for insurgents trying to overthrow an internationally recognized government. The major problem is that dwelling exclusively on this dimension of terrorism leads to neglect of its indigenous sources. To claim, for example, that the dominant characteristic of the IRA is Marxism is highly misleading. Irish terrorism against the British preceded both Marx and the establishment of the Soviet Union. It derives from the particular historical situation of Ireland and from relationships between Protestants and Catholics, not from Communist subversion. In fact, the Provisional IRA split from the Official IRA precisely because of the latter's vaguely Marxist bent. It is worth noting that the Marxist ideology of the Officials dictated that they wait for the right conditions rather than actively try to bring about the revolution. The Provisionals were too impatient to wait for the historical tide to turn.

Most terrorist organizations are indiscriminate in their pursuit of foreign assistance. They exclude no donors on principle. The acceptance of support does not, however, bind clients to the wishes of their patrons, as the United States has learned in trying to compel or restrain even the most dependent of allies, such as South Vietnam or Israel.

The belief that terrorism is part of the international power struggle between East and West obscures perception of the diversity of types and forms of terrorism. There is not one terrorism but many terrorisms. For example, critical distinctions exist between separatist and revolutionary terrorism. Nationalists in divided societies stand a much better chance of acquiring popular support than would-be revolutionaries in Western democracies. The ideological attractiveness of revolutionary movements is greater in authoritarian regimes, but here the government's repressive capability deters potential supporters. Terrorist organizations have different objectives, potentials for popular support, and organizational capabilities. They employ a variety of tactics within the context of a common strategic conception, based on compensating for their lack of numbers with extreme and shocking violence designed to intimidate and demoralize rather than defeat the enemy.

The omission of terrorism of the right from the universe of terror-ism that the state-sponsored theory covers is a serious flaw. In West Ger-many, France, and Italy neo-fascist organizations have been responsi-ble for numerous casualties. Their acts are often highly indiscriminate, such as the bombing of the Bologna railroad station. In Northern Ire-land, Protestant paramilitaries attack Catholics just as the IRA targets Protestants. In Latin America the governments who practice repressive techniques at home are not restricted to Cuba and Nicaragua. Nor is the use of violence abroad. We have only to remember the Chilean-sponsored assassination of Orlando Letelier in Washington. Right-wing death squads, linked to police and military, have been responsible for thousands of deaths and "disappearances." The terrorism that weakened the civilian regime in Turkey so that it fell to a military coup d'etat in 1980 was due to right as much as left extremism. The Weimar Republic succumbed to Hitler, not to Communists.

Looking only at state-sponsored terrorism also implies either that there is no terrorism not instigated by governments or that, if so, it is unimportant. However, significant terrorist campaigns are possible without external support. Of all Latin American governments, Peru [has experienced] . . . the most serious terrorist challenge. Although the Sendero Luminoso organization is said to be Maoist in orientation (the meaning of this description in unclear, other than the implication that revolution is to be rural rather than urban), it is thought to be completely independent of foreign assistance.

Ascribing terrorist motivation to world Communist aggression provides an easy answer to a hard question. Simplicity of explanation is a virtue, but terrorist motivations are in reality extremely complicated. Some par-ticipation in terrorist organizations is inspired by the psychology of group dynamics or individual personality. The longer a group is in existence, the more likely is its isolation from reality and reliance on fantastical con-ceptions of struggle. Other terrorist actions may be motivated by rival-ries among competing terrorists groups, such as the different Palestinian factions. The June [1985] hijacking to Beirut may have resulted from a desire by more militant Shi'ite factions in Lebanon to show that they, like the Palestinians, could coerce Israel into releasing prisoners. Such a demonstration of power would aid them in the Lebanese political arena. Ideology rarely seems to be a strong motivating factor, although religious and political beliefs may be a stronger force among Shi'ites than among secular groups. Terrorists usually disdain theorizing and talking. Their strongpoint is action.

The state-sponsorship argument is in many ways distressingly similar to theories put forward by the French military during the Algerian war. Advocates of what was called "guerre revolutionnaire" doctrines denied that the Algerian rebels were motivated by indigenous nationalism. They blamed international Communism and its supposed tool [Egyptian leader] Nasser. The idea of appearing as the defender of the West against aggression from the East was more heroic than appearing as a colonial occupier. French participation in the ill-fated Suez expedition was dictated by the desire to end what was mistakenly thought to be critical Egyptian aid to the FLN. Toward the end of the war it was discovered that the major contributors to FLN finances were Algerian workers in France.

Some of the international alliances posited in the geopolitical interpretation of terrorism also seem implausible in light of local realities. The Soviet Union may profit by Middle Eastern anti-Americanism, but that Iran and Shi'a Muslims should be acting in the interest of the Soviet Union seems unlikely, despite Syrian support for Iran in her war [in the 1980s] with Iraq. How can the bitter conflict between Syria and the Arafat faction of the PLO be explained, if both are subservient to the Soviet Union? What accounts for the hostility between Lebanese Shi'ites and Palestinians? The tendency to equate the PLO, seen somehow as a monolith, with the most radical Palestinian factions rather that with [PLO leader Yasir] Arafat obscures the complexity of relationships within the Palestinian nationalist movement. Furthermore, if the PLO was the linchpin of worldwide connections among subnational terrorist groups, then the destruction of the PLO in Lebanon after the 1982 Israeli invasion should have significantly reduced international terrorism. Yet the frequency and the destructiveness of terrorist acts [subsequently] . . . increased.

The theory of terrorism as undeclared war also assumes that the reactions of Western societies have been weak and vacillating. The news media are singled out for blame. One criticism is that media coverage presents terrorism as justifiable and heroic, because the "liberal" press is both morally ambivalent and naive about the Soviet threat. Another is simply that media attention encourages terrorism by providing the publicity terrorists seek. Liberal democracies in general are accused of lacking resolve. Their governments are reluctant to condemn or penalize terrorism, perhaps because the public, misled by a biased media, fails to understand the immediacy of the threat. References to local conditions and political grievances which may inspire terrorism are rejected as attempts to excuse violence. According to . . . Secretary of State [George Shultz], American public opinion should [have been] more determined and united in order to overcome the self-condemnation and defeatism, "wallowing in self-flagellation or self-doubt," he [saw] about him.

The believers in the Soviet aggression theory feel that critics and skeptics fail to understand that attitudes toward terrorism must be founded on value judgments. Objectivity is inappropriate. Violence is justified in terms of its ends. Directed against the West it is always illegitimate and immoral. Moral ambiguity or questioning of American principles is harmful to democracy. It is essential that the public understand clearly this simple moral distinction between good and evil, between friends and enemies. Only through this comprehension can our resolve be stiffened to combat terrorism effectively.

This interpretation of society's reactions to terrorism suffers from a number of deficiencies. Certainly the news media (with some exceptions) tend to both sensationalize and trivialize terrorism, and in any reporting of the act a message is communicated to the audience. This is true of the treatment of most social phenomena, and violence is more newsworthy than orderly behavior. However, the press rarely portrays terrorists sympathetically or describes their motivations in any detail. The emphasis of their coverage is on the plight of the victim. The public acquires little concrete information about terrorism from television coverage, which is their main source of information. People watch television for its entertainment value, not its contribution to knowledge. Furthermore, the main source of information for reporters is the government. Consequently the government's viewpoint is likely to be presented more comprehensively than that of the terrorist. That terrorists seek publicity and that representatives of the media can be irresponsible are unchallengeable assertions. However, it is not the case that the public gets from the media a positive or coherent view of the terrorist.

The argument that Western governments have shown weakness before the terrorist threat is also puzzling. Extensive domestic terrorist campaigns were defeated by both West Germany and Italy. Great Britain has shown no signs of permissiveness with regard to the IRA, nor has the Spanish government surrendered to the demands of the Basque ETA. Both West Germany and France have adopted significantly harsher policies over the past decade. West Germany went so far as to intervene militarily outside her borders for the first time since World War II (at Mogadishu in 1977). The European Community has agreed on a coordinated response. Terrorism is prominent on the agenda of Western summit conferences.

The sticking point in the area of cooperation remains the right to grant political asylum. The United States is an important offender in this regard, since American courts habitually refuse to extradite members of the IRA. Yugoslav officials are also critical of the United States for tolerating violent Croatian organizations. Nevertheless rather than irresolution the evidence points to a trend toward more hard-line policies. Perhaps the lack of allied support for the U.S. role in Central America is the source of the contention that the West is weak toward terrorism.

The charge that moral ambivalence or confusion underlies an unwillingness to perceive the terrorist threat realistically may reflect a Manichean world view that divides opinion into opposing camps: realists who recognize danger and suspiciously liberal idealists who think that the Soviet Union is peace-loving. It allows for no middle ground. . . .

In conclusion, the framework of assumptions and policy prescriptions based on an interpretation of terrorism as a reflection of state rivalries, particularly the Cold War struggle, is an attempt to draw universal principles from a partial picture of reality. State sponsorship is part of the problem of terrorism but it is not all of the problem. A more comprehensive, integrated theory of terrorism is required. The assistance of states is one of the facilitating factors in the development of terrorism but not the single cause. It is distressing that the advocates of the view that state sponsorship is the determinant of terrorism . . . doubt the integrity and judgment of those who disagree with them. It is even more disturbing that a policy of using force against terrorism might be adopted without adequate examination of the validity of the assumptions upon which the recommendation is founded. It is appropriate to urge the American public to develop an understanding of terrorism, but this comprehension must be based on objective analysis, unburdened by prior commitment to rigid ideological beliefs. The American government must also recognize that the public's unwillingness to support a policy of force may not reflect miscomprehension. Reasoned analysis suggests that some of the assumptions behind the state-sponsorship view are questionable and that military intervention may not be a feasible alternative.

17

The Superpowers, Foreign Policy, and Terrorism

Donna M. Schlagheck

Terrorism is a flexible, highly adaptable political instrument. Its usefulness in nationalist struggles for autonomy or liberation is well known and frequently employed. Increasingly, terrorism is used to promote the ideas and objectives of radical ideologies, while governance by terror continues on the left and right of the political spectrum. Terrorism also has become an instrument of foreign policy since World War II, particularly important, some claim, to the repertoire of the two superpowers. Since 1945, the international political environment has been changed by three developments that have elevated the use and importance of terrorism, particularly for the Soviet Union and the United States.

1. World War II ended with many of the old, great powers left prostrate. Germany, France, and Great Britain saw world politics lose its Eurocentric focus; the US-USSR relationship took center stage, and the two new "super" powers began a long-term ideological rivalry.

2. The Soviet-American rivalry, with its strong ideological underpinnings, had to manifest itself in an age of nuclear weapons. The United States ended its war with Japan by detonating nuclear devices over Hiroshima and Nagasaki in 1945. Four years later, the USSR successfully detonated its first atomic bomb, ushering in the age of apocalyptic warfare. The destructive power of nuclear weapons now provides the two superpowers with the capability of destroying most life on the planet. Consequently, the United States and Soviet Union have sought to compete in ways more indirect and with lower risks. To avoid a direct conflict and the exchange of nuclear firepower that might escalate into a global holocaust, the United States and USSR carry out an arms race and arms control talks, conduct clandestine activities and covert operations, act through proxies, and sponsor and engage in terrorism to promote their interests. These activities are less costly and less risky than direct conflict; most are also deniable.

3. With the emergence of the Third World (Latin America, Africa, the Middle East, and Asia) as the focus of Soviet-American rivalry, terrorism came into its own as an instrument of foreign policy. The European theater had come to hold too high a risk for costly conflict. The large Red Army presence and the American nuclear umbrella offsetting it, together

Note: footnotes have been deleted.

with NATO and Warsaw Pact forces poised along the Iron Curtain, have made Europe an extremely dangerous site for open U.S.-Soviet conflict. At the same time, the war that left the great European powers incapacitated after World War II also weakened their grasp on their colonies. In the Middle East, Africa, and Asia, irregular and unconventional resistance against colonial powers increased; guerrilla warfare and terrorism became popular weapons in many struggles for independence. The presence of indigenous groups using terrorism to achieve political goals provided an opportunity for the Superpower rivalry to express itself in and through many organizations and conflicts in the Third World.

The Superpower-terrorism "connection" assumes many forms. It may take the form of support for groups using terrorism against friends or allies of the rival superpower, or against that superpower directly. "Support" includes providing funds, weapons, training, political endorsement or other logistical assistance (passports, intelligence, use of diplomatic facilities, etc.) to groups that use terrorism. The support may be channeled through a proxy or delivered directly by the superpowers' own military and intelligence services. Cuba frequently is identified by the United States as a Soviet proxy in Latin America and Africa, while expatriate Cubans in the nationalist-terrorist group known as Omega 7 are considered American proxies due to attacks on Chilean and Cuban officials. U.S. aid to Afghani *mujahedeen* resisting Soviet occupation and Soviet support of Palestinian efforts against what they consider Israeli occupation of Palestinian lands are further examples of the indirect Soviet-American conflict that often involves terrorism, proxies, and allies. Neither superpower officially admits to sponsoring terrorism or publicly endorses terrorism, and the evidence to substantiate their involvement is scarce, indirect, or frequently unavailable. Given the "plausible deniability" that attends superpower involvement with terrorism, the following two sections address the diverse schools of thought on terrorism and foreign policy. Ranging from denial to international conspiracy networks, this area is perhaps the most speculative of all approaches to international terrorism. . . .

SOVIET FOREIGN POLICY AND TERRORISM

. . . The Soviet Union does not deny it supports revolutionary groups, but it does reject the labeling of their tactics as "terrorist." The Western view of the Soviets' foreign policy supporting revolutionary groups is split into two schools of thought. The "international terrorist network," as it has come to be known, is the more radical, conspiratorial view of Soviet foreign policy and terrorism; Soviet "opportunism" is the alternate approach to Soviet involvement with international terrorism. Both groups interestingly refer to much the same body of evidence to support their claims.

The "international terrorist network" is a theory that most international terrorism is organized, funded, armed, supported, and directed by the Soviets to weaken the Western democracies without risking nuclear war (see Figure 1). The "international terror network" is looked on as one part of a broader Soviet campaign that also includes disinformation, espionage, subversion, and the phony "peace offensive," all intended to undermine the Soviets' enemies. Journalist Claire Sterling was one of the first to popularize the idea of an international terrorist conspiracy to undermine the Western industrialized democracies. She wrote in 1981 that "direct control of the terrorist groups was never the Soviet intention. All are indigenous to their countries. All began as offshoots of relatively nonviolent movements that expressed particular political, economic, religious or ethnic grievances." The assassination attempt against Pope John Paul II by a Turk, Mehmet Ali Agca, with alleged Bulgarian and KGB connections, stirred broader interest in the

international terrorist network. In 1983, in *The Grand Strategy of the Soviet Union*, Edward Luttwak argued that Soviet support for terrorist groups came in response to the failure of more traditional Soviet measures. It was only when it became clear that the Soviet Union was ineluctably losing the support of the trade unions and left-wing mass movements of the West that the Soviet leaders began to accept terrorists as useful allies. . . .

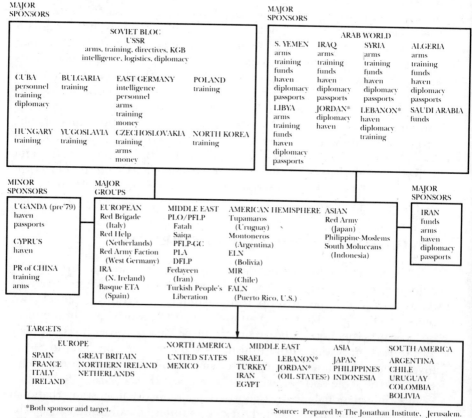

Figure 1. **International Terrorism: Sponsors, Terrorists, and Targets, 1980**

By 1984, Ray Cline (formerly with the CIA) and Yonah Alexander argued in *Terrorism: The Soviet Connection* that terrorism had become indispensable to the Soviets' efforts to undermine western democracies and hasten the end of capitalism.

The evidence used to support the "international terrorist network" theory is often circumstantial and open to different interpretations. Many groups that use terrorism espouse Marxist-Leninist ideology—e.g., West Germany's Red Army Faction, Italy's Red Brigades, the Irish National Liberation Army, and the Popular Front for the Liberation of Palestine (PFLP). The Soviet Union has publicly supported some of these groups in the media and at the United Nations and defended and legitimized their use of violence "in the struggle for national self-determination and against imperialism." Soviet and Eastern-bloc weapons often have been found by Western governments fighting these groups, although the international traffic in weapons undermines the persuasiveness of such evidence. The Israeli discovery of Russian maps in 1978 in Palestinian camps in Lebanon, and the 1985 capture of Nidia Diaz, commander of the Salvadoran Marxist Central American Revolutionary Workers Party, provide stronger evidence of Soviet contacts and terrorist training in Soviet and other socialist states. Nidia Diaz kept a journal that was captured with her; in it, she recorded that Salvadorans were training abroad in Bulgaria, East Germany, Vietnam, and the Soviet Union. Other Western states have expelled Soviet diplomats, complaining that KGB operatives were assisting local terrorist groups. In 1978, Italy expelled twenty-two Soviets for alleged ties to the Red Brigades, and in 1983 the Republic of Ireland expelled three Soviet diplomats for allegedly supplying weapons and funds to the Provisional IRA. In 1985, the Israelis announced [the] finding [of] evidence that thirty-five Lebanese Shi'ites had been trained in small arms and explosives in the Soviet Crimea.

In addition to the Soviets or other friendly socialist states providing funds, weapons, and political support, the "international terrorist network" theory often argues that contacts or networking among different groups is instigated and facilitated by the Soviet Union or its allies. When members of the Baader-Meinhof Gang went to Lebanon and Jordan to train with the PFLP in 1970, some traveled by way of East Berlin (others went by way of Paris). The Patrice Lumumba Institute in Moscow, which offers many non-Soviets an opportunity to study on scholarship, is another means by which the Soviets allegedly put future terrorists in contact with each other. Marxist members of the Sandinista government in Nicaragua have spoken of training they received in North Korea and alongside Palestinians in Beirut in the early 1970s; and . . . the presence of Cuban, East German, and Soviet advisers in Nicaragua . . . [has been] taken as further evidence of the Soviet conspiracy to destabilize governments in Latin America. The Palestine Liberation Organization also is identified with the Soviet Union; Chairman Arafat has made numerous visits to Moscow and has also traveled to East Germany,

Yugoslavia, Bulgaria, and Hungary, in addition to numerous meetings with Cuban officials in Beirut. Camps set up in Libya, Syria, Algeria, Iraq, Lebanon, and South Yemen to assist Palestinians training for conflict with Israel have been opened to European and Latin and North American terrorists. The British government found evidence that the assassins of Lord Mountbatten trained in a Marxist PFLP camp and the Spanish government has reported that ETA Basque terrorists have trained in Cuba and Czechoslovakia. In its campaign to arrest all RAF members in the late 1970s and early 1980s, the West German government reported finding evidence that RAF members had also trained in South Yemen and Libya, and had links to terrorist groups in Italy, France, the Netherlands, Belgium, Iran, Lebanon, and the United States.

Skeptics reject the claims of a Soviet conspiracy to fund, arm, and direct an international terrorist network. Soviet political and logistical support for the causes that some terrorist groups pursue, skeptics argue, is not sufficient evidence to support the claim of a Soviet "conspiracy." The Soviets may exploit opportunities to stir up trouble in Western or pro-Western nations, but that does not in itself constitute a conspiracy. No evidence of direct Soviet or KGB control of terrorist groups has been produced, disbelievers frequently point out. As a state favoring change in the international status quo, the Soviet Union predictably will support terrorist groups, skeptics concede, but the issues and grievances that terrorists cite are not Soviet creations. Critics of the conspiracy theory point out that the desire to believe in a communist conspiracy is very strong, even when the evidence is weak. Michael Stohl has identified the key—but dangerously circular—logic in the conspiracy theory: since the Soviet Union is an anti-status quo power, benefiting from the chaos and anarchy terrorism causes, the Soviet Union must be the source of international terrorism.

In addition to the skeptics (who recognize evidence of Soviet support for terrorist groups but do not conclude that a conspiracy exists), there are several experts who conclude that the "conspiracy" theory is a Western fabrication altogether. Thomas Raynor, in *Terrorism: Past, Present, Future* (1982), argues that the Soviets shy away from groups like the RAF and Red Brigades because they are undisciplined and hurt the revolutionary cause with their brand of terrorism. Raynor recognizes Soviet and satellite aid to "wars of national liberation," but points out the lack of hard evidence of a network of terrorist groups. Alexander Cockburn contends that the terrorist network was essentially the product of "the rumor mill of a few Western propagandists talking to one another about a fantasy concocted by the C.I.A." . . . The harshest opponent of the conspiracy is Edward S. Herman. In *The Real Terror Network*, Herman argues that the "terror network" is part of a new "red scare" designed to rally anti-Soviet sentiments in the West. The "real" terror network, according to Herman, is the one led by the United States that supports governments that rule by torture and terror. For example, the Shah of Iran used the state security force, SAVAK, to terrorize his political opponents; SAVAK was trained by the CIA. United States aid to the Nicaraguan contras, the Afghani *mujahedeen*, and the UNITA forces led by Jonas Savimbi in Angola and Namibia are also cited by the discreditors of the "international terror network" theory. Both superpowers are accused of involvement with international terrorism based on claims they support or conspire with terrorists.

UNITED STATES FOREIGN POLICY AND TERRORISM

. . . In January 1961 Nikita Khrushchev and John F. Kennedy gave speeches that reflected how U.S.-Soviet competition had begun to evolve. Khrushchev vigorously declared his intention to support wars of national liberation, and Kennedy called on the U.S. military to build a counterinsurgency program. The Soviets supported efforts to alter the international status quo, and the United States set out to train forces to preserve it. Terrorism allegedly entered the United States' foreign policy repertoire by way of the counterterror programs that became the centerpiece of the "global struggle" with communist subversion. Where the Soviet Union supports insurgencies, the United States responds by training counterinsurgency forces to meet the subversion. . . .

The Phoenix Program

In 1961, President Kennedy ordered five hundred military advisers to South Vietnam. The army's Special Warfare Center at Fort Bragg, North Carolina, sent four hundred of its Special Forces (Green Berets), who, with CIA personnel, set up the Civilian Irregular Defense Groups (CIDG) to train South Vietnamese villagers to protect themselves from terrorist and guerilla attacks. Within a few years the Special Forces and CIA were working separately on counterinsurgency projects. By 1965, Special Forces were training Vietnamese in "ambushing, raiding, sabotaging and committing acts of terrorism against known VC (Viet Cong) personnel." The idea of turning the enemy's use of terrorism against him had become popular. In 1965, the CIA also established its own counterterror (CT) teams. "CIA representatives recruited, organized, supplied, and directly paid CT teams, whose function was to use Viet Cong techniques of terror—assassinations, abuses, kidnappings, and intimidation—against the Viet Cong leadership." . . .

The Phoenix Program coordinated South Vietnamese and American police, military, and intelligence units in a three-year assault on the Viet Cong Infrastructure (VCI). Critics of Phoenix have described it as the high point of countering terror with terror, a coordinated program of assassination and murder. The U.S. House of Representatives Foreign Operations and Government Information Subcommittee Report in 1971 gave Phoenix a mixed review, acknowledging that VC leaders and supporters were the targets, but that "many of the more than 20,000 suspected VC killed under the program known as Phoenix were actually innocent civilians who were victims of faulty intelligence." ... Between 1968 and 1971, Phoenix accounted for 20,587 VC killed (the Government of South Vietnam reported 40,994 killed), and another 28,000 captured. Stopped after 1971 when news of the program leaked to the public, Phoenix remains an early hallmark of American counterterrorism.

CIA and Political Murder

After the 1973 coup in Chile that deposed the government of Salvador Allende, the U.S. Senate began an inquiry into intelligence activities carried out by the CIA against the Chilean government. The Senate Select Committee to Study Governmental Operations with Respect to Intelligence Activities, chaired by Senator Frank Church of Idaho, investigated CIA involvement in the 1973 coup and other alleged CIA assassination plots involving foreign leaders. . . .

The Church Committee . . . documented CIA covert action in Chile from 1962 until 1973, which culminated in the overthrow and death (possibly suicide) of Marxist President Allende. The CIA, the Select Committee recommended, should be barred from three types of covert activities:

1. All political assassinations,
2. Efforts to subvert democratic governments,
3. Support for police or other internal security forces which engage in the systematic violation of human rights.

In addition to political assassinations, U.S. governmental agencies' involvement with security forces (e.g., Iran's SAVAK and the Phoenix Program in South Vietnam) that used torture and terrorism to counter political unrest and subversion came under closer scrutiny.

The United States and Counterinsurgency in Latin America: Reports of Torture, Disappearances, and Death Squads

. . . Critics of United States foreign policy in Latin America now criticize a new form of U.S. interventionism: the United States allegedly exports its counterinsurgency doctrine through schools run by the American security establishment (CIA and military forces), e.g., the School of the Americas. In what appears to be a second conspiracy theory of international terrorism, the U.S. doctrine of counterterror allegedly has become the primary military and police objective in Latin America. Rather than training police to combat crime and the military to defend against external threats, Latin American security forces have shifted their focus to subversion and insurgency. With U.S. guidance, critics argue, Latin American security forces have transformed themselves to conduct irregular, internal warfare against their own people using torture, terrorism, and mass murder to stop subversion. In his study of paramilitary and state terror in Central America, Michael McClintock (an employee of Amnesty International) presents evidence that "personnel of the CIA and U.S. regular army work closely with and perhaps control top members of the Salvadoran military responsible for formulating counter-terror policy, and directly with the intelligence agencies responsible for executing policy through torture and political murder." The United States response to these allegations points out that close U.S.-Salvadoran collaboration has helped bring right-wing paramilitary death squads under control. . . .

Similar allegations of U.S. counterinsurgency training that Latin American security forces have used against civilians have implicated previous governments in Guatemala and Argentina. Investigative journalist Jack Anderson reported in August 1981 that the United States was paying Cuban expatriates to train security forces in Guatemala, and in 1982 the *Washington Post* announced that Special Forces were training Guatemalan officers. Following a coup in 1982, Amnesty International reported that the new regime killed twenty-six hundred peasants in its first six months in power. Guatemala elected a popular government in 1986 and death squad activity has declined, but estimates of civilian deaths since the CIA helped overthrow the government of Jacobo Arbenz in 1954 range upwards of sixty thousand. The "dirty war" in Argentina . . . that the security forces conducted from 1976 until 1983 took approximately thirty thousand lives. The mass murder and terror have been blamed in part on the "counterterror doctrine" that Argentina's military, intelligence and police forces adopted in response to increasing terrorism from the ERP and the Montoneros. The counterinsurgency and counterterror training was provided at the Inter-American Police Academy and the School of the Americas (Panama), now closed.

SUMMARY

Interesting parallels emerge in allegations of U.S. and Soviet sponsorship of international terrorism. The two superpowers have carried their rivalry into the turbulent politics of the Third World, where insurgency and counterinsurgency attract outside interest. For the superpowers, sponsorship or involvement in international terrorism may offer opportunities to promote their interests and influence, opportunities not available through other, more traditional channels. The temptation for the superpowers is the same one experienced by groups employing terrorism to achieve nationalist or ideological goals: important ends can be used to justify terrorist means. The documentary record remains too incomplete to conclude with any certainty that the Soviet Union or the United States sponsors international terrorism. As a potential instrument of foreign policy, however, international terrorism must be considered as part of the potential repertoire available to either the United States or the USSR in their global rivalry.

18

Explaining
International Terrorism:
The Elusive Quest

J. Bowyer Bell

[Since the 1970s] . . . we have apparently lived in a time of terror—aerial hijackings, car bombs, assassinations, the slaughter of innocents, hostages, and urban guerrillas—the politics of atrocity. The contemporary, post-industrial Western world seems particularly vulnerable to bloody spectaculars as the complex technology is attacked or warped to the uses of the gunmen: diplomats may be held in a basement along the banks of the Nile at Khartoum and the terrorists' demands arrive on our evening television news, not weeks later by forked stick. And there are ample prophets of doom who correctly indicate matters may grow worse. The fanatics may poison the water or spread plague or build their own nuclear device. Many see even the present threat as crucial, seriously threatening Western civilization, eroding the peoples' confidence in governance, disrupting our complex and fragile world. Some anticipate escalation. Others note that incidents appear to be increasing. Few, certainly in the United States, delight in the time of terror, understand the motives of the militants, or view the future without alarm. All want answers. . . . And after . . . twenty years there is still no consensus about . . . the terrorists, about their goals, avowed and perceived, and about what might be done. There are, however, all sorts of explanations concerning the phenomenon, some self-serving, often discipline-based, many speculative, and most arising from long-held political and ideological positions. And out of the welter of explanations some have proved more appealing, logical, even convincing.

Nearly everyone, understandably, wants convincing, logical, and simple explanations. Terror, then, however defined, has been deeply disturbing: random, irrational, elusive, beyond reach of law or retaliation, messianic, and alien. Some observers, however, have increasingly found matters not so uncertain. They have focused on discovered or suspected linkages not only between patron states who aid or direct terrorists but also between various revolutionary organizations. Authors and analysts of generally conservative posture have found conspiratorial nets, implying at minimum that many strands lead to Moscow or the capitals of Moscow's friends. At one time or another leaders as diverse as the Socialist President of Italy and the Republican Secretary of State [George Shultz] have indicated that their nation's problems with terror have in part an Eastern origin. Some have found the communist hand nearly everywhere; and no one denies that Moscow and Havana and other, especially Arab radical, states aid revolutionaries engaged in various armed struggle—often quite openly. This everyone agrees may not be the whole story. There are voices of caution and even the most devout advocates of a KGB terrorist conspiracy admit that the origin of every massacre can not be traced to Moscow or Havana or Tripoli, that matters may be more complex. Complex or not, the fashion [during the 1980s was] . . . to stress the nets, the links, the contacts, and conspiracies. A global communist conspiracy means that terrorists, perhaps unwittingly, are part of a rational design. The enormous complexities of special cases, historical backgrounds, individuals' predilections, varying ideologies and contradictory ambitions can be ignored. These are merely the surface turmoil of a cold, simple Soviet calculation. There need be no complexities in a conspiracy nor need for a complicated mix of special, parochial responses. The threat is clear, the means are patent—the search for a response, then, must begin at the center of the terrorist web. Many analysts feel that they have now eliminated the complexities.

The international conspiracy is essentially an aspect of Soviet policy, although often through proxies that may be several removes from direct Russian control. Some analysts accept that there is a vast [distance] . . . between the gunmen slaughtering for a very special cause, even fascism, and a Moscow center; while others tend to see the sinister Soviet hand everywhere and everywhere close to the action. For both, an enormous amount of the world's terrorist din would be stilled if the Russians closed down their advocacy. This, given the nature of the Soviet state and Marxist-Leninist thought, seems unlikely. So an international communist conspiracy exists and will continue to exist. And, unlike some conspiracy theories blaming our ills on the masons or heretical religions, the analysts have considerable evidence.

First, there is no doubt [of] nor does the Soviet Union make any effort to hide the involvement of Moscow in the revolutionary world. Radical and friendly governments are aided and maintained in as diverse settings as South Yemen and Cuba. More to the point, authenticated liberation movements, some overt acting as a counterstate seeking legitimacy and others covert [and] visible only in exile offices, are welcomed and aided— potential friendlies of the future. Not openly avowed, other revolutionary organizations have been able to count on Moscow for aid and comfort, introductions and access to training and weapons. Many individuals, real or potential radicals, are Soviet guests; and others are sponsored by distant organizations engaged in dubious pursuits. On a far deeper level the Soviets run their own agents into organizations of interest from the far left of Italy, beyond the Communist Party, to the dedicated peace groups. At times independent revolutionaries may for various reasons be involved in Soviet active affairs. In general the Soviets run intelligence and covert operations within the revolutionary world—as do many states—that ranges from absolute control to none. Almost the same spectrum of involvement from host of liberation movements to undeclared agent at the cutting edge of the killing can be found in each of the Warsaw Pact countries with a degree of Russian control ranging from total except for the nationality of the involved down to a watching brief. There are all sorts and conditions of Soviet intelligence, military, party, educational, social and medical, cultural and press institutions engaged in world revolution, overtly, covertly. There may be conflicts, contradictory directions, and varied purpose, but the central intent is to further the policy of the state.

This is the controlled core of the Soviet revolutionary effort; but surrounding the heartland are a circle of allied states indebted to Moscow in varying degrees—Vietnam or Cuba or Ethiopia—who may for mutual interest or in repayment for past or future favors become involved in Soviet-supported revolutionary adventures. Some may even initiate such steps without prompting or guidance as has been the case with Cuba from time to time. Some of these Soviet proxies may oppose each other and yet hew to certain Soviet policies—for a long time, off and on, this has been the case with Syria and Iraq. Where the real advantage to Russia appears is when such a regime follows its natural bent—as Moscow anticipated— without any prompting or control necessary. Russian weapons given to Syria may in time appear far away, indeed, in combat that Moscow would prefer to ignore. Sometimes the transfer from Syria to Palestinians is not a matter of plausible denial but simply convenience and sometimes from Libya to a whole host of esoteric causes unforeseen. At one more step away from the center, the rich revolutionaries may even pass on aid and comfort to the weaker, sell to worthies without their own friends, or at times resell for profit. In this increasingly murky world of fleeting organizations, agents without ideology, transient gunmen, and desperate radicals, control ebbs; but the big picture in the conspiracy theory remains stable. The dark underworld of revolution and terror on the installment plan is simply the forging ground for violence with predictable targets and carefully selected audience. The ultimate purpose is to destabilize the West. Armenian gunmen shooting down a Turkish diplomat in Los Angeles may be an event far from Moscow's control but is still grist to the mill, still part of the conspiracy, still not isolated from the Russian purpose.

Within the conspiracy, then, are those Soviet actions that clearly abet terror and those that create an appropriate atmosphere for violence. And there are those acts, encouraged or . . . [not] by Moscow, [which] add to the turmoil. There is also other evidence of conspiracy proffered. First, again no matter how defined, the great mass of terrorist organizations claim to be Marxist-Leninist. All may be special, some a step beyond Mao not to mention Marx, others may be wedded to parochial conditions, but all purport to be following the shining path of socialism. There are, it is true, neo-fascists, religious fanatics, rightists, pure nationalists, tribal terrorists, and cults of violence; but mostly the gunmen stand on the left. Not only do they stand on the left but also they operate mostly against the West. They may claim the old communists in Moscow or Peking have sold out but the targets they seek are in Paris or London or Tel Aviv. Practically everyone is anti-imperialist and the epitome of contemporary imperialism is a NATO meeting. Thus no matter what the cause, from vengeance for Islam to the freedom of Corsica, a NATO power is the enemy—and behind NATO lies the Great Satan of Amerika. It is true that a few revolutionary guerrillas seem to find the NATO-circle to be irrelevant like the Armenians or the Tamils of Sri Lanka and a few even find the United States tolerable like the Provisional IRA who depend on Irish-American patriots for support. This excludes from consideration those freedom fighters Washington . . . supports. In sum, terrorists operate almost entirely outside the Marxist-Leninist world (no urban guerrillas in Kiev), against Western targets (no Soviet embassies bombed), or within Western arenas. Even those campaigns isolated in the developing world unconcerned with NATO or Moscow still seem to disturb Western interests. In other words the terrorists *say* they are communists of different sorts and *act* the part if in different ways.

Consequently, we have ample evidence that Soviet Russia is engaged in a long-term policy of encouraging militant revolutionary movements. Secondly, Soviet allies, especially outside the Warsaw Pact, are often deeply involved in revolutionary-terrorist support. Thirdly, many terrorists advocate Marxist-Leninist ideologies, profess admiration of Moscow or Havana or congenital revolutionary centers, and target the West. Finally, the answer as to Who-gains? seems to be the enemies of the West and of global stability. Thus to explain the present apparent wave of world terrorism the simplest answer is that a communist conspiracy most easily fits the evidence. And the existence of a conspiracy gives order and form, makes comfortable the complicated, fits a great many perceived notions about international structures and conjures up a familiar and quite real demon.

It is hardly surprising that long-term militant anti-communists accept the existence of the terrorist conspiracy. It fits. It is even less surprising that many Western security forces, who tend to see a wide spectrum of disorder and crime as terrorism, are inclined to exaggerate the threat—the involved always do—and find the conspiracy theory comforting. The targets, too, often prefer to find an alien enemy than look too closely at their nations' internal flaws and vulnerabilities: outside agitators and imported gunmen, especially when they do exist in real life, have always had a certain attraction. Then, too, those regimes considered if not illegitimate at least unsavory prefer a popular opponent rather than a risen people. South Africans see themselves beating back a communist conspiracy rather than maintaining an odious racist system of tyranny. Finally, those nations who have pursued a harsh antiterrorist policy, have employed the techniques and tactics of counter-terror like the Israelis, deploy along with the particular reasons and justifications in the importance for the West to recognize the threat and then respond in ways not unlike their own. In sum, a conspiracy for which there is ample evidence also fills a variety of real and perceived needs. And the prime argument against the conspiracy is to dredge up the old adage of experts and analysts and observers, mostly in ivory towers or far from responsibility, that matters are more complicated. Matters *always* seem more complicated to specialists and the truth is always simple.

[Alas], the world of terror *is* more complicated no matter the evidence and appeal of the conspiracy out of Moscow. More disheartening is that the various anti-terrorist strategies proposed instead of a counter-terror anti-communist crusade are not very appealing to the practical. First, the advocates of order would eliminate the avowed causes of terror. There would be no PLO if Palestinian nationalism were recognized—and there might be no Israel either. The avowed aims of many terrorists and most revolutionaries are zero-sum options[—they] can only be achieved with the destruction of the opponent. All just demands cannot be sated: separatists would destroy the center, millenarians would bomb down the system, and some gunmen want simple vengeance or to rewrite history or, as the two young men who hijacked the TWA plane out of Athens [in June, 1985], to die for the cause. No more can the second great decent option, apply the rule of law, work alone or even in conjuncture with the security forces. International law is at best a weak reed and the terrorists elusive—in any case laws do not prevent murder and those most restricted by regulation are the threatened. What law can stand in the way of a nation or dissuade a true believer, give a gunman second thought or turn the bomber into a criminal in his own mind? And so finally we are left with the proposition that by any quantitative measuring stick terrorism is not a terminal threat, few are killed, few vulnerable technologies have been damaged, few gunmen threaten order, many seeking the prominence of television coverage rather than the power that should come from their revolver. All this is true. Terrorism is not new—once trains were hijacked, now planes; kings and presidents have long been vulnerable; a century ago anarchist bombers moved across continents in orbits as dreaded as present jackals. Terrorism probably is not escalating despite jiggling statistics to prove the case. Terrorists have not followed any of the dreadful academic scenarios escalating to nuclear bombs or spreading anthrax to the millions or bombing life to a halt. No matter, the public *perceives* terrorism as a major threat. The politics of atrocity exaggerated by television and the anguish of authority cannot be permitted to continue uncountered without eroding public morale. So something must be done.

And the communist conspiracy is only a partial answer. The world is much more complex. Terror arises from all sorts of conditions and most of all from the opportunity to act in open or fragile societies. Communism has little to do with many national struggles and even avowed Marxist-Leninists often operate far beyond the control of a Moscow center, high in the Andes of Peru or the swamps of the south Sudan. They may unwittingly or consciously be doing Russia's work but again they may take from Moscow and go their own way. And that way is manifold, diverse, difficult of analysis, elusive to diagram. The contemporary revolutionary ocean is murky, cut with unexpected currents, dark with layered temperatures and ateem with fish elegant or awful.

There are many conspiracies and many contacts. All those involved want an erosion of the isolation of the revolutionary vocation, the comfort of association with their fellow rebels, the agitational support of friends, the exchange of ideas and experience. At times real governments, especially but hardly alone Marxist-Leninist regimes, may offer logistical aid and comfort, sanctuary may be given, training and funds and money made available, schooling or passports promised or resolutions at the United Nations [passed]. There are some proxies, owned and operated, by masters in Tripoli or Moscow or even Washington. There are those up to dirty tricks and black agents of distant powers and thrones. The ocean shifts and flows constantly, friends come and go. Old nets collapse and are blown away, not to be replaced. Telephone numbers and ideological postures change. New people come into the center of the circle, old ones grown tired. No one from the IRA now remembers how to run the old Middle Eastern routes and every one of the Eritreans remembers when Russia deserted them to make a deal with Addis. The Kurds still have no friends and the rebels in Mozambique no program. The new currents do not seem helpful this year but next year there may be a neap tide. For the IRA or the Eritreans, for most, there is no conspiracy but a community of interests, a shared vocation, a ragged book of telephone numbers, a few friends without names, and if need be a sense of which current to swim against. The fanatics out of Persia will find a warm spot perhaps filled with exotic creatures, perhaps even kept warm for a time with heat funded in Moscow, perhaps not. It is a dark, shifting world of intuition, emotive response, dissolving arrangements, uncertainty, tacit understanding, vague, fluid, violent and uncertain and in the heel of the hunt not especially amenable to academic, analytical investigation, not easy to reveal with numbers, charts, and graphs, not sufficiently explained by conspiracy theory, and not likely to drain away soon.

So what is to be done? The people of the West, properly, want something to be done. If terrorism were just or even largely a communist conspiracy, then a trim course could be plotted against outside agitators and indigenous dupes. If justice could be given, then only the psychopaths would be left in a drained terrorist ocean. But absolute justice is impossible. And just [as] the law will not work ... the harsh face of security has not. And insisting that the terrorist ocean is murky—and it is—and that the phenomenon is complex—and it is—is not especially helpful nor likely to calm the justifiably anxious. The problem is there is no solution. That is the very bad news. . . .

Finally, there is good news. Essentially we live in a world so stable that the few and truly desperate have turned to the tactics of terror. Despite gross international tensions, the threat of Armageddon, the bloody regional wars, the plagues and famines and constant coups, despite the interesting times, we live in promising times. Terrorism is little more than the muzak of a world that has avoided the worst and can hope for better. Driven young men with pistols in a paper bag are not going to destroy us—only we can do that.

III

The Control of
International Terrorism

Terror. A disarmingly simple word. But it holds widely varying meanings for different people. As is noted throughout this book, there exists little agreement over the phenomena to which the term applies.

However different the world view of different observers, nearly all share a repugnance for the activities perceived as terrorism. No actor accepts being labeled a terrorist for the term is pejorative.

Yet the ranks of alleged terrorists show few signs of decreasing. Terrorism is practiced by a widening circle of actors—both revolutionaries and governments. Terrorism appears to be growing in frequency and lethality, and its capacity to terrorize continues, spectacularly if spasmodically. The fear terrorism instills extends its shadow over every corner of the globe.

Terrorism's advent has stimulated energetic efforts to bring it under control and has generated much discussion about the most effective response. "Indeed," as one reviewer noted, "the problem of 'What is to be done?' is central to much of the literature."[1] The search for appropriate countermeasures has, like efforts to define terrorism itself, proven elusive.

RESPONSES TO TERRORISM:
PROBLEMS OF CONCEPTUALIZATION

Those wishing to combat international terrorism have experienced great frustration. Why have measures to contain the spread of terrorism not succeeded? Among the sources of failure, the inability to discover the causes and accurately characterize the behavior to be deterred is basic. As one set of experts concluded,

> The problem with the prevention and suppression of "terrorism" arises in part because there is no clear understanding of the causes leading to conduct constituting "terrorism." The international community has been unable to arrive at a universally accepted definition of "terrorism" and [this has con-

185

tributed to the fact that countermeasures have] so far failed to control such activity.[2]

As another study put it, "there is no one internationally accepted definition of terrorism—a fact which, indeed, constitutes part of the problem in helping shape national attitudes about the scope of violence that many states remain prepared to tolerate or even support."[3]

This aspect of the difficulties underlying approaches to the control of international terrorism gained recognition in the aftermath of the United Nations' first effort to investigate terrorism in 1972. The Resolution (No. 3034) that resulted "led to the creation of three committees to 1. Define terrorism, 2. Examine the causes of terrorism, and 3. Propose measures to prevent terrorism."[4] In recognizing the differences and connections among terrorism's characteristics, causes, and control, the UN's approach was logical, but the results proved unproductive in the absence of a consensus about how these three goals were to be realized.

As the readings in **Parts I** and **II** should make abundantly clear, disagreement about the character and the cause of international terrorism remains pronounced. And without agreement on these preliminaries, it is understandable why agreement on the response to terrorism is unlikely, perhaps impossible. The criteria for evaluating possible controls are obscure without consensus on terrorism's character and causes. Like a disease which cannot be treated until it is first accurately diagnosed, so the plague of terrorism cannot be prevented until it is first defined, and successful strategies of control are contingent upon understanding its causes.

Those persuaded by one particular image of terrorism's character and cause are inevitably drawn to a particular set of policy recommendations, while those persuaded by a competing image inevitably embrace an entirely different set of policy prescriptions.

There are many issues which provide examples of this link between perceptions of what terrorism is and what produces it, on the one hand, and prescriptions for its effective cure, on the other hand. For purposes of illustration, consider the diametrically opposed views of whether conciliation or repression are viable remedies (see Table 1). Those advocating the former approach see terrorism rooted in frustrations with political oppression and deprivation; they recommend addressing these root causes in order to reduce it. Long-term reforms and short-term conciliatory policies are proposed. Those advocating the latter approach see terrorism springing from the rational decisions of extremists to rely on political violence; they advise prevention by the promise of swift and severe retaliation.

These differences about the character and cause of terrorism thus are the basis for the disagreement between those who see virtue in negotiation of terrorists' demands and those who see compromise as a vice and insist that terrorism is a problem to be deterred at its incipience. Likewise, these differences underlie the differences between those who see the use of

**TABLE 1   The Postulated Cause of Terrorism and Its Proposed Remedy:
Two Postures**

Are There "Root" Causes?	Proposed Remedies
	Find Cures
Yes	1. **Alleviate the sources of discontent:** "Measures to prevent international terrorism [require] study of the underlying causes of those forms of terrorism and acts of violence which lie in misery, frustration, grievance and despair." — U.N. Resolution, Nov. 2, 1972
	2. **Permit the oppressed to participate in the political process:** "The question for those with any power to bear on the problem is how to divert the terrorists from their terrorism. The obvious answer is to give their cause the hearing which is their primary demand." — Stephen Segaller, 1987
	Prevent and Deter
No	1. **Threaten terrorists with harsh reprisals:** "The root cause of terrorism is terrorists....Deterrence works on terrorists just as it does on anyone else." — Benjamin Netanyahu, 1986
	2. **Retaliate against the states that support international terrorism:** "A truly effective concerted action against terrorism is possible, but only on the basis of the strategy first advocated by the nineteenth-century Russian terrorists of 'hitting the centre,' meaning the main sponsors of international terrorism." — Walter Laqueur, 1987

military retaliation as playing into the hands of terrorists (by mobilizing sympathy for the cause and thereby paradoxically promoting rather than curtailing it) and those who regard the use of force necessary to combat terrorism.

The search for solutions thus springs from radically different assumptions about the nature and sources of terrorism, and these assumptions strongly affect conclusions about the wisdom or futility of contemplated remedies. What to one serves as a policy around which an effective counterterrorist program might be constructed is to another a plan that will only exacerbate the problem by provoking the very result that the plan was designed to solve: recourse to future terrorist actions. One man's solution is another man's problem. In seeking to prevent terrorism, when a democratic government suspends civil liberties and issues shoot-to-kill orders of suspected terrorists, does it curtail or strengthen the terrorist movement by allowing the terrorists to succeed in their goal of driving the democracy to desperate and unpopular repressive measures? The answers are often unclear. A counterterrorist program that may succeed in one location may backfire in another. Hence, promise and/or peril may result when the same countermeasure is deployed. In inspecting proposed controls, we are confronted with a series of incompatible clichés and conclusions: "concessions only encourage terrorists' appetite for further terrorism" as opposed to "concessions can redress the grievances that lead to terrorism," or "terrorism requires a long-term solution" as opposed to the claim that "terrorism cannot be cured but it can be prevented by preemption."

Opinion about the feasibility of finding controls also ranges across a broad spectrum. At one extreme are those who feel that obvious solutions, such as swift and severe retribution, are available. These maintain "that terrorism can be minimized, if not entirely eliminated, within a state if the government is fully determined to use all its potential powers of coercion."[5] At the other extreme are those who recognize neither permanent solutions nor the existence of effective deterrent measures, a position represented by Walter Laqueur's view that "the issues that give rise to terrorist activity are often simply not soluble."[6] In between are those (recall J. Bowyer Bell) who envision "no easy solutions" but maintain that while the flame of terrorism cannot be extinguished it can be reduced through the carefully selected application of responses fit to the peculiarities of each situation. "It's a problem to be managed, not to be solved,"[7] and "We cannot expect completely to eradicate terrorism. But we can aim to reduce significantly terrorism's significance on the international agenda,"[8] are expressions of this intermediate opinion about the prospects of curbing international terrorism.

In this context, Peter C. Sederberg observes that the Reagan administration's antiterrorism policies often appeared incoherent because they reflected many of the fundamental contradictions contained within the debate about the response to terrorism. The ambivalence and incompatibilities of its counterterrorism approach,

> ... bombing one sponsor of terrorism and trading arms to another—even if unwise in its particulars may [have been] an inevitable characteristic of any serious counter-terrorist program. We may pine for simple solutions and pronounce inflexible principles of "no negotiations, no concessions," only to find this quest for consistency undermined by the complexity of the problem.[9]

Thus, there appear to be few absolutes or universally applicable prescriptions. Generalities about the validity of various propositions regarding the control of terrorism are dangerous, and their applicability is likely to decay over time "as terrorist groups adjust to newly instituted counterterrorist measures."[10] The obstacles to finding effective answers to international terrorism are substantial. As Brian M. Jenkins describes them:

> When terrorists ... innovate, it is only to overcome a specific countermeasure. Terrorists ... have virtually unlimited targets, and this reduces the require-

ment for tactical innovation. When confronted with security measures, terrorists merely alter their tactics to obviate the security measures or shift their sights to other vulnerable targets. Because terrorists can attack anything, anywhere, any time, and governments cannot protect everything, everywhere, all the time, terrorists always retain a certain advantage.[11]

Against these barriers to control, there is some evidence that "in fact a variety of counterterrorist programs have been tried over the years with mixed success,"[12] and that "although the number of incidents has not declined . . . on the whole progress has been substantial" in some countries as "the direct result of determined and deliberate efforts."[13]

Let us review current thinking about the challenge of controlling international terrorism by considering the diversity of opinion about the feasibility of various counterterrorist policies expressed in policy debate.

To do so, we must begin by reiterating the fact that the approaches considered to counter the threat of terrorism are as varied as opinions about international terrorism's character and causes. No inventory can be exhaustive; for just as the methods of terrorists are constantly adapting to accommodate new challenges and take advantage of new opportunities, so, too, the response of governments about the ways to prevent or reduce the threat of terrorism is also constantly changing. Consider, for example, the diverse "policy options" identified by one authority as potential components of an anti-terrorist campaign:

1. Attempt to find long-term solutions to the underlying causes of terrorism. . . .
2. Increase the size and powers of the security forces. . . .
3. Introduce capital punishment for terrorist activities. . . .
4. Enact legislation limiting rights of assembly and increasing controls over the members of society by way of identification cards, registration of residence and extensive use of computerized files. . . .
5. Establish a 'third force' or special military units to cope with terrorist attacks. . . .
6. Announce a policy of 'no negotiations' with terrorists. . . .
7. Increase physical and procedural security. . . .
8. Introduce internment without trial or special legal procedures designed to limit intimidation of witnesses. . . .
9. Place legal limits on the ability of the media to report terrorist acts. . . .
10. Introduce special anti-terrorist legislation which may mandate a combination of the above or other measures. . . .
11. Make it illegal for individuals or private organizations to pay ransom to terrorists or to take out ransom insurance and place legal duty on people to report hostage takings to the police. . . .
12. Promote and become a signatory to international treaties providing for extradition or trial of captured terrorists, suspension of air services to countries providing safe haven for hijackers, etc. . . .

13. Research and develop alternatives to hostage negotiations. . . .
14. Suggest that terrorist groups be encouraged to adhere to the norms articulated by the customary laws of war, the Geneva Conventions, and the Nuremberg Principles. . . .
15. Develop and deploy highly intrusive technologies as preemptive moves (for example, technologies for monitoring and surveillance). . . .[14]

This survey demonstrates that the search for answers has been extensive and that the policy responses to the goal of countering terrorism are best characterized by their variety. Other inventories, of course, would necessarily reflect the same diversity. For example, another survey of approaches to counterterrorism includes in its list banning arms sales to terrorist-sponsoring nations, denying entry to suspected terrorists, improving extradition procedures, imposing tougher immigration and visa requirements, improving collaboration among security organizations, gathering intelligence, enhancing security measures, developing amnesty programs to redirect terrorists to alternative occupations, expanding public awareness, strengthening legal and social measures, intensifying military and police measures, controlling arms and explosives, and encouraging media self-regulation.[15] The options are highly varied, and the advantages of each proposed option seem destined to remain the subject of debate, for no single remedy serves as a panacea, and each has costly consequences associated with it. For example, military retaliation, "far from deterring future action, may solidify a previously unstable group."[16]

As the readings that follow illustrate, the debate about methods revolves around a series of interconnected issues: Are the policies effective? Ethical? Compatible with other values such as the preservation of civil liberties and democratic procedures? Do they require multilateral (international) cooperation, or can they be engineered through unilateral (national) solutions? Can technology provide a barrier? Is terrorism best combated through proactive or reactive measures? Can international terrorism be addressed through legal or institutional procedures? What are the relative benefits and costs of counterterrorist measures defined by the categories prevention, protection, and prosecution?[17] And if, as alleged, "There is no force more terroristic than a national state at war,"[18] by what means if any is the terrorism of sovereign states to be contained?

Let us approach these questions by considering some of the ideas advanced about them in the readings.

REFLECTIONS ON THE CONTROL OF INTERNATIONAL TERRORISM: SELECTIONS

As noted, the rise of international terrorism since the 1960s has stimulated determined efforts to contain its spread and deter its occurrence. "Impediments and Prerequisites to Counter-Terrorism," by Conor Cruise

O'Brien, exposes the limitations of alternative responses and the reasons why previous efforts have met with only marginal success. These failures stem in large part, O'Brien argues, from inaccurate images of international terrorism's character and causes, which fail to give proper recognition to the motives inspiring terrorists. Unfortunately, prevailing stereotypes mask the disparate sources of international terrorism and the varied motives of terrorist movements, and these mistaken images "serve mainly to confuse debate." Misperceptions range from the "sentimental" to the "hysterical," with the former distorted by empathy with struggles for national liberation and the latter by unwarranted hatred and the consequent belief that a "hawkish" response can cure the problem.

O'Brien examines the dangers of these stereotypes and the responses they rationalize to show why "the prospects for ending terrorism through a negotiated settlement are not bright" and why the combating of terrorism through hawkish approaches only legitimizes violence and may inadvertently encourage further terrorist actions. The record of past efforts that relied on these "solutions" reveals their deficiencies. But, concludes O'Brien, whereas "it is not possible to extirpate terrorism from the face of the globe, it should be possible to reduce the incidence and effectiveness of terrorism." "Coordinated international action" is recommended for this purpose, led by the two superpowers, the United States and the Soviet Union. (One suspects that O'Brien would not approve of the Reagan administration's unsuccessful search for a consistent policy, which substituted unilateral retaliation for multilateral action.)[19] By implication, O'Brien also may be presumed to favor counterterrorism strategies guided by the goal of maintaining a proper balance between respect for freedom and a capacity for decisive and resolute action. This presents a substantial challenge.

This preference stresses the importance of identifying and adhering to a coherent set of principles to manage the threat of international terrorism. What principles should guide the search for methods to combat terrorism? Different observers provide different answers. Among them, Walter Laqueur's cautious perspective commands wide respect. In "Reflections on the Eradication of Terrorism," he argues that approaches to counterterrorism must recognize the diversity among alleged terrorist groups. Different types need to be distinguished and counterterrorist strategies need to be specifically tailored to deal with these alternate modes. Central to the capacity to cope with terrorism is an accurate image of its character (how it should be defined) and its origins (what causes it). At the core of these questions, Laqueur maintains, is the fundamental relationship between the extent of terrorist action and the level of repression practiced by governments seeking to combat it. To Laqueur, a negative relationship between governmental repression and terrorist activity is evident: the more severe the repression, the less frequent terrorism becomes. Dictatorships, he observes, are immune from terrorism, whereas "hardly a major democratic country has entirely escaped it." Hence terrorism is best curbed by policies that punitively repress terrorist tactics, not by remedies that seek to reduce the grievances of the discontented and dispossessed. This approach is diametrically opposite those who aver that the answer lies in action to change the political, social, and economic soil in which terrorism is perceived to be rooted, as represented by Richard E. Rubenstein's claim that "No solution to the problem of terrorism is conceivable that does not reconnect politicized young adults to society by involving them in mass-based movements for change."[20]

Laqueur also examines other aspects of putting an end to terrorism and advances insightful if controversial conclusions about the dubious utility of a variety of allegedly naive recommendations.

These reflections raise the critical question of the criteria by which the response to terrorism is to be ethically evaluated. In "Framing a Moral Response to Terrorism," James Turnstead Burchael cogently argues that "the background, identity, and purposes of terrorists must be known if one is to frame a moral response to them." Like others,[21] Burchael believes the moral reaction must acknowledge the vast variety of purposes, tactics, and circumstances that are a component of the "terrorist" syndrome to construct a reaction that is not only effective but also morally justifiable. To manage this task, Burchael turns to moral and legal principles and assesses their relevance to approaches proposed to counter terrorism. Although he sees terrorism as empirically different from conventional warfare, Burchael seeks to evaluate the applicability of five ethical doctrines on warfare in the Western tradition to counterterrorism. His informed interpretation of these principles provides perceptive observations about the character of counterterrorist strategies and the moral dilemmas they pose.

The preceding three essays in **Part III** summarize the major philosophical, practical, and moral issues in discussions of the control of terrorism. The six that follow evaluate the alternate types of counterterrorism programs available.

Perhaps the most frequently advocated types of response are "proactive" ones—those which propose to hit terrorists actively and aggressively. This punitive approach has tended to be articulated most vociferously in the immediate wake of spectacular acts of terrorism that elevate the general feelings of frustration and powerlessness experienced by governments in their dealings with elusive terrorist groups. In "Proactive Responses to Terrorism: Reprisals, Preemption, and Retribution," Neil C. Livingstone examines the nature of these policy responses in light of the attention given them by President Reagan's National Security Decision Directive 138 (3 April 1984) which announced a willingness and intent by the United States to go beyond condemnation and reaction and "to consider military action in advance of actual incidents to prevent them from occurring or to punish terrorists in the aftermath of an attack." That policy initiative also laid great stress on state terrorism and on punishment of governments alleged to support terrorism abroad. Secretary of State George Shultz

(13 April 1984) expressed the thinking behind the U.S. quest for an active program when he asserted that it was "increasingly doubtful that a purely defensive strategy can even begin to cope with the problem."

These "proactive" policies, examined in light of history and political theory, embrace tactics which, in Livingstone's view, may in some ways undermine their usefulness. They encompass inherent practical dangers, and can violate moral and legal principles, thereby threatening to reduce those governments which employ them to the level of those they seek to combat. Thus, Livingstone warns that risks are inherent in a policy that requires, for instance, acceptance of the loss of innocent lives as a collateral consequence of military retaliation. Whereas it is tempting to "hit back" at terrorists, for example, in the absence of an ability to identify the perpetrators, their location, and their sponsors, it is nearly impossible to strike back with force without attacking bystanders who had nothing to do with the terrorist movement. To retaliate militarily is not only likely to destroy innocents but also to respond precisely as the terrorists hoped; "terrorism may be aimed at deliberately provoking repression, reprisals, and counterterrorism, which may ultimately lead to the collapse of an unpopular government."[22]

These risks to the conviction that "swift revenge and/or preemptive attack is the answer" notwithstanding, Livingstone concludes that "the threat posed by international terrorism and its patrons is so serious that there is need by the liberal democracies of the West to protect their moral order and values with the judicious use of force." In the end, therefore, he condones the use of these proactive measures, arguing "When living in the jungle, it is best to observe the laws of the jungle." At issue, of course, is how the line is to be drawn between legitimate and illegitimate uses of military force in fighting terrorism. Do the ends justify the means? Under what conditions?

Most efforts to address the question of counterterrorism have viewed the problem from the perspective of the targets of terrorist attacks (as Livingstone does from the point of view of liberal democracies from the West). The policy recommendations that are advanced typically prescribe policy actions designed to deter the actions undertaken by terrorist groups, rather than confronting the political conflicts that escalate long-standing disputes into terrorist activities. As Christopher C. Joyner advises in this context, "If there exists an end to terrorism, it lies not in measures of prevention, protection, or prosecution taken by any government. Rather, it is to be found in addressing the deep-seated political and psychological grievances that motivate terrorists."[23] This advice may or may not be cogent. But regardless, it is true that in most cases terrorism and counterterrorism are conflicts between unequals. If this characteristic is emphasized, then the feasibility of an alternative to military force becomes a salient issue.

In this context the views of Stephen C. Cohen and Harriet C. Arnone, who perceive "Conflict Resolution as the Alternative to Terrorism," are representative.[24] They see the primary task as the management of the underlying conflicts which prompt terrorism, contending that the ultimate solution to protracted conflict is its resolution, not its mere reduction. For this, they and others of this perspective argue that the Breeding grounds for terrorism should be modified by attempts to facilitate conflict resolution through enhancement of each adversary's identity, creation of new symbols, enfranchisement of elements within each of the conflict groups, enhancement of internal development, and use of indigenous third parties. The advantages of this alternative response over conventional approaches to counterterrorism are suggested by those who adhere to the "root-causes" theory of terrorism's origins (see **Part II**) and emphasize terrorism as a political and strategic problem (see **Part I**).

Consistent with this reasoning is the position of those who accept the proposition that one man's terrorist really is another man's liberator and that revolutionary terror and regime terror are often indistinguishable. These observers thus argue that terrorist groups share many practices with national governments dealing with enemies both within and beyond their borders. If this is so (that is, if Richard Falk's proposition is correct, that terrorism exhibits a dual face and shows itself as a practice of both revolutionaries and governmental functionaries), then the control of terrorism is considerably more complex indeed. Curtailing terrorism requires modification of the practices of states and not just management of the activities of insurrectionists. But policing the foreign policy and internal conduct of states is extremely difficult because international law gives sovereign states wide (some would say unrestrained) room for maneuver.

Still other dimensions of international terrorism serve as obstacles to its control. For example, a number of observers have recognized the extraordinary impact of technology on both the emergence and control of international terrorism.[25] Technological innovation has created an environment conducive to the practice of terrorism across national borders. With modern technologies, terrorists are better able to manipulate the media and have at their disposal a wide array of sophisticated weapons, including impact grenades, anti-armour rockets, long-delay timing devices on bombs, liquid explosives, remotely controlled vehicles, plastic handguns, and the like: "technological advances are creating a new range of small, portable, cheap, relatively easy to operate, and highly destructive weapons which, if produced on a large scale, will undoubtedly find their way into the hands of terrorists."[26] But technological innovations also have created a variety of techniques (for example, metal detectors at airports) that have facilitated the control of terrorist activities by expanding the capacity to protect potential targets. These technologies also have made possible effective security at airports and embassies. To some, therefore, terrorism is largely a technological problem that can be combated with more sophisticated applications.

Perhaps no technological innovations have greater impact than those in the nuclear energy and weapons sphere.[27] Over 300 nuclear-related "incidents" were observed between 1966 and 1985.[28] The potential risks of supply disruptions caused by "techno-terrorist" attacks of energy facilities were underscored in a U.S. Energy Department report issued in February 1989. That report warned that "enemy-related terrorism in the United States would be a particularly significant threat" and that "even in the absence of a superpower confrontation, there is the possibility that potential Third World adversaries could sponsor attacks on the energy infrastructure of the United States."[29] Hard-to-detect plastic explosives, hand-held missiles, and electronic surveillance gear make politically motivated acts of sabotage feasible, as acts in Europe and elsewhere suggest.

In "Responding to the Threat of Nuclear Terrorism," Louis René Beres explores the substantial threat posed by the existence of nuclear explosives and radiological weapons and by the practice of nuclear reactor sabotage.[30] The opportunities these technologies present to terrorists have increased with the dispersion of nuclear production facilities worldwide and the vertical and horizontal proliferation of nuclear weapons. As the evidence in his essay summarizes, this threat is not to be minimized, for the use of nuclear terrorism could lead to mass annihilation. To respond to this threat, Beres interprets the problem primarily from the vantage point of the most vulnerable country, the United States. In identifying the available policy options, Beres astutely warns that sole reliance on "hard-line" methods "may only reinforce the antagonism and intransigence" of terrorist groups. Instead, a balanced approach is recommended which carefully weighs the type of terrorist groups which states hope to deter and the aspirations that motivate them.

Beres convincingly explains why strategies employing both negative sanctions and positive rewards are sometimes appropriate (depending on the purposes and values of terrorist groups). In calculating the relative advantages and disadvantages, Beres accentuates the risks of combating terrorism vindicatively with the use of force. In his opinion, this is likely to demonstrate not resolve but weakness and hence play into the hands of nuclear terrorists, stimulating rather than curtailing their temptation to turn to the extreme of exploiting nuclear vulnerabilities. His analysis also exposes the related dangers to the protection of civil liberties. Underlying the entire discussion is the thesis that pursuit of a globalist, Cold War foreign policy by the United States might encourage recourse to nuclear terrorism, because those aims may rationalize continuation of military approaches to Third World political problems by the United States and thereby incite the very terrorist tactics most feared.

Technology also becomes a factor in the control of terrorism through its contribution to global communications. Terrorism is theatre. Terrorists, Brian M. Jenkins has remarked, "want a lot of people watching and a lot of people listening, not a lot of people dead."[31] To counter terrorism's threat, a number of observers accordingly have stressed the role of the media in the process. Some ascribe to it great potency as a cause of terrorism (recall **Part II**) and see in its manipulation a solution: control terrorism by controlling the media which gives terrorism its theatric effect.

Like all alternatives, opinions on the potential utility of methods relying on this approach are divided. For example, consider the perspective on the issue offered by Bruno S. Frey in "Fighting Political Terrorism by Refusing Recognition."[32] Terrorists, he submits, are rational, goal-oriented actors who take measured risks in order to attain satisfaction of their demands. Part of their decision calculus is demonstrably premised on the expectation that terrorist actions will elicit great publicity. He recommends the creation of an international information regime whose rules would deny terrorists the public attention they seek, thereby reducing the perceived benefits of terrorist acts. This prescribed approach is designed to complement existing policies of counterterrorism, but differs in that it is an active rather than passive strategy.

The assumption behind this approach—that terrorist activity is designed to attract attention and arouse sympathy—seems unassailable. In Margaret Thatcher's words, terrorism thrives on "the oxygen of publicity" provided by the media. But the conclusion from this assumption—that the denial of recognition will reduce the incidence of international terrorism—is open to dispute. In "Why We Need More But Better Coverage of Terrorism," Patrick Clawson maintains that "the media should not be viewed as potential enemies [but] instead be seen as likely allies who can contribute much toward the elimination of terrorism." Because "terrorism has long flourished in the absence of mass media," Clawson suggests that what is needed is expanded coverage of terrorist acts, accentuating its "horrible nature" in order to challenge terrorists' propaganda and arouse public opinion about the repugnant character of terrorists' methods and motives. The practicality of this approach is contingent, it would appear, on the probability that responsible journalists will see and describe particular terrorist actions in the same negative way as do their primary targets.

The difficulties posed by reaching agreement on "the facts" and by a policy requiring government management of the news—the danger of crossing the line to censorship—are also acknowledged. And the limits to the approach are not dismissed, because Clawson insightfully acknowledges that unsupportive media coverage is unlikely to moderate terrorists sponsored by states. Clawson's advocacy of media self-regulation offers an interesting counterpoint to the approach proposed by Bruno Frey and to others who go even further by proposing "outright media restrictions to deal with these perceived problems."[33]

Another perspective is offered on methods to combat terrorism by those who see terrorism defined best by what terrorists do—their repertoire of tactics—and by the political and strategic aims they pursue. If terrorists are distinguished by the techniques they use—bombings, kidnappings, skyjackings, sabotage, hostage takings—then the search for a remedy turns to instruments of *protection* of targets to deny terrorists the opportunity to practice these methods so easily.

William Gutteridge reviews the practicality of these largely "reactive" or "prophylactic palliatives"[34] in "Countering Terrorism: Evaluating the Options." Emphasizing the need "not to overreact to the terrorist threat," he also states that the threat is sufficient so that "the option of inaction is not really available." But "neither terrorism nor the grievances in which it is rooted can be entirely eradicated. So the problem is one of balance—how to contain terrorism, diminish it and eliminate particular forms of it without necessarily reducing the quality of life and the liberties of the individual."

This relatively modest goal can be accomplished by "distinguishing the variety of motivations and grievances that inspire terrorism" and by dealing with the "clearly different categories of terrorist activity" with different measures.

Among the approaches reviewed, Gutteridge stresses the importance of involving the public in efforts to undermine the terrorists' morale and logistic support, and regards international cooperation "as a prerequisite for real progress in the fight against international terrorism." When these preconditions are met, the problems of identifying the terrorist, addressing the issue of frontiers, and coordinating diplomatic sanctions and military responses become feasible. This capacity for achievement is demonstrated by a review of the progress that has been made with respect to air piracy, kidnappings, and hostage taking. He describes the positive contributions of antiterrorist conventions, which in his opinion appropriately endorse the principle of "no concessions." Countering terrorism, he concludes, "is not a small law and order matter for security forces to deal with." Terrorism does not lend itself to a purely legal remedy, and "need not depend on formal treaties." Rather, the problem can be contained by creating a climate in which reliance on terrorist tactics is increasingly difficult.

Although morality and legality are to be distinguished, they both are highly relevant to discussion of the methods by which international terrorism might be controlled. To those who see terrorism as a method of fighting oppression, terrorism is sometimes morally and legally justifiable. To those who see terrorism as a form of violence targeting innocents, terrorism cannot be morally or legally justified.

Likewise, there exists considerable debate about the legality of many counterterrorist programs conducted by states. "The issue of the legitimacy of the use of force to combat terrorism," notes one commentator, "lies at the heart of the current debate."[35] Some agree with his position that "the use of force to combat terrorism is an acceptable response under customary international law."[36] Others, however, dispute this interpretation and point to contradictions and ambiguities in international law which undermine the legal right of states to use force against terrorists and strengthen the legal right of liberation movements to use force to free themselves from tyrannical oppression when they assert they are acting as "lawful combatants."[37] As one U.S. authority, Abraham D. Sofaer, notes, "the legitimacy of political violence is a notion that has worked its way deep into international law enforcement."[38] Yet the standards and legal rules are unclear and imprecise, which leaves terrorism beyond legal control, largely unregulated. Although numerous international conventions and declarations have enunciated opposition to state assistance of terrorist acts (such as the 1983 Madrid concluding document of the Conference on Security and Cooperation in Europe [CSCE] review committee), these statements uniformly have been condemnations without sanctions, and effective multilateral resistance to state sponsorship of terrorism through collective measures has been rare and modest. As Yonah Alexander notes, "the failure of the international community to fully recognize terrorism as criminal behavior and low-intensity warfare has encouraged the growth of terrorist activity."[39]

The uncertain place of law in the effort to arrest international terrorism is a topic that is directly related to debate about its definition and determinants. Legal approaches and their applicability to the control of terrorism are evaluated comprehensively by Paul Wilkinson in "Fighting the Hydra: International Terrorism and the Rule of Law." Depicting terrorism as "only one among many methods of struggle," Wilkinson proceeds from the premise that "context is all in the analysis of political violence." He explores the weaknesses of international legal measures to regulate international terrorism, but he argues that these do not preclude the future construction of an effective counterterrorism regime. To coordinate a concerted response to terrorist activity, agreement must be reached about the mixture of norms and principles that states could embrace.

The prospects of confronting international terrorism through institutional approaches are explored further by Seymour Maxwell Finger in "The United Nations and International Terrorism." In contrast to William Gutteridge, Finger argues the capacity of existing UN resolutions and conventions to make a difference. They are worth the effort, Finger answers, because they establish legal norms, encourage collaboration among states, and legitimize unilateral and multilateral retaliation against those responsible for terrorist acts. Finger submits that "mere condemnation of such acts is insufficient" and that practical procedures must be implemented and enforced. Examination of the impact of the rules and regulations created by the UN's International Civil Aviation Organization suggests the kinds of actions which might be taken in other areas to reduce the incidence of international terrorist activity through institutional instruments.

The essays in **Part III** have shown that, like efforts to unravel the riddles about the character and cause of terrorism, so, too, efforts to respond to it are fraught with myths and uncertainties. Proposed solutions have often failed because they were based on false premises about terrorism's nature and determinants. In "Responses to Dissident Terrorism: From Myth to Maturity," Peter C. Sederberg seeks to cut away the conceptual underbrush obscuring thought about the control of terrorism in order to disentangle sense and nonsense, reality and myth. His review and synthesis provide a summary and fitting conclusion to the problem, for it subjects to critical evaluation many of the issues introduced previously.

This is an ambitious undertaking because discussion of the response to terrorism has been dominated by advocates of overly simplistic solutions, he argues. These range from hard-line proponents of severe retribution to proponents of conciliatory approaches and of the alleviation of grievances presumed to cause terrorism. Both polar positions, Sederberg argues, are mythical because they are based on unwarranted assumptions about the nature of terrorism and the factors which produce it. To avoid these errors, he identifies the considerations relevant to the construction of an adequate response. For example, terrorist movements' ideological aims should be taken into account, as should the level of external support received for their cause. These factors vary considerably across terrorist movements, rendering the search for an "all-purpose" counterterrorist policy inadvisable. Instead, Sederberg suggests, the solution embraced should fit the particular actor and its goals and circumstances.

Armed with a recommended set of analytic principles, Professor Sederberg then proceeds to evaluate critically a number of the possible remedies recommended in the previous readings, including legal procedures, repressive measures, non-military pressure, military reprisals, improved security, retribution campaigns, military intervention, conciliation and concessions, negotiations, and reform. Weighing the evidence and theories behind these alleged remedies with an eye to the differences between their short- and long-range advantages and disadvantages, Sederberg convincingly shows why it is an illusion to hope for a sure cure in confronting the "myriad forms of dissident terrorism around the world, much less the different cases of establishment terrorism. Those attempting to deal with terrorism," he concludes, "must act with maturity and restraint so that the cure does not cripple or kill the patient." Left unanswered is the question, Can the world muster the political will and wisdom to act in a more mature and responsible manner to the threat of international terrorism?

NOTES

1. Shaul Bakhash, "The Riddle of Terrorism," *The New York Review of Books* 34 (24 September 1987), 12.

2. Cited in Jay Mallin, "Terrorism as a Military Weapon," in Yonah Alexander and Seymour Maxwell Finger, eds., *Terrorism: Interdisciplinary Prespectives* (New York: McGraw-Hill, 1977), 93.

3. José Luis Nunes and Lawrence J. Smith, Rapporteurs, *Terrorism* (Brussels: North Atlantic Assembly, 1989), 3.

4. Donna M. Schlagheck, *International Terrorism* (Lexington, Mass.: Lexington Books, 1988), 122.

5. Grant Wardlaw, *Political Terrorism* (Cambridge: Cambridge University Press, 1982), 69.

6. Cited in Bakhash, 12.

7. U.S. Ambassador Edward Marks, as cited in Rushworth M. Kidder, "The Fear of Fear Itself," *The Christian Science Monitor* (13 May 1986), 17.

8. L. Paul Bremer III, "Countering Terrorism in the 1980s and 1990s," *Current Policy* No. 1135 (Washington: U.S. Department of State, 22 November 1988), 1.

9. Peter C. Sederberg, *Terrorist Myths* (Englewood Cliffs, N.J.: Prentice-Hall, 1989), 130.

10. U.S. Department of State, *Patterns of Global Terrorism: 1987* (August 1988), 4.

11. "Defense Against Terrorism," *Political Science Quarterly* 101 (No. 5, 1986), 777.

12. Sederberg, 136.

13. Nunes and Smith, v.

14. Wardlaw, 66-68.

15. Rushworth M. Kidder, "Countering the Threat of Terrorism," *The Christian Science Monitor* (21 May 1986), 15.

16. Ibid., 15.

17. This classification of approaches is proposed in Christopher C. Joyner, "In Search of an Anti-Terrorism Policy," *Terrorism: An International Journal* 11 (No. 1, 1988), 29-42.

18. Richard E. Rubenstein, *Alchemists of Revolution* (New York: Basic Books, 1987), xvii.

19. Edward A. Lynch, "International Terrorism: The Search for a Policy," *Terrorism: An International Journal* 9 (No. 1, 1987), 1-86.

20. Rubenstein, 228.

21. For example, Jenkins, "Defense Against Terrorism."

22. Brian M. Jenkins, *International Terrorism: A New Mode of Conflict* (Los Angeles: Crescent Publications, 1975), 5.

23. Joyner, 40.

24. *Journal of Social Issues* 44 (No. 2, 1988), 175-189.

25. Neil C. Livingstone, "The Impact of Technological Innovation," in Uri Ra'anan, et al., eds., *Hydra of Carnage* (Lexington, Mass.: Lexington Books, 1986), 137-153.

26. Jenkins, *International Terrorism*, 19.

27. Not to be dismissed is the threat posed by terrorist use of chemical weapons, which are possessed by no less than twenty countries (Nunes and Smith, 24).

28. Ibid., 22.

29. "Energy Department Alerts Companies to Growing Threat of Terrorist Attacks," *The State* (Columbia, S.C.: 6 February 1989), 1A, 7A.

30. See Jeremiah Denton, "International Terrorism—The Nuclear Dimension," *Terrorism: An International Journal* 9 (No. 2, 1987), 113-123, as well as Brian M. Jenkins, "Will Terrorists Go Nuclear?," *Orbis* 29 (Fall 1985), 507-515.

31. *International Terrorism*, 3.

32. *Journal of Public Policy* 7 (April-June 1987), 179-188.

33. Nunes and Smith, 20.

34. Joyner, 40.

35. Franz W. Paasche, "The Use of Force in Combatting Terrorism," *Columbia Journal of Transnational Law* 25 (No. 2, 1987), 377.

36. Ibid., 378.

37. Jenkins, "Defense Against Terrorism," 779.

38. "Terrorism and the Law," *Foreign Affairs* 64 (Summer 1986), 906.

39. Cited in *Executive Intelligence Review* (22 August 1986), 53.

19

Impediments and Prerequisites to Counter-Terrorism

Conor Cruise O'Brien

Terrorism is disturbing not just emotionally and morally but intellectually, as well. On terrorism, more than on other subjects, commentary seems liable to be swayed by wishful thinking, to base itself on unwarranted or flawed assumptions, and to draw from these assumptions irrational inferences, muzzily expressed. . . .

[Many observers exemplify] a dovish, or sentimental, variety of wishful thinking on the subject of terrorism. There is also a hawkish, or hysterical, variety. Each has its own misleading stereotype (or stereotypes) of the terrorist. Let us look at the stereotypes:

Sentimental stereotype. According to this stereotype, the terrorist is a misguided idealist, an unsublimated social reformer. He has been driven to violence by political or social injustice or both. What is needed is to identify the measures of reform that will cause him to desist. Once these can be identified and undertaken, the terrorist, having ceased to be driven, stops.

Hysterical stereotype. Less stable than the sentimental variety, this can be divided into subvarieties:

(a) The terrorist is some kind of a nut—a "disgruntled abnormal" given to "mindless violence." ("Mindless violence" may be applicable to the deeds of isolated, maverick assassins. As applied to the planned activities of armed conspiracies, it is itself a mindless expression.)

(b) The terrorist is nothing more than a thug, a goon, a gangster. His "political" demands are simply a cover for criminal activity.

(c) The terrorist is an agent, or dupe, or cat's-paw of the other super-power. (He might, of course, be a nut or a goon as well as a dupe.)

These stereotypes serve mainly to confuse debate on the subject. There is no point in arbitrarily attributing motives, nice or nasty, to the terrorist. It might be more useful to look at the situations in which terrorists find themselves and at how they act, and may be expected to act, given their situations. . . .

201

Terrorists have a grievance, which they share with members of a wider community: the division of Ireland, the division of Palestine, the inroads of secularism into Islam, or whatever. But they also have, from the moment they become terrorists, significant amounts of power, prestige, and access to wealth, and these constitute vested interests in the present, irrespective of the attainment or non-attainment of their declared long-term political objectives.

The sentimentalist thinks of the terrorist as driven to violence by grievance or oppression. It would be more realistic to think of the terrorist as hauling himself up, by means of the grievance or oppression and the violence it legitimizes, to relative power, prestige, and privilege in the community to which he belongs. For an unemployed young man in a slum . . . , for example, the most promising channel of upward social mobility is his neighborhood branch of the national terrorist organization. There are risks to be run, certainly, but for the adventurous, aggressive characters among the unemployed or the otherwise frustrated, the immediate rewards outweigh the risks. In this situation the terrorist option is a rational one: you don't have to be a nut, a dupe, or an idealist.

I don't mean that the terrorist is necessarily, or even probably, insincere about the national (or religious or other collective) grievance or in his hatred toward those seen as responsible for the grievance. On the contrary, hatred is one of the things that keep him going, and the gratification of hatred is among the rewards of the terrorist. The terrorist is not just a goon, out for the loot. His political motivation is genuine. But there are other rewards in his way of life as well as the hazy reward of progress toward the political objective. The possession of a known capacity and willingness to kill confers authority and glamour in the here and now, even on rank-and-file members in the urban ghetto or in the village. On the leaders it confers national and even international authority and glamour, and independence from financial worries.

If we accept that the terrorist's way of life procures him immediate rewards of that nature, and that he is probably not insensible to at least some of the rewards in question, it seems to follow that he will probably be reluctant to relinquish those rewards by voluntarily putting himself out of business.

The situation thus outlined has a bearing of a negative nature on the notion that there are "negotiated solutions" to the "problems" that "cause" terrorism.

First of all, a negotiated solution—being by definition an outcome that offers some satisfaction to both parties—will be inherently distasteful to terrorists and their admirers, accustomed as these are to regarding *one* of the parties (Britain, Israel, or another) as evil incarnate.

Second, to exploit that genuine distaste will be in the interest of the terrorists, in relation to the reward system discussed above. So pride and profit converge into a violent rejection of the "negotiated solution"—

which therefore is not a solution to terrorism. . . . [Therefore] the prospects for ending terrorism through a negotiated settlement are not bright, . . . But the insistence that a negotiated solution *can* end terrorism actually helps the terrorists. It does so because it places the responsibility for continuing terrorism equally on the terrorists and those they seek to terrorize. The enhanced respectability with which the terrorist is thereby invested gives him a foretaste of success and an encouragement to persevere. This is the opposite of what the dovish advisers desire, but it is the main result of their ill-advised endeavors.

Not only do doves sometimes help terrorists, but some hawkish advisers also give inadvertent aid and comfort to the forces they abhor. The combating of terrorism is not helped by bombastic speeches at high levels, stressing what a monstrous evil terrorism is and that its elimination is to be given the highest priority. I'm afraid that the most likely terrorist reaction to such a speech, whether it comes from a President, a Secretary of State, or other important official, is: "You see, they *have* to pay attention to us now. We are hurting them. Let's give them more of the same." And it all helps with recruitment. A movement that is denounced by a President is in the big time. And some kind of big time is what is most wanted by the aggressive and frustrated, who constitute the pool on which terrorist movements can draw.

What applies to speeches applies *a fortiori* to unilateral military action against countries harboring terrorists. Whatever short-term advantages may be derived from such attacks, a price will be paid—in increased international sympathy for the "cause" of the terrorists in question, and so in enhanced glamour and elbow room for them, all tending to legitimize and so facilitate future "counterattacks."

Nor does it help to suggest that terrorism is about to be extirpated—because it almost certainly isn't. Today's world—especially the free, or capitalist, world—provides highly favorable conditions for terrorist recruitment and activity. The numbers of the frustrated are constantly on the increase, and so is their awareness of the life-style of the better-off and the vulnerability of the better-off. Among the better-off themselves are bored young people looking for the kicks that violence can provide, and thus for causes that legitimize violence, of which there are no shortage. A wide variety of people feel starved for attention, and one surefire way of attracting instantaneous worldwide attention through television is to slaughter a considerable number of human beings, in a spectacular fashion, in the name of a cause.

Although the causes themselves hardly constitute the sole motivation of the terrorists—as terrorists claim they do—they are not irrelevant, either. The cause legitimizes the act of terror in the terrorist's own eyes and in those of others belonging to his nation, faith, or culture. Certain cultures and subcultures, homes of frustrated causes, are destined breeding grounds for terrorism. The Islamic culture is the most notable example.

That culture's view of its own rightful position in the world is profoundly at variance with the actual order of the contemporary world. It is God's will that the House of Islam should triumph over the House of War (the non-Moslem world), and not just by spiritual means. "Islam Means Victory," [was] a slogan of the Iranian fundamentalists in the Gulf War. To strike a blow against the House of War is meritorious; consequently, there is widespread support for activities condemned in the West as terrorist. Israel is one main target for these activities, but the activities would not be likely to cease even if Israel came to an end. The Great Satan in the eyes of Ayatollah Khomeini—and of the millions for whom he [spoke—was] not Israel but the United States. The defeat of Israel would, in those eyes, be no more than a portent of the impending defeat of the Great Satan. What the West calls terrorism should then be multiplied rather than abandoned.

The wellsprings of terrorism are widespread and deep. The interaction between modern communications systems and archaic fanaticism (and other sources of resentment and ambition) is likely to continue to stimulate terrorist activity. In these conditions, talk about extirpating terrorism—and unilateral exploits backing such talk—are likely to be counterproductive. They present terrorists with a "victory," merely by the fact of being able to continue their activity. Similarly, solemn promises never to negotiate with terrorists can play into the hands of terrorists. Terrorists holding hostages can force a democratic government to negotiate. . . . If the democratic government then pretends that no negotiation took place, this helps the credibility of the terrorists, not that of the democratic government.

It is not possible to extirpate terrorism from the face of the globe, but it should be possible to reduce the incidence and effectiveness of terrorism, through coordinated international action. The Reagan Administration's efforts to get better cooperation in this matter from the European allies [were] justified in principle but flawed in practice. They [were] justified because the performance of several European countries in relation to international terrorism has often amounted to turning a blind eye for commercial reasons. . . .

[Unfortunately], the President's remonstrances [lacked] the moral leverage they [needed] to have. They [lacked] such leverage because a very wide international public [saw] the Reagan Administration itself as engaged in supporting terrorism in Central America, in its backing for the contras in Nicaragua. Public cynicism about American anti-terrorist rhetoric [was] increased by the strong component of Cold War ideology that the Reagan Administration [had] been putting into its anti-terrorism, implying that almost all terrorism has its ultimate roots in the Soviet Union. Most of the interested public outside the superpowers tends to see each superpower as calling the terrorists whom it favors "freedom fighters" while reserving the term "terrorists" for the "freedom fighters" favored by the other side. That view of the matter is debatable, but the point, in the present context, is that it is shared by so many people that it inhibits effective international cooperation against international terrorism.

Such cooperation is unlikely to have a strong impact unless both superpowers are prepared to participate in it. Bringing about such cooperation will be difficult but is not inconceivable. Limited superpower consensus has emerged, in the second half of the twentieth century, on at least three occasions: in 1956, against the Anglo-French-Israeli invasion of Egypt; in 1963, against the continued existence of the secessionist "state" of Katanga; and in 1977, against the supply of arms to South Africa.

Can limited superpower consensus be attained for coordinated action against terrorism? I think it can, especially if international terrorist activity grows to the degree that it begins to pose a clear threat to international peace and stability—not just as these are perceived by one superpower but as perceived by both. There is a historical precedent, flawed—like all such precedents—but suggestive. This is the case of the Barbary pirates, who used to operate in the Mediterranean, out of North African ports. In the seventeenth and eighteenth centuries, rivalries between the European powers provided the Barbary pirates with conditions propitious to their activities, much as global rivalries tend to protect state terrorism today. The Barbary pirates were a general nuisance, but they were a worse nuisance to some powers than to others, and so the enemies of the powers for whom the pirates were making the most trouble were apt to give the pirates a helping hand from time to time. In the first half of the nineteenth century, however, the powers decided, in effect, that the pirates should be treated as a common enemy: the enemy of the human race, *hostes humani generis*. With that change in international approach, piracy was brought under control in the Mediterranean.

International terrorism has yet to reach the stage that Mediterranean piracy reached in the nineteenth century. Terrorism is a worse nuisance to one superpower—the United States—than it is to the other. Democratic societies, committed to freedom of information and having governments necessarily sensitive to changing public moods, are far more vulnerable to terrorist blackmail, and offer a far more stimulating environment for terrorist activity, than closed societies like the Soviet Union. (We are often told that there is no terrorist activity in the Soviet Union; in reality we don't know whether there is terrorism or not. But the fact that we don't know and that the Soviet public doesn't know would certainly be advantageous to the Soviet authorities in coping with any terrorists that they may have.)

So the Soviets have no clear and present incentive to join in international activity against terrorism. On the contrary, they have given cautious aid and encouragement to some forms of terrorism (less than right-wing propagandists suggest, but more than the left admits). But it would be wrong to conclude, as most right-wing analysts do, that the Soviets are operating under a doctrinal imperative to destabilize the West. The Soviet authorities—despite their ideological bravado—know well that a destabilized West could be extremely dangerous, and specifically dangerous to the Soviet Union. The superpowers do have an elemental common interest—in survival. That is why limited superpower consensus has been possible in the past, and that is why it remains a possibility for the future with regard to terrorism. Such consensus could take the form of a joint warning that any country harboring terrorists would no longer be allowed to invoke its sovereignty as a protection against international intervention. Once superpower agreement had been reached, that warning could be embodied in a mandatory resolution of the Security Council.

We are very far indeed from that point, though here as elsewhere thought should not treat present actuality as if it were eternal. . . .

20

Reflections on the Eradication of Terrorism

Walter Laqueur

I

...How to eradicate terrorism? Moralists believe that terrorism is the natural response to injustice, oppression and persecution. Hence their seemingly obvious conclusion: remove the underlying causes and terrorism will wither away! This sounds plausible enough, for happy and content people are unlikely to commit savage acts of violence. Although this may be true as an abstract general proposition, it seldom applies in the real world, which is never quite free of conflicts.

The historical record shows that, while in the nineteenth century terrorism frequently developed in response to repression, the correlation between grievance and terrorism in our day and age is far less obvious. The record also shows that in more recent times the more severe the repression, the less terrorism tends to occur. This is an uncomfortable, shocking fact that has therefore encountered much resistance. But it is still true that terrorism in Spain gathered strength only after General Franco died, that the terrorist upsurges in West Germany, France and Turkey took place under social democratic or left-of-center governments, that the same is true with regard to Peru and Colombia, and that more such examples could easily be adduced.

Terrorism has never had a chance in an effective dictatorship, but hardly a major democratic country has entirely escaped it. There is a limit to the perfection of political institutions, and, however just and humane the social order, there will always be a few people deeply convinced that it ought to be radically changed and that it can be changed only through violent action. The murder of Sweden's prime minister, Olof Palme, is just one illustration that shows that "objective factors" cannot account for the actions of a fringe group.

Nationalist-separatist terrorism has been doing better than that of the extreme left and right, and it is not difficult to understand why. National groups and minorities usually have grievances, and some of them may be quite justified. In some instances, they can be put right; in others assuaged, but frequently neither may be possible. In an ideal world, each

Note: some footnotes have been deleted, and another has been renumbered.

group of people, however small, claiming the right of full independence and statehood, should receive it. But in some cases, given the lack of national homogeneity and the intermingling of ethnic and religious groups, no basic redress may be feasible.

Even at this late date, it may be possible for the Turks to accept responsibility for the Armenian massacres during World War I, to apologize to the descendants of the victims, and to show contrition. But an Armenian state on Turkish territory . . . would be an absurdity: Armenians no longer live in eastern Turkey, nor do they have any intention of settling there. Nor would a Sikh state in the Punjab be viable. The Sikhs, in any case, are not an oppressed minority in contemporary India: the president of India is a Sikh and so are most of India's military leaders. The majority of Sikhs do not even want a state of their own.

The Basque Homeland and Liberty group (ETA) and the Corsican militants are also fighting for independent statehood. But even if these ministates would be viable, which is uncertain, these groups' demands are by no means shared by most of their fellow countrymen, let alone by the majority populations in either the Basque region or Corsica, which are of different ethnic backgrounds (Spanish and French, respectively) from the terrorist groups.

Nor is it certain that the establishment of new, independent states would put an end to terrorism. On the contrary, there could well be an intensification of the struggle between various terrorist groups, between moderates who want to proceed with the business of statehood and radicals who claim that what has been achieved is only a beginning and that the borders of the new state should be expanded. The Tamils in Sri Lanka have been fighting with as much relish against each other as against their common enemy, and there is no reason to assume that this would stop if they were to get a state of their own.

The high tide of PLO activities both on the political and the terrorist level was in the mid-1970s. True, even then much of Middle Eastern terrorism had only a tenuous connection with Israel but was indigenous to the region. Since then this trend has become even more pronounced: some of the terrorist groups, such as Abu Nidal's or Abu Mussa's, serve the highest bidder among the Arab governments. They have killed considerably more Arabs than Israelis. As for Shi'ite terrorism, this never had much to do with Israel except at times when the Israelis happened to get in the Shi'ites' way.

No effort should be spared to pursue the peace process between Arabs and Israelis. But few serious students of this conflict argue that if a Palestinian state were to come into existence in the foreseeable future, terrorism would decrease. No settlement that recognizes Israel would be to the liking of Palestinian radicals. This does not make the search for a solution of the conflict undesirable or unnecessary, but there should be no illusions with regard to its likely consequences so far as the persistence of terrorism is concerned.

II

It is frequently argued that there is no defense against extremists willing to sacrifice their lives and that arresting or shooting terrorists cannot solve the problem because the "blood of the martyrs is the seed of the church." Historical experience does not confirm such wisdom.

The number of potential terrorists inside every country is limited. On the basis of a painstaking analysis, a recent study [reached] the obvious conclusion that "the more terrorists in prison, the lower the violence level."[1] This does not, of course, apply to a mass insurrection supported by the overwhelming majority of the population, but it is true with regard to terrorist groups.

Shi'ite propensity to engage in terrorist suicide attacks has been very much exaggerated. True, there have been a few cases, but not more than four or five of such operations. Furthermore, this readiness to commit suicide can be found at all times and for many reasons. Ten members of the Irish Republican Army starved themselves to death—despite the express ban of the Catholic church against suicide; members of Baader-Meinhof also killed themselves, not to mention the mass suicide in Jonestown. When the Japanese authorities asked for kamikaze candidates during the last year of the war, many thousands volunteered and some 4,600 were killed. It is not so much a matter of a specific religion but of fanaticism, and a psychological predisposition. What Voltaire wrote about the subject seems still relevant today: the entire species (of fanatics) is divided into two classes—the first does nought but pray and die, the second wants to reign and massacre.

Terrorism has been stamped out with great ease not only by modern dictatorships; it has been defeated also by governments that are anything but modern. In 1981, Ayatollah Khomeini's former allies from the left, the mujahedeen and some other groups, turned against the new rulers of Iran. They were many and experienced; within three months they succeeded in killing the prime minister, many chiefs of police, half the government and the executive committee of the ruling party, not to mention dozens of members of parliament. Perhaps never before had a terrorist onslaught been so massive and so successful. Yet within another three months, the terrorists either were dead or had escaped abroad. The government acted with great brutality; it killed without discrimination; it extracted information by means of torture; it refused as a matter of principle to extend medical help to injured terrorists. And it broke the back of the terrorist movement. . . .

The power of the state is infinitely greater than that of terrorists, and it will always prevail, provided there is the determination or the ruthlessness to do so. But can a democratic society subdue terrorism without surrendering the values central to the system? Again, experience

[1] Christopher Hewitt, *The Effectiveness of Anti-Terrorist Policies*. Lanham, Md.: University Press of America, 1984, p. 47.

shows that it can be done without great difficulty. The Italian authorities defeated the Red Brigades, while acting strictly within the law, by a mixture of overdue political reform, penetration of the terrorist ranks, and the promise of substantial reduction in prison terms to the penitents. Terrorist movements do not have an unlimited life span. If terrorists realize after a few years that the murder of a few politicians (and many innocents) has not brought them any nearer their goals, their resolve weakens.

The nationalist-separatist terrorists hold out longer, for their basis of support is stronger and they may have assistance from foreign countries. But even in Northern Ireland and the Basque region of Spain, the level of violence [declined in the 1980s], and the Armenian Asala has all but disappeared.

A dialectical process seems to dictate the policy of democratic societies toward terrorists. As long as terrorism is no more than a nuisance, a democracy will rightly resist any attempt to curtail its traditional freedoms. Once terrorism becomes more than a nuisance, once the normal functioning of society is affected, there will be overwhelming pressure on the government to defeat the threat by all available means. Hence the paradoxical conclusion that the more successful the terrorists, the nearer their ultimate defeat. There are exceptions to every rule, but in this case they are few and far between. . . .

III

As internal terrorism has declined in the Western world [during] the last decade and as international terrorism has become more frequent, the need for full international cooperation against terrorism has been invoked a great many times. It is a hopeless undertaking, however, as long as some states sponsor, finance, equip and train terrorists and provide sanctuaries for them. Spokesmen for democratic societies will continue to proclaim that terrorism is abhorred and condemned by the whole civilized world. But the civilized world does not extend that far these days, and proceedings in the United Nations have shown that it is very difficult to have terrorism condemned even on paper, unless some of the leading communist or Third World countries just happen to be on the receiving end of terrorist operations—which helps to clear their minds but, unfortunately, not for very long.

These debates will no doubt go on for many years; it may be wrong to pay too much attention to them. International terrorism is an extra-legal activity, and thus the contribution of our legal experts is bound to have a limited effect. Specific bilateral agreements or pacts among several countries may be of certain value; the exchange of information between NATO countries and others has improved during the last decade, and as a result some terrorist attacks have been prevented. Under certain conditions quiet diplomacy, such as issuing unpublicized warnings, has been of help; in other circumstances preemptive publicity has helped. Most sponsors of state terrorism do not want their involvement to become known. They will, at the very least, temporarily scale down their involvement once they realize that what was meant to be a high-value, low-risk undertaking might escalate into an armed conflict in which the risks are high and the value is at best uncertain.

But truly effective concerted action against terrorism is possible only on the basis of the strategy first advocated by the nineteenth-century Russian terrorists. This is "hitting the center," meaning those rulers of countries who are sponsors of international terrorism. But hitting the center may not be easy for a variety of reasons. The responsibility for a certain terrorist action or campaign cannot always be easily proved. The aggrieved party may find it difficult to provide sufficient hard evidence. Smoking guns are seldom left at the scene of the crime in this kind of business. Even if there is evidence, to reveal it would often mean giving away the identity of well-placed intelligence sources in the terrorist hierarchy, of which there are probably not many.

For a country or a group of countries subject to attacks by international terrorism, there are, broadly speaking, three ways to react. Given the natural inertia of democratic governments and the difficulties involved, the obvious reaction is to condemn the attack but to refrain from any physical act of retaliation. As long as these attacks occur relatively rarely and inasmuch as they do not result in many victims, this is a feasible policy. But lack of reaction is usually interpreted as a sign of weakness, in which case the attacks will become more frequent and murderous. The sponsors of international terrorism resemble in many respects children trying to find out by trial and error how far they can go in provoking the adults until punishment will be meted out to them.

If an escalation in international terrorist attacks does take place, the obvious way to retaliate is to pay back the sponsors in their own coin. As General George Grivas, head of the EOKA (the National Organization of Cypriot Combatants) in Cyprus and a man of great experience in the field, once put it: to catch a mouse, one uses a cat, not a tank (or an aircraft carrier). But democratic countries may not have cats, meaning a truly effective covert action capability, or "active measures," to use the well-known Soviet term. Even if they have a capability of this kind, they may find it difficult to use, be it because terrorist acts are much easier to carry out in open societies than in dictatorships or because those who engage in covert action on behalf of a democratic country are not normally permitted to kill enemy leaders. In the United States there is an absolute prohibition by presidential order.

What alternatives exist? In some cases diplomatic action may have some success; on other occasions economic sanctions may have a certain impact, but only if there is agreement between the major Western countries. Otherwise, in the absence of "cats," retaliation takes the form of military action. Such escalation involves risks: innocent people are likely to get killed, and those who retaliate will be blamed for creating a new dangerous situation. This has been the fate of the Israelis, who for a long time combined covert action with surgical air strikes (which, on occasion, hit the wrong target). It was also the fate of the United States after the strike against Libya in April 1986: those who retaliate become attackers, and there will be a great deal of handwringing and dire warnings. No government will lightly take such a course of action. It will only do so if it has good reason to believe that the alternative—refraining from counteraction—would have fateful consequences, and if public opinion at home is so strongly in favor of retaliation that it cannot safely be ignored. This is particularly true with regard to a superpower, whose freedom of action is by necessity more restrained than that of a small country. The more powerful a country, the stronger the constraints to act cautiously, for everything a major power does is important; it may turn a local incident into an international conflict. . . .

21

Framing a Moral Response to Terrorism

James Tunstead Burchael

It would perhaps be misleading to address the ethics of terrorism and response to terrorism by accepting without question the fashionable presumption that terrorism is a development so discontinuous with the traditions of warfare that is deserves unconventional moral scrutiny. On the contrary, terrorism, like the many enlargements of savagery before it, is a lineal descendant of traditional warfare. It can best be understood and evaluated by analogy with conventional conflict. And I am increasingly of the opinion that it raises not old questions about new kinds of combat but new questions about all the old forms of war. It is warfare's newest and most sobering progeny. . . .

There are . . . three realities that terrorism introduces into the field of belligerency that move beyond the well-staked battleground of conventional warfare:

1. Terrorism is the warfare of the desperate.
2. Terrorism is a warfare of solidarity: a people against a whole people.
3. Terrorism is a warfare of selective targeting.

A MORAL ESTIMATE OF TERRORISM AS WARFARE: *NEMO ME IMPUNE LACESSIT*

Now let us follow up the [proposition] that terrorism is in fact not a rejection of warfare but the resort to new and disconcerting measures that are the direct offspring of what we had previously grown familiar with as conventional warfare. To put the thesis to the test, let us see what results if we attempt to apply the traditional ethical doctrine on conventional warfare to the response to terrorism.

The tradition distinguished between the right to go to war (*jus in bellum*) and rightful conduct in war (*jus in bello*). Much of what has passed as moral discrimination between armaments and tactics in war, as defined by treaties, laws, and military codes of discipline, is little more than convention. It simply states what most warring nations agree not to do in order not to risk the same in return. We do not butcher prisoners because

Note: footnotes have been deleted.

we want ours to survive. This is a convention, and indeed a desirable convention. But it is not a canon of morality, as if there would be clear reasons why it would be moral to protect prisoners but also moral to shoot active combatants.

This concentrates the fullest weight of moral inquiry and decision making on the *jus in bellum*: what justifies going to war in the first place? According to the Western tradition of justified warfare, there are five principal requisites for a war to be morally undertaken:

1. Action by a legitimate national authority.
2. A just grievance.
3. The exhaustion of other alternatives.
4. A reasonable likelihood of success.
5. More good foreseen than evil.

Let us see whether these criteria can be applied to counterterrorism.

Action by a Legitimate National Authority

The issue here is not whether a government faced by terrorists is such an authority but whether its adversaries are. The international convention is that nations declare war only on other nations. We are brought to ask, however, whether this need necessarily be so.

A problem presented by terrorism is that while it is in fact an act of armed belligerency—an act of war—it is treated legally as if it were instead an act of crime. While the terrorizing group is acting in solidarity, the nation that is the object of its belligerency acts on the fiction that it faces only individual miscreants and restricts itself to dealing with those persons who can be convicted of actual crimes. International law may need to supply a new category or, better, an extended category of warfare. If a whole people is in fact actively mounting hostilities against a nation (think of the Kurds against Iran, Iraq, and Turkey, or the Mafia against Italy, or the French connection against the United States), then the target nation ought have some deliberative and formalized way of declaring the terrorist group as a whole its adversary. Thus, for instance, the Irish Republican Army Provos as a group might be declared by Great Britain to be its adversary at war. Any member of the belligerent group, not just one who was convictable of violent acts of terrorism, would be at risk of capture.

In the international legal community, the first moves have already begun to accommodate terrorism and its opposition within the conventions of warfare, just as had been done years before for insurgency. But in the meantime sovereign nations are left relatively free to decide whether to acknowledge terrorist enemies as formal belligerents. To date few have been willing to do this.

Furthermore, since terrorism is often undertaken by peoples who are in arms precisely because they have been denied the opportunity for national self-determination, they cannot be represented by a recognized government. The nations they oppose use this as an excuse to deny them legitimate recognition as conventional belligerents, but this is often a self-serving exercise of political self-interest. That way, the dissidents can be classified as criminals instead of as belligerents. . . .

It is the legal convention among nations that we recognize established governments as representing the national populace. But there are some countries where this not true. Is our first obligation of fellowship to the unpopular government or to the people? Are there ways in which we can render the government its formal due while also supporting the people's just claims on our aid? And if this is impossible, then should we not on occasion withdraw our recognition of a government and establish our links of fellowship with other, more credible representatives of the people? If a government is our terrorist adversary, could we not declare war on that government without declaring war on the population? For that matter, could we not declare war on a nonnational group that has in effect entered into systematic hostilities against us? These are possibilites worth considering.

Current moral inquiry on the subject of terrorism has been puzzling over the acceptability of preemption. This may not be the best way of approaching the question. It is only by regarding terrorist activities as distinct acts of criminal violence that we could speak of preemption. The criminal law does not easily permit authorities to move against persons who are contemplating a crime. But if a group is described and declared to be at war, then an action to fend off their intended strike is not preemption but part of a continuing campaign. Once again, the ethical picture depends on the model one chooses to use. If terrorism is merely a crime, then it must be dealt with by according due process to individual persons for individual actions. If it is a state of belligerency, then it must be dealt with by warfare and by the restraints appropriate to warfare.

For any response to a terrorist group to be ethical, then, a nation must acknowledge popular leadership in its adversaries as pragmatically as it recognizes de facto governments after coups, and it must consider the group as a whole as its true challenger.

A Just Grievance

As in the criterion of legitimate authority, the question here is not so much whether a government has a just grievance in defending itself against terrorists but what grievances the terrorists are wanting to redress. . . .

A nation that must address a terrorist adversary, then, has the highest moral obligation to discern what the terrorists have experienced and what are their complaints. That nation must, ironically, make a reflective moral appraisal of the grievances of its adversary before allowing itself to respond with the use of force. In the face of passion and anger, the offended and affronted government is morally compelled to use patience and dispassionate objectivity. Granted the heroic difficulty of such objectivity, it may be that nations should turn to detached, judicious outsiders to render their opinion before any decision is made. A moral decision to move into war against terrorists requires mighty patience and discernment of grievances.

Exhaustion of Other Alternatives

The first alternative always to be considered is the satisfaction of terrorists' demands, and nothing could be less agreeable to their target nation.

The natural instinct of all victims of terrorism is outrage and the desire to retaliate. But leaders of state and of the armed services, perhaps more than any other citizens, have the duty not to operate on instinct, especially this sort of instinct, for it is most likely to increase the force of the vortex of violence. . . .

I am not making the case that terrorists should be given satisfaction simply because they have indulged in violence. My point is that terrorists should not be denied redress and satisfaction simply because they are terrorists. It is in the national interest not to be blinded by outrage but to ascertain whether we are dealing with people who are themselves the victims of earlier, and possibly more grievous, injury: injury that we may have inflicted or conspired in or from which we can give them relief. To fail in this inquiry out of anger is to fail in one of the primary duties of patient statecraft.

When there is no justice in terrorist demands, then the next alternative is measured retaliation: purposefully restrained, with the promise of harsher reprisal to follow. Should that not stay the hand of terrorism, then is the time to declare that belligerency has begun. After that, the strategy is not to await further strikes in order to strike back but to move to capture or to destroy the terrorists. . . .

Reasonable Likelihood of Success

The only success is peace, and the only steady ground under peace is justice. A nation must ask whether a belligerent response to a terrorist attack will quench hostility or only foment more determined resistance and widespread sympathy. Will it enlarge the conflict? Will it rupture the relations we now maintain with the sponsoring group? They may only be civil and formal, but even so they may offer access to reconciliation that rupture would remove. Would a belligerent response lead to confrontation with a more formidable patron power?

Every nation must ask its people, especially its military and its police, to absorb outrage when no reasonable advantage is likely to accrue from a hostile response. It must be endured. Once again, one sees the difference between an adversary group of terrorist criminals and an adversary nation. The one group may much more easily be neutralized by armed response than the other, which ultimately cannot be either squelched or destroyed. It must be rendered peaceable, and this is not deftly done by belligerent response.

On the other hand, the principal service of war is to make people once again prefer peace. Not until the two peoples loathe the war more than the price they must pay for peace will they cease their hostilities. And there are some injustices so despicable that men and women will count their lives cheap in resisting them. It is this sort of readiness to sacrifice oneself that we must be noticing in our terrorist adversaries, especially if they are an entire people. There is little reasonable likelihood of success against such a people except by coming to terms.

More Good Foreseen than Evil

The primary risk in responding to terrorism is the moral danger to the respondent: what brutalization of character do we incur if we enter into comparable hostilities or, on the other hand, if we stand idly by? By striking out at terrorists, one may seize the advantage. But by striking out intemperately, a nation may sacrifice the advantage of moral sympathy from other nations. The difficulty in applying this criterion for justified belligerency is that one must compare such incommensurables: human life with property, urgent needs of the moment with long-term values, individual welfare with the common good.

The ultimate good is the creation of peace. Every response to terrorism must have as its desired outcome that the terrorist people would eventually become allies. Thus we must measure how far we can go in destroying their dignity and driving them into insensate and irredeemable hostility.

When terrorism is an act of covert warfare initiated by another state and all parties know that, we face a severe conflict. Do we wish to suppress public mention of the true source of the violence in order not to exacerbate what remains of our public relationship, or is the crisis so acute and our opportunity to prevail so likely that we would choose a public showdown? What response is vigorous enough to maintain the respect that may discourage further attempts at terrorism yet not so headlong that we are entrapped into needless forfeiture of life and property? Is there a response available that might cope with the terrorist program itself but that, once introduced into accepted usage, would find us as an especially vulnerable and exposed potential victim?

THE GOAL: PEACE NOT CAPITULATION: *OPUS JUSTITIAE PAX*

Many conflicts come to apparent cloture through the capitulation of one party to another, yet peace is not really created, and a resentment is left to fester until another more violent day.

The criteria for rightful entry into belligerency against another power offer an array of challenges to those in public office who must determine how to respond to terrorism. The just war test meets the terrorist situation well: well enough to lead to the expectation that terrorism will eventually be seen not as an anomaly in international relations but as one more of the degenerate progeny of conventional warfare.

Weapons development early in this century had elicited three distinct reactions. Some thought the new devices were horrendous and therefore immoral. Others thought they were so horrendous that people would become more reluctant to engage in war. Still others thought that they were indeed horrendous but that they only brought out more clearly how horrendous all warfare had always been. The realities of terrorism may justify all three conclusions. Terrorism is indeed savage and inhumane. It is a moral quagmire into which a nation steps at its peril, for it may be as bottomless as quicksand. And yet it brings to the light the essential character of warfare, which, despite conventions and mutual restraints, is a form of inhumane savagery that threatens at any moment to break loose into uncontrollable destruction. Inquiry into the nature and ethical imperatives of terrorism is sound only if we do not imagine that it is inhumane by contrast with war, which is humane. Conventional warfare is conventionally inhumane.

There is a double paradox about peace being the desired outcome of belligerency. On the one hand, you may not be preserving the peace by refusing to fight. Thomas Jefferson, who had explicitly renounced any resort to warfare, eventually sent the navy to suppress the Barbary pirates. He explained, "Against such a banditti, war had become less ruinous than peace, for then peace was a war on one side only." Yet on the other hand, armed intervention can destroy the possibility of peace when its target is a resolute group of men and women who believe themselves to be defending their families, their homes and homeland, their faith and their freedom: in short, the precious things people are willing to die for. Every decision to use force or to abstain from force can be justified only by its realistic claim to make peace more possible.

22

Proactive Responses to Terrorism: Reprisals, Preemption, and Retribution

Neil C. Livingstone

The options for combating and suppressing terrorism can be visualized as a continuum of response moving from stoicism, static defensive measures, and diplomatic initiatives at one pole to the force options at the opposite end of the spectrum. In this connection, proactive responses to terrorism can be separated into three categories: reprisals, preemption, and retribution. All can be viewed as coercive measures short of war, although each is also applicable in the context of general warfare. All three proactive forms of response have a legal justification under Article 51 of the U.N. Charter, which reserves to nations the inherent right of self-defense. If we accept the fact that terrorism, especially that sponsored and supported by foreign governments, is a form of aggression, then the United States may adopt and employ proactive measures as a traditional form of self-help while still attempting to find peaceful long-term solutions to the problem.

[Hugh] Tovar has argued that force should be used "whenever we judge that it is justified and feasible" and not simply as a last resort, maintaining that to regard it as a final option would, in effect, mean that it would never be employed. Although the United States should be free to consider armed strikes against terrorists at any time, nevertheless every feasible and effective option short of force should be explored before crossing the force threshold. The operative term here is *effective*. If the only effective response is force, then the liberal democracies of the West should not shrink from using force to protect their interests, citizens, and property. Force, moreover, may be used in some cases even more effectively in combination with other forms of retorsion and coercion short of hostilities designed to isolate, weaken, and punish sponsoring states....

Force is a deterrent to terrorism. Nevertheless, the resort to force by a democratic society is always a difficult and usually reluctantly reached decision. Because democratic societies are founded on the rule of law, there is a natural tendency to want to solve international problems by diplomacy and recourse to other legal devices rather than by force.

Note: footnotes have been deleted.

However, the threat posed by international terrorism and its patrons is so serious that there is need by the liberal democracies of the West to protect their moral order and values with the judicious use of force.

REPRISALS

Reprisals, defined as coercive measures directed by a state against another state in response to (or 'in retaliation for') illegal acts of the latter for the "purpose of obtaining, either directly or indirectly, reparation or satisfaction of the illegal act," are as old as history itself and recognized under international law. Reprisals involve the exaction of punishment on those who have committed an illegal act for which there is no other form of peaceful redress. For them to be legal and recognized under international law, reprisals cannot be capricious and open-ended and must conform to certain carefully defined conditions and limitations. . . . [To] be legitimate, reprisals must be precipitated by a prior illegal act, preceded by an unsatisfied demand for peaceful redress of the injury, and in proportion to the initial action.

Other limitations governing reprisals include prohibitions against injuring innocent third parties, continuing reprisals after reparations have been made by the guilty state, engaging in reprisals against reprisals, and resorting to reprisals before all peaceful means to obtain redress have been exhausted. To be legal, reprisals must also be carried out by states. Until the 1856 Treaty of Paris, private citizens who had suffered injury or loss at the hands of a national from another country could receive authorization from their own government to carry out reprisals—usually the seizure of property—against fellow citizens of the national who was responsible for the original offense. Even the U.S. Constitution provides for the granting of letters of marque and reprisal by the Congress, a privilege specifically denied to the states.

One of the problems with the traditional legal limitations on reprisals is the insistence that all peaceful remedies be exhausted before carrying out any form of retaliation. As the Israelis have maintained in disregarding efforts at peaceful redress before undertaking military reprisals in southern Lebanon, such efforts would be a waste of time and unlikely to produce tangible results. Furthermore, many observers hold that only a very short window exists wherein reprisals against terrorists are relevant and can be effectively linked to a precipitating terrorist incident. Under normal circumstances, such a window for military action is probably no more than seventy-two hours. After that, the horror of the original terrorist incident generally recedes, and both the public and world opinion begin to have difficulty in connecting the original action to the response. To be most effective, recent military experience suggest, reprisals should be swift and discriminating, or in other words whenever possible directed at those specifically responsible for the actual terrorist incident.

Public attitudes in the West reject notions of collective responsibility where members of a whole group or nationality are held responsible for the actions of a minority—which in most cases they are powerless to influence—and punished accordingly. During the 1984 hijacking of a Kuwaiti jetliner to Tehran by Shiite terrorist, two Americans were brutally murdered and others abused and tortured simply because they were Americans. The American public was outraged at the thought that nationality alone was justification enough for murder. . . . To adopt a policy of indiscriminate reprisals against whole populations for the terrorist crimes of a few is to accept the distorted value system of the terrorists and become like them.

Criticism of reprisals also comes from those who believe that they are a cruel and ineffective strategy for dealing with terrorism. . . . Critics of such . . . policies contend that reprisals . . . simply feed the cycle of violence . . . without materially affecting the terrorists and guerrillas who are the real source of the problem. [The] 1983 shelling of the Chouf Mountains in Lebanon by the U.S. battleship *New Jersey* following attacks on U.S. Marines could not reasonably have been expected to punish those specifically responsible for the incidents. Although enemy command and forward observation positions were hit, reportedly killing high-ranking Syrian military personnel, the naval bombardment also inflicted casualties on the civilian population of the region without having a real impact on those who actually carried out the attacks on the marines. Using the *New Jersey* to fight terrorists is rather like employing a sledge hammer to kill a bothersome flea.

When considering military reprisals against terrorists, a number of suggestions relating to practical, legal, moral, and public relations issues must be given careful weight. Reprisals should be carried out as soon after the terrorist attack as possible so as not to permit the public to lose sight of the original incident which provoked the retaliation. And whenever possible, there should be a direct, provable link between the target of the reprisal and the terrorist incident. Striking at a terrorist training camp, for example, where members of a particular group that carried out the terrorist attack were trained, or at a facility where a particular bomb was assembled would generally be good targets that the public would understand.

The law of proportionality should always be borne in mind. Public opinion in the United States will never accept massive retaliation for a minor offense; it will be regarded as mean-spirited and beneath the dignity of a great power.

According to Michael Walzer, although a terrorist attack may be aimed at innocent civilians, "the reprisal must not be so aimed. Moreover, the 'reprisals' must take care that civilians are not incidental victims of their attack." Thus, whenever possible, civilian targets should be avoided, although as [U.S.] Secretary of State [George] Shultz has contended, some civilian casualties may be an inevitable product of reprisal scenarios.

Terrorists have a propensity for locating their installations near hospitals and in heavily populated civilian districts precisely because to do so affords them protection and raises the stakes to any nation eager to carry out reprisals. Nevertheless, to punish large numbers of innocent civilian noncombatants as a side product of military strikes against terrorists is generally a poor policy and one likely to bring censure on the country initiating the reprisals. Such behavior runs the risk of making the states in opposition seem little different from the terrorists and augurs for smaller, more surgical operations designed to minimize casualties to innocent parties.

Reprisals against states that sponsor terrorists and use terrorism to achieve their national purposes always run the risk of precipitating either a general state of war or additional terrorist attacks. . . .

Reprisals should be overt, rather than covert, if they are to have a cathartic effect on the victimized nation or serve as a deterrent to future attacks. While deniable missions and other black work can disrupt terrorist operations and punish terrorists for past transgressions, reprisals must be publicly acknowledged to have maximum impact.

Finally, the choice of the appropriate instrument with which to carry out a reprisal is all important. Without a full range of options in this regard, a nation can find itself employing the wrong instrument to achieve the right effect, a sure formula for eventual disaster. A measured response to intimidation and violence is required, ranging from low-signature, highly surgical operations to air strikes and full-scale military operations.

By contrast to Napoleon, who viewed reprisals as "a sorry recourse," reprisals have utility in combating terrorism. Nevertheless, they must be employed with restraint and then only when other alternatives do not exist. There is moral and legal justification for states carrying out reprisals against terrorists and their supporters, but reprisals remain an imprecise method of dealing with the problem. To be successful, reprisals generally require a rational adversary who can be intimidated into showing restraint rather than suffering the consequences that might flow from a particular reprisal. Moreover, if reprisals are to serve as a real deterrent, the state that threatens retaliation in the event that it suffers some injury at the hands of terrorists must be prepared to carry out its reprisals expeditiously and without hesitation or vacillation if an attack occurs. Otherwise threats of retaliation will have little credibility, and the victimized nation will suffer the second indignity of being seen as a paper tiger.

PREEMPTION

Preemption can be defined as striking in advance of hostile action to prevent its occurrence and to avoid suffering injury. Preemption involves many more difficult questions than reprisals since it takes place before an actual terrorist attack or injury is suffered and therefore amounts to a response without a prior illegal action. Preemption is not designed to punish or deter, as are reprisals, but rather to protect; in other words, it is designed to prevent a terrorist attack from being carried out and thus to avoid the related deaths, injuries, and destruction.

Preemptive responses run the risk of relinquishing the moral high ground that derives from being the victim of an attack and therefore entitled to some form of redress, including the possibility of reprisals. In fact, a nation carrying out a preemptive attack may appear to the rest of the world as an aggressor rather than a potential victim, and in order to win acceptance of its action, the nation engaged in the preemptive attack will have to make a strong and persuasive public case to justify its action. This, however, can be exceedingly difficult and in some instances impossible. Few potential terrorist attacks can be verified in advance. Intelligence collection and analysis is an imprecise science, and policymakers often are required to make decisions based on imperfect intelligence where conclusions represent only probabilities, not hard facts. As a result, intelligence officials may only be able to advise policymakers that there is a 70 or 80 percent probability of a particular attack occurring, and they will be forced to decide whether that level of certainty is enough to act upon. The lower the level of certainty, the greater the incumbent risks in taking preemptive action. . . . Thus, preemptive strikes against terrorists raise serious practical and public relations issues, which will tend to discourage policymakers from such a course of action in all but the most high-consequence and solidly documentable circumstances.

"When you see a rattlesnake poised to strike," President Franklin Delano Roosevelt once observed, "you do not wait until he has struck before you crush him." Nowhere is it written that the United States must absorb terrorist onslaughts before striking back. From the standpoint of self-defense, offensive action may well be justified; hesitation by policymakers to strike first in the face of a bona-fide threat from terrorists will be roundly condemned by their own citizens, especially if their restraint permits a terrorist outrage to occur that results in extensive destruction and loss of life.

The problem of preemption is brought into sharp focus by the prospect of terrorists armed with weapons of mass destruction or conspiring to strike at a critically sensitive or high-consequence target. The outcome of such an attack would likely be too terrible for a president to accept, and therefore he would have to make every effort to prevent the attack from occurring.

In this connection, preemption need not automatically entail air strikes or the insertion of commando teams to attack a specific facility or group of people. The United States has, for example, been engaged, along with other Western nations, in a quiet struggle to disrupt terrorist operations and communications through a process of disinformation, dirty tricks, and so-called black work. For example, Western intelligence operatives posing as illicit arms merchants have sold terrorists defective weapons and equipment. In one case ultrasensitive detonators were given to a group of terrorist bomb builders who lost their lives when the bomb they were loading into a vehicle went off prematurely.

The following guidelines are proposed to govern acts of preemption. Just as conspiracy to commit a crime is illegal from the standpoint of domestic law, so too should conspiracies by foreign terrorists to harm the interests, citizens, and property of the United States be deemed illegal in advance of the actual attack and as appropriate justification for preemptive action. In this regard, the United States should invoke the right of self-defense and mount an effective campaign to explain the underlying reasons motivating its action.

Preemptive action should represent a last resort when no other remedy exists to prevent a terrorist attack from occurring. When advance information is obtained describing a forthcoming terrorist attack, publicly or privately threatening a patron state or the country where the attack will occur with certain reprisals if it permits the attack to be carried out may be a more effective strategy than preemption. Because preemptive strikes necessarily involve violations of another nation's sovereignty and thus could be considered a form of aggression, every effort should be made to get the nation where the terrorists are located to deal with the problem utilizing its own methods and legal procedures. If, however, a nation repeatedly demonstrates an inability . . . or an unwillingness . . . to take appropriate action, then it should not be necessary for a potential victim nation to waste time once more and leave itself vulnerable to attack before striking to eliminate the threat.

The amount of force used should be adequate to remove the threat and no more. Any disproportional use of force runs the risk of undermining the position of the threatened state and ultimately is itself a threat to the peace (with the preemptive strike viewed simply as a pretext for aggression). Moreover, any preemptive action should be highly discriminate and clearly defined so as to prevent the needless loss of life.

If the United States desires to prevent injury from occurring to its national interests, citizens, and property, it must be prepared—as a last resort—to preempt terrorist attacks. Anything less is a policy without teeth.

RETRIBUTION

In response to the bloody massacre of Israeli athletes at Munich in 1972 and a wave of attacks on Israeli diplomats, aircraft, supporters abroad, and other targets, the government of Prime Minister Golda Meir concluded that "current methods of dealing with terrorists had become obsolete overnight" and that a "new approach to the terrorist threat had to be devised." The enemy in this case was the shadowy Palestinian group known as Black September, which had been established by Yasir Arafat and the high command of the PLO as a deniable unit without offices and formal infrastructure that could carry on the terrorist struggle while the PLO itself moved toward public respectability.

The Israeli answer to the challenge was to create a new organization committed to fight fire with fire. Known as the Mivtzan Elohim ("Wrath of God"), its members were drawn from the Israeli defense and intelligence establishment. In the months that followed, the Israelis relentlessly struck back at the Black September terrorists, conducting daring raids into Beirut to kill the top leadership of the organization, tracking down Palestinian operatives in Europe and other locations and assassinating them, and broadcasting a message to terrorists everywhere that Israeli lives could not be taken with impunity.

In July 1973, a Wrath of God operation in Norway went sour, and a young Moroccan waiter was mistakenly killed in the belief that he was Black September's operations chief, Ali Hassan Salameh. Apparently the waiter, who bore a striking resemblance to Salameh, had been set up by the Black September agents who knew that the death of an innocent man would bring public censure down on the Wrath of God. Although the Wrath of God purportedly was disbanded after the Norwegian incident, its work continued under the direct auspices of the Mossad, and it was not until 1979 that Salameh was actually killed. By late 1973, however, Black September had ceased to exist, its remaining members demoralized and fearful of being assassinated. The activities of the Israeli counterterrorist operation had not ended Palestinian terrorism but had certainly disrupted its operations and undermined its capability to carry out sophisticated attacks. . . .

Today the United States should give serious consideration to restructuring its antiterrorist force to approximate the unit created by the Israelis. This new unit should be given the responsibility of taking the offensive against international terrorism, and should be trained to deal with this challenge equally well on paramilitary, intelligence, and investigative levels. This force would carry the war to the terrorists, turning the hunters into the hunted by disrupting their lines of communications and supply, gathering intelligence, infiltrating their organizations, sabotaging their weapons and plans, exposing their operations to friendly governments, and buttressing normal police investigative and assault tactics. The United States should work closely with and support any friendly government and its police and security apparatus to track down terrorists and ensure that they are punished for their crimes, no matter how long the hunt may take or how far afield it may range.

Today terrorists are still one of the least likely categories of international criminal to be caught and punished, and this has a corrosive impact on the international order because it serves to embolden terrorists who otherwise would have to be fearful for their own lives. The only durable way to remedy this situation is to turn up the heat and by so doing make it clear to terrorists that they will be pursued until they are caught and punished. This determination will communicate to state sponsors of terrorism that a cost will be attached to their support and they themselves are not immune from the retribution exacted by victimized Western governments.

"Keep running after a dog," goes the old saying, "and he will never bite you." By taking the war to the terrorists, it will be possible to keep them off balance, sow suspicion within their ranks, undermine their sources of support, and erode their confidence. They will be forced to stay constantly on the run and to expend scarce resources for their own security that might otherwise have gone to buying arms and underwriting new operations.

A policy designed to target the actual terrorists responsible for specific crimes is infinitely more humane than blasting heavily populated villages in reprisal air raids or shelling them with 16 inch guns from a battleship. By targeting clearly identified terrorists and relentlessly pursuing them, it will be possible to ensure that the guilty are punished and the innocent spared. . . .

CONCLUSION

The United States may yet perish as a nation of the delusion that it is necessary to be more moral than anyone else. There exists today a void in the international milieu composed of countries that do not subscribe to the laws and civilized norms that are the bedrock of the international system—nations . . . which observe traditionally accepted rules of behavior only when it serves their purposes. Similarly, transnational terrorists and third-force groups have added a new dimension of instability and peril to the international scene, sometimes at the behest of patron states and at other times to achieve their own agendas. To maintain a posture of national innocence and inaction in the face of such threats is to run the risk of catastrophe. When living in the jungle, it is best to observe the law of the jungle.

All three force responses discussed . . . involve considerable risk and controversy. In some respects, all three options fly in the face of traditional U.S. self-perceptions, which hold that the United States does not need to resort to so-called dirty forms of warfare, even in self-defense, because to do so would compromise its own values and standing in the world community. The United States perceives of itself as a good and benign nation, slow to anger but righteous in its wrath, the kind of power reminiscent of old Hollywood adventure films where the hero throws away his sword after knocking the villain's weapon from his hand and then disposes of the fellow with his fists.

This does not mean that moral and legal considerations should be disregarded; quite the contrary. It is merely to suggest that we do not cease to be moral beings simply because we engage in nasty, low-intensity forms of conflict. The various proactive strategies for dealing with terrorism must be judged in the context of the circumstances in which they are employed, the limitations placed on the use of force in any of its manifestations, and the ends that each response is designed to achieve. In the words of Admiral James D. Watkins, "No response to terrorism ever will be absolutely clean or pure in its morality to all people. We do not live in a world of perfect absolutes, so we must do the best we can with the information available to us." Those who allege that the Western democracies run the risk of becoming like the terrorists they oppose by adopting proactive options to suppress and defeat them are engaging in a cruel form of deception and falsehood, which only encourages and emboldens terrorists who want the United States to be paralyzed with indecision and moral vacillation. It is a sad commentary on the times that it is necessary to reassert our obvious superiority, by any conceivable yardstick, to the terrorists and their sponsors whose only politics are those of fear and murder and whose only law flows out of the barrel of a gun. It is time to stop apologizing for taking appropriate measures to protect societies from enemies bent on destruction.

The demand for probative, or court-sustainable, evidence of a particular foreign terrorist group's culpability or affirming the complicity of a specific sponsoring state is an impractical standard and has contributed to the impression on the part of terrorists that the United States is inhibited from responding meaningfully to their outrages. The amount and quality of intelligence available will always fall something short of optimal. . . .Thus the United States should not insist on absolute evidence before employing force against terrorists; a functional standard of guilt appropriate to the threat will suffice.

Neither should there be an absolute requirement to obtain public endorsement and support of every contemplated action against international terrorism. This, too, would have a chilling effect on the ability of the United States to wage war against terrorists. The president and other elected officials should do what is required to protect the nation regardless of considerations relative to the support any action enjoys in the polls. Force, in the abstract and irrespective of an actual terrorist incident, will never garner a great deal of public support. Public officials therefore must be prepared to lead public opinion rather than simply follow it.

In conclusion, Oliver Wendell Holmes, Jr. once observed, "Between two groups that want to make inconsistent kinds of worlds, I see no remedy except force." The obvious superiority of the Western liberal democracies over the forces challenging them gives moral authority and license to their actions. Terrorists and their sponsors operate on the assumption that the United States will never use force. It is time to prove them wrong.

23

Responding to the Threat of Nuclear Terrorism

Louis René Beres

In an age that brings together terrorism and nuclear technology, an overriding question comes immediately to mind, one that assumes particular importance for the United States: What would happen if future instances of anti-U.S. terrorism were to involve the threat or use of nuclear weapons (i.e., nuclear explosives or radioactivity) by insurgent groups? Is this country and its president prepared to deal with such fearful contingencies? Or does the record of recent American impotence in the face of conventional terrorism suggest even greater levels of vulnerability?

The questions are compelling. In the hazardous flux of world affairs, the spectre of nuclear terrorism is particularly frightful. Understandably, fresh visions of desolation now kindle apocalyptic imaginations, reinforcing already-troubled feelings of powerlessness and frustration. And as if this were not disturbing enough, America's elected leaders have normally remained frozen, like the chorus in a Greek tragedy, distraught at a march of events they seemingly cannot control.

The threat of nuclear terrorism *is* fraught with disquieting possibilities. Potentially it confronts all states. But the threat to the United States is the most immediate. For this reason, this essay will explore the problem primarily from the perspective of the United States, with a view toward illuminating characteristics of the problem in general. My thesis is that it is too soon to despair. There are steps that can be taken, measures that can be implemented, to reduce the danger. With these moves, the United States could begin to take the first critical steps back from a portent that now glows as a numbing hallucination.

WHO ARE THE TERRORISTS?

Before the United States can reduce the risk of nuclear terrorism, however, the U.S. president must understand the difference between lawful and unlawful insurgencies. And this understanding must be based upon more than the desolate intuitions of geopolitics. Specifically, it must rest upon well-established jurisprudential standards that reflect not only international law but also the most cherished elements of the American political tradition.

The Reagan administration embraced only one standard of judgment concerning American foreign policy: anti-Sovietism. Human rights had nothing to do with this standard. It follows that efforts to overthrow allegedly pro-Soviet regimes were always conducted by "freedom fighters" (even where these efforts involved rape, pillage, and mass murder), while efforts to oppose anti-Soviet regimes (even where these efforts were undertaken by the most oppressed and downtrodden peoples of genocidal regimes) were always conducted by "terrorists."

Consider President Reagan's press conference of March 1985, where he stated that the 17 blacks assassinated by South African police were not "simply killed," but were the excusable casualties of "rioting." Moments later, reacting to a question about Nicaragua, the president defended the use of force against a "Communist tyranny." In other words, implied Mr. Bush's predecessor, rebellion against apartheid must always be peaceful, but opposition to Sandinista rule must always be violent.

With this view, black South Africans, although understandably unhappy to be victims of a uniquely repressive regime, were instructed to be "patient" as the U.S. continued with its policy of "constructive engagement." At the same time, contra rebels—widely and authoritatively associated with the execution of noncombatants in Nicaragua and with death-squad activities in El Salvador and Honduras—were embraced by the president as "our brothers." These "freedom fighters," said the president on March 1, 1985, "are the moral equal of our Founding Fathers."

The Reagan administration had based its selective regard for human rights on pure bravado. As a result, many of the world's peoples saw the United States as an *affliction*, and certain insurgent groups throughout the world were provoked to accelerate their activities against the United States. In other words, by its failure to recognize the connection between regime terror and insurgent terror, the United States rendered itself increasingly vulnerable to terrorism in general and to nuclear terrorism in particular.

What lesson is to be learned from this? It is that the true danger of terrorism lies not in the guerrilla camps of Central America and southern Africa. The enemy lies in ourselves. By supporting invidious regimes in pursuit of anti-Soviet advantage, the U.S. risked sparking a sustained and potentially catastrophic insurgency against the United States.

Yet, American foreign policy is not the only source of possible nuclear terrorism against this country. Even if there were a dramatic transformation of current policy orientations under the Bush administration, a significant hazard would remain. To reduce this hazard, major improvements are needed in preventing terrorist access to assembled nuclear weapons, nuclear power plants, and nuclear waste storage facilities. Included in these improvements are measures to contain the spread of nuclear weapons to additional countries.

THE NATURE OF THE THREAT

To undertake acts of nuclear terrorism, insurgent or revolutionary groups would require access to nuclear weapons, nuclear power plants, or nuclear waste storage facilities. Should they seek to acquire an assembled weapon, terrorists could aim at any of the tens of thousands of nuclear weapons now deployed in the national or alliance arsenals of the United States, the Soviet Union, France, England, India, and China. Moreover, because the number of nuclear weapons states is certain to grow, such terrorists are destined to have an enlarged arena of opportunity.

Should they seek to manufacture their own nuclear weapons, terrorists would require both strategic special nuclear materials and the expertise to convert them into bombs or radiological weapons. Both requirements are now well within the range of terrorist capabilities. Some 260 commercial nuclear power plants are operating in the non-Communist world today, each with the capacity to produce bomb-capable plutonium. And approximately twenty plants in seventeen countries can now process plutonium from spent reactor fuel.

Significantly, the amounts of nuclear materials present in other countries will probably expand further. Pilot reprocessing plants to extract weapons-usable plutonium from spent reactor fuel rods signal dangerous conditions. Unless immediate and effective steps are taken to inhibit the spread of plutonium reprocessing and uranium enrichment facilities to other countries, terrorist opportunities to acquire fissionable materials for nuclear-weapons purposes could reach very high levels.

To manufacture its own nuclear weapons, a terrorist group would also require expertise. It is now well-known that such expertise is widely available. In 1977, the Office of Technology Assessment (OTA) produced a report titled *Nuclear Proliferation And Safeguards*. After a general description of the two basic methods of assembling fissile material in a nuclear explosive (the assembly of two or more subcritical masses using gun propellants and the achievement of supercriticality of fissile material via high explosive), the report stated that "militarily useful weapons with reliable nuclear yields in the kiloton range can be constructed with reactor-grade plutonium, using low technology." Indeed, it continued, "given the weapons material and a fraction of a million dollars, a small group of people, none of whom had ever had access to the classified literature, could possibly design and build a crude nuclear explosive device."[1]

Another path to nuclear capability by terrorists could involve the sabotage of nuclear reactor facilities. It is now apparent that such acts could pose monumental problems for responsible government authorities. This is especially apparent in the aftermath of the Soviet nuclear accident at Chernobyl in the spring of 1986.

What can be done to protect against sabotage of nuclear reactors by terrorists? According to the *Report of the International Task Force On Pre-*

vention of Nuclear Terrorism, a project of the highly-esteemed Nuclear Control Institute in Washington, D.C.:

1. Denial of access to nuclear facilities should be the basic consideration in protecting against sabotage.
2. Thorough vigilance against the insider threat is needed.
3. Guard forces should be thoroughly trained and authorized to use deadly force.
4. The basis used for designing physical protection of nuclear plants should be reviewed to ensure that it accurately reflects the current threat.
5. Power reactors should have adequate security provisions against terrorists.
6. Research reactors should have adequate security provisions against terrorists.
7. Reactor safety designs should be reexamined to protect against an accident caused by terrorists.
8. IAEA (International Atomic Energy Agency) physical protection guidelines should be reviewed and updated.
9. Protection standards should be spelled out unambiguously.[2]

In the end, however, efforts at "hardening the target" will not be enough. Although physical security measures are indispensable, an all-consuming preoccupation with guards, firearms, fences, and space-age protection devices would be counterproductive. A *behavioral* strategy of counter-nuclear terrorism, one that is directed toward producing certain changes in the decisional calculi of terrorist groups and their sponsor states, is a prerequisite.

UNDERSTANDING THE ADVERSARY: BEHAVIORAL STRATEGIES

A behavioral strategy must be based upon a sound understanding of the risk calculations of terrorists. Until the special terrorist stance on the balance of risks that can be taken in world politics is understood, we will not be able to identify an appropriate system of sanctions. Although terrorists are typically apt to tolerate higher levels of death and injury than states, there *is* a threshold beyond which certain costs become intolerable.

To understand this threshold, we must first recall that there is no such thing as "the terrorist mind." Rather, there are a great many terrorist minds, an almost unbelievable potpourri of ideas, methods, visions, and objectives. To seek a uniformly applicable strategy of counter-nuclear terrorism, therefore, would be foolhardy.

Contrariwise, in spite of the obvious heterogeneity that characterizes modern terrorism, it would be immensely impractical to formulate myriad strategies which are tailored to particular groups. What must be established is a limited and manageable number of basic strategies that are formed according to the principal types of terrorist group behavior. By adopting this means of "blueprinting" effective counter-nuclear terrorist action, policymakers can be presented with a decision-making strategy in which options are differentiated according to the particular category of risk-calculation involved.

This is not to suggest that each terrorist group is comprised of individuals who exhibit the same pattern of behavior, i.e., the same stance on the balance of risks that can be taken in pursuit of particular preferences. Rather, each terrorist group is made up, in varying degrees, of persons with disparate motives. Since it is essential, from the point of view of creating the necessary decisional strategy, that each terrorist *group* be categorized according to a particular type of risk-calculation, the trick is to identify and evaluate the leadership strata of each terrorist group in order to determine the predominant ordering of preferences.

In terms of actually mounting an effective counter-nuclear terrorist strategy, therefore, governments must organize their activities according to the following sequence of responsibilities:

1. Appraise the terrorist group under scrutiny for the purpose of identifying leadership elements.
2. Appraise the leadership elements for the purpose of identifying predominant patterns of risk-calculation.
3. Examine the decision-making strategy for the purpose of identifying the appropriate type of counter-nuclear terrorist strategy, i.e., the strategy that corresponds with the identified pattern of risk-calculation.

In so organizing their counter-nuclear terrorist activities, governments can begin to develop a rationally conceived "behavioral technology" which distinguishes contingencies of reinforcement according to the particular type of terrorists involved. To deal effectively with the prospective problem of nuclear terrorism, it is essential to correlate deterrent and remedial measures with the preference orderings and modus operandi of the particular terrorist groups(s) in question.

EXAMPLES OF THE THEORY

For example, if a terrorist group displaying the self-sacrificing value system of certain Shiite factions in the Middle East were to threaten nuclear violence, it would be inappropriate to base deterrence on threats of physically punishing acts of retaliation. Here, negative physical sanctions, unless they are devastating enough to ensure destruction of the group itself, are bound to be ineffective. Indeed, such sanctions might even have the effect of a *stimulus*. Instead of orthodox threats of punishment, deterrence in this case should be based upon threats which promise to obstruct preferences which the terrorist group values even more highly than physical safety.

Such threats, therefore, should be directed at convincing terrorists that the resort to nuclear violence would mitigate against their political objectives. To support such threats, steps would probably have to be taken to convince the terrorists that high-order acts of violence are apt to generate broad-based repulsion rather than support. As long as the threatened act of nuclear violence stems from propagandistic motives, terrorists who associate such violence with unfavorable publicity may be inclined to less violent strategies.

Deterrence in this case might also be based upon the promise of rewards. Such a strategy of "positive sanctions" has been left out of current studies of counter-terrorism; yet, it may prove to be one of the few potentially worthwhile ways of affecting the decisional calculi of terrorist groups with self-sacrificing value systems. Of course, in considering whether this sort of strategy is appropriate in particular situations, governments will have to decide whether the expected benefits that accrue from avoiding nuclear terrorism are great enough to outweigh the prospective costs associated with the promised concessions.

The reasonableness of such a strategy is also enhanced by its probable long-term systemic effects. Just as violence tends to beget more violence, rewards tend to generate more rewards. By the incremental replacement of negative sanctions with positive ones, a growing number of actors in world politics, terrorists as well as states, are apt to become habituated to the ideology of a reward system and to disengage from the dynamics of a threat or punishment system. The cumulative effect of such habituation is likely to be a more peaceful and harmonious world and national system.

For another example, we may consider the case of a terrorist group which exhibits a preference ordering very much like that of an ordinary criminal band, i.e., its actions are dictated largely by incentives of material gain, however much these incentives are rationalized in terms of political objectives. If such a terrorist group were to threaten nuclear violence, it would be as inappropriate to base deterrence on threats of political failure or negative public reception as it would be to threaten self-sacrificing ideologues with personal harm. Rather, deterrence in this case should be based largely upon the kinds of threats that are used to counter orthodox criminality.

This is not to suggest, however, that threats of physically punishing retaliation will always be productive in dealing with this type of terrorist group. Even though this particular type, unlike the self-sacrificing variety considered in the first example, is apt to value personal safety in its ordering of preferences, threats to impair this safety may be misconceived. Indeed, a great deal of sophisticated conceptual analysis and experimental evidence now seems to indicate that, in certain cases, the threat of physical punishment may actually prove counter-productive.

Contrary to the widely-held conventional wisdom on the matter, taking a "hard-line" against terrorists may only reinforce antagonism and intransigence. Recent experience indicates that physical retaliation against terrorists often causes only a shift in the selection of targets and a more protracted pattern of violence and aggression. The threat of physical punishment against terrorists is apt to generate high levels of anger that effectively raise the threshold of acceptable suffering. This is the case because anger can modify usual cost/benefit calculations, overriding the inhibitions ordinarily associated with anticipated punishment.

To this point, the discussion of negative sanctions has been limited to physical punishment. However, there is considerable evidence that *all kinds* of negative sanctions, economic as well as physical, stiffen rather than diminish terrorist resistance. Whatever the nature of negative sanctions, they appear to generate anger which causes terrorists to value retaliation (or counter-retaliation, whichever the case may be) more highly than the objectives that have given rise to terrorist activity in the first place.

For a third example, we may consider the case of a terrorist group which exhibits a primary concern for achieving one or another political objective, but which lacks a self-sacrificing value-system. If this sort of terrorist group were to threaten nuclear violence, it would be appropriate to base deterrence on a suitable combination of all of the negative and positive sanctions discussed thus far. This means that steps should be taken to convince the group that: 1) nuclear violence would mitigate against its political objectives; 2) certain concessions would be granted in exchange for restraint from nuclear violence, and 3) certain physically punishing or otherwise negative acts of retaliation would be meted out if nuclear violence were undertaken.

In deciding upon what, exactly, constitutes a suitable configuration of sanctions, governments will have to be especially discriminating in their manner of brandishing threats of physical punishment. In this connection, it is worth noting that threats of mild punishment may have a greater deterrent effect than threats of severe punishment. From the vantage point of the terrorist group's particular baseline of expectations, such threats—when threats of severe punishment are expected—may even appear to have positive qualities. Catching the terrorist group by surprise, such threat behavior is also less likely to elicit the high levels of anger and intractability that tend to override the inhibiting factor of expected punishment. Moreover, the threat of mild punishment is less likely to support the contention of official repression, a contention that is often a vital part of terrorist groups' strategies for success.

In reference to the actual promise of rewards as an instrument of deterrence, governments may find it worthwhile to consider whether a selected number of particular concessions would produce a gainful net effect. In other words, recognizing that threats of severe punishment produce rationality-impairing stress, which in turn produces greater resistance rather than compliance, governments may discover that the promise of rewards communicates feelings of sympathy and concern, which in turn diminish terrorist resistance. With such an understanding, governments may begin to delimit the particular concessions which they are prepared to make.

A fourth and final example that illustrates the need to correlate deterrent and situational measures with particular preference orderings centers on the case of terrorist groups spurred on by the need for spectacular self-assertion. From the standpoint of preventing nuclear violence, this type of terrorist group presents the greatest problems. Faced with terrorist groups who long to act out the urgings of Bakhunin, Sorel, and Fanon, governments may be confronted with genuine psychopaths and sociopaths. Clearly, since the preference that would need to be obstructed in this case is neither political success nor personal profit, but the violent act itself, and since personal safety is unlikely to figure importantly in the terrorist's risk-calculus, deterrence of nuclear terrorism must be abandoned altogether as a viable strategy. Instead, all preventive measures must concentrate upon limiting the influence of such terrorists within their particular groups and maintaining a safe distance between such terrorists and the instruments of higher-order weapons technologies.

If the apparent danger is great enough, governments may feel compelled to resort to a "no holds barred" counter-terrorist campaign. In such cases, governments must be aware that the inclination to escalate violence would signify the erosion of power. Violence is not power. Where the latter is in jeopardy, the former is increased. Understood in terms of anti-terrorism measures, this suggests that the imprudent escalation of violence by public authorities can destroy power. Taken to its outermost limits, such escalation can lead to rule by sheer violence and the substitution of "official" terror for insurgent terror.

NUCLEAR TERRORISM: FORMS AND EFFECTS

Nuclear Explosives

The low-technology nuclear explosives that might be manufactured by terrorists could range anywhere from a few hundred tons to several kilotons in yield. The destructive potential of such explosives would depend on such variables as type of construction, population density, prevailing wind direction, weather patterns, and the characteristic features of the target area. Such potential would be manifested in terms of three primary effects: blast (measured in pounds per square inch of overpressure); heat (measured in calories/cm^2); and radiation (measured in roentgen equivalent man—rem—a combined measure that includes the radiation absorbed dose—rad—and the relative biological effectiveness—RBE—or the varying biological effectiveness of different types of radiation).

Relatively crude nuclear explosives with yields equivalent to about 1,000 tons of high explosive would be far easier to fabricate than explosives with yields equivalent to about 10 kilotons of high explosive. Nonetheless, explosives with a yield of only one-tenth of a kiloton would pose significant destructive effects. A nuclear explosive in this limited range could annihilate the Capitol during the State of the Union Address or knock down the World Trade Center towers in New York City. An even smaller yield of 10 tons of TNT could kill everyone attending the Super Bowl.

In assessing the destructiveness of nuclear explosions, it is important to remember that such explosions are typically more damaging than chemical explosions of equivalent yields. This is the case because nuclear explosions produce energy in the form of penetrating radiations (gamma rays and neutrons) as well as in blast wave and heat. Moreover, a nuclear explosion on the ground—the kind of nuclear explosion most likely to be used by terrorists—produces more local fallout than a comparable explosion in the air.

Radiological Weapons

Radiological weapons are not as widely understood as nuclear explosives, but they are equally ominous in their effects. Placed in the hands of terrorists, such weapons could pose a lethal hazard for human beings anywhere in the world. Even a world already dominated by every variety of numbing could not fail to recoil from such a prospect.

Radiological weapons are devices designed to disperse radioactive materials that have been produced a substantial time before their dispersal. The targets against which terrorists might choose to use radiological weapons include concentrations of people inside buildings, concentrations of people on urban streets or at sports events, urban areas with a high population density as a whole, and agricultural areas. The form such weapons might take include plutonium dispersal devices (only 3.5 ounces of plutonium could prove lethal to everyone within a large office building or factory) or devices designed to disperse other radioactive materials. In principle, the dispersal of spent nuclear reactor fuel and the fission products separated from reactor fuels would create grave hazards in a populated area, but the handling of such materials would be very dangerous to terrorists themselves. It is more likely, therefore, that would-be users of radiological weapons would favor plutonium over radioactive fission products.

The threat of nuclear terrorism involving radiological weapons is potentially more serious than the threat involving nuclear explosives. This is because it would be easier for terrorists to achieve nuclear capability with radiological weapons. Such weapons, therefore, could also be the subject of a more plausible hoax than nuclear explosives.

Nuclear Reactor Sabotage

In the aftermath of the Chernobyl disaster, even the average layperson has become familiar with the meaning of "reactor-core meltdown." Such an event, in which a reactor deprived of its temperature-controlling coolant melts in its own heat and produces lethal clouds of radioactive gases, could be the objective of future terrorism. Significantly, incidents involving violence or threats of violence at nuclear facilities at home and abroad are already a matter of record.

In comparison with a low-yield nuclear explosion, a reactor-core meltdown and breach of containment would release a small amount of radiation. However, the consequences of such an event would still involve leakage of an immense amount of gaseous radioactive material that could expose neighboring populations to immediate death, cancer, or genetic defects. To better understand the nature of the threat, we must first try to understand the fundamentals of nuclear reactors.

Essentially, these reactors may be characterized as giant teakettles that turn water into steam. The steam is piped to large turbines that turn generators. When a typical teakettle is operating at full power, the radioactivity in its fuel core can reach 17 billion curies, enough—in principle—to kill everyone on the planet. Within the uranium fuel rods in the core, the fission reaction can unleash energy to drive the temperature above 4,000 degrees Farenheit—a temperature hot enough to melt through all protective barriers.

From the standpoint of radiation discharged, the consequences of a successful conventional attack upon nuclear reactors could equal those of the worst accidental meltdown. This form of nuclear terrorism could result in moderate to major releases of radioactivity into the environment. Additional problems would arise through release of the inventories of spent fuel customarily located at reactor sites. Early fatalities are possible, although late cancers and genetic effects would dominate. In densely populated countries deaths could number in the tens of thousands.

Whatever form nuclear terrorism might take—nuclear explosives, radiological weapons, or nuclear reactor sabotage—its effects would be social and political as well as biological and physical. In the aftermath of a nuclear terrorist event, both governments and insurgents would be confronted with mounting pressures to escalate to higher-order uses of force. With terrorists more inclined to think of nuclear weapons as manifestly "thinkable," both governments and terrorists would find themselves giving serious consideration to striking first.

Like Camus' Caligula, who kills because "there's only one way of getting even with the gods . . . to be as cruel as they," a number of terrorist groups could turn to nuclear weaponry as a new instrument of vengeance. Faced with such threats, governments would find it necessary to choreograph their own macabre dances of death, meeting savagery with savagery in a quest for security that might reveal only impotence. In the wake of such widespread dislocation, madness would be celebrated by all sides as the liberating core of survival, and sanity would dissolve into insignificance.

THE PROBLEM OF CIVIL LIBERTIES

In the preceding examples, some of the prospective sanctions available to counter-nuclear terrorist strategists entail measures that might be injurious to such values as social justice and human rights within states. Of special interest in this connection are options involving:

1. A total, no-holds-barred military-type assault designed to eradicate the terrorist group(s) altogether; and/or
2. A protracted, counter-terrorist campaign utilizing "classical" methods of informers, infiltrators, counter-terror squads, assassinations, agents provocateurs, and raids.

The first option, however effective it might be, is apt to be most destructive of essential citizen rights. Hence, governments contemplating such an option must pay close attention to the necessary trade-off between efficacy and liberty that is involved. Since this option would almost certainly be repugnant to the most deeply-held values of liberal, democratic societies, governments, before resorting to this option, would have to be convinced that its prospective benefits were great enough to outweigh its probable costs. In fact, short of its use at the situational level where higher-order acts of terrorist violence have already taken place, it is unlikely that this option will be taken seriously in democratic states. Rather, we are likely to see its adoption only by the world's most blatantly anti-democratic regimes.

This no-holds-barred military option is problematic for another reason. Not only might it incite reasonable fears of military/police repression among the population, it might also confer a genuine combatant status upon the terrorists. As a result, the terrorist group(s) would more likely acquire the cast of an underdog army than that of a criminal band.

The second option is also apt to score high marks on the efficacy dimension, but its effects on essential citizen rights need not be injurious. This is not to suggest that a protracted counter-terrorist campaign utilizing classical methods of apprehension and punishment would necessarily be any less repulsive to liberal, democratic societies, but that such a campaign might be conducted on a comparatively less visible and clandestine basis. An additional virtue of such quiet operations would be the avoidance of sympathy-generating publicity for the terrorist group(s).

In the final analysis, the problem of conflicting values which emerges from the consideration of harsh deterrent counter-measures can be resolved only by careful comparison of the costs and benefits involved.

In general, the optimal counter-nuclear terrorist strategy is one in which effective counter-action leaves the prevailing network of citizen rights and privileges unimpaired. Barring this possibility, however, the requirements of effective strategies should be tempered by concern for those freedoms which are assured by humanitarian international law.

REDEFINING NATIONAL INTERESTS: PLANETIZATION AND FREEDOM FROM NUCLEAR TERRORISM

In the final analysis, the effectiveness of international strategies of counter-nuclear terrorism will depend upon the tractability of pro-terrorist states. Real effectiveness, therefore, requires commitment by all states to unity and relatedness. To realize this commitment, all states will have to work toward the replacement of our fragile system of *realpolitik* with a new world politics of globalism.

Preventing nuclear terrorism must thus be seen as one part of an even larger strategy, one that is geared to the prevention of all forms of international violence. It would be futile to try to tinker with the prospect of nuclear terrorism without affecting the basic structure of modern world politics. This structure is integral to all possibilities of an atomic apocalypse, and its re-visioning and reformation is central to all possibilities for survival.

The capacity to prevent nuclear terrorism is inseparable from a new consciousness by our national leaders. Amidst the precarious crosscurrents of global power relations, states must undertake prodigious efforts to resist the lure of primacy, focusing instead on the emergence of a new sense of global obligation. And these efforts must be undertaken very soon. The great French Enlightenment philosopher, Jean Jacques Rousseau, once remarked: "The majority of nations, as well as of men, are tractable only in their youth; they become incorrigible as they grow old." Understood in terms of the imperative to change direction in the search for peace, this suggests that unless these nations achieve such a change before losing their "youth," the chances for later success may be lost forever.

What is required, then, is a nuclear regime which extends the principles of nuclear war avoidance to the problem of nuclear terrorism. The centerpiece of this universal regime must be the cosmopolitan understanding that all states, like all people, form one essential body and one true community. Such an understanding, that a latent oneness lies buried beneath the manifold divisions of our fractionated world, need not be based on the mythical attractions of universal brotherhood and mutual concern. Instead, it must be based on the idea that individual states, however much they may dislike each other, are tied together in the struggle for survival.

The task, then, is to make the separate states conscious of their emerging planetary identity. With such a re-visioning of national goals and incentives, states can progress to an awareness of new archetypes for global society. Since all things contain their own contradiction, the world system based upon militaristic nationalism can be transformed into an organic world society.

To succeed in this task will be very difficult. But it need not be as fanciful as some would have us believe. Indeed, before we take the shroud measurements of the corpse of human society, we must understand that faith in the new forms of international interaction is a critical step towards their implementation.

If all of this sounds grandly unpolitical, it is because politics as usual cannot prevent nuclear terrorism. And if it all sounds hopelessly idealistic, it must be realized that nothing can be more fanciful than continuing on the present course. To be sure, today's idealists in foreign affairs— those who would seek to leave militaristically nationalistic states behind, whimpering in the corners of their egos—have little cause for optimism. Their search to actualize new forms of international interaction is unlikely to succeed. But it is the only search with even a remote chance of success; the only search worth conducting. It is, therefore, the only approach worthy of the term "realism."

From the point of view of the United States, and President George Bush, there is only one immediate imperative: to end our singular preoccupation with Cold War theology. By casting every issue of foreign policy within the limiting context of Soviet-American competition, the U.S. has endorsed an inscrutable logic whereby many of the most repressive regimes are included in the "Free World," and where U.S. military intervention on behalf of "freedom" becomes self-justifying. As a result, the victims of regime terror and of U.S. interference with self-determination often identify America as their enemy, a tragic and humiliating association that ensures American vulnerability to insurgent terror.

In *The Plague*, Camus tells us: "At the beginning of the pestilence and when it ends, there's always a propensity for rhetoric. . . . It is in the thick of a calamity that one gets hardened to the truth—in other words, to silence." As long as the U.S. continues to stand in the ruins of thought, ruins created by its frenzied and perpetual enmity with the Soviet Union, it will be unable to avoid the more tangible ruins of terrorism. And if there is no progress beyond the facile tenets of *realpolitik*, these ruins might well be generated by nuclear explosives or radioactivity. Before a livable society could be born from the ashes, a gravedigger would have to wield the forceps.

NOTES

1. U.S. Congress, Office of Technology Assessment, *Nuclear Proliferation And Safeguards* (New York: Praeger, 1977).

2. *Report Of The International Task Force On Prevention Of Nuclear Terrorism*, 25 June 1986, 10-11.

24

Why We Need More but Better Coverage of Terrorism

Patrick Clawson

The discussion about media coverage of terrorism has focused on how much should be reported, particularly about counterterrorism activities. That is the wrong question. What should be asked instead is, how can media coverage contribute to the fight against terrorism? The media should not be viewed as potential enemies who would damage the anti-terrorism effort unless kept carefully in check. The media should instead be seen as likely allies who can contribute much towards the elimination of terrorism. By approaching the media as possible friends rather than as likely enemies, government officials can expect the media to be more sympathetic and open to their concerns.

HOW THE MEDIA CAN HELP

Ample media coverage is vital to generating awareness of the magnitude of the terrorist threat. Sporadic coverage could lead to a public perception that terrorism is not likely to be a serious or lasting problem, and therefore little needs to be done on a regular basis to combat it. Without broad support for a sustained struggle, public officials will not be ready or able to take the difficult steps needed to combat terrorism—to provide the funds, to train the forces, or to implement security measures that inconvenience the public. In short, only extensive coverage will generate the attention needed to secure the resources necessary for an effective anti-terrorism program.

Furthermore, in times of a hostage-taking crisis, media coverage can provide public officials with vital information, since the media often have greater ability than [government] officials to get up close to the action and to report it quickly. . . . Reporters also have greater access to the terrorists themselves, who often refuse to speak to government officials. For these reasons, the [U.S.] government already relies on . . . the . . . electronic

Note: footnotes have been deleted.

media for fast-breaking news. By using this information rather than dupli-
cating it, . . . government[s] can devote more resources to analyzing information and putting it into context.

Solid journalism documents the isolation of terrorists from society and
exposes the criminality of terrorist acts. Such coverage by no means adds
to the support for terrorist groups. Quite the contrary, the more the public learns about terrorist organizations, the less likely is any assistance from
those who might be sympathetic to the cause the terrorists champion.
Publicity about the details of the IRA's terrorism has reduced its support
from Irish-Americans who want to see a united Ireland. To be sure, terrorists can draw strength from reporting that magnifies their importance
and publicizes their world-view, and such coverage can be vital for radical
groups that depend upon voluntary recruits and donations. The problem
in such cases, however, is with the quality of the reporting, not with the
amount of publicity.

At times, media coverage can prevent further deterioration of a
situation. Jerry Levin, the CNN reporter held captive in Lebanon for over
a year, [argued] that he [owed] his life to the extensive coverage given his
captivity, since that coverage caused his captors to be concerned about
the possible impact of his death. Letting a kidnapper vent his frustration
by talking in front of a camera or into a microphone can help defuse
tension.

Some have suggested that publicity encourages terrorism, or even that
terrorism would end were it not for media coverage. To take two examples: Michael Davies, president of the Associated Press Managing Editors
and editor of the *Hartford Courant*, has said, "Publicity is the lifeblood of
terrorism. Without it, these abominable acts against the innocent would
wither quickly away." In a similar vein, Ted Koppel wrote, "Without
television, international terrorism becomes rather like the philosopher's
hypothetical tree falling in the forest—no one hears it fall and therefore
it does not exist."

Certainly publicity can be useful to terrorists in magnifying the impact
of their actions; many terrorists have learned to posture for prime-time
coverage. Nevertheless, these statements exaggerate the importance of
the media in four ways. As noted above, the more the public knows about
a terrorist group, the less likely it is to support that group. Second, lack
of coverage is likely to have little impact on terrorists who rely on state
sponsorship; they do not need publicity to generate recruits or sympathy.
Third, the behavior of terrorists often responds primarily to local politics,
despite some of the antics that may be staged to win media attention.
Most important, terrorism has long flourished in the absence of mass
media. The medieval Assassins thrived and struck fear in the hearts of
government officials when news of their actions was spread mostly by
word of mouth. In the contemporary Middle East, terrorist bombings
are common in countries to which Western television reporters have little
access, including Iraq, Syria, and Iran. . . .

CONTROLS ON THE MEDIA?

The initial impulse of some observers contemplating problems with media coverage of terrorism is to propose controls on the media. The idea of legal controls is not new nor is it the preserve of conservatives. Andrew Young, then the U.S. ambassador to the United Nations, proposed federal laws to restrict press coverage of terrorist incidents in 1977. . . .

Any attempt to impose legal controls on the media would face serious practical problems. For one thing, legal controls [by a national government] could not cover the foreign media and so would be ineffective at keeping information secret. . . .

Furthermore, proposals for legal controls do not consider the competitive nature of journalism. . . . Timely newsbreaks can "make" a reporter's career. Thousands of people compete intensely for the few slots at the top of the prestige ladder in television and print journalism. It is unrealistic to expect that all of them will refrain from reporting what could be the big break of their career at the request of some official they barely know. Nor is it likely that an editor, under pressure to show that his paper or station can outperform its many rivals, will agree to sit on a scoop at the urging of some unknown [governmental] voice. . . . Once one station or newspaper has reported an item, the competitive pressure can force others to follow quickly.

Equally important, attempts at control will lead to a confrontational attitude towards the government from the media, thus undermining a key potential source of support for counter-terrorism. As discussed below, by working together with the media rather than by attempting coercion, the government can achieve many of its aims, since editors generally agree that information that would genuinely threaten national security should be withheld.

Finally, consistent with [American] constitutional freedoms, prior constraint of the press is only acceptable . . . in the most extreme circumstances. . . .

For these reasons, controls over press coverage have found little support from those who might at first consideration be thought to be sympathetic, including staunch conservatives in the media and terrorism experts. . . .

Experts on terrorism have noted that any attempt to impose media blackouts is likely to force terrorists to escalate the level of violence in order to attract more attention. . . .

THE SOLUTION: CLOSE WORKING RELATIONS BETWEEN PUBLIC OFFICIALS AND THE MEDIA

Rather than devoting their efforts to media blackouts, public officials could more productively concentrate on developing closer working relations with the press in order to promote responsible journalism in the coverage of terrorism. Cooperation between the media and the government must be a two-way street. Just as the media should delay reporting some sensitive information, the government should ensure that media representatives are well informed about anti-terrorism operations.

Recognizing that nearly everything is going to get out eventually anyway, public officials should provide the information openly, rather than waiting for leaks they cannot control. A "no comment" policy can encourage irresponsible leaks. . . . Officials who provide information to the media can place it in a proper context. If they—not some anonymous leaker— provide the information, the officials can then embargo its use until a certain time, when disclosure would no longer hurt a planned rescue or reprisal. Note that the government's concern is often about the timing of a report. For instance, delaying a report about plans for a hostage rescue can be crucial to allowing that operation to proceed. In this context, the electronic media have a particularly heavy responsibility. . . .

If the media and government officials working on counter-terrorism are well acquainted with each other, a relationship of mutual confidence is more likely, and contacts during a moment of crisis would be easier to arrange. . . . Furthermore, background briefings by government officials could help those in the media prepare themselves for terrorist episodes by gathering information on antiterrorism policy, terrorist methods, and terrorist organizations. . . .

A first step toward improving media coverage of terrorism would be to implement the recommendation of the Vice-President's Task Force on Combatting Terrorism [1986], "The government must improve its communications with the media during a terrorist attack. At the same time, the media must maintain high standards of reporting to ensure that the lives of innocent victims and national security are not jeopardized. . . . Regular meetings between media and government officials on the coverage of terrorism could contribute to more effective government-media relations."

25

Countering Terrorism: Evaluating the Options

William Gutteridge

"All that is necessary for the triumph of evil is that good men do nothing."

—Edmund Burke

With this quotation the opening speaker, a senior British policeman, set the tone for a recent seminar on terrorism, held in Washington D.C. Terrorism, it is generally accepted, imposes a responsibility on individuals, as well as on states and international organizations, that cannot be shrugged off. Recent events, notably negotiations by the United States and France with Iran over the release of hostages, have, however, exposed an inconsistency of response amounting to different interpretations of the nature of that responsibility. Though in some other circumstances a policy even of inertia may conceivably be appropriate, in the face of terrorism as it has developed over the last twenty years, the option of inaction is not really available. Terrorism compels a response precisely because it challenges democratic values. Without action to combat it, democratic societies are likely to be undermined and possibly destroyed.

It is, however, essential not to overreact to the terrorist threat. Giving counter-terrorist measures priority over all other considerations may inspire the imposition of draconian provisions which could themselves pose a threat to democracy and cause a particular democratic society to destroy itself—to commit, as it were, political suicide. This is indeed what the more sophisticated, rational terrorist may actually have in mind, and certainly seemed to be the case with the Baader-Meinhof gang in the Federal Republic of Germany in the 1970s.

Neither terrorism nor the grievances in which it is rooted can be entirely eradicated. So the problem is one of balance—how to contain terrorism, diminish it, and eliminate particular forms of it without unnecessarily reducing the quality of daily life and the liberties of the individual.

IDENTIFYING THE TERRORIST

A main instrument in the essential step of identifying the terrorist is the active cooperation of the public, in order especially to affect morale and to undermine the logistic and other support that is necessary for the survival of the terrorist undercover. This public cooperation has to be sustained in the face of the inherently unpopular, but nevertheless indispensable, covert intelligence gathering procedures and surveillance that are essential to the process of seeking out the terrorist. Separating a possibly sympathetic and often morally justifiable cause from the brutal criminality of the terrorist act carried out in its name requires a sensitive public relations strategy on the part of the police and other security agencies. Well-timed, accurate, and if possible, spontaneous intelligence, shared nationally and internationally, is essential for combating terrorism, as it is also for defeating increasingly sophisticated criminal enterprises, which are quite often actually linked to it.

Distinguishing the variety of motivations and grievances that inspire terrorism is in turn vital to the gathering and application of intelligence. There are clearly different categories of terrorist activity. Essentially national terrorism, such as that practiced by the Irish Republican Army (IRA) and Euskadi Ta Askatasuna (ETA) has to be distinguished from international or state-sponsored terrorism operating far from the point where it originates. Terrorist acts carried out by liberation movements such as the African National Congress (ANC) in South Africa may be subordinate to a broad-based political strategy and only incidental to it, but they are violent crimes and there is no alternative but to treat them as such.

The consensus at the Washington seminar, among analysts and counter-terrorist practitioners alike, was to support treating terrorist acts as the already legally defined crimes they usually are. The progress made in combating the IRA in Northern Ireland once this principle was accepted is well documented. The political dimension, the question of association, is a separate matter for governments rather than for the police. Without this clear distinction, the application of justice is always likely to be obscured by residual sympathy for an apparently just cause. The overlap between politically motivated terrorism and violent and intimidatory crime is consequently an important factor assisting the mobilization of the public behind the forces of law and order.

ANTI-TERRORIST INSTRUMENTS

The adequacy of national legal provisions and of the powers that they give to the police and other forces is a matter for continuous reappraisal. The British Prevention of Terrorism legislation, enacted by the Labour Government of 1974 after the Birmingham bombings on a temporary but so far regularly renewable basis, necessarily imposes some restrictions on the freedom of the individual. Powers to detain suspected individuals pending investigation and to exclude others from mainland Britain seemed to be the minimum consonant with combating the evil. The European Convention on Human Rights facilitates the raising of complaints about the treatment of suspect terrorists in EEC countries.

Whether the acts under investigation are defined as terrorist or are simply criminal, some legally controlled or monitored interception of communications, including telephone tapping, is inevitable. In Britain this extends, particularly in relation to drug trafficking (often, incidentally, a source of funds for terrorists) to customs as well as security officers, but the responsibility for control lies directly with the Home Secretary and is formally subject to a system of annual quotas. The Special Branch of the police is responsible for other, more direct forms of information gathering by observation.

A relatively new aspect of counter-terrorist methods is analysis of financial transactions, which is becoming increasingly difficult with the introduction of more or less instant electronic transfer of funds. At the same time, as happened in the Aldo Moro kidnapping in Italy, traditional police methods such as detailed forensic examination of available evidence, even the obvious fingerprinting, are sometimes neglected. But even more important are arrangements for the storage of the accumulated data, and for its retrieval.

In combating the Red Brigade, the willingness of the West Germans to allow the Italians access to their police computer proved vital. International cooperation is generally regarded as a prerequisite for real progress in the fight against international terrorism, but there are reasonable doubts about the utility of formal treaties for this purpose. Harmonization of law and police practices on the basis of mutual understandings seems in several directions likely to be more profitable.

THE PROBLEM OF FRONTIERS

In no aspect of terrorism is international cooperation more central than in dealing with problems arising outside the borders of the national state principally affected. These problems are compounded by the freedom of movement which is encouraged by democratic societies and by modern modes of transport. The ease with which terrorists based in one country can take refuge or sanctuary in another has been increased by steps taken towards improved international cooperation in other directions.

This is particularly the case in Western Europe, where the adoption within the European community of the principle of freedom of movement and employment for its citizens has led to a progressive downgrading of transfrontier checking. Differential laws with regard to the control of firearms, notably in the United Kingdom, impose some restraints, but the situation is affected adversely by a number of inbuilt factors. There are, for instance about 360 largely unmanned open road crossing points over the border between France and Switzerland. The links of several Western European countries with their former colonies facilitate entry by people from the majority of the world's ethnic groups, thereby incidentally assisting the infiltration of determined terrorists. Guestworkers also provide cover, as does the accepted facility for East German refugees to obtain passports in the Federal Republic, and by extension EEC documents. The implications of a system of external visas for EEC countries collectively and for a standard computer-readable community passport were discussed at the seminar. Resistance in the U.K. to the issuing and carrying of any identity document is an example of the obstacles to such procedures, which prevail on the grounds that they infringe individual liberty.

Significantly, since the Washington seminar, a review by Lord Colville QC of the current British Prevention of Terrorism Act has not only recommended that the act be made permanent, but expresses the "grave misgivings" of the police and security services about the removal of frontier controls in Europe by 1991 and suggests that new movement through the proposed Channel Tunnel will pose more "formidable" problems. The powers of exclusion of suspected terrorists from mainland Britain, seen as a system of internal exile, should be dropped, but the powers of arrest and detention on reasonable grounds of suspicion of involvement in terrorism should be made permanent. At the same time, the civil rights protections for suspects, contained in the provision of the Police and Criminal Evidence Act, would be extended to those arrested under the Prevention of Terrorism Act. This conscious concern to balance effective counter-terrorist measures with the maintenance of civil rights is based on the assumption that terrorism has become a fact of life that a civilized democratic society has to accommodate.

Once a terrorist act has been committed, attempts to apprehend the criminals involved and to bring them to justice assume primacy. In this respect, it is not only the exchange of information that is critical in terms of international cooperation, but the legal restraint on police and security forces, but not the terrorist, from crossing borders in hot pursuit. Once the terrorist has been caught, a combination of legal, judicial, and political considerations affects the chances of his extradition. A leading Italian jurist pointed out, during discussion of this issue, that the need is to "unify terminology" and to achieve a greater measure of "judicial harmonization." For these purposes a clear demarcation between a political act and a terrorist crime should be established. The concept of a political offense justifying asylum ought, however, to be sustained, but perhaps with modifications.

INTERNATIONAL
AND COORDINATED TERRORISM

By definition, international terrorism, whether state-sponsored or not, poses more difficult problems even than essentially national movements like the IRA and ETA. While state sponsorship in the shape of weapons, money and training has clearly increased and is exemplified by the mushroom growth of terrorist bases in Lebanon from whatever source they are supported, there is doubt as to the extent of actual control and direction exercised over terrorist activities. The evidence is inevitably largely circumstantial, mainly because a sponsor need do no more than prime the pump of a group whose objectives and methods it assumes to be congruent with its own. Thereafter, most groups can readily become self-sustaining, generating more funds by investment in activities such as drug trafficking, or by extortion, protection rackets, or bank robberies.

Proof of state direction of specific terrorist activities is always hard to come by and will inevitably be doubted. Even if responsibility is proved, the decision to make an appropriate response is fraught with political difficulties. It inevitably shifts the emphasis from the crime that has been committed to its political motivation and raises questions of legitimacy (in both directions) and whether the cause in itself is just. It puts to the test the collective will, and in so doing strains the links in alliances. Coordinated diplomatic sanctions, restricted aircraft landing and overflying rights, prohibition of immigration, exclusion of students, trade restrictions, and embargoes on technological transfers are all possible and may be effective if they achieve the isolation of the guilty party.

The military solution is generally regarded as the last resort, reserved for use where the offending state or regime is already relatively isolated. Even so, at the Washington seminar, strong reservations were expressed. The legal basis for such action, even in self-defense, is dubious, and its regular use would imply a shift in the foundations of international law. In the case of U.S. action against Libya, it might be deemed to have been a short-term success in deterring the training of terrorists and initiating terrorist action on Libyan soil. In the longer term, and certainly in other circumstances, it might well prove counterproductive. There would, for example, be significant strategic risks in appearing to call the Soviet bluff by taking similar action against Syrian targets. The burden of proof, the question of international legality and the difficulty of precise execution all combine to make direct military action of this kind a difficult option. The use of overwhelming force by a major power against the territory or installations of a small one is by definition likely to create more problems than it seems at the time to be able to resolve. In general, the use of force by a state can be seen as an expression of frustration at its failure to achieve its objectives by peaceful means. Individual political activists who resort to violence similarly claim that there is no legitimate alternative left open to them. This is, however, an analogy that should not be carried too far! It assumes rationality on both parts and an objective that is conceivably negotiable.

AIR PIRACY

Hijacking, the seizure of an aircraft in the air or on the ground, has been over the last two decades one of the most common forms of terrorism. It tends to attract maximum media attention, usually involves a large number of hostages from different countries, and has the advantage, in terms of publicity for the terrorist cause, of being relatively long and drawn out. Though governments and the civil aviation industry were unprepared for the phenomenon, preventative and deterrent measures have had considerable success in reducing the number of incidents.

The use of armed sky marshals, particularly in the United States and Israel, though effective up to a point, has in most parts of the world taken second place to precautions on the ground. Security checks of passengers and baggage, with the delays they involve, have achieved popular acceptability in many countries. Even with improving technology, the gap permitting human error remains wide. Quality, training and efficiency of security staffs can easily be nullified by overworking them in long shifts. Carelessness or inexperience, as the Air India disaster demonstrated, can even at a comparatively well-disciplined airport bestow on the terrorist the good luck he usually needs to be successful. Security and customs procedures are only really effective when supported by rapidly conveyed intelligence on international networks. Liaison between law enforcement agencies, airport authorities, and the aviation industry generally is still primitive in many countries. Only belatedly are security systems being built into new airports at the design stage—a condition regarded by experts as essential.

The response of terrorists to the progressive tightening of precautions, and to the presumably many occasions on which they have been thwarted, is to look to new methods. More attempts to create havoc in check-in areas and to sabotage aircraft by gaining access on the ground can be expected. More sophisticated and well-organized groups may seek, by posing as airline staff, to take crews hostage before they reach the aircraft, or to intimidate them by seizing their families in their homes. Attempted infiltration of sleepers among passengers has been suspected. Precautions against such threats will inevitably, because of costs in money and time, raise problems of commercial viability. Intensive interrogation of passengers before departure, already adopted by El-Al, is now being tentatively tried by some other airlines when there is a special state of alert.

Two issues tend to dominate debates about the handling of aircraft hijack incidents. Some security authorities give priority to immobilizing the aircraft, either by denying refuelling or obstructing takeoff, while others are doubtful whether this improves the chances of a successful outcome. Similarly, establishment of the criteria to be used in deciding on a military assault hinges around the priority to be given to the safety of each and every hostage. The murder of a hostage has been used as an indicator that negotiation is futile, but to some this kind of sacrifice is unacceptable even though the risks of attempting to resolve a situation prematurely by force have been shown to be even greater. The dilemma posed, especially for democratic governments, between determined counter-terrorism and responsibility for the lives and liberties of individual citizens is in the forefront at all stages in this kind of war. Terrorist threats and intimidation are aimed at exploiting what is difficult on humanitarian grounds to reconcile and justify. Their efforts to win sympathy by driving an emotional wedge between governments and people are a major ingredient in the sensation factor on which the media inevitably feed. In the end nothing seems more newsworthy than the threatened disaster to individuals, which officials or politicians appear to have it in their power to avert.

KIDNAPPING AND HOSTAGE TAKING

Kidnapping and holding to ransom in kind or cash of individuals can attract attention for longer than a large-scale hijack, depending always on the character and status of the individuals held. The arbitrary value placed on a human life is related by implication to the capacity to pay. A shrewd terrorist whose objective is really money may decide that in some circumstances 25,000 pounds [or dollars] is more likely to be paid than 2,500,000 pounds and demand accordingly. A business or other organization may be tempted to respond in accordance with its ability to pay up to dangerously high limits in terms of its own viability. Governments may have decided and agreed with others to make no concessions to terrorists, but sometimes justifiably rationalize partial payment as a tactic that can lead to the resolution of the incident and the apprehension of the terrorist.

ANTI-TERRORIST CONVENTIONS

A policy in principle of no concessions is now widely subscribed to by governments even outside Western Europe, but in practice there is backsliding in a variety of forms. Rigid adherence to the code is eroded by expediency and by humanitarian appeals to hearts rather than minds. It does, however, depend on the conviction that it is failure and frustration that discourages terrorists even more than the threat of death, and that concessions are almost bound to encourage them to try again. The prospects of governments legally prohibiting concessions in the shape of the payment of ransoms by businesses or families willing to pay for the lives of individuals are poor and constitutionally very difficult. They are left, even if they set a good example in this respect themselves, with the problems of demonstrating that the interests of the state and the community lie first in combating the terrorist threat by the best means available, and that those of the particular individual who may be taken hostage are subsidiary.

The Italian government's refusal to negotiate the release of Prime Minister Aldo Moro, who was then murdered, appears to have been the beginning of the rather abrupt decline of Red Brigade terrorism. British governments have indicated that they would not bargain for the release of a kidnapped minister. The consensus at the seminar was that there should be no real concessions to terrorist demands. The problem for governments is to develop such a consensus among people at large or firmly to shoulder unpopular leadership responsibility in the longer-term interests of international order.

In a sense the same applies to government's relations with the media. The imposition of censorship or arbitrary blackouts on information will inevitably be counterproductive in a free society. Publicity may give heart to terrorists, but censorship will breed rumors and alarm conducive to a mood of capitulation. Where reporting is liable to put operations or the lives of hostages at risk, then an agreement on temporary restraint on publication can be sought. Where this sort of convention is achieved, as it has been in Britain for the time being, it is likely to be tenuous and has to be accompanied by liberal access and freedom to publish information at other times.

NEW DIMENSION OF POLITICAL VIOLENCE

Speculation about nuclear terrorism or the possibility of large-scale chemical and biological contamination carries with it obvious dangers. The margin between widespread awareness of the dangers to put the population on its guard and encouragement by familiarity is a fine one. Increasingly, however, there are some fields of political violence where the onus for preventing it depends to a greater extent than ever before on the cooperation of ordinary members of the public. Major terrorist organizations such as Action Directe and Black War in France, and Revolutionary Cells (RZ) in Germany, have begun to use antinuclear, antiapartheid, and other causes as justifications for action. They have no particular commitment to the cause and are in effect exploiting the sympathies of legitimate campaigners.

More sinister, in some ways, is the infiltration of respectable humanitarian and other groups by small cells of individuals who will not stop at force, firebombs, and small explosive devices, under cover of vegetarianism, animal rights, or antivivisection but with the object of destabilizing society and fomenting antiestablishment sentiment. In the Netherlands, actions in the name of the antiapartheid cause, but against the wishes of the main AA groups and the ANC itself, have caused serious damage over the last two years to stores and petrol stations.

CONCLUSION

In an important sense, these examples of low-level political violence beginning to merge with mainstream terrorist activities constitute a significant pointer to the requirements of counter-terrorist strategy. The coordination of policy internationally first requires determined political will on the part of governments. But if governments are to sustain it in time of crisis when the dilemmas are sharply apparent, then they have deliberately to educate populations concerning the danger of terrorism. It is not a small law and order matter for the security forces to deal with; as it is, developing terrorism can be a major threat to human rights, and its countering requires the alertness as well as the active cooperation of ordinary people. Stemming the progressive institutionalization of violence in Western societies begins with the clear understanding that terrorism, at whatever level, is not a legitimate means of protest or achieving change. Given the climate induced by a real awareness of the danger, the prospects for consistent cooperation in all the directions already mentioned would be much brighter and need not depend on formal treaties, the breaking of which tends to create diplomatic crises.

26

Fighting the Hydra: Terrorism and the Rule of Law

Paul Wilkinson

. . . Before proceeding to a discussion of the problems of international response to terrorism, including the use of international law, it is important to define the scope of the subject. It is wrong to equate terrorism with violence and insurgency in general. Some journalists and politicians have tried to use it as a synonym for guerrilla war, but terrorism is a special mode of violence which, since the late 1960s, has more often than not been used entirely alone, in a pre-insurgency situation. And it is this type of attack—spasmodic bombings, shootings, kidnappings—which has been the characteristic modern pattern in western democracies. Terrorism can be briefly defined as *the systematic use of murder, injury, and destruction, or threat of same, to create a climate of terror, to publicize a cause, and to intimidate a wider target into conceding to the terrorists' aims. . . .*

Context is all in the analysis of political violence. In view of the enormous diversity of groups and aims involved, generalizations and evaluations covering the whole field of modern terrorism should be treated with considerable reserve. Oversimplified analysis of phenomena tends to induce simplistic and dangerous proposals for panaceas. It is a snare and a delusion . . . to assume that there is some quick-fix solution to the whole problem of modern terrorism. For what we are really contending with is a hydra. As soon as the authorities believe they have cut off the head of one movement, another arises in its place. Terrorism is one of the ugliest manifestations of the intractability of human conflict. It is inextricably interwoven with the whole complex of interactions in the international system and the reactive behavior of all actors in the system. One cannot envisage a world without the pervasive element of terror violence unless one assumes a change in the whole nature of international organization and human behavior. . . . Anyone who claims to have a total solution to terrorism in a democracy is either a fool or a knave. This does not mean that there is nothing democracies can do about reducing terrorist violence. There are measures of proven effectiveness which they can undertake while remaining true to their basic values. But such measures are bound to be limited not only by the fundamental requirement that they must be consistent with the maintenance of basic civil rights and

253

democracy, but also by the inherent complexities in the causation and development of political violence.

Let us examine more closely some of the aspects of these complexities which help to explain the manifest weaknesses of international law and organization for dealing with the problem of international terrorism on both a global and a regional basis.

One of these aspects is the existence of a number of regimes in the international system which systematically resort to coercive intimidation in order to control their populations, to suppress dissent, and maintain themselves in power. It is sometimes assumed that although the large-scale violations in human rights can or should provoke international condemnation and pressure on the regime on the part of democracies, there is nothing inherently conducive to international conflict in this situation. But does a state such as the Soviet Union only become a threat to peace when it decides to embark on a military crusade of ideological expansionism? Not so. A regime's persistent use of state terror against its own citizens in itself has profoundly disruptive implications for foreign relations. Other states—especially those which are militarily weaker and contiguous with the violator state—will feel a sense of threat and danger in such behavior. They will be naturally frightened and suspicious of a state that treats its own population so ruthlessly. Those states which feel insecure will tend to band together in defensive alliances. Bipolarization and the formation of alliance blocs, both on global and regional levels, are likely to ensue. The populations and governments of foreign states are likely to find themselves appealed to by victims of oppression. Fugitives from persecution will seek refuge behind the safety of their frontiers. Support organizations for the oppressed populations of terroristic regimes will form. Diplomatic and political interventions to secure improvements in human rights are likely to be mounted. When they are attempted they almost inevitably lead to a deeper polarization between the violator state and the part of the international community which respects human rights. Severe violations of domestic human rights by states are therefore also to be seen as substantial obstacles to improved international relations, the relaxation of tension and the development of trust and cooperation.

Regimes of state terror also tend inevitably to provoke movements of resistance and opposition at home and abroad. If they cannot mount a successful campaign in their original homeland as a result of the severity of the state repression, they will try to do so from abroad. In response the regime of terror instinctively reaches for the weapon of state-sponsored international terrorism to silence and destroy its exiled opponents. In a notorious example, Stalin sent an agent to London to murder the dissident writer Georgi Markov, using a poison-tipped umbrella. Qaddafi [has sent] his hit-squads to hunt down leaders of opposition movements living as refugees in Western Europe and the United States.

These and many other examples show how the very existence of terroristic states in the international system is conducive to the escalation of state-sponsored international terrorism. But they are also conducive to terrorism in two other crucial respects. First, by attempting, if only with limited success, to export ideologies of revolution and to establish client movements and regimes dedicated to coercion for revolutionary ends, they constantly multiply the number of groups and states capable of employing terrorism. They significantly increase the number of sanctuaries, training areas, and sources of arms, cash, diplomatic and propaganda support for international violence. Each newly-established revolutionary regime thus becomes an additional launching-base and conduit for the promotion of further international terrorism. . . .

Second, in an international system which is inherently anarchic due to the lack of a single supranational legal sovereign, the terror states are able to block any effective global effort against international terrorism. Asking the Soviet Union to join in such a system would be like inviting a Mafia chief to take control of the police force. The Soviets and their communist allies regard what we consider sponsorship of international terrorism as being ideologically necessary and entirely justified assistance to "national liberation" and "fraternal revolutionary movements," i.e., a vital tool of their foreign policy.

Far from being able to act effectively on this issue, the member states of the UN have not been able to agree on a definition of international terrorism. The discussion in the Ad Hoc Committee set up in 1973 in the wake of the Munich Olympics massacre in 1972 was vitiated by a fundamental split between those states who wanted to concentrate all the attention on the terror of colonial and racist regimes and assistance to national liberation struggles and those Western states which were primarily seeking UN action to prevent factional terrorism against the innocent.

These fundamental differences of values and ideologies rule out for the foreseeable future any general international legislation designed to deal with the broad range of terrorist crimes in general. But limited progress has been made in international legislation to deal with the very specific examples such as aircraft hijacking and the protection of diplomats. States of almost all ideological hues have gradually come to recognize that their civil airliners and airports cannot gain immunity from aircraft hijacking simply by pretending that it does not happen. The Tokyo Convention on Offences and Certain Other Acts Committed On Board Aircraft (1963) set out for the first time the jurisdictional guiding principles which require all contracting states to make every effort to restore control of the aircraft to its lawful commander and to ensure the prompt onward passage or return of the hijacked aircraft together with its passengers, crew, and cargo. The Hague Convention (1970) requires all parties to extradite apprehended hijackers to their country of origin or to prosecute them under the judicial code of the recipient state. And the Montreal Convention (1971) extended the scope of international law to cover sabotage and attacks on airports and grounded aircraft, and laid down the principle that all such offenses must be subject to severe penalties.

Likewise, the even more radical states came to recognize that *their* diplomats and embassy premises are as much at risk as everyone else's from the growing plague of attacks on diplomatic targets. Castro's Cuban representatives in the U.S., for example, have been the targets of anti-Castro exile groups such as the Omega 7. And the Soviet Union ranks as one of the most victimized states in the league of those states subject to attacks on their diplomats abroad. Hence there is very little opposition in principle to the idea of international legal measures aimed at helping to deter, prevent, and punish the assassination and kidnapping of diplomats. After the spate of diplomatic kidnappings in their region between 1968 and 1971 the Organization of American States formulated a Convention to Prevent and Punish Acts of Terrorism Taking the Form of Crimes Against Persons and Related Extortion that are of International Significance. And there is a UN Convention on the Prevention and Punishment of Crimes Against Internationally Protected Persons, including Diplomatic Agents, adopted by the General Assembly in 1973. The OAS convention sought to define attacks against internationally protected persons as common crimes, regardless of motives, thus making it possible to apply the *aut dedere aut punire* (extradite or prosecute) formula which has been used in most efforts at international legislation on terrorism.

But are these worthy Conventions of practical use? The case of diplomatic terrorism appears to demonstrate their virtual irrelevance. Implementation has inevitably to be left to the contracting states authorities. If the receiving state is weak and ineffective in providing for the security of diplomatic missions, all the sending state can do to help protect its representatives is to protest and to improve the physical security of the embassy buildings and diplomatic residences. The result is obvious from statistics on international terrorism: attacks on diplomats have continued unabated and the profession is still the favorite target of international terrorists worldwide.

In the struggle to suppress aircraft hijacking the value of the Tokyo, Hague, and Montreal Conventions also appears to be only marginal. What has really helped to reverse the rising curve of hijackings was a combination of the system of comprehensive personnel and baggage searches at aircraft boarding gates and the dramatic successes of hostage rescue missions such as Entebbe and Mogadishu, which vividly demonstrated to the terrorists that the authorities could hit back and inflict crushing defeats on the hijackers. There is only one specific contribution from international law which can be said to have played a key role in this battle. Bilateral agreements between states of completely opposed ideological color *have* been effective. For example, the Anti-Hijack Pact between the U.S. and Cuba (1973) was an arrangement of mutual convenience. Castro had become as weary of receiving the criminals and psychopaths who hijacked U.S. flights as the U.S. government had of losing aircraft and passengers to Havana. The Anti-Hijack Pact helped to ensure the return of aircraft, crew, passengers, and hijackers. In effect it bolted the door to the favorite refuge of U.S. aircraft hijackers. . . .

In sum, while there is always scope for trying to strengthen these global international conventions and to pressure more states into ratifying and implementing them, these alone are almost useless. They are a classic illustration of the inadequacy and weakness of international legal measures in dealing with violence and intimidation. There is simply no machinery for sanctions against offending or defaulting states which alone could ensure enforcement. Small wonder that the state sponsors of international terrorism feel free to treat the international law with derision and contempt. . . .

Western governments and public opinion may, not unnaturally, respond to the upsurge of terrorist violence in the third world in a different way. When they see their diplomats and embassies hit, their soldiers and civilians victimized and seriously endangered, some will advocate withdrawing altogether from the high-risk zones. Others demand immediate use of military force to preempt or to retaliate against terrorist organizations and their state-sponsors. The first of these options is not really a practicable policy for the U.S. . . . with vital economic and political interests, alliances, and strategic commitments in every part of the world. . . .

As regards the use of military options, of course, Western military units stationed abroad must defend themselves if they are attacked. . . . But it is one thing for military units to aid the civil power, to exercise the right of self-defense, and to rescue hostages. It is quite another for them to carry out military raids on foreign soil with the aim of preempting, destroying, or punishing terrorists. Such raids will inevitably be seen internationally as acts of war against sovereign states. Almost inevitably, innocent civilians will be killed or injured. This is unavoidable even when raids are restricted to terrorist bases, because almost invariably they base their headquarters in areas of civilian population. There is a grave danger of losing the support of both domestic and international opinion when such raids cause the loss of innocent lives. A great power like the U.S. cannot afford to disregard international opinion or to undermine its moral credibility. In any case it is notoriously difficult to identify and locate the perpetrators of the terrorism one is trying to punish. It is even more difficult to prove beyond reasonable doubt the links between the terrorists and an alleged state sponsor. Most dangerous of all, any military offensive of this kind is almost bound to provoke retaliation and escalation. A military action which starts with raids on selected targets may well end up in the launching of lateral attacks indiscriminately on the population of the host state, or even in a full-scale war.

Terrorism is certainly an evil, but it is by no means the worst evil. It pales into insignificance when one compares it with the lethality and destructiveness of a major civil or international war. Those who have the responsibility for determining the response of Western governments to international terrorism must be aware of these pitfalls and risks. They should always ensure that they have tried to use all the available non-military methods of bringing strong pressure to bear against pro-terrorist states. There is a whole range of non-military options available. States guilty of promoting and instigating terrorist attacks can be arraigned and condemned in the court of world opinion, by concerted Western action at the UN and in other international fora. Individual diplomats from terrorist states who abuse their role can be declared *persona non grata*. Whole diplomatic missions from rogue states can be drastically reduced or expelled. Formal diplomatic relations can be broken. A concerted Western embargo against the export of high technology goods, weapons, and services can be organized. Products from the rogue states can be boycotted. Against medium-sized and small terrorist states such actions are likely to be extremely effective if they are backed by a sufficient number of industrial countries.

A cool and considered response to terrorism drawing on a judicious mixture of all these types of pressures and inducements is much more likely to be successful in bringing a reduction in terrorism without taking the real risks of substituting far more dangerous levels of conflict in the place of the evil one is attempting to combat. The true Grotian response by Western states to terrorism must combine firmness with a commitment to act within the framework of the rule of law. Heaven knows this rule of law internationally is pathetically weak. But it is all we have got. If powerful Western states disregard the inhibitions of international law and use means against terrorism which are totally disproportionate to the threat, they will risk increasing the very anarchy in which terrorists flourish.

27

The United Nations and International Terrorism

Seymour Maxwell Finger

In response to the dramatic increase in terrorist incidents . . . the United Nations has focused greater attention on this serious threat. On 26 June 1985, the fortieth anniversary of the signing of the UN Charter, Secretary General Javier Perez de Cuellar observed:

> In these past days and weeks, the world has faced repeated instances of terrorism in the form of bombings, hijackings and the taking of hostages. The victims have been hundreds of innocent people who have harmed no persons and no cause. Mere condemnation of such acts is insufficient. Effective international action is required. Resolutions and conventions have been adopted in the past by the General Assembly and the International Civil Aviation Organization, outlawing hijackings and the taking of hostages. These provide a vital framework for counter-measures. It is tragically evident, however, that new, multilaterally coordinated efforts are urgently required to deal with this terrible phenomenon, which is beyond the capacity of any one country to handle alone.

That October, the Security Council condemned terrorism "in all its forms" and specifically the hijacking of the Italian cruise ship *Achille Lauro*; and on 17 December 1985, the Council adopted unanimously Resolution 579 which:

1. *Condemns unequivocally* all acts of hostage taking and abduction;
2. *Calls for* the immediate safe release of all hostages and abducted persons wherever and by whomever they are being held;
3. *Affirms* the obligation of all states in whose territory hostages or abducted persons are held urgently to take all appropriate measures to secure their safe release and to prevent the commission of acts of hostage taking and abduction in the future;
4. *Appeals* to all states that have not yet done so to consider becoming parties to the International Convention against the Taking of Hostages adopted on 17 December 1979, the Convention on the Prevention and Punishment of Crimes against Internationally Protected Persons Including Diplomatic Agents adopted on 14 December 1973, the Convention for the Suppression of Unlawful Acts

Note: footnotes have been deleted.

against the Safety of Civil Aviation adopted on 23 September 1971, the Convention for the Suppression of Unlawful Seizure of Aircraft adopted on 16 December 1970, and other relevant conventions;

5. *Urges* the further development of international cooperation among states in devising and adopting effective measures which are in accordance with the rules of international law to facilitate the prevention, prosecution, and punishment of all acts of hostage taking and abduction as manifestations of international terrorism.

Earlier that month, the General Assembly, by a vote of 118-1 (Cuba) and two abstentions (Israel, Burkina Faso), adopted Resolution 40/61 (9 December 1985), which [condemned] unequivocally "as criminal, all acts, methods and practices of terrorism wherever and by whomever committed;" [appealed] to non-party states to ratify the relevant conventions; [called] upon all states "to fulfill their obligations under international law to refrain from organizing, instigating, assisting or participating in terrorist acts in other states, or acquiescing in activities within their territory directed toward the commission of such acts," and to take all appropriate measures "to prevent terrorist attacks against civil aviation and other forms of public transport."

These resolutions [stood] in welcome contrast to the earlier reluctance of many states to condemn international terrorism in unequivocal terms. Unfortunately they are not binding on states, much less on terrorist groups which governments can not or will not control. Even international conventions, which are legally binding, have often been ignored, as did Iran in the American hostage crisis of 1979—81. Clearly, states whose interests are threatened must frequently either take unilateral or multilateral action or stand by in frustration and impotence.

Do resolutions and conventions make any difference and are they worth the effort? I think yes, for several reasons: they establish legal norms, even though these may be breached; they encourage cooperation among interested and willing governments; and they help to legitimize unilateral or multilateral actions against those responsible for terrorism. . . .

[Inspection of the history of the United Nations' performance with respect to, and posture toward, international terrorism, with particular reference to *The Convention on the Prevention and Punishment of Crimes Against Internationally Protected Persons, The Convention Against Hostage Taking,* and *The Convention for the Suppression of Unlawful Seizure of Aircraft,* suggests the progress which has been realized. But that record also suggests the limitations and deficiencies of efforts by the United Nations to impede international terrorist activities. It is therefore] clear that international law against various forms of terrorism must be strengthened both substantively and procedurally. Compliance will be imperfect, often egregiously so, as long as nation-states remain the world power centers and many of them are prepared to flout or ignore international law when it suits their immediate national goals. Then, too, there are countries like

Lebanon, where the government is unable to control terrorist actions even against itself.

These difficulties notwithstanding, every effort must be made to reduce or eliminate ambiguity and strengthen the automaticity of sanctions. Laws can be made less ambiguous if they deal with specific actions that are defined as crimes regardless of alleged political motive; for example, hijacking, kidnapping, *deliberate* killing or maiming of children or other innocent civilians, sending of letter bombs or other explosives through the international mail, and the export of violence to countries and people not party to the conflict. There should be no quibbling about labels, "terrorist" or "freedom fighter." As [T. M.] Franck and [B. B.] Lockwood have observed: "Terrorism is an historically misleading and politically loaded term which invites conceptual and ideological dissonance." A crime is a crime, regardless of pretext.

A constant effort must be made to strengthen existing legal instruments and adopt new conventions, as required, and these instruments must be enforced.

At the present stage of international law and organization, enforcement of the law is not in the hands of the UN or ICAO [International Civil Aviation Organization]; it must be the job of governments. If all governments are not prepared to enforce the law and to apprehend and punish the criminals, then those governments that are ready to act must do so decisively and cooperatively. A government can be excluded from cooperative efforts to enforce the law only by itself.

Action is required not only against the terrorists themselves but also against those governments which assist, protect, or harbor them. This should include not only sanctions by governments but also nongovernmental action; for example, a boycott by the International Federation of Airline Pilots Associations (IFALPA). Timidity in taking such actions has brought heavier burdens to Western European countries that are trying to contain terrorism than to [sponsors of terrorism such as] Libya and Syria, whose failure to cooperate handicaps the enforcement of international law.

Governmental and non-governmental actions against terrorism are not substitutes for law. On the contrary, they are essential supplements if the law is to have any meaning. They should include not only police work to apprehend criminals but also swift and sure punishment. Intelligence work involving various national agencies and cooperation among such agencies is crucial. Paying informants and offering reduced sentences to criminals as an inducement to inform are useful tools. Constant work to improve security and vigilance at airports, embassies and other vulnerable installations must go forward; as criminals improve their techniques, so must the law enforcers and defenders.

Let us not mock the weakness of international laws against terrorist crimes. Instead, let us strive for strengthening and enforcing them, no matter what the difficulties and hindrances.

28

Responses to Dissident Terrorism: From Myth to Maturity

Peter C. Sederberg

Calvin: What do you think is the best way to get what you want? Is it better to hold fast and never back down, or to compromise?

Hobbes: I suppose it's best to hold fast when you can, and compromise when you must.

Calvin: That's a lot more mature than I think I care to be.

—Bill Watterston, "Calvin and Hobbes"

MYTHICAL SOLUTIONS TO TERRORISM

When victimized by a terrorist outrage, many people, including political leaders, understandably want to strike back, to inflict a painful retribution on those responsible. Such an emotional reaction provides a powerful, though not necessarily rational, underpinning to one myth about how best to deal with terrorism. The myth of severe retribution, in its extreme form, perceives those resorting to terrorism as "mad dogs," and death is the only cure for the threat posed by a mad dog. Those who unleash mad dogs on the world—the terrorist-sponsoring states—must also be dealt with severely.

Paul Johnson, an advocate of the counterterrorist hard line, asserts: "It must be made clear to the master killers of Tehran and Tripoli that there can be no ultimate hiding place for them either, that the arm of civilization is long and sinewy and may be stretched out to take them by the throat." Johnson goes on to suggest that the Western nations determine "the limits beyond which the terrorist states will not be allowed to pass, and let us perfect a military instrument of fearful retribution when and if those limits are ever crossed."[1] Johnson cites the 1982 Israeli invasion of Lebanon as precisely the kind of operation he advocates. He fails to note, however, the extent to which this "drastic treatment" developed into a weeping sore on the Israeli body politic.

In contrast, the other mythic solution exaggerates the capacity of conciliation to cure terrorism. Rather than emphasizing the ruthless character of the perpetrators of terrorism and the cynical manipulations of their sponsors, this myth stresses the origins of frustration felt by those who feel driven to resort to terrorism. By recognizing the conditions that nurture extremist politics, this myth encourages a counterterrorist policy aimed at alleviating the root causes of radical discontent. Not surprisingly, this approach tends to play down the role of external sponsors just as the opposing myth stresses the significance of such support.

Richard E. Rubenstein offers an interpretation of dissident terrorism that understands it as being largely rooted in a crisis of "social disconnection" existing between militant intellectuals and the masses they wish to lead. Terrorism represents "an intellectual attempting to shoot his way out of isolation."[2]

> Based on this understanding, Rubenstein suggests that the most effective counterterrorist device yet discovered is a popular mobilization for significant change. Domestic terrorism can be averted, in the long run, only when there are mass-based organizations capable of linking the youthful intelligentsia to the people.[3]

Few establishments under siege, however, are likely to be enthusiastic about policies providing political "therapy" to alienated intellectuals, nor are they able to make the kinds of concessions that would satisfy radical demands.

These two myths pose some other instructive contrasts. The myth of retribution stresses immediate response at the expense of long-term solutions; the myth of social cure, by focusing on presumed underlying causes, fails to address immediate security concerns. Moreover, although violent reprisals to terrorist provocations might reinforce the conditions nurturing the desperation that gives rise to terrorism, meaningful reform may well increase anger with the remaining grievances and, in fact, could stimulate extremists who feel threatened by any moderate solution.

If we consider terrorism to be a particular form of coercive tactic selected by a variety of groups pursuing different purposes, then context becomes more important in determining appropriate response. When context changes, appropriate response also varies. As J. Bowyer Bell simply admonishes, "Know thy terrorist," although he admits such advice is more easily offered than followed.[4]

Among the factors that should affect the shape of response to dissident terrorism are the following:

1. **The ideological aims of the dissident groups.** We might expect that groups desiring the destruction of the established order (nihilists) and/or its radical transformation would not be open to much compromise of their political objectives. Desire for greater autonomy within the established political order or independence from it, when this devolution does not threaten the survival of the established state (for example, the aspirations for independence possessed by a colony) offers greater promise for negotiated settlement.

2. **The relative isolation/representativeness of the dissident group.** Punitive actions against fringe elements may be more successful than those against groups who are strongly supported by a significant segment of the population.

3. **The role of terrorism in the overall dissident strategy.** As dissident groups become more representative and as they more successfully organize their communities for resistance, the relative role of terrorist tactics may well diminish. A regime that attempts to delude itself that a full-scale rebellion is only an isolated band of "criminal terrorists" courts disaster.

4. **The significance of external sponsors.** If a group is a puppet, then pressure on the master may work. The more autonomous the dissident movement, regardless of whether it receives external support and approval, the less effective will be those counterterrorist policies that ignore internal dynamics to concentrate on external conspiracy theories.

Our identification of these broad considerations to be taken into account when formulating responses to terrorism suggests why an "all-purpose" terrorist policy cannot be prescribed.[5] Moreover, while external sponsorship and conspiracy undeniably comprise an element of global terrorism, the diversity of sponsorship and the complexity of its nature make it impossible to substitute facile consistency for serious analysis. Paul Wilkinson correctly notes the following: "Over-simplified analysis of [terrorism] tends to produce simplistic and dangerous proposals for panaceas. It is a snare and a delusion for any democratic government to assume that there is some quick-fix solution to the whole problem of modern terrorism."[6] And, in fact, a variety of counterterrorist programs have been tried over the years with mixed success.

RESPONSES TO TERRORISM

Attachment to one or the other of the mythic responses to terrorism impoverishes our understanding of the range of available options that are actually at the disposal of regimes (and nonstate actors). These options, all of which have been tried to some degree at one time or another, arise not from some systematic theory of counterterrorism so much as reactions to different situations and opportunities. We must, therefore, attempt to identify the elements that affect the degree of success enjoyed by a variety of particular actions and policies.

Legal Responses to Terrorism

Arguably, our first response to terrorism, whether dissident or establishment, should be to look to legal remedies. We should ask: Do laws exist that, if effectively enforced, could reduce the threat of terrorism, or do new legal regulations need to be devised? This does not mean that the other responses are necessarily illegal, although they may be; rather, the law presumes to define the arena within which other policies might be pursued. Generally, domestic law, backed by a sovereign political authority, defines and defends legal boundaries more successfully than does international law. However, both domestic and international legal remedies to terrorism deserve consideration.

Successful laws combine repression and reconciliation, at least to some extent. Certainly law enforcement involves restricting some behavior, but the process of law formation also reflects other considerations, from fundamental legal norms (like due process), which need to be preserved, to political objectives other than simple repression. Effectively enforced laws, moreover, can both dampen existing terrorist outbreaks and discourage terrorist campaigns in the future.

Domestic Legal Remedies. When faced with an outbreak of dissident terrorism, many countries devise new laws to strengthen the ability of the government to respond effectively. Among the measures approved in Western nations plagued by terrorism since 1970 are harsh penalties for acts defined as terrorist (for example, hijackings, political kidnappings); creation of special courts and prosecutors to try those accused of terrorism; restrictions on the freedom of movement both internally and across national boundaries (for instance, the new visa regulations imposed by France after a series of bombings in Paris in the latter part of 1986); and restrictions on media reports of terrorist incidents.[7] Of course, new laws mean little if they cannot be enforced, and countries confronting terrorism typically reinforce their police, sometimes creating specially trained units to carry out counterterrorist enforcement.

Such measures, though understandable reactions in the context of domestic turmoil, create certain problems in a liberal democratic system. Grant Wardlaw, in an analysis of German counterterrorist legislation, identifies a number of disturbing initiatives.[8] One such measure is the "job ban" (*Berufsverbot*), which created a process for determining "the suitability of individuals to be hired for or maintain a tenured status in the German civil service."[9] Although similar "loyalty" provisions exist in other legal codes (the U.S. code, for example, denies public employment to those advocating the violent overthrow of the government), the Germans have apparently applied the provisions broadly and with a certain enthusiasm, sometimes using the most tenuous connection with a radical group to terminate someone's employment. In other instances, the law was apparently used to fire people who simply criticized the government.[10] Another controversial legal measure involves restrictions on and surveillance of lawyers who defend radicals.[11]

The vigorous, perhaps excessive, German legal response to terrorism contrasts with the more moderate Italian actions. The threat to stability represented by the Red Brigade in Italy surpassed anything that confronted Germany in the same period. Italian judicial response and enhanced law enforcement contributed to a plummeting of terrorist attacks from about 2,500 in 1979 to fewer than 100 in 1986.[12] This dramatic reduction was brought about without a ban on public employment of people suspected of radical leanings or the creation of special nonjury courts to try accused terrorists (as were set up in France). Italian security forces have attempted to minimize arbitrary surveillance measures, which they believe only contribute to a siege mentality. Italian success seems largely attributable to judicial firmness in the existing Italian courts combined with improved police work (infiltration of the Brigades, clemency for former radicals who cooperate with law enforcement officials, and so on).

Closely related to the formulation of new legal remedies is the enhancement of police powers. As domestic turmoil deepens, the ability of conventional police forces to deal with the attacks may be severely taxed. Although tempting, the militarization of the police forces or, even more serious, the use of regular military units for domestic law-and-order missions represents a grave escalation of response that may well subvert the constitutional order as readily as the terrorist attacks themselves. Wardlaw argues, though, that there may be some terrorist events that even specially trained and equipped police may find difficult to handle, such as the seizure of a major installation.[13]

To prepare for such a circumstance, joint military/police operations must be planned, or a special military force created and carefully trained. The United States, Great Britain, and West Germany have all created such forces. The potential cost of ill-planned militarization of the struggle against terrorism was amply illustrated by the response to the takeover of the Palace of Justice in Bogota, Colombia on November 13, 1985. The Colombian government refused to negotiate and called in the armed forces to break the siege; in the resulting battle, at least 100 people died, including eleven supreme court justices.[14]

Wardlaw makes a number of sensible observations concerning the development of vigorous legal responses to a dissident terrorist threat. First, he notes that "the duty of the government is to balance the extent of the response with the seriousness of the problem and the rights of its citizens."[15] He recommends that any new powers given to courts or police be balanced by legal checks and that emergency provisions be repealed once the crisis has passed. Finally, he cautions that legal measures to combat terrorism usually do not provide long-term solutions: "The pity is that in many instances governments seem almost to have stopped thinking about the 'why' of terrorism once they have introduced police and judicial measures to try to contain it. They fail to see that containment is not equivalent to understanding and solution."[16]

International Legal Remedies.   Since terrorism often transcends the boundaries of individual nation-states, international law constitutes another possible arena of recourse. The emphasis, once again, has been on devising compacts to combat the more blatant forms of international dissident terrorism, such as air piracy, diplomatic hostage taking, and so on.

Attempts to address the problem of terrorism through international law often founder on both the ideological diversity of the world's nations and the presence of an essentially anarchic international system. The absence of a global sovereign authority frustrates the formation and enforcement of international law in areas less contentious than the regulation of international terrorism.

Compacts on terrorism tend to challenge the "sacred" principle of the right to "self-determination," undercutting many efforts to deal with dissident terrorism. Definitions of terrorism generally involve disputes over wars of national liberation fought by presumably oppressed peoples. Communist countries and many Third World states vigorously oppose any measure that appears directed against the Palestinian movement or that might limit the black struggle in South Africa. Somewhat related to the support of national liberation movements is the desire to protect the right of political asylum for those persecuted for their beliefs. Regimes are not above labeling all those engaged in dissent as "terrorists." The task, then, is to delineate the line between "political offenses" and "international crimes."[17] We might expect that conflict over this distinction will usually reflect partisan ideological preferences.

Despite such difficulties that have frustrated efforts to achieve a United Nations agreement on dissident international terrorism in general, some progress has been made with respect to specific terrorist offenses, especially the protection of diplomats and the related area of hostage taking.[18] In addition, several international agreements on air piracy exist, the first dating back to 1963.[19] Finally, regional compacts, such as the European Convention on the Suppression of Terrorism (1977), have been achieved, providing for a greater degree of regional coordination in the struggle against terrorism.[20] Such successes, though, are limited by the absence of effective enforcement.

Repressive Responses to Terrorism

The formulation of new laws, both domestic and international, to combat terrorism entails elements of both repression (behavior regulation) and conciliation. Often, when confronted with an outbreak of terrorism or when fearful that such an outbreak is imminent, a regime may turn to specifically repressive actions. These policies may be within the law or beyond it, either by acting in areas where the law is not clear (especially in the international arena) or by directly violating existing law in the name of some higher order.

A variety of repressive tactics of varying intensity have been tried, some intended to counter and contain ongoing terrorist campaigns, others designed to deter or prevent terrorism over the longer term. Milder forms of repressive, counterterrorist policy include nonmilitary pressure and improved security. More severe alternatives range from immediate reprisals to long-term military intervention.

Nonmilitary Pressure.   Both regimes and nonstate actors have various ways of bringing nonmilitary (though still coercive) pressure on those engaging in or sponsoring terrorism. Among these methods—in order of increasing severity—are programs of public condemnation of terrorist acts and sponsors; expulsion of diplomats from states believed to be supporting terrorism; complete ruptures in diplomatic relations; arms embargoes, and comprehensive economic sanctions. Nonstate actors can also bring forms of pressure on states engaged in terrorism. Airline pilots, for example, have threatened to boycott those countries seen to be tolerating airline hijackings.

Such pressure tactics are generally imposed on the offending states by external actors, whether other states or private groups. Internal pressure, though, may also be brought to bear if the participants have sufficient courage. In Northern Ireland, women, both Protestant and Catholic, have organized protests against the sectarian violence afflicting that community. Even in Beirut, demonstrations have been held to protest the continual kidnappings.

The success of nonmilitary pressure tactics is not easy to determine. After Syria was implicated in the plot to blow up an El Al airliner in April 1986 (a possible reprisal for the United States' attack on Libya earlier that month), Great Britain broke off diplomatic relations and a number of other Western nations, including the United States, followed with more mild diplomatic sanctions. These measures may have contributed to Syria's sense of isolation and a consequent moderation of its support of terrorism in 1987. On the other hand, Syria's frustration with the chaotic situation in Lebanon may be a more significant motive behind its diminished support for extremist groups.

Arms embargoes and economic sanctions would seem to be especially promising means to pressure those engaged in terrorism. Unfortunately, such sanctions have proven notoriously difficult to impose effectively. The basic problem seems to be that the more widespread the adherence to the sanction, the greater the incentive (that is, profit) for those not participating to continue to do business with the target country, especially if that country possesses a highly desirable resource like oil (Iran) or gold (South Africa). Add ideological affinities to this profit motive, and the probability is high that some countries will break ranks with the sanctions movement.

If the target is economically weak or dependent on one or a few suppliers for key imports, sanctions might be more easily imposed and enforced (assuming an ideological consensus among the suppliers). Governments, however, can still find reasons to evade them. As the Iran/Contra mess of 1986-1987 revealed, the United States was not above violating its own arms embargo against Iran in hopes of gaining the release of Americans held hostage in Lebanon.

International and internal pressure against those using terrorist tactics still has much to offer, especially when applied to relatively vulnerable groups or states. Many times, however, those committing or aiding terrorism care little about public opinion outside their own support group and may not be especially susceptible to externally imposed sanctions. Those victimized by terrorism must then look to other means of protecting themselves.

Improved Security.   If countries cannot stop terrorism at its source, they can discourage it by improving the security of likely targets. The intense security at El Al Airlines prevented the bombing attempted in April 1986 when an alert baggage inspector noticed a bag was suspiciously heavy. Good police work, internally and involving cross-national cooperation, interdicts many terrorist plans. It is difficult to estimate the full level of success in this area, because police and intelligence services do not always publicize their accomplishments for fear of compromising their sources of information and methods of operation. In addition, possible targets of terrorist attack, from embassies to nuclear power plants, may be "hardened" to increase the costs to those who might contemplate such attacks. Although difficult to demonstrate conclusively, improved intelligence, successful police work, and increased defense of likely targets may be the most important contributors to the reduction of some forms of dissident terrorism in the late 1980s.

Improved security measures, though they may deter dissident terrorism, do not address the root causes of frustration, and they suffer from their own peculiar shortcomings. Most important, increased police surveillance along with the "hardening" of public buildings, moves a political community away from conditions of noninterference in private lives and access to public spaces associated with a constitutional democracy. Undoubtedly, all of these policies can be justified in the name of public order, and many of us would accept some intrusive measures to lower our anxiety about being a victim of terrorism. We want intelligence services to keep track of those suspected of contemplating terrorist attacks. We concede the need to protect our public buildings, even if this makes them more fortresslike and inaccessible.

But how far should this quest for security go? Should checkpoints be set up throughout our cities? Should the public be completely cut off from their representatives? Should everyone suspected of harboring dissenting views be closely monitored, just in case the person might have links to violent groups? The fear of terrorism, then, can induce a mania for security that undermines the very character of the political system presumably being defended. Terrorism might be defeated, but the political community will not have won. Moreover, improved security in some areas, ironically, may have an unintended side effect of encouraging extremist forces to attack other, softer targets—tourists instead of diplomats; department stores instead of embassies.

Military Reprisals.   Improved security measures, whatever their merits, suffer from another major drawback: They appear relatively passive. Once victimized by terrorism, people might not be content with simply beefing up security and hoping to do better next time. Some will undoubtedly be interested in striking back at those responsible. Military reprisals consist of acts of retaliation for specific offenses directed by one state or group against another.[21] Reprisals obviously may be used in response to other deeds than simply terrorism, but we will confine our attention here to military strikes designed to punish the presumed perpetrators of specific terrorist acts. Reprisals, then, follow upon a particular terrorist event or related events. To be effective, they must be closely tied to the incident being punished. The main instrumental purpose (other than merely venting spleen) is to persuade those engaged in terrorism to cease and desist.

In order to effect a discriminating reprisal, whether internal or international, the retaliating power must have accurate intelligence and the capacity to attack precisely. In the case of the American bombing of Qaddafi's headquarters, which was partly in reprisal for presumed Libyan sponsorship of terrorist attacks in Europe, the planners apparently had the intelligence but chose not to use precise means. Israel, too, has often killed many civilians in its retaliatory air attacks. Moreover, as Livingstone correctly observes, reprisals to succeed assume "a rational adversary who can be intimidated into showing restraint."[22] Retaliation against a powerful and dedicated opponent may result in both high casualities in the attacking force and an escalation of counterreprisals. Such considerations seem to contribute to both American and Israeli restraint in dealing with Syria.

Finally, although reprisals may succeed in intimidating a relatively weak and isolated adversary into ceasing terrorist activities, it fails to address the sources of frustration and anger that give rise to extremist politics in the first place. To attack these roots even more ambitious repressive measures may be undertaken.

Preemptive Strikes.   Preemption "entails striking in advance of hostile action to prevent its occurrence and to avoid suffering injury."[23] Although the primary purpose of preemption is prevention, a demonstrated willingness and capability to preempt may have a deterrent effect over the long run. For these reasons, preemption against dissident terrorism appears to be a seductively attractive tactic.

Preemption, though, suffers certain drawbacks. Most importantly, such strikes "run the risk of relinquishing the moral high ground that derives from being a victim of an attack and therefore entitled to some form of redress."[24] Indeed, the preemptor might very well be preceived as the aggressor, no matter how well founded the basis for the attack. Consequently, the preemptor faces a serious problem of public justification, or else its military success could turn into a moral and political victory for those who are attacked. A preemptive strike, moreover, may purchase a short term success at the cost of intensifying the struggle over the long run.

These substantive risks place a high value on precise intelligence about *who* is planning to do *what* and *when*. Such precision is not easily achieved in counterterrorist intelligence, and, as Neil Livingstone notes, advisors may only be able to identify probabilities, not certainties. The political leadership, then, may be forced to agonize over a potentially costly course of action on the basis of highly imperfect information. For this reason, Livingstone recommends preemption only as a last resort to prevent a terrorist attack that seems almost certainly forthcoming.[25]

Retribution Campaigns.   Simple preemption against a particular attack in the offing may do little to prevent future terrorist attacks, although it may complicate the perpetrator's own security problem. Improved security, while raising the possible costs of engaging in terrorism and protecting some of a community's more important "soft" spots, fails to attack terrorism at its roots. Retribution campaigns hold out the promise of more vigorous repressive measures that may yield longer-term results. These campaigns involve a shadow war against the political infrastructure of an opponent. Livingstone argues that a force should be created capable of "taking the offensive against international terrorism."[26] Such a force would be patterened somewhat after the secret Israeli counterterrorist group *Mivtzan Elohim* (Wrath of God), which waged a running war against those held responsible for the massacre of Israeli athletes at the 1972 Munich Olympics.

Advocates of retribution campaigns suggest that liberal democracies should authorize a covert organization involved in everything from disinformation to assassination. Although this appears to raise some serious ethical questions, Livingstone argues that such campaigns are "infinitely more humane than blasting heavily populated villages in reprisal air raids or shelling them with 16-inch guns from a battleship."[27] Indeed, we could argue that whereas indiscriminate bombings are likely to reinforce the resentment that fuels extremists politics, a careful campaign of retribution probably will generate more fear among those using terrorism than anger among a wider population.

Of course, we can always make a policy look more restrained and "humane" by contrasting it with one still more extreme. Aimlessly shelling the hills around Beirut, for example, could be preferred to blanketing them with the carpet bombings of a conventional B-52 air strike, much less obliterating them with nuclear weapons. Ultimately a policy must be judged on its own merits and not simply on the basis of comparisons with even more dubious alternatives.

Retribution campaigns place severe demands on the intelligence and covert action capabilities of a regime. Livingstone suggests that such an American unit should draw upon the expertise of both the Department of Defense and the Central Intelligence Agency.[28] Personnel would be chosen to reflect a broad range of age, experiences, and lifestyles. He recommends the recruitment of foreign nationals on the lines of the French Foreign Legion. This unit must have the ability to track suspects and engage in successful covert actions, some of which would conceivably involve breaking the laws of our own or those of other countries (for example, burglary, wiretaps, assassination). Blunders in such operations can be costly, as Israel discovered when one of its hit teams killed an innocent man by mistake in Norway in 1973.

Livingstone, to be sure, calls for a "restrictive" charter, an absolute ban on deployment of the unit on U.S. territory, and "prudent congressional consultation."[29] Such organizations, however, are inherently difficult to control because, by their nature, they are highly secretive, and they are engaged in activities that are at least formally illegal. We should also have some qualms about the kind of individual who might be attracted to such service; certainly the French Foreign Legion is not an altogether encouraging model. Moreover, given the experiences of Iranscam, Watergate, and J. Edgar Hoover's use of the FBI to disrupt dissenting groups in the 1960s and early 1970s, we can hardly be nonchalant about the potential for abuse that such an instrument poses. It would certainly not be difficult to imagine a sequence where a retribution campaign against radical dissidents degenerates into establishment terrorism. Indeed, this seems to be the path taken by Uruguay and Argentina in the 1970s.

Covert activities probably constitute a necessary component in any effort to eliminate dissident terrorism. In fact, a regime attempting to control rogue establishment groups would also find it useful to infiltrate these groups for information that could lead to preemptive actions. As a general principle, we should be increasingly skeptical of covert activities as they move from authorized intelligence gathering, to gray areas such as disinformation campaigns, to actions in clear violation of our governing laws and principles, such as assassination.

Military Intervention.   The most extreme repressive response to terrorism originating in another country is a direct military intervention to extirpate it branch and root. Two major military interventions of the past decade have been motivated, at least in part, by the desire to halt some form of terrorism. One of these, the Israeli invasion of Lebanon in 1982, was directed against Palestinian terrorism. The other, the Vietnamese invasion of Cambodia in 1978, was partly motivated by a desire to stop the genocidal establishment terrorism of the Pol Pot regime. The consequences for both of the intervening countries do little to recommend such extreme tactics to others. Each country suffered international condemnation, and each found itself in a protracted conflict from which neither nation has been able to extricate itself fully.

Israel invaded Lebanon presumably to secure its borders against Palestinian infiltration and to support some of its Lebanese allies, but the Israeli leadership saw an opportunity to drive the PLO out of Lebanon entirely. Although initially successful, the invasion mired the Israeli army in a war of attrition against Lebanese Shi'ites and Druze as well as associated it with a major act of terrorism in the Palestinian refugee camps of Sabra and Shatila. The invading army gradually withdrew close to its own border, and by 1987 the PLO fighters were back in Lebanon.

Vietnam attacked its erstwhile ally partly because of the oppression endured by ethnic Vietnamese in Cambodia, and partly because of the calculation that Vietnam could expand its sphere of influence. However, the Vietnamese appear to have underestimated the resentment that fueled several Cambodian guerrilla groups, including the remnants of the Pol Pot regime.

Both interventions raised widespread protests over the violation of the sovereignty and territorial integrity of another state, although both countries had their supporters. The invocation of the principle of nonintervention, even with respect to a regime as murderous as Pol Pot's or an internal situation as anarchic as Lebanon's, demonstrates some of the frailties of the international order. In the absence of a clear-cut consensus on the validity of full-scale military intervention against terrorism—whether dissident or establishment—such actions are likely to be both risky and costly. The United States found out just how costly this can be with the death of its marines in Lebanon in 1983.

When such a consensus can be established, however, "humanitarian" intervention may serve to pacify some forms of communal violence, including terrorism. The United Nations has met with some limited success in this area, as on Cyprus, where UN forces separated warring Greek and Turkish communities.[30] More recently, in 1987, both sides in the communal war in Sri Lanka initially accepted Indian military intervention to help enforce a cease fire and provisional political settlement. It is not yet clear whether the Indians will succeed in mediating the dispute between the Tamil and Sinhalese communities or whether they will find themselves merely caught in a crossfire.

External policing of an internal dispute, although it may be effective at the beginning, does not address the underlying issues that divided communal groups. Unless the sources of frustration and anger can be reduced, the intervening "police force" may find itself first compromised and then targeted. Political solutions, whether short or long term, may require something more than variations on themes of repression; they may demand some forms of conciliation.

Conciliatory Responses to Terrorism

Given their potential risks and costs, repressive strategies, especially the more dramatic ones of retribution campaigns and military intervention, may tend to be overvalued. On the other hand, conciliatory responses are generally rejected out of hand (even though most every regime ends up using them at one time or another). Especially when confronted with a spurt of dissident terrorism, many countries, including the United States, announce a tough policy of "no negotiations/no concessions" with terrorists.

A "hard-line" policy sounds impressive and reflects the conventional wisdom that any form of conciliatory response will only encourage further terrorism. Repression, however, would seem to be most effective against fringe elements—and even there compromise might sometimes be justified. When the dissidents reflect widely shared and deeply held grievances, then an absolute ban on conciliation may prove to be both costly and futile over the long run and may even intensify the conflict.

Concessions.   The short-term conciliatory response to terrorism is to accede to the immediate demands of the perpetrators in order to end a particular incident or campaign. It should come as no great surprise that this idea draws heavy criticism, because it would appear to encourage the successful extortionists, and others who might be inclined to emulate them, to continue or even intensify their activities.

A policy of short-term concessions presumes that the perpetrators make reasonably concrete demands on a government (or private group like a corporation). Among the typical demands that have been met are those for ransom, release of jailed compatriots, and publicity for the dissidents' political program. Dissident demands for structural transformation, in contrast, are not the subject of concessions, although they might be addressed through longer-term reforms (see below).

Concessions to terrorism obviously appear to reward such activities and may therefore reinforce them. Nevertheless, governments and corporations have often met such demands: Ransoms have been paid, dissidents released, and revolutionary statements published. Although such concessions may seem dubious, a policy that absolutely prohibits them under any circumstances may be unworkable and even ill-conceived.

Grant Wardlaw, who takes a relatively strong stand against concessions to dissident terrorism, emphasizes that his recommendation refers to the dissidents' "political demands."[31] What he means by this is not altogether clear, but it implies that there may be some lesser points that could be conceded. Wardlaw also recognizes the enormous political pressure that can be placed upon leaders in a democracy, especially by relatives, friends, and sympathizers, to gain the release of loved ones.

Even these rather grudging qualifications indicate that the costs and risks of concessions must be balanced against potential benefits, and concessions cannot be absolutely dismissed. For example, should a regime reject out of hand the exchange of a small concession—say, the publication of the dissidents' political manifesto—for the safe release of many hostages and the peaceful surrender of the perpetrators? Rejection of this concession is by no means the obvious choice. Perhaps more substantive concessions may be justified when compared with the costs of a policy of no compromise.

Nor should we accept, without qualification, the proposition that making concessions to terrorism necessarily leads to more terrorism. The causal path is far more complex than this. Minor concessions may carry little weight in the deliberations of those who contemplate the risks and benefits of further terrorist action. The probability of some payoff is only one part of the decision to engage in terrorism, and a government making a concession to resolve an immediate problem may counter the presumably increased incentive for future terrorism by raising its cost. If, for example, likely targets are hardened, intelligence improved, and police counterterrorist capabilities strengthened, further terrorist attacks may become too costly, regardless of past successes.

These observations do not mean that governments should give in to all demands. Generally, there may be sound reasons for resisting, even at some risk to hostages' lives. The point is, rather, that empty axioms like "no concessions to terrorists" are not a substitute for serious analysis and judicious assessment of the potential risks and benefits, as far as they can be identified. If the concessions needed are relatively minor or if the failure to make some concession is likely to be catastrophic, then "contingent concessions" might be made.[32] Fringe groups might be given minimal concessions and later subjected to reprisals and repression. More serious challenges, however, may require something more than ransom payoffs or prisoner exchanges—the situation may demand conciliatory reforms. In either the case of short-term concessions or long-term reform, conciliatory responses to terrorism involve negotiations with the perpetrators.

Negotiations.   Even Grant Wardlaw, who rejects making substantive concessions to groups using terror tactics, recognizes the need for some flexibility in counterterrorist policy. He states that "a 'no concessions' policy should not imply a 'no negotiations' one."[33] Israel probably approaches the latter case, but it is not clear that this rigid rejection of most negotiations has deterred terrorism; it may arguably lead to an escalation of terrorism as the Palestinian dissidents attempt to gain some recognition. In any case, patient hostage negotiations, in particular, have been successful under some circumstances in gaining the release of the hostages with little or no damage to the regime's position.

Negotiation may be either a short-term reaction to a particular terrorist event, sometimes intended to buy time to design an appropriate repressive response, or a longer-term process aimed at reducing the intensity of the conflict between the contending sides in a political struggle. Even though it may seem reasonable to at least talk with one's adversaries, all negotiations involve potential risks and costs.

First, such discussions, even when no concessions are contemplated, may confer a kind of legitimacy craved by those resorting to terrorism. For this reason, the Israelis refuse to negotiate with the PLO. Such recognition will be especially significant in a relatively open society, where negotiations may proceed in the glare of the media.

Moreover, once negotiations begin, pressure may build for concessions initially rejected by the government. Public expectations may increase, making it difficult for the government to break off negotiations and implement more repressive countermeasures. At a minimum, therefore, the government should have a clear idea of its limits and be willing to stick by them when entering into a negotiating process.

Finally, the character of the negotiations will vary with the significance of the group using terrorism. Negotiations with fringe movements must be tightly controlled so that no significant concessions are made that might encourage other extremist elements. In contrast, if the group engaged in terrorism is representative of a significant disaffected community and/or terror tactics represent only one element of a more encompassing military and political strategy, then negotiations must necessarily be more flexible, long term, and substantive.

Reform.   Those condemning the "soft-line" or conciliatory responses to terrorism tend to focus on the "terrorist" and little more. If terrorism, however, is viewed as a tactic that a variety of groups may use, then such a quick dismissal may neglect a long-term strategy of reconciliation that could prove quite capable of reducing or eliminating the sources of terrorism. If the groups using terrorism have a broad base of support and substantive grievances, then consideration should be given to the possibility of reform to meet these grievances.[34]

Structural reform to lessen the underlying grievances of those who instigate (or tolerate) terrorism smacks of the kind of "surrender to terrorism" that many commentators reject. Certainly such an alternative is largely irrelevant if those committing terrorism are either on the margins of society or pursuing some absolutist ideological fantasy—whether that of nihilist destruction or genocidal purification. If the objectives are more limited, reasonably concrete, and widely supported, then some strategy of structural reform may have to be pursued.

The devolution of power to a previously dominated community seems to provide the clearest cases where these conditions hold. The alienated population may simply have limited aspirations for greater autonomy (or even independence) and may not threaten the core interests of their rulers. In many cases of resistance to colonial rule, the imperial power simply cut its losses and agreed to independence. The struggle against the British occupation of Palestine by those seeking the foundation of Israel after the end of World War II and in Cyprus in the 1950s involved actions that at least the British viewed as terrorist. Yet the British Empire had entered its twilight era, and continued military occupation of these territories in the name of resisting terrorism would probably have proven costly and fruitless.

Even where the British succeeded in crushing a native resistance movement, as with the Mau Mau in Kenya in the 1950s, they moved rapidly to give the restive colony its independence, turning power over to Jomo Kenyatta, whom they had earlier jailed as a terrorist. To argue that decolonization was a mistake because one should not reward terrorism seems largely irrelevant.

Decolonization, admittedly, provides perhaps the most straightforward example where substantive change can alleviate the sources of terrorism and other forms of dissident violence. When the people demanding autonomy are more closely integrated in an existing state, the willingness and ability of the government to respond may be much more limited. Algeria was considered to be a part of metropolitan France when violent Arab resistance to continued French rule began in 1954. The ensuing struggle was both long and bitter, and it involved acts of both dissident and regime terrorism, especially during the famous Battle of Algiers (1957). Nevertheless, by the early 1960s, French President Charles de Gaulle was ready to negotiate Algerian independence, even though the French army possessed military superiority over the rebels, in order to end what he believed was a bloody, useless drain on French resources. In retrospect, de Gaulle's action is considered one of courageous statesmanship, not a surrender to terrorists.

The Palestinians present a more intractable case of bitter grievances and stubborn resistance to significant reforms to meliorate these frustrations. The desire for an autonomous Palestinian state conflicts with the core interests of Israel and, in part, accounts for the Israeli insistence that the PLO is nothing more than a "terrorist organization." On the other hand, the more radical Palestinians have made little secret of their desire to destroy the "Zionist entity," a position that hardly encourages moderation on the part of their opponent. Yet the recent willingness of the PLO to accept Israel's right to exist seems to present opportunities for negotiation and accommodation, if the Israeli government can find a way around its refusal to deal with "PLO terrorists."

We could multiply the examples of the use of reform to counter the causes of terrorism further, but these should suffice to illustrate several points. First, the relevance of reform to the problem of terrorism depends on what we might term the *representativeness* of those using terrorism. The more that dissident groups reflect widespread grievances, then the more relevant reform may be as a response.

Second, the more concrete and specific the changes needed and the less they threaten the core interests of establishment groups, the easier it will be to institute them. Nevertheless, as the French experience in Algeria makes clear, even relatively significant interests may be compromised if the costs of defending them appears unacceptably high.

Third, reforms often stimulate resistance on the part of extremists on both sides of the struggle. Radical dissidents may fear the erosion of their base of support; intransigent elements of the establishment may resist any concessions that appear to threaten their privileges. Both may escalate the level of violence in an effort to frustrate reform policies. A regime, therefore, must possess sufficient resources to assuage the moderates while controlling the radicals on all sides.

Finally, we must recognize the moral questions raised by proposals for conciliation. Such programs often entail offers of amnesty to those guilty of acts of terrorism. When the imperial powers withdrew from their Asian and African colonies, they released many prisoners accurately accused of terrorist acts.

In a world of perfect justice, those who indiscriminately attack non-combatants would not benefit from such amnesty. In an imperfect world, rigid adherence to a principle of retribution may lead to still more bloodshed. With cases of compromise like those described, the terrorism that occurred must be placed in a wider political struggle, and responses to terrorism must be weighed in relation to broader political objectives. In a perfect world, moral choice is clear; in our world, moral dilemmas are real.

CONCLUSION: RHETORIC AND ILLUSION IN COUNTERTERRORISM

The rhetoric that usually surrounds the discussion of responses to terrorism tends to emphasize "tough-minded" repressive approaches that tolerate no mention of compromise or possible justice in the claims of those resorting to terrorism. At most, demands are made for them to abandon their violent resistance before consideration might be given to their concerns. Such rigid responses decline in relevance as the groups resorting to terrorism increasingly represent broad communities and widely shared frustrations.

One illusion afflicting many hard-line responses involves denying such support may exist and a consequent blindness to the nature of the problem. As long as Israel dismisses the PLO as simply terrorists, or the South African government refuses to recognize the African National Congress, it is difficult to see how the cycle of violence in these two countries can be moderated. On the other hand, apologists for those using terrorist tactics may be deluded in the opposite way; that is, they exaggerate the representativeness of the perpetrators and the justness of their cause.

The presence of such illusions begs the following question: How are we to distinguish an extremist fringe from a broadly based movement when both claim to act in the name of the people? Although this question cannot be definitively answered outside of the relevant political context, we might suggest one guideline: By their *other* actions. An extremist faction, isolated from broader support, will be little more than their terrorist activities. A widely based revolutionary movement may still use some terror tactics, but these will be subordinated to an overall politico/military strategy that possesses demonstrably deeper organizational roots. Widespread support does not serve to excuse the resort to terrorism, but it is a fact that has to be taken into account when weighing responses to it.

Realistically, responses to terrorism must be gauged to the different character of the diverse elements that resort to this tactic, and the result may be apparent inconsistency. Truly murderous, deviant elements can only be repressed, preferably in the least destructive fashion involving improved police work as opposed to massive retaliation. As the perpetrators become more representative, responses must necessarily become more sophisticated and, perhaps, more conciliatory.

No single-minded policy is likely to prove satisfactory in dealing with the myriad forms of dissident terrorism around the world, much less the different cases of establishment terrorism. Those attempting to deal with terrorism must act with maturity and restraint so that the cure does not cripple or kill the patient. They must also act with intelligence; both in the sense of military/police intelligence and the wisdom to recognize what they confront.

NOTES

This essay is a revised and abridged version of "What is to be done?" in Peter C. Sederberg, *Terrorist Myths: Illusion, Rhetoric, and Reality*, (Englewood Cliffs, N.J., Prentice Hall, 1989), pp. 128-160.

1. Paul Johnson, "The Cancer of Terrorism," in Benjamin Netanyahu, ed., *Terrorism: How the West Can Win* (New York: Farrar, Straus & Giroux, 1986), 37.

2. Richard E. Rubenstein, *Alchemists of Revolution: Terrorism in the Modern World* (New York: Basic Books, 1987), 13.

3. Ibid., 16.

4. J. Bowyer Bell, *A Time of Terror; How Democratic Societies Respond to Revolutionary Violence* (New York: Basic Books, 1978), 269.

5. Rubenstein, *Alchemists of Revolution*, 229.

6. Paul Wilkinson, "Fighting the Hydra: International Terrorism and the Rule of Law," in Noel O'Sullivan, ed., *Terrorism, Ideology, and Revolution: The Origins of Modern Political Violence* (Boulder, Colo.: Westview Press, 1986), 210.

7. See, for example, the country studies in William Gutteridge, ed., *Contemporary Terrorism* (New York: Facts on File, 1986), and Juliet Lodge, ed., *Terrorism: A Challenge to the State* (New York: St. Martin's Press, 1981).

8. Grant Wardlaw, *Political Terrorism: Theory, Tactics, and Countermeasures* (New York: Cambridge University Press, 1982), 121-126.

9. Ibid., 122.

10. Ibid., 122-123.

11. Ibid., 124.

12. William Echikson, "Italian Terrorism Plummets," *Christian Science Monitor*, 27 March 1987, 1 ff.

13. Wardlaw, *Political Terrorism*, 100.

14. George Rosie, *The Directory of International Terrorism* (New York: Paragon House, 1987), 76-77.

15. Wardlaw, *Political Terrorism*, 126.

16. Ibid.

17. See the discussion of Nicholas N. Kittrie, "A New Look at Political Offenses and Terrorism," in Marius H. Livingston, ed., *International Terrorism in the Contemporary World* (Westport, Conn.: Greenwood Press, 1978), 354-375.

18. Wardlaw, *Political Terrorism*, 110-115.

19. Ibid., 115-118.

20. Ibid., 114-115.

21. Neil C. Livingstone, "Proactive Responses to Terrorism: Reprisals, Preemption, and Retribution," in Neil C. Livingstone and Terrell E. Arnold, eds., *Fighting Back: Winning the War Against Terrorism* (Lexington, Mass.: Lexington Books, 1986), 120.

22. Ibid., 124.

23. Ibid.

24. Ibid.

25. Ibid., 124-126.

26. Ibid., 127.

27. Ibid., 128.

28. Ibid.

29. Ibid.

30. See Richard B. Lillich, *Humanitarian Interventions and the United Nations* (Charlottesville: University Press of Virginia, 1973).

31. Wardlaw, *Political Terrorism*, 70.

32. Ibid., 75.

33. Ibid., 73.

34. James Tunstead Burtchaell, "Moral Response to Terrorism," in Livingstone and Arnold, eds., *Fighting Back*, 204.

Acknowledgments (continued)

Richard Shultz. Published by permission of the *Journal of International Affairs* and the Trustees of Columbia University in the City of New York.

Gary G. Sick. *SAIS Review*. Reprinted by permission of the *SAIS Review*, Vol. 7, No. 1. Copyright 1987 by the Johns Hopkins Policy Institute, SAIS.

David Fromkin. Reprinted by permission of *Foreign Affairs*, Vol. 53, July 1975. Copyright 1975 by the Council on Foreign Relations, Inc.

Paul Johnson. Reprinted by permission of the *NATO Review*, Vol. 28, No. 5 (Oct. 1980).

Walter Laqueur. Copyright ©1976 by *Harper's Magazine*. All rights reserved. Reprinted from the March issue by special permission.

William B. Quandt. Abridged and titled from testimony before the Subcommittee on Civil and Constitutional Rights, U.S. House of Representatives, Hearings on Terrorism, August 26, 1985.

Michael Stohl. Prepared especially for this book by the author.

Martha Crenshaw. Prepared especially for this book by the author.

Richard E. Rubenstein. From *Alchemists of Revolution: Terrorism in the Modern World*, by Richard E. Rubenstein. Copyright ©1987 by Richard E. Rubenstein. Reprinted by permission of Basic Books, Inc., Publishers.

Rushworth M. Kidder. Reprinted by permission from *The Christian Science Monitor* ©1986 The Christian Science Publishing Society. All rights reserved.

Paul Wilkinson. *Terrorism and the Liberal State*, 2nd ed., (New York University Press, 1986). Reprinted by permission of the publisher, Macmillan Education, Ltd, and the author.

David C. Rapoport. Prepared especially for this book by the author.

L. John Martin. Excerpt from *Terrorism: An International Journal*, Vol. 8, No. 2. Copyright ©1983. Reprinted by special permission from Taylor & Francis.

Martha Crenshaw. Abridged and titled from testimony before the Subcommittee on Civil and Constitutional Rights, U.S. House of Representatives, Hearings on Terrorism, August 26, 1985.

Donna M. Schlagheck. "The Superpowers, Foreign Policy, and Terrorism." Reprinted by permission of the publisher, from *International Terrorism: An Introduction to the Concepts and Actors* by Donna M. Schlagheck (Lexington, Mass: Lexington Books, D.C. Heath and Company, Copyright 1988, Lexington Books).

J. Bowyer Bell. "Explaining International Terrorism: The Elusive Quest." Abridged and retitled from testimony before the Subcommittee on Civil and Constitutional Rights, U.S. House of Representatives, Hearings on Terrorism, August 26, 1985.

Conor Cruise O'Brien. Copyright ©1986 by Conor Cruise O'Brien, *The Atlantic Monthly*, June 1986. Reprinted by permission of the publisher and author.

Walter Laqueur. Reprinted and retitled by permission of *Foreign Affairs*, (Vol. 65, Fall 1986). Copyright 1986 by the Council of Foreign Relations, Inc.

James Tunstead Burchael. Reprinted by permission of the publisher from *Fighting Back: Winning the War Against Terrorism*, edited by Neil C. Livingstone and Terrell E. Arnold (Lexington, Mass: Lexington Books, D.C. Heath and Company. Copyright 1986, D.C. Heath and Company).

Neil C. Livingstone. Reprinted by permission of the publisher, from *Fighting Back: Winning the War Against Terrorism*, edited by Neil C. Livingstone and Terrell E. Arnold (Lexington, Mass: Lexington Books, D.C. Heath and Company. Copyright 1986, D.C. Heath and Company).

Louis René Beres. Prepared especially for this book by the author.

Patrick Clawson. Published by permission of *Orbis: A Journal of World Affairs* and the Foreign Policy Research Institute.

William Gutteridge. Copyright 1988 by William Gutteridge. From the *Journal of Defense and Diplomacy*, Vol. 6 (April 1988). Published by special permission.

Paul Wilkinson. From the *Harvard International Review*, Vol. 7 (May–June 1986). Reprinted by permission of the *Harvard International Review* and with the permission of the author.

Seymour Maxwell Finger. Reprinted from *The Jerusalem Journal of International Relations*, Vol. 10, No. 1. Copyright 1988, by special permission of the publisher, the Johns Hopkins University Press.

Peter C. Sederberg. Prepared especially for this book by the author.

Parliamentary Power v. executive

State formation > Spain r. ?

Economics — issues difficult.

I.B. History (U.S. civil war)

Compare + contrast process of state formation.

form + function.

Spain de centralizes.
w/ limits

Scotland de
centralize w/.

76/77

9/8